ATTACKING RURAL POVERTY
How Nonformal Education Can Help

The International Council for Educational Development (ICED) is a nonprofit research organization concerned with improving the contribution of education to social and economic development throughout the world. ICED's staff, consultants, and governing board are multinational.

The present study was largely financed by the World Bank, with supplementary funds from the Ford Foundation.

ATTACKING RURAL POVERTY
How Nonformal Education Can Help

Philip H. Coombs
with
Manzoor Ahmed

a research report for the World Bank
prepared by
the International Council for Educational Development

edited by
Barbara Baird Israel

THE JOHNS HOPKINS UNIVERSITY PRESS
Baltimore and London

Originally published, 1974

Paperback edition, 1974
Second printing, 1978
Third printing, 1980

Library of Congress Cataloging in Publication Data

Coombs, Philip Hall, 1915–
    Attacking rural poverty.

    Bibliography: p. 273
    1. Education, Rural.   2. Underdeveloped areas—
Agricultural education.   I. Ahmed, Manzoor, 1940–
joint author.   II. International Bank for Reconstruction
and Development.   III. International Council for
Educational Development.   IV. Title.
LC5146.C65   1974   370.19′3   73-19350
ISBN 0-8018-1600-9
ISBN 0-8018-1601-7 (pbk.)

PREFACE

This study is part of a continuing effort by the World Bank Group to improve the assistance it gives to developing countries in the field of education. By sponsoring its publication, the Bank hopes to stimulate both professional and public discussion of issues which are central to its purpose: helping the world's poor countries improve the condition of their people through economic and social development.

In a general sense, the relationship between education and development is self-evident. It is difficult to define, however, and perhaps impossible to measure with any assurance. Yet the need for better definition and assessment has become increasingly acute.

Typically, education absorbs a high and rising proportion of national budgets in developing countries. The absolute number of illiterates has steadily increased, however, and significant improvements in the quality and scope of formal educational systems have been rare and exceedingly difficult to achieve. In part, this can be attributed to rapid population growth caused by declining mortality rates without a corresponding reduction in fertility. In these conditions, there is a disproportionate increase in the ratio of school age children to total population, so that educational budgets are strained merely to keep abreast of numbers.

But this is by no means all of the problem. Even if physical facilities and teaching staffs were adequate and essential reforms of structure and curricula were achieved, it is doubtful that formal education as presently conceived could satisfy many of the most crucial developmental needs. In most developing countries, for example, a very high proportion of the population is engaged in agriculture, often at the subsistence level. In this area, not only is the need for increased productivity especially acute, but the incidence of literacy and other essential skills is exceptionally low, among adults as well as children. If productivity is to be increased, enhancing the prospects of overall development and improving the pattern of income distribution, some means must be found to meet the basic educational needs of the population concerned.

The Bank has long felt that an important part of the solution might lie in the improvement and expansion of nonformal education if it could be effectively organized, financed and administered. For a number of years, both the Bank and its affiliate, the International Development Association (IDA), have probed the possibilities by financing specific projects in various countries. Many other organizations, public and private, have accumulated valuable experience in this field, in both rural and urban areas.

The Bank's main objective in commissioning the present study was to obtain an overall review and synthesis of this experience. Cooperation has been freely given by governments, international agencies and private institutions. Both the main study and a large body of supporting case materials, too numerous to publish in this volume, are valuable to the Bank for the further development of policy and the formulation of projects. We hope the results will be equally useful to others, and especially to the governments of developing countries. It must be emphasized, however, that specific policy conclusions contained in the study are those of the authors, and may not necessarily reflect the views of the World Bank.

DUNCAN S. BALLANTINE
Director, Education Department
World Bank

TABLE OF CONTENTS

LIST OF TABLES

Table
No.   *Page*

GLOSSARY

Acronym	Name	Country
ACPO	Acción Cultural Popular	Colombia
BSD	Banque Sénegalaise de Développement	Senegal
CADU	Chilalo Agricultural Development Unit	Ethiopia
CAR	Centre d'Animation Rurale	Senegal
CD	Community Development Programme	India
CER	Centre d'Expansion Rurale	Senegal
CFA	Communauté Financière Africaine	Senegal, Upper Volta
CIMMYT	Centro Internacional de Mejoramiento de Maíz y Trigo (International Maize and Wheat Improvement Center)	Mexico
CRAD	Centres Régionaux de l'Assistance pour le Développement	Senegal
EC	Extension Centres	India
FPR	Formation Professionnelle Rurale	Senegal
FTC	Farmer Training Centres	Kenya
IAAP	Intensive Agricultural Area Programme	India
IADP	Intensive Agricultural District Programme	India
IDC	Industrial Development Centre	Nigeria
INACAP	National Vocational Training Institute	Chile
IRAM	Institut de Recherche et d'Application des Méthodes de Développement	Senegal
IRRI	International Rice Research Institute	The Philippines
KTCCA	Kotwali Thana Central Cooperative Association	Bangladesh
MTTS	Mobile Trade Training Schools	Thailand
NCCK	National Christian Council of Kenya	Kenya
OCA	Office de Commercialisation Agricole	Senegal
ORD	Office of Rural Development	Republic of Korea
PACCA	Programme on Agricultural Credit and Cooperation in Afghanistan	Afghanistan
PACD	Presidential Arm for Community Development	The Philippines
PPP-R	Promoción Profesional Popular-Rural	Colombia
PPP-U	Promocion Profesional Popular-Urban	Colombia
PRRM	Philippines Rural Reconstruction Movement	The Philippines
RIP	Rural Industries Project Programme	India
RRW	Rural Reconstruction Worker	The Philippines

RTC	Rural Training Center	Senegal
SATEC	Société d'aide technique et de coopération	Senegal
SCC	Social Communications Center	The Philippines
SENA	Servicio Nacional de Aprendizaje (National Apprenticeship Service)	Colombia
SIET	Small Industry Extension Training Institute	India
SISCOMA	Sociéte Industrielle Sénégalaise de Construction Mécanique et de Matériel Agricole	Senegal
SISI	Small Industry Service Institute	India
SODEVA	Société de Développement de la Vulgarisation Agricole	Senegal
SSIDO	Small-Scale Industrial Development Organization	India
TANU	Tanganyika African National Union	Tanzania
TTDC	Thana Training and Development Center	Bangladesh
VIC	Vocational Improvement Center	Nigeria
VLW	Village Level Worker	India

International and Bi-Lateral Organizations

Acronym	Name
FAC	Fonds (français) d'aide et de Coopération
FAO	Food and Agriculture Organization
FED	Fonds Européen de Développement (European Development Fund)
ICED	International Council for Educational Development
IIEP	International Institute for Educational Planning
ILO	International Labour Organization
ODA	Overseas Development Administration
OECD	Organization for Economic Co-operation and Development
SIDA	Swedish International Development Agency
Unesco	United Nations Educational, Scientific and Cultural Organization
UNICEF	United Nations Children's Fund
USAID	United States Agency for International Development
WHO	World Health Organization

INTRODUCTION

No problem is of greater worldwide concern today than the poverty that shackles one-third of the world's people. The well-publicized economic gap between nations—the "haves and have-nots"—is one dimension of this problem. The gap between cities and rural areas is another. And the gaps within rural areas are yet another. It is clearer now than perhaps it was a decade or so ago that only through concerted efforts to develop rural as well as urban areas can the peoples of the world's poorest nations take the first steps beyond sheer subsistence.

Because of the importance of education for present as well as future generations, the focus of this study turns on types of educational efforts, outside the formal school system, which seem to offer potential for helping in the monumental tasks of rural development. The study is particularly concerned with nonformal programs to increase the skills and productivity of farmers, artisans, craftsmen, and small entrepreneurs.

Nonformal education, though not a recent phenomenon, has received little systematic study. Therefore, we should like to emphasize that our researches are but an initial effort to map a complex and uncharted territory and to open it up for further investigation by others. We hope, however, that the results of even this initial exploration will provide some fresh insights and guidance of practical value to those practitioners who grapple daily with the problems of rural poverty and with questions of how education can help break the cycle.

This study, initiated and supported by the World Bank, was carried out by the International Council for Educational Development (ICED) over the past two years. More or less simultaneously, ICED has also conducted a complementary study sponsored by UNICEF on nonformal education for rural children and youth, the preliminary findings of which are published in New Paths to Learning for Rural Children and Youth. Though the present study is concerned with programs for employment and productivity and deals generally with older age groups, it will be seen that there are many connections between the two projects.

ICED is extremely grateful to the many individuals and agencies in developing countries whose cooperation made this study possible. We are similarly grateful to a variety of international and bilateral aid agencies for their very substantial contributions to this study, from its inception to its completion. They provided useful advice and documentation, arranged group meetings and individual interviews with staff members, prepared special working papers and commentaries, facilitated the field work of ICED teams, and in some cases seconded their own staff experts to these teams. Most recently, these agencies participated in several informal interagency meetings in Europe and the United States to critically review an earlier draft of this report, and produced many useful suggestions for improving it.

In particular, ICED thanks the International Institute for Educational Planning (Unesco) which, as a partner in this study, contributed the research time of a staff member and consultant; the International Labour Office for releasing an able staff person for one year to serve as Deputy Director of the ICED study; the Food and Agriculture Organization for contributing its experts to ICED's field work; Unesco staff members for supplying many useful leads and stimulating ideas; the United Nations Development Program for providing useful documentation and for reviewing draft reports; the United Kingdom's Overseas Development Administration for arranging valuable professional contributions to the ICED study by the Institute of Education at the University of London and the Agricultural Extension Centre of the University of Reading; the Central Educational Research Institute (CERI) of the Republic of Korea for their research assistance; the bilateral aid agencies of France, Sweden and the United States for their help in identifying and examining noteworthy programs; the Ford and Rockefeller Foundations for similar help on case studies and for facilitating ICED's field work.

Without the contribution in time and talent of these agencies, this study could not have been made. It is important to state clearly here, however, that they are absolved of any guilt for what is said in this report, which is the sole responsibility of the authors and ICED.

We express our gratitude also to the Board of Trustees of ICED, an international group including members from developing countries, for their time and close attention to reviewing drafts of this report and for their expression of general agreement with its findings and conclusions.

Our special thanks go, of course, to the World Bank, the prime sponsor of this study, for the helpful intellectual collaboration of its staff members and for its support of ICED's freedom of action in carrying out the study.

Special mention must be made of two ICED colleagues who contributed importantly to this report. Sven Grabe, on leave from ILO as deputy director of this study during its first year, authored three of the case studies and generated a plethora of valuable ideas and insights which found their way into this report after his departure. Roy Prosser, who arrived at ICED while the report was being written, found time despite his heavy duties as deputy director of ICED's UNICEF study to review all drafts and to contribute many valuable criticisms and improvements.

The study was financed mainly by funds from the World Bank, with supplementary support from the Ford Foundation. Carrying it out required at several stages supreme efforts by our secretarial staff and research assistants that went well beyond the call of duty. It is difficult to thank them sufficiently.

PHILIP H. COOMBS
Vice Chairman of ICED
Director of Studies

Essex, Conn.
August 1973

ATTACKING RURAL POVERTY
How Nonformal Education Can Help

1: BACKGROUND OF THE STUDY

This report is addressed to planners and policymakers who are concerned with improving the conditions of life in the vast rural areas of the world's poorest countries. It presents the main findings of an international research study designed to assist their efforts. The study was commissioned by the World Bank in January 1971 and carried out over the next two years by the International Council for Educational Development (ICED), with help from numerous developing countries,[1] multilateral and bilateral assistance agencies, and other organizations.

Genesis of the Study

The study grew out of a widespread conviction among development experts by the end of the 1960s that greater emphasis should henceforth be given to developing the *rural* areas of poor nations and that this would require, among other things, fresh approaches to meeting the educational needs of rural populations.

In retrospect it was clear that development efforts in the previous two decades had followed a lopsided pattern. The main thrust had centered on the modernization of urban areas, particularly on industrialization, and while notable progress had been made in many countries, the great majority of the people—those living in rural areas—had benefited relatively little. As a consequence, the social and economic gap between the modernizing urban sectors and the poverty-ridden rural sectors of these societies was widening ominously. Imbalances in the pattern of national development threatened further progress, even in the cities.

Education was part of this imbalance. For many years the dominant strategy everywhere had been to achieve rapid quantitative expansion of the existing educational system substantially in its old image, in the belief that this would equalize opportunity and generate the human skills and leadership needed for general development. Measured by statistics of enrollments, this expansionist strategy had made spectacular gains. Yet as the developing nations entered the 1970s they found themselves, without exception, in the throes of a deepening educational crisis. It was not only a financial crisis, it was a crisis of serious maladjustment, taking many forms, between inherited educational systems and the realities of their rapidly changing societies.[2]

---

[1]Afghanistan, Colombia, Ethiopia, India, Indonesia, United Republic of Kenya, Republic of Korea, Malawi, Mexico, Nigeria, the Philippines, Senegal, United Republic of Tanzania, Thailand, and Upper Volta.

[2]For more details see: P. H. Coombs, *The World Educational Crisis: A Systems Analysis* (New York and London: Oxford University Press, 1968); World Bank, *Education Sector Working Paper* (Washington, D.C., September 1971); International Commission on the Development of Education, *Learning to Be: the World of Education Today and Tomorrow* (Paris: Unesco; London: George G. Harrap & Co., 1972).

National development in general was suffering from this educational crisis but rural people were its most serious victims, for three main reasons. First, urban areas had been strongly favored in the allocation of scarce educational resources. Second, the incompatibility between what schools were teaching and what the people needed to learn was most severe in rural areas. Third, educational policies had equated education largely with formal schooling; hence the important learning needs of children and adults outside school, who constituted the great majority of the rural population, were being seriously neglected.

This set of circumstances—in much clearer focus by 1970 than earlier—prompted a strong new interest by policymakers in what came to be called *nonformal education* (see definition later in this chapter).

The World Bank shared this heightened interest in nonformal education, particularly as it related to the Bank's concern for agricultural and rural development. Having entered the education field in 1962, the Bank by mid-1971 had made educational loans totaling $431 million and planned to increase its lending rate in the educational field at least threefold over the next few years.[3] But most of the loans processed by its Education Projects Department had been for formal education. In 1970 two important policy questions led the Bank to commission the present study: (1) to what extent could the Bank's education financing be extended to *nonformal* educational programs, and (2) what strategy should the Bank pursue in this field and what might be the most promising and appropriate types of projects to support?

Since the field of nonformal education had never been critically and systematically analyzed, it seemed reasonable to hope that the results of this study would be of interest and value not only to the Bank but also to other assistance agencies and the developing nations themselves, who faced similar questions.

The Focus and Key Questions

The study set out with a clear operational objective in view: to develop—on the basis of examining past experience, present evidence and any fresh ideas—improved information, analytical methods and practical guidelines that would be useful to those actually involved in planning, implementing and evaluating programs of nonformal education geared to rural development.[4] While the study was not expected to discover answers to fit all situations, it was intended to help planners and decision-makers to view any specific situation in a broad and systematic perspective, to see their options more clearly, and to assess the short- and long-term implications of each option more judiciously.

Since nonformal education covers a diversity of topics, clienteles and objectives, the scope of the study was confined for practical reasons mainly to programs aimed at increasing rural employment, productivity and income—in general, those programs designed to improve the knowledge and skills of farmers, rural artisans and crafts workers, and small entrepreneurs. Necessarily this left for future study other important objectives and programs of great concern to the Bank and others.

---

[3]World Bank, *Education Sector Working Paper*, September 1971, P. 14. The Bank actually did increase its new education loans from $79.9 million in fiscal year 1970 to $180.4 million in 1972.
[4]Excerpts from the agreed terms of reference of the study are contained in Appendix A.

Specifically, this study asked the following questions in examining a selected sample of nonformal educational programs:

Pre-planning diagnosis: How should an area be sized up *before* deciding on any particular nonformal educational activity, in order to (1) ascertain that area's special educational needs for development, (2) identify the priority learning objectives for each such group, and (3) identify other educational and development activities in the same area to which any new educational program should be related?

Choosing an educational delivery system: What alternative educational approaches would be possible and which one would best meet the above needs and objectives, using the available resources and reinforcing and drawing strength from other educational and developmental activities in the same area?

Costs and required resources: How should the actual or potential costs of any nonformal educational program be estimated in order to determine its resource requirements, practical feasibility and probable efficiency? How should the availability of resources be assessed, including unconventional resources that might be tapped?

Innovative solutions: In the event that standard educational models will not suffice, what possible new approaches might achieve a massive enlargement of educational services—using, for example, low-cost mass media, indigenous learning processes, and other underutilized human and material resources?

Evaluation of nonformal programs: What criteria, methods and types of evidence could best assess the internal efficiency (cost effectiveness) and the external productivity (cost-benefit relationships) of such programs? Even where precise quantitative measurement is impossible, can specific steps be identified for improving these critical relationships between costs and results?

How the Study Was Conducted

Four main research steps were taken. First, extensive discussions were held with experts in numerous international and bilateral assistance agencies, foundations and research organizations to gather information and obtain suggestions on possible "cases" to be examined. Second, a wide assortment of documents—many of them unpublished and restricted—were assembled and critically reviewed. Third, analytical working papers were prepared on a number of topics and programs. Fourth and most important, a diversified sample of ongoing nonformal education projects and programs was selected in Africa, Asia and Latin America and examined in the field by ICED research teams in close collaboration with local personnel. Finally, all of the evidence and ideas collected in the previous steps were sifted and anlyzed in the preparation of the present general report.

Case studies and field notes on the twenty-five selected programs listed in Table 1.1 comprise the main empirical basis for the analysis and conclusions of this report, though much additional evidence from other programs and sources has also been used. Preparing the case studies proved to be a much larger task than anticipated, for three reasons. First, it soon became apparent that a larger number of programs should be examined than originally planned in order to

Table 1.1
Nonformal Education Programs Analyzed by ICED

Country	
	Agricultural Extension Programs
Republic of Korea	• Farmer Education Program of the Office of Rural Development (ORD)*
Senegal	• Operation Productivite of Societe d'aide technique et de cooperation (SATEC)*
	Farmer Training Programs
Kenya	• Farmer Training Centres (FTCs)
Senegal	• Rural Training Centers (RTCs) of the Formation Professionnelle Rurale Program (FPR)*
The Philippines	• Rice Production Training Program of the International Rice Research Institute (IRRI)*
Colombia	• Rural Mobile Skills Training Program: Promocion Profesional Popular-Rural (PPP-R) of National Apprenticeship Service of Colombia (SENA)*
	Training Programs for Rural Artisans and Entrepreneurs
Thailand	• Mobile Trade Training Schools (MTTS)*
Nigeria	• Vocational Improvement Centres (VICs)*
India	• Industrial Development Centres (IDCs)*
	• Small-Scale Industrial Development Program of Small-Scale Industrial Development Organization (SSIDO)*
	• Rural Industries Projects Program (RIP)*
	• Gujarat Entrepreneurship Development Program*
Senegal	• Rural Artisan Training Centers (RATC) of Formation Professionelle Rurale (FPR)*
	Cooperative Self-Help Programs
India	• Community Development Program(CD)
Senegal	• Animation Rurale*
The Philippines	• Philippines Rural Reconstruction Movement (PRRM)
Tanzania	• Cooperative Education System of the Cooperative Union of Tanganyika*
Bangladesh	• Comilla Project of the Academy for Rural Development
Colombia	• Accion Cultural Popular (ACPO)*
	Integrated Rural Development Programs
Sudan	• Gezira Development Scheme
India	• Intensive Agricultural Development Program (IADP)
Ethiopia	• Chilalo Agricultural Development Unit Project (CADU)*
Afghanistan	• Programme on Agricultural Credit and Cooperation in Afghanistan (PACCA)*
Mexico	• Puebla Project of the International Maize and Wheat Improvement Center (CIMMYT)
Malawi	• Lilongwe Land Development Programme

NOTE: This table includes only programs examined by ICED in some detail and reviewed in later chapters of this report. Programs marked by an asterisk (*) are included in ICED case study reports. Not included here are numberous additional programs on which useful but less detailed information was gathered and examined.

6

have a broad enough sample to support valid generalizations. Second, contrary to earlier expectations there was far too little evidence on crucial aspects of the selected programs to support an adequate analysis; hence direct field investigations had to be undertaken in most cases, thereby multiplying the research time and travel requirements. Third, it became necessary in these circumstances to write up the findings on most programs more fully and formally than had been intended so that they could be checked back for accuracy and completeness by experts and officials in the countries visited.

In the end, ICED staff members and consultants visited fifteen developing countries in connection with the present study and observed all but two of the twenty-five programs listed in Table 1.1.[5]

It would have been impossible to impose a single analytical formula on such a diversity of cases or to obtain standardized quantitative data for making comparisons across national lines. Nevertheless, since we were interested in comparative analysis wherever possible (not limited to quantitative aspects), the various cases were examined in as uniform a manner as possible. The "Guidelines for Case Studies" used by all research teams (see Appendix B) provided a checklist of the specific types of data that were to be collected wherever possible and a set of evaluative questions to be answered insofar as the evidence permitted. As will be seen in the analytical sections of this report, this approach yielded a number of interesting comparisons and contrasts.

It would have been impossible to impose a single analytical formula on such a diversity of cases or to obtain standardized quantitative data for making comparisons across national lines. Nevertheless, since we were interested in comparative analysis wherever possible (not limited to quantitative aspects), the various cases were examined in as uniform a manner as possible. The "Guidelines for Case Studies" used by all research teams (see Appendix B) provided a checklist of the specific types of data that were to be collected wherever possible and a set of evaluative questions to be answered insofar as the evidence permitted. As will be seen in the analytical sections of this report, this approach yielded a number of interesting comparisons and contrasts.

The Underlying Education Concepts

We should introduce at the outset several educational concepts and definitions that are basic to the common analytical framework of the present study and to a companion study for UNICEF on nonformal education for rural children and youth.[6]

In formulating these concepts we began with a *functional* view of education, in contrast to the structural and institutional approach used in most

[5]The countries visited are listed in footnote 1. Later, mainly in connection with the UNICEF study but with benefit to the World Bank study, ICED visits were made to five additional developing countries: Brazil, Jamaica, Malaysia, Mali and Sri Lanka (Ceylon).

[6]Several months after the World Bank study was launched, ICED undertook a closely connected study, sponsored by UNICEF, that shared the same general analytical framework but focused on different kinds of programs and on a different clientele—namely, rural children and youth. Wherever possible, the field work for these companion studies was coordinated and in various other ways they benefited each other, as will be seen by later references in this report. A preliminary report submitted to UNICEF in the spring of 1973 has since been published: *New Paths to Learning: For Rural Children and Youth,* ICED Publications, Box 601, West Haven, Connecticut 06516. A final report to UNICEF is scheduled for publication in 1974.

educational planning and administration. This obliged us to start our analysis with the learners and their needs, and to move only then to the question of what educational means might be most appropriate for meeting these needs. This, as we saw it, put the horse before the cart.

We also began with the conviction (later underscored by Unesco's International Commission for the Development of Education) that education can no longer be viewed as a time-bound, place-bound process confined to schools and measured by years of exposure.[7]

These considerations led us to adopt from the beginning a concept that equates *education* with *learning*, regardless of where, how or when the learning occurs. Thus defined, education is obviously a continuing process, spanning the years from earliest infancy through adulthood and necessarily involving a great variety of methods and sources. We found it analytically useful, and generally in accord with current realities, to distinguish between three modes of education (recognizing that there is considerable overlap and interaction between them): (1) *informal* education, (2) *formal* education, and (3) *nonformal* education.[8]

Informal education as used here is the lifelong process by which every person acquires and accumulates knowledge, skills, attitudes and insights from daily experiences and exposure to the environment—at home, at work, at play; from the example and attitudes of family and friends; from travel, reading newspapers and books; or by listening to the radio or viewing films or television. Generally, informal education is unorganized and often unsystematic; yet it accounts for the great bulk of any person's total lifetime learning—including that of even a highly "schooled" person.

Formal education as used here is, of course, the highly institutionalized, chronologically graded and hierarchically structured "education system," spanning lower primary school and the upper reaches of the university.

Nonformal education as used here is any organized, systematic, educational activity carried on outside the framework of the formal system to provide selected types of learning to particular subgroups in the population, adults as well as children. Thus defined, nonformal education includes, for example, agricultural extension and farmer training programs, adult literacy programs, occupational skill training given outside the formal system, youth clubs with substantial educational purposes, and various community programs of instruction in health, nutrition, family planning, cooperatives, and the like.

There are important similarities and differences between formal and nonformal education as they exist today. They have been organized to augment and improve upon the informal learning process—in other words, to promote and facilitate certain valued types of learning (such as reading and writing) that individuals cannot as readily or quickly acquire through ordinary exposure to their environment. These two modes of education are sometimes similar also in pedagogical form and methods.

---

[7] The Commission observed that, "The school's importance in relation to other means of education...is not increasing, but diminishing." *Learning To Be*, p.83.

[8] These particular terms leave something to be desired, but they seemed less ambiguous and less distorted by usage than the various alternatives we considered. It is not without significance that the standard lexicon of education in all the major languages is tied almost exclusively to *formal* education and provides no precise and well understood vocabulary for discussing what we have termed informal and nonformal education.

Nonformal and formal education generally differ, however, in their sponsorship and institutional arrangements and often in their educational objectives — and the groups they serve. Other important differences will emerge in later chapters. It should be said, however, that there is no sharp dividing line between them. Moreover, their differences occasionally merge in "hybrid" programs combining significant features of both.

There is growing agreement that, ideally, nations should strive to evolve "lifelong learning systems" designed to provide every individual with a flexible and diversified range of useful learning options throughout his or her lifetime. Any such system obviously would have to synthesize many elements of informal, formal and nonformal education. In fact, every country, even the poorest, already has a substantial start on such a system. The need now is to visualize the various educational activities as potential components of a coherent and flexible overall learning system that must be steadily strengthened, diversified and linked more closely to the needs and processes of national development.

Structure of the Report

This introductory chapter has explained the background of the research study that underlies this report — its origins; its objectives, scope and limitations; its design and methods; and its conceptual framework.

The remaining chapters of Part One are devoted mainly to a presentation of the basic evidence. Chapters 3 through 7 contain thumbnail sketches of the twenty-five examples of nonformal education in action that were selected for special study, including comment on certain of their strengths and weaknesses. To place these selected cases in broader perspective, however, Chapter 2 leads off with an overview of rural education today in the developing world and a discussion of the character and magnitude of future tasks for nonformal education.

Part Two is the main analytical section. Chapter 8 contains a critique of "agricultural knowledge systems," and Chapter 9, a corresponding critique of training programs for rural artisans, craftsmen and small entrepreneurs. The other three analytical chapters focus on critical issues common to all kinds of nonformal education programs: educational content, methods and media (Chapter 10); the economic aspects of nonformal education and the applicability of cost-effectiveness and cost-benefit analysis (Chapter 11); and finally, issues of planning, organization, management and staffing (Chapter 12).

Many conclusions and suggestions emerge at various points in the analytical chapters of Part Two. These are drawn together in Part Three.

2: AN OVERVIEW
OF RURAL EDUCATION

To confine our attention exclusively to the limited categories of nonformal education that are the focus of this study could result in a distorted picture of the whole. Thus, before we examine these particular types of programs it will be helpful to present a broad-brush picture of the larger rural education scene, including both the present condition and the foreseeable future needs.

Three Critical Factors:
Population, Land, and Employment

Rural people comprise the vast majority of the population in the developing world and virtually all of them are potential clients for nonformal education— whether they live on farms, in villages, or in rural market towns.[1] In the poorest and least developed countries (such as Burundi and Upper Volta) 90 percent or more of the total population lives in rural areas; only in a few exceptional cases (Uruguay, for example) is the rural population in the minority (see Chart 2.1).

Despite continuing migration to urban centers, in most nations the rural population will increase substantially in the decades ahead. UN projections show an overall increase in the rural populations of the less developed regions from 1.91 billion in 1970 to 2.62 billion by 1990. In South Asia, which even now has some of the most densely populated rural areas of the world, the rural population will, according to these projections, increase from 888 million in 1970 to 1.36 billion by 1990.[2] To take a fairly typical example: Thailand's planners have projected growth in urban population from 15 percent of the total in 1970 to 25 percent by the year 2000; but over the same period they project an expansion of the rural population from 30.6 million to 57.0 million.[3]

Moreover, because of high birth rates and rising infant survival rates, child and youth populations are typically growing faster than the overall population. In the majority of developing countries, more than 50 percent of the total population is under twenty years of age, compared with only 30 to 40 percent in Western Europe and North America (see Table 2.1). Consequently, their proportionately smaller adult labor force must bear a greater burden of educating and supporting the young and caring for the aged and infirm. Furthermore, active participation in the work force must typically begin at an earlier age than it does in more economically advanced nations.

---

[1]There are no standardized cross-national definitions of urban and rural. Many developing nations classify all communities with as few as 1,500 or 2,500 inhabitants as urban, but this understates the "ruralness" of such countries.

[2]World Bank Group, Trends in Developing Countries (Washington, D.C., 1971).

[3]Thailand, National Economic Development Board, "Report of the Working Group on Rural Manpower and Employment," mimeographed (Bangkok, 1971).

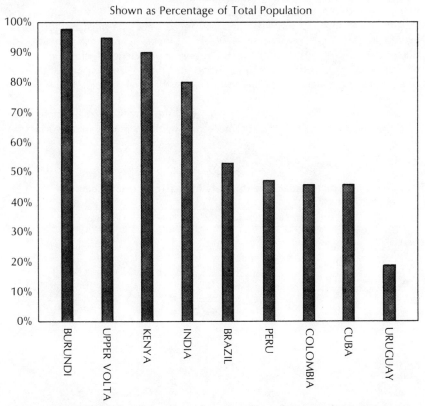

Chart 2.1
Rural Population in Selected
Developing Countries

Shown as Percentage of Total Population

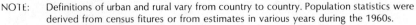

NOTE: Definitions of urban and rural vary from country to country. Population statistics were derived from census fitures or from estimates in various years during the 1960s.

SOURCE: U.N. Dept. of Economic and Social Affairs, Statistical Office of the U.N., *Demographic Yearbook 1970*, (New York: United Nations, 1971). Table 6.

These powerful population trends have major implications for agricultural production, land use, and rural employment. All these in turn have major implications for rural education.

To keep pace with the food and fiber requirements of the steadily growing population and to allow for a modest rise in living standards, agricultural production in the developing world must increase at a substantially higher annual rate in the future than in the 1960s (see Chapter 8, p. 114). With the dwindling supply of reserve land, these future increases must come largely from higher yields per acre. To get these higher yields, millions of farmers—including many of today's subsistence farmers—not only must have better production supplies and incentives but also must learn better farm management and improved production technologies.

More intensive cultivation can help somewhat to reduce rural underemployment (provided that labor-saving machinery is used sparingly), but it cannot

11

solve the massive and mounting rural unemployment problem that has become a central concern of national leaders. The pressure of growing population on limited arable land is creating an ever greater need for off-farm employment opportunities to absorb the excess rural labor force. It is clear from the experience of the past two decades that these new jobs must be generated mainly in the rural areas themselves. The cities—even those that are industrializing rapidly, often with capital-intensive production techniques—cannot sustain the demands for employment, for housing, and for a multitude of public services which continuous migration of the rural unemployed brings in its wake.

Nor can new urban industries prosper and grow without mass markets in rural areas, and such markets can emerge only with increased rural production

Table 2.1
Population Under Twenty Years of Age in Selected Countries

Country	Total Population	Population Under 20	Bank (%)
Kenya (1969-C)	10,942,705	6,397,954	59
Colombia (1964-C)	17,484,508	9,921,569	57
Jamaica (1965-E)	1,808,700	1,008,500	56
Brazil (1960-C)	70,119,071	37,073,924	53
Korea, Republic of (1966-C)	29,159,640	15,391,966	53
Thailand (1960-C)	26,257,916	13,818,635	53
Ethiopia (1967-E)	23,667,400	12,412,900	52
India (1970-E)	550,376,000	284,038,000	52
Tanzania (1967-C)	12,313,469	6,306,968	51
U.S.A. (1970-C)	203,211,926	76,970,400	38
Japan (1970-C)	103,720,060	33,730,500	33
France (1968-C)	49,654,556	16,008,300	32
Sweden (1970-C)	8,076,903	2,234,663	28

SOURCE: U.N. Department of Economic and Social Affairs, Statistical Office of the U.N., *Demographic Yearbook 1970* and *Demographic Yearbook 1971* (New York, 1971, 1972).

E = Estimate   C = Census

employment and widely distributed purchasing power. Here we see the inter-dependence between urban and rural development. The concentration of national governments and external agencies in past years on urban modernization, to the neglect of rural areas and people, has produced serious distortions in national development. The assumption that rapid urban industrialization would spread dynamic forces and benefits automatically to the rural areas has proved illusory. Actually the spread effect has been generally weak or nonexistent. As a result, the gap between urban and rural populations has widened ominously, giving rise to grave economic and social inequities as well as to political tensions.

Moreover, in those select rural areas that have enjoyed an unusual spurt in agricultural output and income, such as the Green Revolution districts of Southeast Asia, the marked tendency has been for the greatest benefits to go where they went before — to the more progressive, better-off farmers and large landholders. In the absence of land reform and other distributive measures, the old power structure and hierarchical social patterns have not yielded to the solvent of a cash economy; instead they have often solidified.

The Nature of Rural Development and Education's Role

Several conclusions of prime importance to the context and intellectual framework of this study emerge from the above considerations. It is clear, first, that future national plans of developing countries must provide for a better balance and integration between rural and urban development, and for much more emphasis than previously on rural areas. Beyond this there will be a need for broader-gauged rural development strategies that take into account all the critical factors, forces and problems outlined above and that are geared to a more realistic range of rural development goals and criteria.

Until recently, rural development was considered almost synonomous with agricultural output, and rising statistics of farm production were seen as the prime indicator of rural progress. But a new and broader vision of what rural development means is now evolving and replacing this simplistic view.

Long-Range Development Goals

This larger view — reflected in the goals set for the UN Second Development Decade — equates rural development with the far-reaching transformation of the social and economic structures, institutions, relationships and processes in any rural area. It conceives the goals of rural development not simply as agricultural and economic growth in the narrow sense but as *balanced* social and economic development, with emphasis on the *equitable distribution* as well as the creation of benefits. Among the goals are the generation of new employment; more equitable access to arable land; more equitable distribution of income; widespread improvements in health, nutrition and housing; greatly broadened opportunities for all individuals to realize their full potential through education; and a strong voice for all rural people in shaping the decisions and actions that affect their lives. These, of course, are long-range goals, but they provide the guidelines for shorter-range actions and the framework for rural development strategies.

13

It follows from this view that rural development calls for a massive and multipronged effort, not simply to boost production but to create and spread employment and to root out the fundamental causes of poverty, disease, ignorance and injustice, which continue to afflict more than half the world's population.

The Development Process

How does education fit into this broader conception of rural development? Even to begin to answer the question we found it essential to start with a reasonably clear and realistic picture of the *process* by which rural development gets started and then unfolds. The general literature was of little help in this regard. Although much attention has been given by scholars to evolving general theories of national development (mainly the *economic* elements), surprisingly little has been given to describing and explaining the nature and processes of rural development. We were obliged, therefore, to improvise.

We started with the premise that in most situations a forward thrust in agriculture is one of the essentials for initiating a broader rural development process. But a spurt in agriculture itself requires a combination of circumstances, one of them—but only one—being that farmers must learn and apply improved ways of farming. Rural development, we hypothesized, is the resultant of many interacting forces. Education must be one of them—education taking many forms and touching many people; but in the absence of essential complementary forces, education, least of all conventional primary schooling, cannot alone precipitate a dynamic process of rural development.

Once agricultural development is firmly under way the process spreads to other economic sectors. Increased farm income, particularly if widely distributed, generates new demands for an ever-widening assortment of goods and services, both agricultural and nonagricultural. Village artisans, craftsmen and small shopkeepers feel the stimulus; nearby market towns, if sufficiently responsive to the new demands, become major growth points for a broader self-sustaining variety of rural development.

As part of this process, many new products and technologies penetrate the area, greater specialization and division of labor take place in the economy and employment structures of the villages and rural hub-towns. If other conditions are right, the hub-towns grow and become increasingly important commercial, administrative and cultural centers for the surrounding agricultural area, and important bridges between the villages and the more modern outside world. Of central interest to this study is the fact that out of this complex process new types of tasks and jobs arise, calling for new skills and knowledge to deal with the new services, products and technologies previously unfamiliar to the area.

While the general anatomy of rural development described above may be similar in broad outline for different areas—if and when they get moving—there is no standardized path for all. Even within the same country rural areas often differ greatly in their historical background and traditions, in culture, language and religion, in social patterns and political structures. Especially important to our present concerns, rural areas differ widely in their natural resource endowments and basic development potential, in their present stage of development and economic infrastructures, and in their readiness to advance further. At the one extreme one finds, in close proximity to burgeoning cities, high-potential villages that are modernizing rapidly and sharing in urban progress. At the other end of the spectrum one finds poorly endowed rural communities, largely isolated in every respect from the larger society and economy and shockingly remote from the twentieth century. Most rural areas, of course, fall somewhere between these extremes, moving at their own pace from subsistence farming into a cash economy linked to a larger system.

Given these varied circumstances, there is no single formula for achieving rural development in all situations, nor is there a standard formula for the kinds of education needed to promote that development. Nevertheless, in all instances education, broadly conceived, has an unprecedented opportunity to contribute to generating new employment and advancing rural development. But to exploit this opportunity the architects and managers of educational programs—particularly work-oriented programs—must anticipate and respond to new skill demands and knowledge requirements and prepare both young people and adults to meet them. It is here that the great flexibility and adaptability of nonformal education become so important.

We return now to a closer look at the kinds of education needed in rural areas to feed into the process of rural development. Then we shall examine to what extent these needs are currently being met through the informal, formal and nonformal educational opportunities in rural areas.

Educational Needs for Rural Development

The educational needs for rural development referred to earlier are numerous and diverse, but they can be usefully grouped under four main headings.[4]

(1) **General or basic education:** literacy, numeracy, an elementary understanding of science and one's environment, etc.—what primary and general secondary schools seek to achieve.

(2) **Family improvement education,** designed primarily to impart knowledge, skills and attitudes, useful in improving the quality of family life, on such subjects as health and nutrition, homemaking and child care, home repairs and improvements, family planning, and so on.

(3) **Community improvement education,** designed to strengthen local and national institutions and processes through instruction in such matters as local and national government, cooperatives, community projects, and the like.

(4) **Occupational education,** designed to develop particular knowledge and skills associated with various economic activities and useful in making a living.

Clienteles for Occupational Education

These four types of education are needed by both young people and adults, male and female. As this study is mainly concerned with occupational education, we list below the principal subgroups and their specific requirement for skills and knowledge.

---

[4]For a related discussion of the minimum essential learning needs of rural young people, see ICED's report to UNICEF, *New Paths to Learning For Rural Children and Youth* (Essex, Conn., September 1973), Chapter 2.

(1) Persons directly engaged in agriculture: In most rural areas, especially in those at the early stages of development, farmers, farm workers and those engaged in animal husbandry, fishing and forestry make up most of the active labor force and are the largest audience for nonformal occupational education. They include, it should be emphasized, not only adults but also many young people, and not only boys and men but often girls and women.

The specific learning needs of those engaged in agriculture vary greatly according to the ecological and agricultural pattern of the particular area (rainfed areas, for example, have different requirements than irrigated areas), the state of agricultural technology and markets, and the characteristics of the farmers. Small subsistence farmers, for example, have quite different learning requisites than do progressive commercial farmers. (See Table 2.2.)

(2) Persons engaged in nonfarm artisan and entrepreneurial activities: The main hope for increasing rural employment and broadening the distribution of income lies in the growth of nonfarm rural enterprises—nourished by an increased demand for agricultural supplies and services and new consumption patterns of increased farm incomes.

While increased demand for traditional skills (e.g., tailoring and dressmaking, barbering, masonry and carpentry) often can be accommodated by indigenous training processes, the newer skills associated with modern technologies (e.g., modern food processing, repair and maintenance of farm machinery, motor vehicles, radios and television, electric and diesel pumps, typewriters and cash registers) must be created by new training processes or the modification of existing ones.

(3) Rural administrators and planners: Effective rural development calls for broader plans and strategies which require a new breed of rural development planners and administrators, capable of diagnosing the major elements of any rural situation, selecting priorities in consultation with others, evolving workable plans and tactics, and then mobilizing available resources and implementing plans.

In addition to these more general rural planner/administrators, there is need for competent managers for more specific purposes, such as managing rural cooperative societies, health services, water supply, and credit and transport services. Meeting their educational needs is likely to require some formal training followed by a variety of nonformal educational experiences.

The types of learning needs of some of the above subgroups are illustrated in Table 2.2.

The Poverty of Present Rural Learning Environments

Rural areas today have relatively poor educational resources for meeting the diverse needs outlined above. Especially in areas beyond the immediate geographic orbit of a major city, there is a lack, first, of many of the diverse

Table 2.2
Illustrative Rural Occupational Groups and Their Learning Needs

Groups	Types of Learning Needs (at varying levels of sophistication and specialization)
A. Persons directly engaged in agriculture 1. Commercial farmers 2. Small subsistence and semi-subsistence farm families 3. Landless farm workers	• Farm planning and management; rational decision-making; record keeping; cost and revenue computations; use of credit • Application of new inputs, varieties, improved farm practices • Storage, processing, food preservation • Supplementary skills for farm maintenance and improvement, and sideline jobs for extra income • Knowledge of government services, policies, programs, targets • Knowledge and skills for family improvement (e.g., health, nutrition, home economics, child care, family planning) • Civic skills (e.g., knowledge of how cooperatives, local government, national government function)
B. Persons engaged in off-farm commercial activities 1. Retailers and wholesalers of farm supplies and equipment, consumer goods and other items 2. Suppliers of repair and maintenance services 3. Processors, storers and shippers of agricultural commodities 4. Suppliers of banking and credit services 5. Construction and other artisans 6. Suppliers of general transport services 7. Small manufacturers	• New and improved technical skills applicable to particular goods and services • Quality control • Technical knowledge of goods handled sufficient to advise customers on their use, maintenance, etc. • Management skills (business planning; record keeping and cost accounting; procurement and inventory control; market analysis and sales methods; customer and employee relations; knowledge of government services, regulations, taxes; use of credit)
C. General services personnel: rural administrators, planners, technical experts 1. General public administrators, broad-gauged analysts and planners at subnational levels 2. Managers, planners, technicians, and trainers for specific public services (e.g., agriculture, transport, irrigation, health, small industry, education, family services, local government, etc.) 3. Managers of cooperatives and other farmer associations 4. Managers and other personnel of credit services	• General skills for administration, planning, implementation, information flows, promotional activities • Technical and management skills applying to particular specialties • Leadership skills for generating community enthusiasm and collective action, staff team work and support from higher echelons

modernizing influences from which people of all ages learn *informally* and acquire most of their lifelong education. The second handicap is, of course, the severe shortage of *organized* educational programs—both formal and nonformal—that can assist in the modernization of rural areas.

Informal Education

In urban centers visited by ICED teams not only were there many more, and more accessible, schools than in rural areas, but there were many modern economic activities, media (newspapers, magazines, books, movies, radios and television broadcasts) and modern consumer goods—all the hallmarks of modern life. Thus, even without going to school or participating in a nonformal education program, persons living in such an environment are exposed to many modernizing educational influences and, if motivated, can learn much on their own to advance their employment opportunities and the quality of their lives. (They can also, of course, learn many socially undesirable things.)

In contrast, the rural areas visited had far fewer of these educative resources. A repeated question concerning literacy, for example, was what persons in a remote, traditional rural area would find to read after they went to the trouble of learning how. In such circumstances, both formal and nonformal educational programs face a much more difficult task than they do in urban areas. They cannot count nearly so much on educative forces of the environment to accelerate and reinforce their efforts; on the contrary, their efforts often are countered by traditional educative influences.

Formal Education

Rural areas also suffer from inadequate formal educational opportunities. Ordinarily, the objectives and curriculum of formal schools relate mainly to only the first of the four sets of needs listed earlier—i.e., general education— and contribute marginally, if at all, to the other three (although vocational schools may help develop occupational skills pertinent to the local economy). Yet rural primary schools are benefiting far fewer rural young people than official educational statistics imply.[5] The familiar enrollment/age ratios furnished by ministries of education, and by Unesco on an international scale, are usually heavily inflated with pupils who are repeating grades or who are older than the normative age population on which the ratio is based. Even more important, they conceal the high rate of dropouts among young children who leave school—usually never to return again—before they have learned to read, write or count. Thus many children included in the school statistics are actually destined for a life of illiteracy. This is particularly the case in rural areas, where the dropout rate at every grade level is usually considerably higher than in urban primary schools.

A Unesco study in Latin America in the 1960s revealed the sharp contrast between the numbers completing primary education in rural and urban areas. In Guatemala, for example, of every 1,000 *urban* children starting primary school in 1962, 496 could be expected to complete six grades, whereas of 1,000 *rural* children starting school, only 35 would finish six grades. In Colombia, the same study showed 273 *urban* children completing five grades as com-

[5]For a fuller discussion of this point, see ICED, *New Paths to Learning*, Chapter 3.

pared with 37 *rural* children (of every 1,000 enrolled in the first grade); in Uruguay, the comparable figures were 736 *urban* children to 417 *rural.*[6]

Though one can construct from official school statistics a profile of the *in-school* youth group in a country, it is far more difficult to obtain such a profile of the *out-of-school* youth group, broken down by age cohorts and amounts of previous schooling. It is obvious, however, that in most rural areas of developing nations the out-of-school group constitutes the vast majority of the whole population from, say, 10 to 20 years old. For all practical purposes, they are beyond the reach of formal education and must be served, if at all, by nonformal education programs. From our own samplings, we would guess that in most poorer rural areas today fewer than one in every four young people reaching 14 years of age—sometimes fewer than one in ten—has achieved functional mastery of reading and writing. And many of these, regrettably, may have lost this ability after a few years for lack of opportunity to use it.

The laudable target of achieving universal primary education by 1975 or 1980, which the developing nations themselves set under Unesco's auspices in the early 1960s, has proved far more difficult to attain than expected. Given the steady expansion in the number of school-age children (typically 2 to 3 percent annually) plus the rising unit costs of schooling and increasingly severe financial constraints on educational expansion—not to mention the costly reforms and improvements needed in rural schools—universal primary schooling seems a more distant goal in many countries today than when the target was set.

Meanwhile, primary schools, instead of serving as the great equalizers of opportunity they were meant to be, have become great discriminators. In the poorest rural areas they have, at best, equipped only a small minority of the new generation for the venture into a more modern life. The great majority of young persons seem destined to perpetuate the familiar cycle of ignorance and poverty.

This serious deficit in primary schooling compounds enormously the tasks of nonformal education, which not only must follow up primary education with further learning (a mammoth task in itself) but also try to rectify the deficit left by the formal schools. Yet the pattern of nonformal education programs that has evolved thus far is grossly inadequate to these tasks and seriously imbalanced in relation to the educational needs of different groups, both children and adults, in rural communities.

Nonformal Education

In our cursory survey of rural nonformal education we found comparatively few programs concerned with *general or basic education*. The most notable exceptions were adult literacy programs, which exist in one form or another in most developing nations (though typically they serve only a minute fraction of the rural adult population). There are also occasional "school equivalency" programs designed to provide school dropouts or unschooled youngsters an opportunity to make up whatever formal schooling they missed, sometimes

---

[6]Unesco, "Statistical Measurement of Educational Wastage Drop-out, Repetition and School Retardation," Working Paper prepared for the International Conference on Education, 32nd Session, Geneva, 1-9 July 1970, ED/BIE/CONFINTED 321 Ref. 1 (Paris, June 24, 1970) Appendix D. Mimeographed.

opening the possibility of reentry into the formal system. The most interesting of such programs was the rural education system in Upper Volta, which attempts to provide rural teenagers in three years the equivalent of a four-year primary education coupled with orientation and practical skills development in modern agriculture.[7] By and large, however, nonformal programs for general education are few, the common (but mistaken) assumption appearing to be that the regular schools take care of this kind of learning.

There are many educational programs for *family and community improvement* but typically they are fragmented, limited in scale and weak. It is common to find in the same rural area a series of small, separate programs for health, nutrition, home economics, family planning, cooperatives, local government, sports and recreation, etc.—all aimed at much the same audience, yet sponsored and operated by different public and private agencies with little, if any, coordination or cooperation.

On the other hand, *occupational education* typically claims the largest share of nonformal education in the rural areas of developing nations, with farmer education far in the lead. Even here, however, usually only a small fraction of the potential clientele is being effectively served, and these programs are often of such poor quality and spread so thin that they have little impact.

Moreover, farmer programs largely ignore the important role of women in agriculture, who comprise a large part of the agricultural labor force in many developing countries. In parts of Asia, for example, women often do most of the rice planting and also help with the harvesting. In many parts of Africa women do as much farming as men and sometimes more. In some areas, family-subsistence crops are customarily grown in the "women's fields" and cash crops in the "men's fields." Women often handle the marketing of crops, keep records and exercise important farm management functions. It follows, therefore, that the educational needs of girls and women for knowledge of improved agricultural practices may often be at least as great as the needs of boys and men. (See Table 2.3.) So-called women's programs are typically on a token scale and are designed with the implicit assumption that the place of rural women is solely in the home.

General education and occupational skill training programs for out-of-school adolescents typically range from scarce to nonexistent. Programs for developing nonfarm rural skills for artisans and small entrepreneurs are also scarce, and those that do exist are often ill-adapted to actual needs. We do not intend by these observations to ignore or disparage the many instances in which competent and strenuous efforts have been made, with considerable success, to meet important learning needs of rural people through nonformal education. But unfortunately these cases are in the minority and are dwarfed by the magnitude of the needs.

Few nations have yet made a serious effort to look at rural nonformal education as a whole in relation to their practical development needs. And fewer still have attempted to harmonize the scattered efforts of various public and private bodies in nonformal education. There is no one body responsible for maintaining an overview of all such activities, for projecting future needs, or for encouraging collaboration among different program sponsors. In nations where

---

[7]Sven Grabe, *The Rural Education System in Upper Volta,* ICED Case Study No. 14 (Essex, Conn., April 1972).

Table 2.3
Participation of Women in the Agricultural Labor Force
In Selected Countries—1960

Country	Total Agricultural Labor Force Number (in thousands)	Women Employed in Agricultural Labor Force	
		Number (in thousands)	Percentage of Total Agricultural Labor Force (%)
Thailand	11,342	5,735	51
Upper Volta	2,322	1,093	47
Senegal	1,212	539	44
Haiti	1,891	835	44
Malawi	1,483	590	40
Tanzania	4,180	1,650	39
Kenya	2,867	1,080	38
India	137,568	49,106	36
Korea, Republic of	5,433	1,521	28
Indonesia	24,471	6,788	28

SOURCE: International Labour Office, *Labour Force Projections*, 1965-1985, 1st ed. (Geneva, 1971). Table 3.

private educational initiatives are welcome, interesting and successful programs of nonformal education have been created by voluntary organizations.[8] But the limited resources of these organizations usually restrict such programs and consequently they benefit only a fraction of the rural population.

In summary, most rural areas in developing countries are characterized by poverty in their educational as well as in their economic resources. The informal learning environment, while often rich in culture and tradition, lacks those influences and material resources, such as print and other media, that would add to the general fund of knowledge and skills to promote development. Organized educational programs, both formal and nonformal, serve but a minority of young people and adults, and thus far have reinforced the neglect of important rural learning needs among out-of-school children and youth, among women, and among small subsistence farmers.

The reasons for these educational imbalances and the overall deprivation in rural areas are, of course, complex and beyond the scope of this chapter. Nevertheless, we should note that in general the educational conditions of rural areas are at least in part traceable to policies at national and international levels, and particularly to past and present patterns in the allocation of educational resources.

---

[8]A variety of these are described in J.R. Sheffield and V.P. Diejomaoh, *Non-formal Education in African Development* (New York: African-American Institute, 1972).

The Distorted Allocation of
Educational Resources

In most developing nations both the absolute amounts and the percentage share of total public revenues and of the gross national product devoted to formal education have substantially increased over the past ten to fifteen years. Recently, however, this rising percentage curve has been flattening as education encountered stiffer competition from other claimants on public funds.

There is no available basis for measuring comparable trends in nonformal education. Expenditure figures are simply not obtainable, except for occasional individual programs. They are tucked away under countless budgetary rubrics of many different organizations, public and private. Furthermore, in many nonformal education programs a substantial portion of the real costs is not recorded anywhere since they are in the form of contributed services and facilities.[9]

The General Pattern

Even without detailed statistical evidence, however, one can sense the general pattern of the allocation of educational resources in a developing nation by looking at the formal education budget, noting the scale and character of the principal programs of nonformal education, and spot-checking urban and rural educational activities. The following generalizations, formulated on the basis of ICED's research and field observations, seem to apply in most developing nations:

- Formal education receives the lion's share of total public educational outlays, in both urban and rural areas; nonformal programs get only a fractional share.[10]
- Urban areas receive a disproportionately large share of both formal and nonformal educational resources relative to their population.
- Formal educational expenditures in poorer rural areas benefit only a few of the children and youth, generally those from economically better-off families.
- The meager public resources for nonformal education in rural areas are devoted largely to adult programs (especially farmer education).
- The few nonformal programs for young people often benefit only those who are still attending school; programs to meet the needs of the out-of-schoolers, who constitute the great majority, are generally scarce.
- Potential resources for nonformal education in rural areas are often underutilized or untapped: physical facilities and equipment could be

---

[9]Expenditure figures on nonformal education are almost as difficult to obtain in industrialized nations. Even a cursory review makes clear, however, that nonformal education is much more extensively developed in the industrialized countries. A study of the United States in the 1950s by H.F. Clark and H.S. Sloan concludes that the outlays of certain major U.S. business corporations on nonformal education for their employees and customers rivaled in size the budgets of the largest universities. See *Classrooms in the Factories*, (Rutherford, New Jersey: Fairleigh Dickinson University, Institute of Research, 1958).

[10]In most Latin American countries, for example, there are from 200 to 350 times as many primary schoolteachers as field-level agricultural extension agents. FAO, *State of Food and Agriculture 1972* (Rome, 1972), p. 137.

22

used in spare hours; the expertise of local master craftsmen, progressive farmers, entrepreneurs and government specialists posted in rural communities could be harnessed for part-time instruction; and educated but underemployed adolescents and young adults could share their general education with others.

The Pattern of External Assistance

External assistance agencies have tended to reinforce this lopsided pattern of educational resource allocations. While it was not feasible for ICED to make a detailed statistical breakdown of educational assistance outlays (again because nonformal education is often hidden under many different rubrics and combined with noneducational items), even a cursory review of agency reports supports the following conclusions:

- External assistance for formal education has greatly exceeded that for nonformal education;
- Assistance for nonformal education has gone disproportionately to urban areas;
- Multilateral assistance for nonformal education is highly fragmented and reflects the specialized biases and narrow perspectives of different agencies;
- A high proportion of externally assisted nonformal education projects in rural areas has been on a pilot scale with relatively short periods of assured support, thus leaving in serious doubt their long-term continuity, enlargement and impact.

Unesco, the United Nations agency with prime responsibility for education, has had a long standing interest in nonformal adult education programs but has devoted only a small share of its total budget and staff time to nonformal education. Two notable exceptions to Unesco's generally minor activities in this field are its major program in "fundamental education" in the 1950s and, more recently, its experimental program of functional literacy (largely financed by UNDP). Like the national ministries of education with which it works most closely, Unesco's dominant interest has been in formal schooling and teacher training.

In the field of skill training, Unesco has concentrated on formal vocational schooling, while ILO has concentrated on various kinds of nonformal skill training programs. Both agencies, however, have primarily emphasized developing skilled manpower for modern urban uses; rural skill needs have been relatively neglected, though ILO has recently given more attention to rural skill training.

FAO has been very active in assisting rural nonformal education. While its major emphasis has been on programs for adult male farmers, it has also encouraged nonformal education services for rural women (mainly in home economics) and for rural youth (especially 4-H type clubs). WHO has encouraged and assisted programs for improved family health, though only on a limited scale in rural areas. UNICEF, in concert with the specialized UN agencies, has directed a substantial share of its resources to improving the diet, health and educational opportunities of rural children, but until recently the bulk of its educational support has been for formal schooling.

The education loan projects of the World Bank have been associated very largely with formal education. In noneducation loan projects, however, nonformal training components have been receiving increasing attention.

The patterns described above are the heritage of past policies and perspectives. Major changes in outlook and policies are currently taking place which could result in a much larger role for nonformal education over the next ten years. Unesco, FAO and ILO, for example, have all cooperated closely in the present study, for the avowed purpose of getting ideas that might be useful in broadening and strengthening their own program activities in nonformal education. In a recent revision of its policy guidelines, UNICEF reduced its emphasis on formal education in favor of increased attention to nonformal education. At the present writing, nonformal education is one of three top-priority subjects of the U.S. Agency for International Development in the field of human resource development. In developing nations as well, there is growing recognition of the urgency of doing more through nonformal means to meet the educational needs of rural people and rural development, and there is deep concern with finding more effective methods and strategies for accomplishing this. We now turn to a look at the strategies for increasing productivity and employment opportunities—the major focus of this study.

Four Approaches to Rural Extension and Training

The search for more effective approaches should logically begin with a critical appraisal of the approaches of past and present nonformal education programs. For the purposes of this study it has proved useful to group these approaches under four main headings: (1) the extension approach, (2) the training approach, (3) the cooperative self-help approach, and (4) the integrated development approach.

These are not watertight, mutually exclusive compartments; nor are they purely educational classifications. They differ mainly not in their educational principles and methods (which they often share) but in their quite different underlying conceptions and theories of rural development. The descriptions that follow, it should be emphasized, are idealized models. Many actual programs fitting into these general categories differ considerably from the "pure" versions we are about to sketch.

The *extension approach* in its purest doctrinal form involves not just the use of extension methods but at least an implicit conviction that an independent agricultural extension service can, by itself, help transform a static subsistence economy into a dynamic market economy while improving the quality of family and community life. Thus, what may seem on the surface to be simply a pedagogical doctrine and set of educational methods turns out to be a self-contained theory and strategy of rural development. It should be added that few "extensionists" any longer hold strictly to this view, but for more than a decade it had a powerful impact on the agricultural services of some developing regions.

The *training approach,* though sometimes wedded to the extension approach, has a different basic educational tradition and philosophy, more closely allied to institutionalized schooling. In contrast to the extension approach, which emphasizes the communication of information about innovative technical practices, the training approach emphasizes more systematic and deeper learning of specific basic skills and related knowledge. Training programs typically involve assembling learners in a training center—often a residential center—for a sustained period of instruction broken down into a planned succession of learning units combining theory and practice. The pedagogical principles are the same regardless of what specific skills are to be taught. But again, the training approach, as we use the term here, involves more than a particular set of educational principles and methods; in the hands of purist proponents it too involves a narrow, self-contained view and strategy of development, based on the premise that knowledge and skills by themselves can precipitate the process of development.

To be sure, even the "purist" proponents of the extension and training approaches usually do not openly espouse the one-eyed development theory we have attributed to them. Yet this is the only logical inference to be drawn from the positions they often take and from their behavior in particular situations. It would perhaps be most accurate to say that they are unaware of having any overall theory of rural development. Rather, they simply take it for granted (like most other types of specialists) that their particular approach is the key to development, that if it is given high priority things will start moving, and then it will follow as the night the day that all other necessary changes will take place more or less spontaneously.

Although extension proponents maintain that there is a two-way flow of information between specialists and farmers, in practice both the extension and training approaches seem to operate on the assumption that useful knowledge flows mainly in one direction: from outside specialists to the rural clienteles (who are presumed to be unable to diagnose their needs and problems, much less to devise solutions to them). Hence an aura of benevolent authoritarianism pervades many rural extension and training programs, reflecting the conviction that only by the intervention of outsiders with superior knowledge and wisdom can any rural society be jarred loose from its traditional moorings and started on the voyage to modernization.

The *cooperative self-help approach*, on the other hand, starts with the assumption that the complex process of rural transformation must begin with changes in the rural people themselves—in their attitudes toward change, in their aspirations for improvement, and above all in their perceptions of themselves and of their own inherent power, individually and collectively, to better their condition. The chief motive power for rural development, this view holds, must come from within, though once the people are ready to move, outside help of various kinds *in response to their expressed needs* may be essential to sustain progress.

This process of self-discovery and initiative, leading to self-help and self-management, is seen as education—but of a quite different sort than the education provided by formal schooling that tends to alienate rural young people from their environment, and also different from the technical instruction that outside experts provide to rural inhabitants as if they were passive objects incapable of thinking for themselves. There is heavy emphasis in this approach on the building of local institutions for cooperative self-help and governance.

If the enthusiastic proponents of this approach can be faulted, it is mainly on the score that they sometimes exaggerate what self-help and cooperation can accomplish by themselves, whereas considerable outside help often is needed to break important local bottlenecks to rural development.

The *integrated development approach* is highly versatile and eclectic in its ideologies and educational methods. Its hallmark is its broader view of the rural

25

development process and its coordination under a single "management system" of the essential components (including education) required to get agricultural or rural development moving. The management system may be highly authoritarian or it may be designed to provide—at least eventually—an important role for local people in planning, decision-making and implementation. Its cardinal emphasis in all events is upon the rational deployment and coordination of all the principal factors required for agricultural and rural development.

The bulk of existing nonformal education programs in the fields under study here obviously do not coincide perfectly with one or another of these four approaches. Most programs deviate from the pure form, and many combine elements of more than one approach. Nevertheless, the categories outlined above provide a useful initial analytical structure for now examining sample cases from the real world.

3: EXTENSION PROGRAMS IN AGRICULTURE

Almost every developing country now has some sort of organized agricultural extension service. Some have several. Extension services vary considerably, however. Many, for example, operate on a nationwide scale, whereas others concentrate on a particular geographic area. Some attempt to provide guidance on a wide range of farm products, while others specialize in one or two major commercial crops.[1] Many extension services operate independently of other support services (as they do in much of Latin America), while others (for example, in Indonesia) are closely coordinated with companion services.

The balance of this chapter focuses on two contrasting models of agricultural extension: the so-called conventional model, from which the Office of Rural Development (ORD) in the Republic of Korea evolved, and a much more specialized model, illustrated by the Société d'aide technique et de coopération (SATEC) in Senegal.

The Conventional Model

The most prevalent type of extension service in Latin America and in much of Asia today, often referred to as the conventional or classical model, drew its initial inspiration from United States technical assistance. This model, however, is by no means a carbon copy of agricultural extension as it evolved in the United States. It is, rather, an artificial construct fashioned in the early 1940s and early 1950s by professors of agricultural extension in certain land-grant universities—the so-called extensionist school—who sought to make agricultural extension a separate scientific profession with its own basic concepts, theory, principles and methodologies. Their disciples, both Americans and many from abroad who studied at these universities, propagated and helped establish this conventional model in many developing countries in the decade following the end of World War II.

Allowing for certain deviations from country to country, this model has the following distinguishing characteristics:

Objectives. Its prime objective is to persuade and help farmers increase production by adopting improved technical practices. Secondarily it seeks to improve rural family life by teaching home economics to women, and to create modern young farmers through youth clubs of the 4-H type (i.e., clubs for rural young people offering instruction in agriculture and home economics; the four Hs stand for improving "head, heart, hands, and health").

Target groups. The prime audience, in principle, includes all farmers and, secondarily, their wives and adolescent children. Priority is often given, however, to particular classes of farmers, notably the larger and

---

[1]Many extension services in Africa follow the latter pattern as do those concerned with major export crops in Latin America (e.g., coffee in Colombia) and in Asia (especially rice).

more progressive ones, in selected geographic areas or to those growing particular crops.

Organization and structure. The extension service is typically under the ministry of department of agriculture (though it is sometimes attached to an agricultural college or university); it operates independently within the broad framework of national agricultural policies, objectives and priorities. It has a hierarchic structure with a network of professionally trained field agents at the base, supervised and backstopped by more highly qualified administrators and specialists at each of three or four tiers above (e.g., in subdistrict, district, provincial and national offices). See Table 3.1.

Table 3.1
Chain of Command in Extension Services
Kenya, Nigeria and India

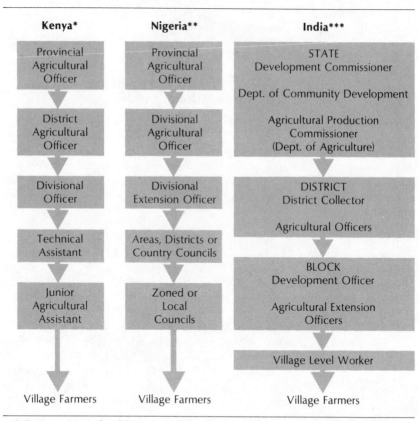

Kenya*	Nigeria**	India***
Provincial Agricultural Officer	Provincial Agricultural Officer	STATE Development Commissioner
		Dept. of Community Development
District Agricultural Officer	Divisional Agricultural Officer	Agricultural Production Commissioner (Dept. of Agriculture)
Divisional Officer	Divisional Extension Officer	DISTRICT District Collector
		Agricultural Officers
Technical Assistant	Areas, Districts or Country Councils	BLOCK Development Officer
Junior Agricultural Assistant	Zoned or Local Councils	Agricultural Extension Officers
		Village Level Worker
Village Farmers	Village Farmers	Village Farmers

*E. R. Watts, "Agricultural Extension in Embu District of Kenya," *Journal of Rural Development,* (1969) p. 69.

**James M. Kincaid, Jr., *Strategies for Improvement of Agricultural Extension Work and Non-Degree Agricultural Extension Work and Non-Degree Agricultural Training in Nigeria,* CSNRD-13 (East Lansing: Michigan State University, Sept. 1968) p. 18.

***Donald G. Green, *Relating Education and Training to Agricultural Development,* ICED Background Paper No. 2, (Essex, Conn., May 1972).

The extension service relies on agricultural colleges and universities (and sometimes on agricultural vocational schools) for the basic preparation of its personnel, while providing its own specialized preservice and inservice training. It relies for its technical "messages" on research organizations and specialists in the ministry of agriculture and the university. It may or may not collaborate with other agricultural support services operating in the field. It considers itself an independent educational service for farmers.

Staff. Its staff includes mainly persons with basic training in agricultural sciences and production technologies and, when available, added special training in the theory and methods of extension. Civil service rank, salary and educational qualifications are lowest at the bottom and highest at the top of the hierarchy. Promotion generally means moving to a higher level; hence the ablest field workers tend to be transferred to desk jobs.

Educational content. The emphasis—often exclusively—is on production technologies; only secondarily if at all is attention given to such economic and logistical matters as farm planning and management, use of credit, procurement of inputs, and marketing of produce. The technical "messages" are usually relayed to local agents from experts at higher echelons in the form of "recommended practices" to be disseminated to farmers through demonstrations and individual consultations. Women extension agents, usually few in number, convey information on recommended practices to housewives on such matters as cooking, food preservation, kitchen gardens, and dressmaking.

Methods. Extension methods spring from a combination of pedagogical, communications and merchandising theories. The aim is to achieve a rapid and widespread adoption of desirable innovations in farm (and household) practices with the local extension worker in the role of "change agent." The stages involved, as seen by extension specialists, are: (1) achieving "awareness" (radio is considered useful here); (2) provoking "interest" (through local meetings, posters, exhibitions, etc.); (3) information and demonstration ("persuasion"), including farmer visits to demonstration plots; (4) "trial" by interested farmers on their own fields; and (5) "adoption" by convinced farmers.[2]

Some extension services concentrate on progressive "leader" farmers, hoping thereby to produce a multiplier effect. Other services reject this method as too "elitist." Some extension services operate special farmer training centers to give more intensive training to leader farmers and other community leaders. (See Chapter 4.)

Costs and finance. Extension services are labor-intensive, especially at the local level where few if any facilities or equipment (other than transport and perhaps demonstration fields) are required. Unit costs (per farmer served) vary greatly according to qualifications and salary levels of employees (particularly local agents), the ratio of agents to farmers, the geographic disposition of farmers (determining the amount of travel time between visits to individual farms), and the extent of ancillary duties

---

[2]These stages are discussed in Everett M. Rogers, *Diffusion of Innovations* (New York: The Free Press, 1962), especially Chapter IV "The Adoption Process"; and Herbert F. Lionberger, *Adoption of New Ideas and Practices* (Ames, Iowa: The Iowa State University Press, 1960), pp. 21-31.

(e.g., clerical work or the supervision of youth clubs) imposed on local agents.

The full operation is typically financed either by the central government or shared with the provincial or state government.[3]

There is extensive literature on the earlier versions of the conventional type of extension service, including considerable evaluative evidence that will be cited later in this report. Hence it seemed worthwhile to choose for a case study a more recent and exceptional descendant of the conventional extension model: the Office of Rural Development (ORD) in the Republic of Korea. A brief summary of the case study follows.

A Sophisticated Version of the Conventional Model

Objective. The Office of Rural Development (ORD) in the Republic of Korea[4] (evolving from the earlier Institute of Agriculture, established in 1957) with extensive U.S. technical assistance. Its main function by adopting improved technical practices. Emphasis is also placed on helping rural families improve their incomes, not only by increasing the yields of their customary crops but also by introducing new crops (such as fruits and vegetables) and taking up sideline farm activities (such as raising hogs or poultry for sale in urban markets) and cottage-industry-type activities in their spare time (e.g., making wigs and embroidered items for export), which can provide income during the long winter season.

Target groups. Farmers, their wives and older children are ORD's prime target groups thoughout the country. Farmers are assistaed in opening up new land and in adopting conservation practices. Other types of farm and home improvements are encouraged and assisted: home economics instruction is provided for women and "handyman" carpentry, masonry and similar instruction for men. More than usual emphasis is given to the training of rural youth in modern farming practices. The 4-H clubs in the Republic of Korea are far more extensive and better supported than those in any other developing country examined by ICED. In addition to the local 4-H clubs, special centers have been established for training 4-H members in the operation and maintenance of agricultural machinery (now being introduced on an expanded scale, in part to overcome farm labor shortages).

Organization. ORD is an operating arm of the Ministry of Agriculture and Forestry, with a relatively high degree of autonomy and its own director. ORD includes (atypically) both the principal national agricultural research facilities and the national guidance (extension) service. This arrangement facilitates close working relations between the two, not only at the national level but also in the field (where there are a number of experiment stations).

Like other national extension services, ORD has several echelons, with offices at the national, provincial and county levels, and below these, local branch offices. Unlike most other national extension services, ORD's extension

---

[3]See Chapter 11 for a discussion of costs and financing of extension in general, which also includes references to the costs and financing of the two case studies summarized in this chapter.
[4]See Manzoor Ahmed, *Farmer Education Program of the Office of Rural Development in the Republic of Korea*, ICED Case Study No. 5 (Essex, Conn., July 1972).

and research activities below the national office are partially financed and managed by lower-echelon governments, thus ensuring a strong local voice in adapting national programs and priorities to special local conditions.

Staff. The staff of ORD includes some 6,000 extension workers—two-thirds working directly in the field and the other third in backstopping positions in county and local branch offices. There is roughly one extension worker on the average for every 425 rural households.

In addition to its regular staff, more than 100,000 local volunteers (mostly leading farmers) have been recruited and given short-term training at farmer training centers. These volunteers serve as leaders of three types of local clubs—4-H youth clubs, farm improvement clubs (for men) and home improvement clubs (for women)—and provide a close linkage between the official extension service and local farm communities.

Even with a generous discount of the official statistics to allow for inactive or marginally active clubs and members, the membership data shown in Table 3.2 reveal an impressive mobilization and involvement of local people in the ORD program.

Methods. The extension techniques used by ORD include all the conventional ones and considerable use of mass media—radio, films, flip-charts, farm bulletins and journals, and traveling libraries (literacy is relatively high).

Appraisal. In its basic conception and design, ORD constitutes a major advance over earlier models of national extension services. And its operation, as observed by an ICED team in late 1971, seemed clearly superior to national extension services observed elsewhere (save for exceptional situations such as those in Tanjore District in India and Jombang District in Indonesia). Nevertheless, ORD has some serious problems and shortcomings. Some stem mainly from budgetary constraints but others run much deeper.

The most fundamental problem concerns the field staff. Several years ago about 90 percent of new recruits had college training and the rest secondary education; by 1971 the proportions were reversed. Turnover is extremely high; many new recruits use ORD as a point of entry into the civil service and

Table 3.2
Office of Rural Development:
Reported Number of Clubs, Members, and Volunteer Leaders
1970

Type of Clubs	Number of Clubs	Number of Club Members	Number of Volunteer Leaders in Club
Farm Improvement Clubs	28,949	356,140	32,582
Home Improvement Clubs	18,189	266,468	19,962
4-H Clubs	29,803	633,481	63,208
TOTAL	76,941	1,256,269	115,752

NOTE: The clubs and memberships reported on above are not all fully active.
SOURCE: Republic of Korea, Office of Rural Development.

then transfer to another service at the first opportunity. Preservice and inservice training of extension workers has been cut back sharply—a dubious economy measure. Extension workers complain of being used by local government officials for office work unconnected with their professional duties, thus curtailing their contacts with farmers.

The reasons for high turnover are not hard to find. An agricultural college graduate can earn about twice as much teaching in an agricultural secondary school as he can as an ORD extension worker; he can earn still more in a nonagricultural job in the city. As an extension worker he would have longer hours and harder work under less attractive conditions, with little chance for promotion. Because of these unfavorable salary and work conditions, more than half the graduates of agricultural colleges are taking employment outside the agricultural system.

A related problem is the evident decline in the quality of the multimedia system which is meant to supplement and reinforce the efforts of extension workers. Budget stringencies have forced a sharp decrease, for example, in the production of instructional films, obliging extension workers to use films that are obsolete.

A third problem is the lack of coordination, both at the national level and in the field, between ORD extension work and complementary support services (particularly agricultural credit) handled by other organizations.

Finally, there appears to be a problem of priorities in the allocation of resources and staff effort among ORD's various stated objectives and programs. In principle, ORD's range of interests is much wider than agricultural production *per se;* its stated goal is rural development, broadly conceived. Yet it appears that such objectives as household improvement, sideline jobs to raise farm family incomes, and the promotion of new and mixed cropping have been subordinated to the traditionally narrow production goals of conventional extension services. The bulk of ORD's effort, as measured by budgetary allocations and personnel assignments, is aimed at increasing agricultural output, particularly rice production (in line with the current national goal of achieving self-sufficiency in rice). A number of knowledgeable economists question whether this heavy stress on rice production at the expense of other commodities makes good economic sense.

Nevertheless, on the basis of scattered circumstantial evidence, ORD's extension efforts over the past decade have probably contributed materially to steady increases—averaging over 4 percent annually in the 1960s—in the nation's agricultural productivity and output, and to the improvement of rural life and incomes. Unfortunately, solid evidence to prove the point is lacking because ORD has made little effort to evaluate its own effectiveness.

Extension as a Catalyst in a Production Campaign

Agricultural extension evolved differently in much of Africa. Instead of building nationwide extension services to serve all areas and a variety of crops and farmers, the African colonial governments generally concentrated their extension efforts on introducing or expanding production of one or another major export crop—such as cocoa, groundnuts, cotton or tea—in particularly favorable regions. One objective no doubt was to improve the welfare of indigenous farmers, but no less important objectives were to generate cash for paying local taxes and to benefit colonial commercial interests.[5]

In these situations, extension services provided the "package of practices" to be followed, while coordinated services supplied necessary physical inputs (seeds, fertilizers, insecticides) and marketing services, usually through marketing boards or private companies. Thus extension became an integral part of a "management system." Often the package of practices was compulsory. Farmers were not merely *taught,* they were *ordered,* under pain of penalty, to observe certain soil conservation rules, to plant specific land to specific crops, to follow prescribed cultivation practices and time schedules, and to sell their products only to designated organizations at designated prices. It is therefore little wonder that farmers generally viewed the extension agent less as a friend and guide than as one more representative of a distant government that was out to exploit them. With independence, these regulatory features of extension services were diminished or discarded.[6]

Yet the concept of making extension an integral part of a larger program to expand output of a major export crop remained very much alive. In the Sudan, for example, it found successful expression in the ambitious Gezira cotton scheme (discussed in a later chapter), thanks especially to unusually imaginative and enlightened management. But also found expression elsewhere in a number of ill-conceived, government-sponsored "crash programs" that ended in disaster. Somewhere between these extremes was the SATEC scheme developed in Senegal.

Société d'aide technique et de coopération (SATEC) in Senegal[7]

Background. In the wake of Senegal's independence, French support prices for a major crop—were to be phased out rapidly. Hence the great majority of Senegal's cash-crop farmers would have to increase their output of groundnuts at a lower price or accept a substantial reduction of income.

SATEC, a quasi-private technical assistance organization, was to help the farmers through this difficult transition period. Initiated in 1964 with aid from the European Development Fund (FED), and Fonds (français) d'aide et de coopération (FAC), the SATEC scheme applied to the major groundnut-producing regions of central Senegal.[8]

---

[5]A. J. Loveridge, "A Survey of British Experience of Non-Formal Education for Rural and Agricultural Development in Developing Countries." Paper prepared for the ICED in cooperation with the Overseas Development Administration and the Institute of Education, University of London, mimeographed (London, April 1972) Chapter 7, Page 13.

[6]The "contamination" of extension with less popular functions such as tax collection did not altogether disappear, however. In East Africa, for example, after independence, part of the job of the agricultural assistant (field-level extension worker) continued to be the collection of loans and enforcement of regulations. Many farmers still perceive the extension worker as an authoritarian and even alien figure.

[7]See Pierre Furter and Sven Grabe, Senegal: Rural Vocational Training Centers, ICED Case Study No. 8 (unpublished).

[8]In 1968 the original SATEC scheme began transformation into a permanent national extension service under the new name SODEVA, with a broadening of its objectives and many changes in structure, methods, staffing and staff training. The description given refers only to the SATEC phase of what has now become known as the SATECDEVA scheme.

The scheme itself was conceived as a specialized educational intervention for supplementing and reinforcing previous rural development efforts, including the program of *animation rurale.*

Organization. The new SATEC organization was essentially a supplier of advice and knowledge and a coordinator and expediter of existing organizations. Credit supplies and marketing functions continued to be handled by existing cooperative societies (some 1,500 of which served groundnut producers). Supply of improved agricultural implements was handled by CISCOMA, a commercial enterprise with its own manufacturing plants near Dakar. Specialized research on groundnuts continued to be the responsibility of the National Agricultural Research Center at Bambey, which had six regional research stations and demonstration fields for adaptive research and verification of recommended practices.

Objectives. SATEC began with the assumption that the technical problems of increasing productivity in groundnuts and millet had already been solved by previous research, though continuing research could gradually improve these solutions.[9] Thus the major remaining problem identified was to improve the communication of knowledge and skills to growers and to help them select the right inputs and implements, adopt more efficient practices, and extend planted areas.[10]

Target groups. SATEC designed educational programs for two sets of farmers: (1) a "heavy" program for larger farmers (over 10 hectares) who had draught animals (oxen) and could be expected to make the largest and quickest contribution to achieving the production targets (a 10 percent increase in overall output per year), and (2) a "light" program directed toward the rest of the farming population.[11]

Educational content. Within this general scheme the learning elements were combined into packages of recommendations on tested seed and fertilizer combinations and instructions concerning soil preparation, planting density, weeding practices and the use of insecticides, translated into simplified instructions on the important steps in every single operation. Farmers were also given help in training oxen.

Management and staff. For rapid diffusion of this program SATEC set up a management and extension staff structure headed by a small management

---

[9]Groundnuts and millet were rotating crops; both were major subsistence as well as cash crops in the SATEC area.

[10]Manpower supply, soil exhaustion and rainfall, not the amount of land available, were seen as the major bottlenecks to increased production. Under prevailing land arrangements, crown lands were allocated to families on the basis of how much they could farm with their own labor. A switch from archaic to more efficient hand tools could help ease the labor bottleneck, expecially in peak periods, enabling a given family to work more land. Even more, the introduction and more efficient use of bullocks could make possible a major breakthrough in the utilization of available land.

[11]This diffentiation was later carried one step further. SODEVA today differentiates between (1) advance farmers—*paysans de point*—comprising 10 to 15 percent of the total and for whom the goal is complete modernization of all farm activities; (2) progressive farmers—*paysans progressistes*—comprising 20 to 30 percent, for whom the objective is full adoption of recommended practices on a portion of their land (excluding the use of oxen if they do not already have them); and (3) traditional farmers, roughly 60 percent of the total, for whom the loosely formulated goal is the adoption of as many recommended practices as possible, but without taking much time of qualified extension advisors.

group (including communications and information specialists) in Dakar. Three regional offices were directed by field managers (agronomist level) covering thirty-nine extension zones. The total field staff included 62 agents and assistant agents at an agricultural technician level (20 of them Senegalese trainees) and 700 extension workers (vulgarisateurs) recruited from among younger growers in the villages who had at least some formal education and sufficient knowledge of French for effective communication with the mostly French-speaking agents. Originally the extension workers were to be part-time workers who would continue to cultivate their land and would receive a small salary from the program (U.S. $33 per month). Eventually, many of them became full-time extension workers.

The technical agents, many of whom had previously worked in agricultural improvement projects in Africa, received mainly inservice training. The extension workers were given a short intensive course in communicating the recommended package of practices to farmers.

Few capital facilities were required other than offices for senior management, regional directors and principal agents. The idea was to keep the whole staff on the move in the field, and for this a generous allowance was provided for transport.

Performance. The SATEC scheme was a well-planned and well-managed campaign, with detailed targets, time schedules and instructions for all, and with maximum independence from national bureaucracies. The scheme got off to an auspicious start; yields and total output rose significantly in the first two years (1964-65 and 1965-66). In the next two years, however, the rains failed, production decreased and farmers became disenchanted with the whole scheme. What went wrong is still debatable. In all events, the whole approach was reexamined, resulting in a decision to reorganize the program drastically.

The two cases described in this chapter—ORD and SATEC—are but a sampling of the experience with the extension approach to agricultural development in developing nations. Between them they highlight the main philosophy and techniques of this approach and reveal several major problems that have plagued extension services practically everywhere. These problems bear particularly on: (1) adequacy of budget, (2) staff recruitment, training and utilization, (3) adequacy of research backstopping and the soundness of recommended practices, (4) priorities among multiple objectives, and (5) coordination of educational activities with essential complementary inputs and services. We shall return in later chapters to a fuller consideration of these problems.

4: TRAINING PROGRAMS IN AGRICULTURE

While extension activities have been the dominant form of farmer education in most countries, more institutionalized and systematic programs have been undertaken for the training of extension workers, and special farmer training centers are increasingly being used to provide deeper training for selected farmers, usually as a supplement to the extension system.

There are many different models of farmer training centers, often with different objectives, clienteles, methods and duration of courses. The farmer training centers in the Korean Office of Rural Development (ORD), for example, mainly give brief (two- or three-day) leadership training courses to selected local farmers who serve as leaders of 4-H and other local farm clubs. The Kenya Farmer Training Centres (FTCs), examined below, are among the most widely known. Formerly they offered long-term training for one or two years for selected young farmers, but now they provide mainly one-week specialized courses for farmers (sometimes accompanied by their wives), designed to encourage them to adopt selected new practices and to serve as a good example for their neighbors. India's new Coordinated Farmer Training Program includes (along with "national demonstration fields," radio discussion groups and functional literacy teaching) farmer training centers located at field research stations. Typically, these Indian centers offer year-long agricultural training for young farmers, shorter-term training—one week or so—for other farmers, and special programs for particular groups, such as farmers' widows who must learn how to manage the family farm.

Most of the centers mentioned thus far are residential, but Rhodesia is reported to have created a network of modest local farmer training centers where nearby farmers gather one day a week for instruction by their extension agent. Tanzania is also moving away from residential farmer training centers to easily accessible local centers. In a few countries special training courses are organized for farmers at agricultural colleges.

This chapter reviews four quite different training models that illustrate both the diversity of practices and the similarity of problems generally found in farmer training centers.[1]

- The Kenya FTCs, in the early 1960s and before, appeared to be doing very effective work, but more recently they have encountered a combination of serious problems that has prompted reconsideration of their basic purposes and design. Similar centers in other East African nations have been undergoing changes from the earlier model.
- The *Rural Training Centres (RTCs)* in Senegal are of more recent vintage and reflect a more classical, long-term "vocational training" approach, comparable in pedagogical theory and methods to industrial training schools. In contrast to the Kenya FTCs and many other farmer

---

[1]The costs and financing of the programs summarized in this chapter are treated in Chapter 11.

training institutions, the Senegalese centers were not conceived of as an appendage of an extension service, rather, they were part of a tripartite rural training scheme that would help equip each rural community with an "elite" team of farmers, artisans and women's leaders who would point the way to modernization.

- The *Rice Production Training Program* of the International Rice Research Institute (IRRI) in the Philippines represents a unique strategy for trying to increase the competence and effectiveness of national agricultural extension services in several rice-producing countries. The program gives special training to key extension officials who in turn, it was hoped, would reproduce this training among their subordinates.

- SENA's program of *Promoción Profesional Popular-Rural (PPP-R)* in Colombia is a special case in which a well-established national training organization that previously had concentrated largely on improving urban industrial skills undertook to extend its services into remote rural areas through mobile training unit.[2]

All these otherwise diverse programs employ pedagogical principles and methods aimed at giving the learner, through a systematic sequence of instructional units combining theory and practice, a basic mastery of certain skills and related knowledge that can serve him for an extended period under a variety of conditions. Extension service, in contrast, are concerned primarily with disseminating specific and immediately useful technical information on new farming practices and at persuading farmers to apply thse new methods.

Many proponents of the training philosophy would draw the distinction by saying that extension is essentially informational, whereas training is more genuinely educational. The two philosophies and sets of methods are, however, more often complementary than contradictory. Still, there are always the questions of what relative emphasis should be given to each function and how to knit them together for maximum combined effect.

The training programs discussed in this chapter are largely or exclusively concerned with agricultural production skills and knowledge. Other rural training schemes concerned with nonfarm occupations are considered in the following chapter. Though to treat these topics separately is somewhat artificial, particularly since farmers need both sorts of skills, it is a realistic reflection of how most training programs are actually organized. Typically, agricultural experts design training programs that concentrate on agricultural skills, while other kinds of training experts create programs that focus on nonagricultural skills.

Short-Term Farmer Training

The architects of the first example we will review—the FTCs in Kenya—were agricultural officers intent on helping Africans who were experienced mainly in traditional subsistence farming to become modern commercial farmers. Over the years the Kenya FTCs have been modified considerably, especially in the length and content of their courses, but their focus has re-

---

[2]For a description and analysis of SENA, see also Frederick Harbison and George Seltzer, "National Training Schemes." In *New Strategies for Educational Development: The Cross-Cultural Search for Nonformal Alternatives*, edited by Cole S. Brembeck and Timothy J. Thompson (Lexington, Mass.: D.C. Heath and Co., Lexington Books, 1972), pp. 195-200.

mained almost exclusively on farming production methods (for men) and home economics (for their wives). Since the Kenya FTCs have served as a model for a number of other developing countries, especially in Africa, it is important to understand why the model has changed through time, what its particular virtues appear to be, and what major problems it has encountered.

Farmer Training Centres (FTCs)

Background. The Kenya model of Farmer Training Centres[3] had its origins in the former Jeanes School, a residential nonformal training center on the outskirts of Nairobi, where courses for practicing farmers and their wives were first introduced in 1934. Farmer training remained an important feature of the Jeanes program until the closing of the school in 1961, and its success had a significant influence on the Ministry of Agriculture's entire approach to farmer education.

In the years immediately following the Second World War and coinciding with the need to resettle African troops, the British agricultural administration, in an attempt to establish a family "group" farming system, introduced a two-year farmer training course at one of its field staff training centers in western Kenya. Although the group farming experiment failed, the training center, redesignated a Farm Institute, continued to devote itself entirely to farmer training courses, shortened to one year. The apparent popularity of the courses and the onset of the Mau Mau rebellion led, between 1951 and 1954, to the opening of two more centers in western Kenya.

Objectives. The success of the residential approach to farmer training was taken into account by the British Colonial Government when the first real attempt was made, in 1954, to bring African peasant farmers into modern commercial farming from which they had previously been largely excluded. To help implement this new policy, steps were taken simultaneously to create a broad-scale extension service, expand the number of farm institutes, promote land consolidation, registration and small-scale farm planning, and qualify African farmers for access to production credit through commercial channels. This ambitious effort to wean thousands of small-scale African farmers from traditional subsistence farming posed a far more complex educational challenge than that of introducing experienced commercial farmers to improved technologies.

Structure. The program of farmer education organized to meet this challenge established an administrative and institutional infrastructure that facilitated rapid expansion after independence. By 1961 there were thirteen farmer training centers, situated mainly in the fertile central region and western areas of Kenya. The National Christian Council of Kenya (NCCK), in a loose association with the government, also began a program of its own to develop rural training centers. These were located to serve major farming districts and covered two million acres in the former "white" highlands which had been

---

[3]Because of the extensive literature on Kenya FTCs, ICED did not prepare a separate case study. The following discussion draws especially on an ICED working paper by Clifford Gilpin which synthesizes much of the evidence in the scattered documentation (much of it unpublished), and on an extensive study of nonformal education in Kenya (particularly Chapter 4) by Roy C. Prosser (now an ICED member), "The Development and Organisation of Adult Education in Kenya with special reference to African Rural Development, 1945-1960" (Ph.D. dissertation, University of Edinburgh, 1971).

subdivided and reallocated to landless Africans. Meanwhile, the government opened eight centers, including a special large-scale farmers' training center for Africans who were taking over European farms intact; a special center for training in tea cultivation; and one for veterinary purposes.

By 1967 there were twenty-seven FTCs, twenty-one run by the government and six by the National Christian Council of Kenya, with a combined total of nearly 1,500 beds. In 1971 the total number of centers remained the same, though new centers have been opened and other closed.

A typical FTC serves fifty to sixty farmers (or farmers and their wives) at a time. It includes one or two dormitory blocks, offices, classrooms, kitchen, and a combined dining room-lecture hall. There is generally a large commercial farm of one hundred or more acres, which is expected to provide income to the center, and a demonstration plot or small-holding. A truck or bus is provided to take participants to and from courses and on educational visits.

Staff. The professional staff of a typical FTC includes a principal (an assistant agricultural officer with four years of secondary schooling and an agricultural diploma), two male agricultural assistants and one female assistant for teaching home economics. Most staff are agricultural production specialists with little or no training in extension methods or teaching. They are part of the general agricultural field service assigned for duty at the FTC.[4]

The FTC principal is responsible to the local district agricultural officer and to the head of the farmer training section in the Ministry of Agricultrue's headquarters in Nairobi. The FTC principal is the liaison with field extension staff through the district agricultural officer. Courses are arranged in conjunction with the district agricultural officer, who is responsible for recruiting farmers.

Educational Activities. Over the years, farmers' courses have gradually shortened in duration, from one year in the mid-fifties to the now prevalent one-week course. Course content has also changed, becoming more specialized and tending to concentrate more on single aspects of cash-crop production or animal husbandry. However, the general course is by no means uncommon. The course subjects are determined by the needs of the particular local farmer group in residence and they vary from place to place. Teaching methodology, however, is standard—a mixture of classroom lecture combined with and related to field work.

While the prime objective of the FTCs has been to give agricultural instruction to farmers, they have also been used for short refresher courses for agricultural field staff. FTCs have also been used by other government departments and agencies for their courses, including 4-H clubs and cooperatives, and for chiefs, local leaders and community development workers. Such courses have normally been held during slack periods in FTCs when local farmers were occupied with planting or harvesting.

Costs. Fees are charged to farmers at the rate of about U.S. $2 (15 Kshs) per week. These fees in no way cover costs, and true recurrent costs are impossible to determine accurately. Budgets are controlled by the district agricultural officer and there is often no special allocation for the FTC. Expenses vary from area to area and income may accrue from different sources, including the FTC commercial farm. The capital costs of new centers have been rising rapidly as

---

[4]Kenya is comparatively well endowed with its agricultural extension service, having an approximate ratio of one technical assistant for every 1,000 farm holdings.

buildings become more elaborate. An estimate for a new FTC in 1970 reached almost U.S. $250,000 (Ik. 100,000). External aid agencies have helped significantly in the building of FTCs and in the provision of bursaries to meet recurring costs.

Recent Problems. During recent years a number of problems in the FTC system have become apparent. These include:

(1) *Serious underutilization of FTC capacity.* For instance, in 1971 40 percent of the places at FTCs were unfilled and 30 percent of the planned courses were cancelled.

(2) *Dramatic drop in farmer attendance.* Attendance of farmers and their wives fell by a third between 1970 and 1971 and by more than 45 percent between 1966 and 1971.

(3) *Severe difficulty in the provision of funds for recurrent cost items.* This has resulted in a number of FTCs having to close for part of a year; in 1971 some closed for as long as six months.

(4) *Inordinately high rate of staff turnover.* In 1967 only seven of the government FTCs kept the same principal throughout the year, and in 1971 only six achieved this.

(5) *Low morale of FTC staff.* This problem is continually referred to in government reports, independent studies and other official documents.

(6) *Increase in the use of FTCs by other departments and agencies for nonfarmer courses.* Calculated on the basis of actual attendance, in 1963 only 6 percent of participants were in nonfarmer courses; in 1966 this proportion had risen to 28 percent and in 1971 to nearly 60 percent. (While increased use of FTCs for nonfarmer courses is undoubtedly desirable in itself, it should not be at the expense of the farmer programs, and may reflect a decline in farmer interest.)

We shall examine some of the above problems in more detail in later chapters; meanwhile, it should be noted that despite the gross underutilization of existing FTCs and the various other difficulties, four new FTCs were scheduled to be built with external aid in the plan period 1970 to 1974.

Appraisal. The available evaluation evidence, though limited and inconclusive, suggests that useful results were achieved by the FTCs (though perhaps less so in recent years). The various partial evaluation studies generally agree that (1) FTC farmers show a higher rate of adoption of recommended practices than other farmers; (2) a high percentage of FTC farmers name FTCs their major source of information on new practices; (3) FTC farmers appear to have influenced neighboring farmers to become early adopters; (4) a high percentage would like to return to an FTC for further training (which appears to contradict the evidence of declining farmer interest); (5) FTC farmers have higher cash incomes and living standards than other farmers.

These findings, however, rest on a very narrow base of evidence. Moreover, they must be interpreted with caution: in particular, the greater innovativeness and higher incomes of FTC farmers may largely reflect the characteristics of many who choose to attend an FTC course.

Toward the end of the decade, initiatives were taken to remedy the conspicuous ills of the FTCs and thus improve their cost-effectiveness and productivity (which is discussed in a later chapter). Recommendations were made that the FTCs be given a separate budget. A Board of Adult Education was set up which included in its brief the improved planning of rural training centers, including the FTCs.

Out of this format has come an interesting new concept—that of the district development center.[5] The Kenya Government policy paper assenting to this provides·for experimentation in two districts. In both there is to be a center serving the training needs of farmers, cooperative development, health and allied requirements, rural trade and industry, community development, and the general needs of youth and adults.

The center is to be administered and staffed through "wings" controlled by the technical departments concerned, and coordinated by a principal of university graduate level. The anticipated effects are: better coordination of activities; improved course quality since there would be mroe staff from differennt disciplines to draw from; improved communication with the field since extension services will be focused on the new center; and more realistic orientation of training to meet the many-sided needs of rural development. The decision has now been made to proceed with this experiment.

Longer-Term Farmer Training

The farmer training scheme in Senegal, briefly sketched below, is a purer and more classical version of the training approach than the Kenya FTCs. The two schemes were designed by professionals with very different backgrounds and outlooks. The Kenya FTCs were conceived by Agricultural officers who believed that extension services needed to be supplemented by more systematic and intensive training for selected farmers, but that the two should operate in unison.

The Rural Training Centres in Senegal, on the other hand, were conceived by vocational training specialists who sought to extend to rural occupations, both agricultural and artisan, basic principles and methods of vocational training similar to those ILO had long recommended for meeting skilled manpower requirements of urban areas. To them, farming was simply another occupation, with its own definable set of skills and body of related knowledge that could be mastered, step by step, to various levels of perfection. They did not see training as an appendage of an extension system (in fact, Senegal had no general extension service at the time), rather, they saw it as part of a broader, highly institutionalized rural training scheme covering agricultural and non-agricultural skills.

The Senegalese Rural Training Centers are interesting also because they were founded on a sociological theory of rural development as well as a philosophy of vocational training. The sociological theory (somewhat at variance with the theory underlying the (*animation rurale* movement in the same country, discussed in Chapter 6) holds that each rural area should have a cadre of elite farmers, artisans and women to show the way and set the pace for modernization—a view that proved rather unpalatable to the nonelite.

---

[5]The idea of a district development center is not altogether new, since the NCCK training centers in Kenya have a number of different training lines. Also, the Ministry of Agriculture has for many years collaborated with the Ministry of Health in the successful operation of a Better Living Institute. What is new, however, is the comprehensiveness of the new center in relation to total development needs of the rural district.

Rural Training Centres (RTCs)

Background. Planning for this pilot project of Rural Training Centers (RTCs) in Senegal[6] began in 1960 and in 1963 agreement was reached with the UNDP to provide support for the initial five-year development phase (1963-67).[7] Primary emphasis in the period was given to constructing facilities, recruiting international experts and training indigenous staff, but relatively ambitious targets were also set for producing initial trainees.

By late 1971 eight centers were in operation: three for farmers, four for artisans (discussed in the following chapter), and one for women. Each of the centers for training leader farmers (*paysans pilotes*) has a capacity of forty. The centers are well equipped with dormitories, instructional space, offices, staff houses and a practice farm.

Target group. Trainees in the farmer centers are young married farmers with farms of no less than two hectares, selected by the local functionary of *animation rurale,* presumably with an eye to their intellectual and potential leadership qualities that would give their training a multiplier effect when they returned home. Part of the rationale of the literacy component is to offset disparities in their educational backgrounds.

Educational activities. Four features of the program content and teaching methods merit emphasis. First, every effort is made to gear the content to the crop patterns and ecological conditions of the participants' home area. Second, the whole course is organized around a full crop cycle and each instruction unit is geared to the current stage of the cycle. Third, the majority of learning time is devoted to practice work in the field—twenty-five to thirty-three sessions out of a total of forty-eight sessions. Finally, the related classroom work puts heavy emphasis on small group discussions rather than didactic lectures. These pedagogical methods are in sharp contrast to the highly academic and didactic instructional approach of the formal programs of agricultural education in Senegal (and most other developing nations). Short courses are also offered on an ad hoc basis.

The original intent had been to make substantial use of visual aids—especially films—but the content of available films proved inappropriate and thus visual aids were deemphasized. There are some reading materials and trainees are provided with *aide memoires* on various instructional units.

Staff. Most of the insturctors are Senegalese, who must be at least eighteen years old and hold a diploma from the college of agriculture or its equivalent. (Those without an agricultural college diploma or its equivalent take one year of special training.) Each center is served by three international experts and six Senegalese instructors. Farmers are organized in groups of eight members for practice exercises and discussions "animated" by a *moniteur.* The total "class" is forty or less at each center.

Performance. The training itself, as far as ICED researchers could determine, has gone quite well, but the program has encountered certain unanticipated

---

[6]Based on Pierre Furter and Sven Grabe, *Senegal: Rural Vocational Training Centers,* ICED Case Study No. 8 (unpublished).

[7]Support was later agreed to for a second phase of three years (1968-71) with the possibility left open for Phase Three support. Though ILO was made the principal executing agency, FAO undertook to assist the women's centers, and Unesco was to incorporate literacy components in the centers.

problems. The number of trainees completing the course during the first phase substantially undershot the target (382 against a target of 700), apparently because of delays in staffing and facilities and problems in recruitment. A total of seventeen Senegalese staff members were trained, against a target of twenty, though some left the employ of the centers for preferred positions in the government service.

A project evaluation study in 1970 indicated that the per-hectare yields of returned trainees rose by 50 to 100 percent or better. Other evidence, however, points to a number of problems in the experience of trainees after returning home. First, the returned trainees, constituting a new elite, were resented by their neighbors. Second, because of the lack of follow-up services for trainees, (including technical advisory services and credit with which to purchase inputs and better implements), many found themselves unable to apply fully the new techniques they had learned and accordingly developed a resentment against the system.

Weighing the relatively high costs of the program against the sparse evidence of benefits, as we will see in a later chapter, presents a difficult problem. Nevertheless, as of late 1971 the Government of Senegal was sufficiently persuaded of the virtues of the Rural Training Centres that it decided to continue and expand them.

Training Extensionists for a Green Revolution

The two training programs reviewed thus far, Kenya's FTCs and Senegal's training centers, have had little connection with the generation of new technology through research; they have taught whatever the best currently available technology seemed to be. In contrast, the rice production training program of the International Rice Research Institute (IRRI) in the Philippines arose directly from a breakthrough in research and a desire to spread its benefits as quickly and widely as possible. It was an unusual initiative on the part of a research organization to strengthen national extension services—not the other way around. The idea was to provide special training to key officials of these services, particularly those officials responsible for training field-level extension workers.

The urgency of upgrading the knowledge of extension agents was dramatically demonstrated by the results of diagnostic tests given by IRRI to several thousand extension workers, extension supervisors and highly trained agricultural experts. The purpose was to assess their ability to identify such things as common pests, diseases and nutritional problems of the rice plant, and to prescribe appropriate chemical treatments for them. On the average, only 25 percent of the questions were answered correctly by extension supervisors and workers from rice-producing areas. The more highly trained agricultural experts did no better. An IRRI official concluded:

> Whatever the reasons, and these vary with situations, the typical extension worker in most Southeast Asian countries lacks background knowledge of rice culture and has had little or no first-hand paddy experience. Moreover, when he lacks the necessary diagnostic skills, he cannot identify the problems in the farmer's field and thus cannot advise him

on appropriate action. Consequently, he is reluctant even to approach the farmer to show him how things might be done.[8]

The Rice Production Training Program

Background. The development of new high-yielding rice varieties in the early 1960s at the International Rice Research Institute in the Philippines presented a major challenge to extension services.[9] The new varieties promised a sharp increase in yield per acre in the rice-producing countries of South and Southeast Asia that could go a long way toward reducing their food deficits. But how was the word to go out to the millions of small rice farmers? Extension agents could not simply hand farmers a sample of the new seeds and tell them to try them out in the usual manner. The new seeds required different treatment: different spacing, depth and timing, heavier fertilization, special water management, a watchful eye for pests and diseases to which the new seeds were not resistant and, if these appeared, prompt application of appropriate chemicals to save the crop.

More complicated still, the new varieties, developed under particular econological conditions in the Philippines, would behave differently elsewhere. Hence adaptive research was needed to provide modified varieties and planting techniques to fit the peculiar circumstances of other areas. Thus the research capabilities of each rice-producing country were also challenged along with the extension services.

Although IRRI had been created solely as a research institute, its officials soon concluded that they would have to venture into the training buiness if IRRI's research results were to pay off quickly. Thus IRRI launched (in 1964) a training program for Filipino extension personnel and by 1967 it had an intensive six-month training program for senior extension officers drawn from many Asian countries and eventually other regions. (See Table 4.1.)

Objective. It was IRRI's expectation that the graduates of the course would go back to their countries to train field extension agents, applying the methods and content of the IRRI course in their own training courses. In this manner, IRRI's training effort would have a broad multiplier effect on upgrading national rice extension programs and would better justify the substantial investment in the program.

Educational content and methods. Three special features of the IRRI training program bear mention.[10] First, the course was timed to follow the full cycle of a rice crop, from land preparation and planting through to the harvest. The participants themselves—often reluctantly at first—did the actual work. They learned, many for the first time, how to *demonstate* to farmers in their own fields. This field work was interlaced with classroom lectures and discussions, taught by a combination of staff extension experts and IRRI's researchers. Second, the participants conducted field experiments of their own, akin to the kind of adaptive research that would be needed back home. Frequently this involved comparative experiments using indigenous varieties they had brought

---

[8]International Rice Research Institute, "Changing the Change Agent—A Step Toward Increase Rice Yields," (Manila, September 30, 1967), p. 2.
[9]Manzoor Ahmed and Philip H. Coombs, *Training Extension Leaders* at the International Rice Research Institute, ICED Cse Study No. 12 (Essex, Conn., June 1972).
[10]IRRI also had shorter courses for extension personnel as well as training for research scientists.

from home. Third, special emphasis was given in the course to techniques of communication and training; trainees had to devise their own two-week course and actually teach it to a group of shor-term trainees from agricultural agencies.

Performance. How effective has the IRRI training program been in achieving its objective of accelerating the adoption of high-yielding rice varieties by special training of key persons in national extension services? In particular, how many IRRI trainees went back home and spread what they had learned to large number of extension workers, and through them to local farmers?

Evidence to answer this question was meager when ICED investigators visited IRRI in late 1971. IRRI had conducted no follow-up study to determine whether and how its more than 200 former trainees were applying their IRRI training.[11] A "hunch" expressed by a senior IRRI official, based on scattered information, was that fewer than 30 percent of them were actually putting their training to intended use; most had been assigned to other duties. Independent evidence gathered by ICED on trainees from India suggested a substantially lower figure.[12] In contrast, in Sri Lanka (Ceylon) a special effort is being made to use virtually all IRRI-trained people to bolster the extension service.

Table 4.1
Trainees in the IRRI Rice Production Training Course
Shown by Country of Origin
1964-1971

Country	No. of Trainees
Philippines	66
India	23
Ceylon	22
Indonesia	19
Pakistan	13
South Vietnam	10
Thailand	9
U.S.A.	9
Laos	8
Burma	6
Fiji	5
Malaysia	3
Others*	18
TOTAL	211

*Includes the following countries with one or two trainees in the rice production training course: Afghanistan, Cambodia, Ghana, Iraq, Japan, Kenya, Korea, Nepal, Nigeria, Sierra Leone, Sudan, Tanzania.
SOURCE: International Rice Research Institute.

[11]We are informed that a study was initiated in late 1972, by Burt Swanson of Wisconsin University, to evaluate the effectiveness of IRRI's training.
[12]The cost-benefit implications of this high wastage rate are discussed in Chapter 11.

The picture appears to be improving as IRRI puts more effort into recruiting and screening appropriate candidates and as more countries recognize the need to strengthen the knowledge and skills of their extension workers as a major means of spreading the adoption of new high-yielding varieties of rice.

Bringing Training to the Farmers

A common feature of the three training programs just reviewed, as well as and of most training programs, is that they oblige the trainees to assemble at a special center to receive instruction, often on a residential basis for a considerable period of time. But what of the farmers in remote rural areas who need training but cannot afford to abandon their daily chores to receive it? The mobile training approach, which brings training to the farmers instead of the farmers to the training, is an alternative possibility which ICED studied in the rural program of SENA in Colombia.

The National Apprenticeship Service's (SENA) Mobile Training

Background. SENA was established in Colombia by government decree in 1957 to provide skill training for employed adults and apprenticeship training for adolescents (aged 14-20).[13] Administratively, it is part of the Ministry of Labor but it enjoys considerable autonomy: its director is appointed by the President of the Republic and its funding comes directly from a special payroll tax rather than through the regular national budget. It has grown rapidly and in 1970 had an enrollment of 268,000 trainees in a wide range of training courses for industrial, commercial and agricultural occupations. During its first decade SENA concentrated on industrial training—mainly to upgrade employed workers—using its own well-equipped urban facilities and standard vocational training techniques, though it also had some activities in the commercial and agricultural sector.

In 1967 SENA began a program called Promocion Profesional Popular-Rural (PPP-R) to provide short-term, low-cost skill training to farmers, farm laborers, rural artisans and small entrepreneurs within their own communities. "Mobile units"—a traveling corps of instructors—were the means to bring training courses to even the most remote areas of rural Colombia.

Objectives. The principal objective of the PPP-R program (and its counterpart for urban areas, the PPP-U) is to improve the skills and increase employment opportunities for underemployed and unemployed workers. A further aim is to slow down the rural-to-urban migration that has led to rapid growth of the country's major cities, with concomitant high unemployment, poor housing for many, and overburdened public services.

Target groups. PPP-R courses are directed to adults and adolescents, men and women, agricultural and nonagricultural workers, but the major emphasis is on skills useful on the farm. The agricultural workers enrolled include land owners (except large landholders), sharecroppers and the landless. There are no educational requirements for entry into courses.

Structure and size. The PPP-R program is decentralized to fourteen regional offices which cover all sections of the country. PPP-R offices are usually housed

---

[13]Based on Stephen F. Brumberg, *Promoción Profesional Popular-Rural of SENA: A Mobile Skills Training Program for Rural Colombia,* ICED Case Study No. 2 (Essex, Conn., June 1972).

at a SENA training center, if such a center is within one of the fourteen PPP-R regions. Actual instruction is offered, however, in temporary facilities in rural communities. Statistically, the PPP-R is SENA's largest program in terms of total enrollments: in 1970 it enrolled 105,000 trainees, or 39 percent of all students enrolled in SENA. It should be noted, however, that the time devoted per trainee is much less on the average—and the unit costs lower—than for urban industrial trainees. For example, the PPP-R enrollment totals include nearly 47,000 migrant workers, each of whom was given a special 20-hour course in cotton picking.

Facilites. The "mobile units" used to bring training to rural communities may be an instructor with a fully equipped instructional vehicle, or just the instructor, who generally brings with him instructional materials, including tools and audiovisual equipment. SENA uses many kinds of transport for its mobile units—even mules and canoes—when necessary to reach remote areas. In most communities, an attempt is made to use existing facilities as classrooms, although there has been some experimentation with prefabricated classroom buildings which can be rapidly assembled at the teaching site.

Methods. Instruction is practical rather than theoretical and there is little lecturing. Instructors rely heavily on demonstrations and trainees are expected to duplicate and practice the lesson. Wherever possible instructors make use of locally available tools and equipment so that trainees can practice what they have learned after completing the course.

Instructors work from detailed training syllabuses prepared by the SENA Documentation Center and use visual materials also provided by the Center. It is up to the individual instructor to alter the content to fit local conditions.

Content. Course offerings are extremely varied. Most are in the categories of agricultural crops, livestock, minor farm industries such as beekeeping, raising rabbits and chickens, and handicrafts. There are also courses in contruction, machinery and mechanics, and in more general fields such as first aid and human relations.

Each course is viewed as a self-contained unit which includes only as much subject matter as can be effectively taught in the time allotted. A course may last from 40 to 120 hours; the average course length in 1970 (excluding short courses for migrant workers) was about 73 hours. Most courses last less than a month and none exceeds three months. Classes last from two to six hours a day. PPP-R courses are provided without charge and are offered at at time of the year and at hours of the day most convenient to local inhabitants.

Staff. More than 300 full-time instructors are assigned to the PPP-R program. In addition, instructors from SENA's eleven agricultural training centers are sometimes seconded to the PPP-R to teach one or more courses.

Instructors are required to have a secondary technical diploma or teacher's certificate in agriculture, with one year of specialization and two years of practical experience. In practice, some instructors have less than the full academic preparation. All instructors take a three- to six-month course at SENA's National Training Center. In addition to pedagogical instruction and technical specialization, the course focuses on the special role of PPP-R instructors as agents of social change in isolated rural communities.

Appraisal. The PPP-R program demonstrates that it is logistically possible to operate a large-scale mobile training program that reaches isolated rural areas at relatively low cost. However, other countries looking at the PPP-R experience need to note some of its special features and some of the initial problems it has encountered and is now endeavoring to remedy. PPP-R has developed as part of a securely established, well-financed national organization with considerable experience in providing occupational training. SENA provided and still provides strong administrative and technical backstopping to the PPP-R program and lends this program some of the prestige SENA has gained throughout Colombia. The incremental cost of adding a mobile rural training program to a large ongoing program is presumably less than that of creating one *de novo* as a separate operation.

The limited evaluative evidence that ICED researchers were able to collect in the field suggests that SENA courses are having significant impact in some situations but much less in others. The impact seems greatest where the SENA courses are arranged in alliance with the land reform agency or some other organization that has devised a broader local development scheme into which the SENA training can be fitted. But unfortunately such situations are far from universal.

There have also been problems of maintaining a competent staff willing to spend so much time away from home in relatively primitive conditions. A further importnat problem has been in the selection and design of courses and content appropriate for each area. SENA officials are well aware of the various shortcomings of this relatively new program—including the serious lack of evaluation measures—and have undertaken to remedy them. To apply such remedies will undoubtedly increase unit costs but chances are it will also greatly improve the learning results and benefits.

This chapter has examined the training approach (as differentiated from the extension approach) as applied to agricultural advancement in four contrasting cases—in Kenya, Senegal, the Philippines, and Colombia. Some of their common features and problems and their comparative advantages and disadvantages will be examined in later chapters. For the present we will turn our attention to other examples of the training approach, applied to rural artisans, craftsmen and small entrepreneurs.

5: TRAINING FOR
NONFARM OCCUPATIONS

The training approach to agricultural skills—discussed in the previous chapter—is usually marginal in scale compared with the agricultural extension approach. When it comes to developing artisan and entrepreneurial skills for off-farm use, however, training usually plays the dominant role and extension is subsidiary. Here the main focus of organized programs is one systematic training at some type of center or institute. On-the-spot advisory services in the extension tradition for small manufacturers and other small businesses generally play a secondary role, if they exist at all.

Skill Requirements in Rural Areas

The distinction between farming skills and nonfarming skills, it should be noted, is in some measure artificial. Farmers generally need a combination of both. A typical subsistence farm family, for example, must not only be skilled in working the soil but be able as well to build and repair simple implements and structures, establish and maintain a water supply, construct bunds and roads, make clothes and produce cottage industry items for sale in the marketplace. The more sophisticated his agricultural technology becomes, the more ancillary skills a farmer requires.

When a small farmer has a need that exceeds his own skills, he is likely to call on the help of a local artisan—generally a part-time farmer who is also a jack-of-all trades, trained through an indigenous apprenticeship system. As the local "blacksmith" the latter may be called upon to produce or repair almost anything made of metal, from a plow or bucket to a broken truck frame. Or as the local "carpenter" he may have to fabricate or repair almost anything made of wood, from tool handles to furniture or a house.

Manpower and training experts (including the ILO) have made far less adequate analysis of rural skills than of modern industrial skills for urban areas, but it is evident that rural skills differ widely, even when they wear the same label. In general, the rural artisan's skills are less specialized and sophisticated but he needs a wider range of skills and more ingenuity in applying them. If a truck needs a replacement part he does not order it from the manufacturer; he makes it himself.

Skill requirements expand rapidly when more advanced technologies begin to penetrate a traditional rural area. New types of farm implements, mechanical rice driers and hullers, bicycles, trucks and bush taxis, diesel and electric pumps, movie projectors and transistor radios—all such revolutionary innovations require new skills for operating them and, even more important, for maintaining them in working order. The indigenous training systems by which traditional skills are passed from father to son, mother to daughter, or master craftsman to apprentice, are often not adequate to handle these new and more sophisticated skills. Hence they must either be modified or supplemented by new skill training programs.

As agricultural development gathers momentum, another set of new skill needs arises, associated with, for example, dispensing and using production credit, operating cooperatives and managing retail stores, farm supply houses, repair businesses or small manufacturing establishments. All of these grow and multiply as part of a broader rural development process.

In a rural economy made up largely of small economic units, the small entrepreneur or the professional manager of a cooperative society plays a crucial role in this unfolding development process. He must not only know the *technical* side of the business—how to manufacture or to service and repair relatively complex products—but he must also acquire increasingly sophisticated *management and commercial skills:* how to handle double-entry bookkeeping and cost accounting; establish inventory controls; procure raw materials and spare parts from distant suppliers; cope with a thicket of government regulations and taxes; market his products in wider and more competitive markets where quality standards spell success or failure.

Originally we had expected to treat training programs for rural artisans and craftsmen separately from those for small entrepreneurs but the distinction often has little meaning: programs wearing a "small entrepreneur" label turned out to be also involved in upgrading the technical skills of employees as well as employers, while programs labeled as "artisan training" included trainees who were destined to become, or already were, self-employed entrepreneurs.

Viewed as a whole, this training field is characterized by great variety, not only because of the diversity of activities and skills involved but also because, in contrast to farmer education, there are no well-established educational models that are widely repeated from country to country. Most of the non-agricultural training programs we encountered appeared to be products of inspiration and improvisation rather than imitation. By and large, however, they fitted one or another of the following categories:

   1. *Technical skills training for older adolescents and young adults* to prepare them for gainful employment (illustrated by Thailand's Mobile Trade Training Schools described below).

   2. *Technical upgrading of existing artisans and craftsmen* (including the self-employed) in order to improve their standards, versatility, productivity, and income (illustrated below by Nigeria's Vocational Improvement Centres and Senegal's Rural Artisan Training Program).

   3. *More comprehensive small industry promotional schemes,* combining organized training for managers and their employees, assistance in securing credit, on-the-spot technical and management consulting services, and other informational and advisory services (illustrated below by three programs in India for small-scale industry and for rural industrial projects).

In a broad sense, these programs share a common goal and all spring from a common training tradition, but as will be seen, they differ markedly in their specific aims, structure, pedagogical methods, content and costs. The Mobile Trade Training Schools (MTTS) in Thailand and the Vocational Improvement Centres (VICs) in Nigeria, for example, offer part-time nonresidential training in borrowed facilities, which has resulted in low unit costs, whereas Senegal's

Rural Artisan Training Program offers full-time, longer courses in well-equipped residential training centers, with much higher unit costs (though perhaps correspondingly larger results). India's small industry promotion programs offer a package of training courses and related support services, whereas the other programs summarized below confine their activities strictly to training (with the partial exception of the VICs in Nigeria).[1]

Surveying the wider scene, we found a dearth of nonfarm skill training programs in rural areas in most developing countries. We also detected a strong inclination on the part of outside professional advisors to prescribe solutions for rural training needs that were strongly biased by their urban backgrounds and industrial training doctrines and standards. It seems doubtful that most of these solutions are appropriate for rural areas.

Developing Young Artisans for Rural Towns

Objectives. Initiated in the early 1960s, the Mobile Trade Training Schools program (MTTS) in Thailand[2] was to provide skill training and improved employment opportunities for out-of-school rural youths and young adults, to meet the increasing requirements for semiskilled and skilled workers foreseen in the national development plan. Priority was at first given to designated "sensitive areas" where antigovernment forces were active, but later the program spread to other areas and by 1972, 54 schools were located in rural towns and provincial centers throughout Thailand.

Target groups. In recent years participation has been limited to older youths and young adults with four or more years of formal schooling.[3] Boys and girls have been admitted in roughly equal proportions and a majority already have some form of employment when they enter the program.

Organization and facilities. The program is now run by the Division of Adult Education under the Ministry of Education but is not considered part of Thailand's formal system of vocational education.[4] The schools are mobile only in the sense that after operating in a particular town for one to three years their equipment and staff are moved to another town. The typical MTTS is located in one or more community buildings made temporarily available to the program, either free of charge or for a rent.[5]

Staff. The full-time staff for a school typically consists of a principal and seven to nine men and women instructors, each teaching one specialty. Formal qualifications for instructors are high, reflecting Ministry of Education standards. They include graduation from a postsecondary technical institute or vocational teacher's college (normally requiring a total of fifteen years of formal schooling). Technical institute graduates must also have a year of teacher

---

[1]The costs and financing of the programs summarized in this chapter are treated in Chapter 12.

[2]Manzoor Ahmed, *Mobile Trade Training Schools in Thailand,* ICED Case Study No. 6 (Essex, Conn., April 1974).

[3]Rural primary schools in Thailand are generally limited to four years; urban schools include seven grades.

[4]The program was formerly operated by the Vocational Promotion Division of the Ministry of Education. The Division of Adult Education which now runs MTTS is in the Department of General Education.

[5]Only one mobile school was actually on wheels, with the work shops located in a fleet of trailers obtained from U.S. Air Force surplus. The trailers remained in fixed position, however, until the time came for redeployment to another town.

training, especially designed for the MTTS program, in the Bangkok Technical School. MTTS teachers receive substantial bonus payments and emoluments over normal scales to attract them away from Bangkok.[6]

Content. Each school offers training in six to eight skills chosen from a standard list and taught according to a nationally standardized syllabus. The courses, in order of their popularity with trainees as indicated by enrollment figures, include: dressmaking, auto-mechanics, tailoring, radio repair, electric wiring and installation, cosmetology and hairdressing, food preparation, welding, typing, bookkeeping, barbering, embroidery, and woodwork. Virtually no printed instructional materials are available (other than the syllabus), but large quantities of raw materials are consumed in the practical work. (See Table 5.1.)

Regardless of the skill involved, all courses are based on a uniform requirement of 300 hours of instruction and practice time, spread over a period of five months. Two daily shifts of three hours are offered (including an evening shift), enabling trainees to choose a convenient time and insuring relatively high utilization of staff and facilities. Two five-month sessions are operated per year.

There are no established standards of achievement; each instructor establishes and administers his or her own final tests and those who pass receive a certificate. (Most trainees who complete the course receive a certificate.)

Performance. From the start of the program to the end of 1970, a total of 51,000 had enrolled (30,000 had completed a course). While this is an im-

Table 5.1
Enrollment and Graduation in 13 MTTSs
for First Session in 1971

Course	Enrollment	Graduation	Percentage of Enrolled Who Graduated
1. Dressmaking	629	419	67
2. Auto-mechanics	522	371	70
3. Tailoring	464	237	51
4. Radio Repair	331	213	64
5. Electric Wiring and Installation	314	213	68
6. Cosmetics and Hairdressing	284	225	80
7. Food Preparation	251	177	70
8. Welding	167	110	66
9. Typing	142	70	50
10. Bookkeeping	97	60	62
11. Barbering	67	37	55
12. Embroidery	30	24	80
13. Woodwork	11	8	73
TOTAL	3,309	2,164	65

SOURCE: Vocational Promotion Division, Ministry of Education, Thailand.

---

[6]All areas of Thailand outside metropolitan Bangkok, including quite large provincial cities, are considered "rural" by Bangkok residents.

pressive number, it is far below the enrollment targets set. The reasons for the wide discrepancy between targets and actual enrollments are not altogether clear. In 1971 the target for forty-five of the schools was 36,000 but enrollments totaled only 23,000. A partial explanation is that the targets were based on the assumption that a third daily shift would be added, which was not done. It is also clear that some courses are more popular than others; these are quickly filled while others are undersubscribed. On the whole, however, the popularity of the MTTS program appears to have remained high, notwithstanding the fact that a tuition fee must be paid by the students.

Appraisal. The managers of the MTTS program feel that it has been highly successful and they want to expand it, with certain improvements. For example, they would like to vary the length of courses for different skills, to adapt them to individual differences, and to enrich them with newly created "programmed instruction" materials.

Critics of the program, particularly economists and educational planners in the government, question the desirability of offering standardized courses for the whole country and of choosing particular courses for a given community without first making a reasonably systematic employment market study. They also criticize the lack of sufficient follow-up to see whether and how former participants are using their training and what benefits have resulted.

The only systematic evaluation attempt in the ten years of the program's life was undertaken by the National Research Council in 1971. While this study provided useful information about trainees, dropouts and graduates of eight sample schools, it provided little evidence on which to judge the program's costs and benefits. According to the Council's survey, just over half of the graduates interviewed had full-time or part-time paid employment and fewer than half of these said they were using in their work the skills learned in MTTS. Most of the graduates in paid employment had had some form of employment before entering the MTTS. The survey did not reveal whether or how much their income had risen. Another quarter of the graduates (mainly women) claimed to be using their MTTS skills at home, but apparently not for income-earning purposes.

Another Alternative to Formal Vocational Training

Notwithstanding certain evident shortcomings of the MTTS program and the sparsity of evidence by which to evaluate its cost-effectiveness and benefits, the potential flexibility, mobility and low unit costs of this approach make it an intriguing possible alternative to full-time vocational high schools, of which Thailand also has a substantial number. A thorough comparative analysis of the cost-effectiveness of these two approaches to vocational education in Thailand would be rewarding but would require a major research effort.

The Vocational Improvement Centres (VICs) in Northern Nigeria—similar in some respects to the part-time low unit cost approach of Thailand's MTTS— also provide an interesting contrast to formal vocational training.

Vocational Improvement Centres (VICs)

Background. The establishment of Vocational Improvement Centres

(VICs)[7] in six Northern Nigerian states was the outcome of a diagnosis by the government that the main impediment to the development of small-scale industries was the low level of skills and the absence of training opportunities for artisans and craftsmen. In 1965, with Ford Foundation assistance, a Business Apprenticeship Training Center was opened at Kaduna. Since then all six northern state governments have set up similar centers and there are now twelve (two in each state) operating in various towns in the entire northern region.

Objective. The objective of the VICs was to upgrade the skills of working artisans and journeymen. It was expected that the trainees would qualify in government trade tests and would be fit to be employed in the government technical services and the modern sector or would open their own small enterprises.

Facilities. The distinguishing feature of the centers is their unconventional flexibility and adaptability. The centers have no physical facilities of their own, no full-time staff (except for an expatriate director, due to leave in late 1972, and two technical instructors in the Kaduna Center), and virtually no minimum entry requirements (except to have worked for two years in the trade). A more conventional feature is that the syllabi are dictated by what is required for the trainees to pass the government trade tests.

The Kaduna Center, for instance, uses classrooms and workshop space provided free of charge by the Kaduna Technical Institute; the Maiduguri Center runs its classes in a primary school and holds practical shop sessions in a local government workshop. Teachers are employed on an hourly basis and are drawn mainly from local private industry, government shops, and the general and technical schools.

Content. All courses are part time; they start at the end of the working day and trainees go to courses four or five days each week for a total of 400 hours of instruction spread over a ten-month period. Most courses prepare trainees for the Grade III (lowest) level trade test but successful trainees may continue their training in order to qualify at Grade II and Grade I levels.

The four basic courses offered in most of the centers are carpentry, auto repair, bricklaying and electrical installation. Considerable time (up to a quarter of the total) is also devoted to English, mathematics and general studies, including storekeeping and elements of business management.

Clientele. An average of 100 trainees attend each center; a majority of them are between 20 and 30 years old. They have limited primary education or no formal education and come from farming families in the area near a center. About half the trainees who completed courses at the Maiduguri Center over the past few years initially had acquired their trade skills in government departments, including the army and the police; about one-third had received their initial training in small private firms (the proportion of trainees from small private enterprises is estimated to be substantially higher in other centers).

In the Kaduna Center, a systematic canvassing of small local industries has formed the basis of recruitment; independent craftsmen and journeymen employed by local, small-scale manufacturers constitute the largest single group among the trainees. A few of the trainees run a business of their own

---

[7]Clifford Gilpin and Sven Grabe, *Programs for Small Industry Entrepreneurs and Journeymen in Northern Nigeria,* ICED Case Study No. 7 (Essex, Conn., April 1972).

(mostly as a spare-time activity) and others intend to set up their own shop in the future. Nevertheless, the courses are geared to the trade tests.

Since the trade tests grant entry into government service as well as middle- and large-scale private industries, the program may be credited with opening up training and modern sector employment opportunities for rural semiskilled workers with little or no formal education (who would not qualify for the regular technical training programs). The good prospects for employment in government or larger industries and the small opportunity cost for the trainee (no fees and after-hour, part-time courses) have kept the demand high for the courses. In 1970, for example, there were 1,000 applicants for 130 places in the Kaduna Center.

Appraisal. Despite special efforts to check on former trainees, ICED researchers found insufficient evidence to reach solid conclusions about the effectiveness of the program. One bit of evidence, which must be interpreted cautiously, is that just over half of the 324 candidates admitted to the Maiduguri Center from 1968 through 1971 sat for the trade tests, and of these seventy-two (22 percent of the total) passed the examination. These results are not as poor as they may seem since the tests are designed for graduates of government trade schools who have had three full years of technical training on top of at least a full primary education. The results also should be judged in light of the low costs of VIC courses (discussed in Chapter 12).

There was no clear evidence by which to measure the impact of the program on the establishment of new rural enterprises, on the generation of new employment, or on the earnings of independent artisans and small industry entrepreneurs. A substantial number of those in government service did enjoy a boost in their earnings, because, by passing the trade test, they gained automatic promotion.

A Formal-looking Nonformal Program

The VICs' use of part-time instructors and borrowed facilities for evening training courses is in stark contrast to the methods employed in the Rural Artisan Training Program which the ILO helped to establish in Senegal. The latter—a meticulously programmed, highly institutionalized, full-time residential training program—would be considered much "sounder" and more "serious" by traditional vocational training specialists. Whether it is the better approach, or even a viable one, in the circumstances of a poor country is a question that merits careful consideration.

Senegal's Rural Artisan Training Program, it will be recalled from the previous chapter, was originally conceived as one component of a tripartite rural training system; other components were addressed to the training of modern farmers and the training of women leaders (in home economics and related subjects). The following summary applies only to the artisan training component.

Rural Artisan Training

Objective. The aim of Rural Artisan Training in Senegal[8] is to develop an elite cadre of rural artisan-entrepreneurs capable of doing any job the farming

---

[8]See Pierre Furter and Sven Grabe, *Senegal: Rural Vocational Training Centers*, ICED Case Study No. 8 (unpublished).

community may require in the way of manufacturing or repairing farm implements or constructing houses; at the same time it does not aim to equip them with urban-type skills that would lure them away from their village. The recruits are young practicing artisans—particularly carpenters and blacksmiths—from rural communities who are anxious to better themselves and are willing to leave their home and business for the better part of a year in order to improve their skills at a full-time, residential regional training center.

Facilities. There are at present five such centers, located near small towns in different regions of Senegal. Each can handle thirty-six trainees and is well equipped with workshops (for metalworking, woodworking and home construction), boarding facilities, office space and staff housing. Recent trainees have helped to build some of these units.

Structure and content. The program stresses minimum technical standards and the mastery of all the types of operations that a rural craftsman may be asked to do. Originally it distinguished sharply between training in woodworking and metalworking, but more recently this distinction has been somewhat blurred in order to encourage the development of multipurpose artisans.

The course is divided into three stages, each usually lasting three months (the trainees return to their homes for three months between stages to catch up with their normal work). The first stage is devoted to individual skill upgrading *(nivellement des connaissances)* to ensure uniform standards of achievement in the group. During the second stage *(fabrication)* trainees manufacture a set of tools for their own use and learn to use them efficiently. The carpenters produce a set of planes, chisels and other basic carpenters' tools and jigs. The blacksmith/mechanics manufacture a comprehensive set of blacksmith's plices, chisels and cutting edges, a hearth and measuring instruments, and tools for mechanical work. The construction craftsmen learn to produce their own brick and bricklaying tools and to build the modernized type of housing and workshops designed under the government's rural housing renewal scheme. The third stage *(confirmation)* is mostly devoted to simulating jobs the trainees are likely to take on after returning home—the manufacture and repair of implements and tools, fabrication of bricks, construction of houses and sheds (mostly for use by the center itself).

Related instruction in blueprints, measurements and the like is mostly provided on the job or in worksheds. Classroom instruction is largely limited to functional literacy and the maintenance of accounts in artisan operations.

The project devised its own standards of performance and does not attempt to achieve equivalence with urban training. Progress is assessed on a continuing basis; there is no final examination.

Staff. Instructors are recruited at an officially recognized skill worker level *(certificat d'aptitude professionelle)*, attained through training in a vocational training institution, at secondary-school level, or through serving a recognized apprenticeship in industry. Recruits are then given two years of special training at one of the artisan centers to which more highly qualified staff has been attached for teacher training purposes. Six trainees can be taken on each year. Most of their training is through supervised practice in a group of regular trainees or (second year) as a leader *(moniteur)* of a group of trainees. They receive a stipend.

Planning. Two difficult problems, which may be of special significance to other developing countries, were encountered in getting the program started: (1) estimating how many well-trained rural artisans would be needed, and (2) determining what the content and level of their skills should be.

There were no reliable figures on the existing supply of rural artisans in Senegal; available estimates were statistically dubious and too wide-ranging to be useful. The membership rolls of the chambers of artisan trades were known to be low because many practicing artisans had not wanted to pay the registration fee. Census figures offered little more help, since artisans who were also farmers could be recorded either way, and most, it was found, were counted as farmers. The technical agricultural services had little to offer. Although they were considering a comprehensive drive to improve farm equipment, there was no way of knowing how this might influence total demand for artisan services. In the end, the size of the scheme had to be determined largely by guesswork.[9]

In retrospect the need for training—or at least the active demand for it—was apparently overestimated. It has proved difficult to fill even the 150 places available each year. One major reason, no doubt, is that most practicing artisans questioned that the opportunity costs of leaving their business for so long would be more than offset by the resulting benefits to their later income. There is some evidence which suggests that they—at least the carpenters—were right.

The second problem—determining the appropriate skill training content and standards—also had to be solved largely by informed guesswork and trial-and-error. The trainees themselves provided information on the types of work they were asked to do by their clients; further clues were gathered from suppliers of new farming equipment and from officials of the agricultural improvement services and the *animation rurale* movement. But there seemed no reliable way of estimating what services farmers would be willing to pay for if well-trained artisans were available to provide them. And there were no government-supported rural works projects under way that would ensure an income for these artisans.

Performance. A tracer study of more than 200 former trainees at the end of 1970 revealed that 153 were active in their trade in a rural area, 24 had given up the trade, and 35 had moved (mostly to nearby urban areas) and could not be interviewed. Those active in their chosen trade estimated that they were making use of between 40 and 90 percent of the new skills learned at the center (disregarding the improvement in their traditional skills). The woodworkers had the highest scores. One-third of this group were training apprentices, which provided a certain multiplier effect. Between 80 and 90 percent of the blacksmith/mechanics said they were earning at least 50 percent more than they had before training. Paradoxically, construction artisans, who scored highest in using their new skills, showed the least improvement in income, presumably because of a general slowdown in the construction industry.

---

[9]To illustrate the problem: three separate enquiries made in the 1960s of the number of artisans in the province of Casamanca resulted in estimates of (1) 228, (2) 558, and (3) 4,100. The degree to which the artisans' trades of Senegal have deteriorated in competition with foreign imports and local factory production is illustrated by the fact that even the highest estimates account for less than 100,000 artisans in a total *adult* population of close to two million.

India's Diverse Programs for Artisans and Small Entrepreneurs

We have reserved to the end some examples drawn from India, which has, of all the developing countries, made the most extensive and diversified efforts to stimulate small industry in both urban and rural areas. Most of the techniques used in Senegal and Nigeria for training artisans and small entrepreneurs can also be found in India, along with a variety of additional ones. India's approach has been more comprehensive and integrated, combining training for both managers and employees with a variety of complementary support services for such small concerns as in-plant consultation; assistance in obtaining credit, equipment, and raw materials; the provision of common workshops and equipment for use by small firms in the same area; and technical assistance on product selection, design and marketing.

The ICED case study of India identifies a variety of efforts in this field but focuses on three in particular:[10]

- *The general small-scale industry program:* This is the largest and oldest of the programs (initiated in 1954) and the most diversified. It comes under the Small-Scale Industry Development Organization (SSIDO), in the Ministry of Industrial Development, Science and Technology, which also oversees the RIP program (see below). Through its extensive facilities and mobile units, this SSIDO program offers training for employers and employees in a wide range of small industries, as well as staff training for itself and other organizations. In addition it provides a variety of other services to small firms. The state governments play a large role in operating the program.

- *The Rural Industries Projects Program (RIP):* This pilot program was undertaken in 1962 to counterbalance the heavy urban bias of the general small-scale industry program. Its own bias is toward relatively "backward" rural areas and small towns farthest from the mainstream of national economic development. Though largely subsidized by the central government, it is operated by the various states with a fairly free hand. Hence the training set-up and methods vary considerably among the forty-nine pilot districts.

- *Recent innovative programs for entrepreneurial training:* In 1970 three development organizations of the State of Gujarat initiated a novel program to train would-be entrepreneurs and to help them get started in business. Later that year, the Government of India launched a similar but more extensive program aimed at helping unemployed engineers and technicians become independent industrial entrepreneurs. Though too young as yet for extensive evaluation, these two programs nevertheless suggest some useful lessons.

In launching the above programs, the Government of India had to face the sticky problem of defining what it meant by "small-scale industry." The decision was to equate "industry" with "manufacturing" and to define "small" as an enterprise with an investment in plant and machinery not exceeding Rs 750,000 (or Rs 1,000,000 in certain cases). This restrictive definition ruled out

---

[10]See John C. deWilde, *Nonformal Education and the Development of Small Enterprise in India,* ICED Case Study No. 4 (Essex, Conn., January 1972).

service industries, though, in practice, repair and maintenance shops are admitted if they produce some spare parts and components ancillary to their main activities. The low financial ceiling has presented problems where the minimum scale for reasonable efficiency is above this limit. It has also posed the policy issue of whether smallness *per se* should be valued and aided, or whether the main aim should be to help small firms become larger and thus generate more employment and income.

The Small-Scale Industry Program

Soon after independence the Government of India, as part of its broader economic development plans, decided to undertake a major effort to promote small-scale industry. Responsibility was entrusted to a new Commissioner for Small-Scale Industry in the (then) Ministry of Commerce and Industry. (It is now a part of the Ministry of Industrial Development, Company Affairs and Internal Trade.)

Objectives. The stated objectives of the new program were to (1) create immediate and substantial employment opportunities at relatively small capital cost; (2) facilitate mobilization of capital and skills that might otherwise remain inadequately utilized; (3) bring about integration of small-scale industries with the rural economy on the one hand and large-scale industry on the other hand; (4) improve the productivity of workers and the quality of small-scale industry products; and (5) ensure equitable distribution of national income and balanced industrial development in different regions in order to provide the basis for a "decentralized" society.[11]

Structure. Over the years the program has grown considerably and has generally adhered to the original concepts. Its various training and extension services—the vital core of the program—are carried out mainly through a network of sixteen Small Industry Service Institutes (SISIs), sixteen Branch Institutes, and fifty-one Extension Centers (ECs), backstopped by a central staff training and research center in Hyderabad called the Small Industry Extension Training Institute (SIET).

Besides these training activities, the Small-Scale Industry Development Organization (SSIDO) provides common facilities for production and testing, assists small industry in improving the design of its products, assesses industrial opportunities and markets, and advises financial institutions on the feasibility of projects submitted for financing.

In addition, SSIDO carries on special programs to (1) facilitate the manufacture of parts and components by small-scale industry for larger industrial establishments, (2) qualify small firms for government contracts, (3) secure a more equitable allocation of scarce raw materials for small businesses, and (4) promote small-scale industrial exports.

Staff. As of 1973, SSIDO had a total professional staff of about 1,000 (most of whom were in the field) to carry out all the training and other functions. Most of the staff were technical specialists on various types of industry or economic analysts and statisticians.

Content and methods. The training courses apply to virtually any type of industry or skill where a need exists. Two main types of courses are offered for employees, primarily to provide the "basics" for those who have on-the-job

---

[11]Ibid, p. 8.

experience but little or no formal technical training: full-time courses for workers sponsored by their employers, ranging from three months to a year; and evening courses on specific topics (e.g., blueprint reading). Such courses are held at SISIs and ECs. The SISIs also have mobile vans to bring training to artisans in rural areas.

The main offerings for managers include: (1) short courses on specific aspects of management (e.g., financial management, cost control, inventory management, marketing, quality control, industrial relations); (2) technical advice and counseling to individual enterprises on various problems (e.g., selection, layout, installation and maintenance of equipment, product specifications, manufacturing methods and processes); (3) seminars and "open houses" on topics of interest to local small businesses (e.g., market prospects for various products, subcontracting, raw material supplies, techniques for increasing productivity); and (4) "intensive campaigns" in outlying areas to arouse interest in specific industrial opportunities and improved productivity.

Performance. According to SSIDO annual reports, the training institutes and centers have trained an average of about 3,500 persons per year in recent years; the mobile vans have given approximately 4,500 demonstrations per year and given training to nearly 6,000 rural artisans; SIET has provided advanced training to more than 300 persons per year (including staff members of the SISIs and ECs and of lending institutions, plus many foreign trainees); and in 1971-72 nearly 88,000 visits were made to individual enterprises and more than 290,000 "advices" were given on technical questions, starting new enterprises, etc., through the distribution of technical bulletins.

Appraisal. These statistics leave little doubt that there has been an enormous amount and variety of activity, though they do not, of course, reveal the quality and effectiveness of the activities, which are extremely difficult to assess, not only because few attempts have been made to evaluate the program but also because it is virtually impossible to separate the respective contributions of the training and other support services. There are ample indications that the program, including the training elements, has had salutory results. But there are also indications that it has failed to keep pace with the increasingly sophisticated requirements of Indian small industry, and that its training and advisory services have declined in quality and effectiveness.

The most serious problem has been the inadequate size and quality of staff relative to the tasks they were expected to perform. Despite the remarkable growth of small industry in India, the staff has expanded relatively little in recent years. And at a time when the increasingly sophisticated needs of small manufacturers called for more competent and experienced staff, unattractive salaries and onerous working conditions have made recruitment of well-qualified staff very difficult. The pressure to expand services and to achieve a good statistical record has resulted in many instances in staff being spread too thin to be really effective.

Another problem has been the recruitment of trainees, particularly for full-time courses. Heads of small enterprises are reluctant to accept the opportunity costs and risks involved in being absent from their businesses or in having any of their key workers absent. They are also fearful of losing a good worker they have trained on-the-job. Workers themselves are often doubtful that the training would lead to a wage promotion since seniority rather than competence is often the basis for promotion in Indian small industry, particularly in units run by the government.

As so often happens in all countries, this program has lost some of its original enthusiasm, vigor and novelty and has tended to become routine and bureaucratic. This point is generally conceded, though ICED researchers were assured by some informed observers that recently, with a renewal of leadership and increased government support, some of the earlier enthusiasm is being restored.

Despite the foregoing problems and a number of other difficulties that beset it, the Indian program for small-scale industry—after nearly two decades—can still be said to be very much alive and continuing to render useful services.

The SSIDO program described above has mainly benefited small-scale industry in the major urban centers, though to some extent the mobile units reached out to lesser cities and towns. Earlier efforts to encourage rural industry—particularly through the Khadi and Village Industries Commission and the Community Development Program (see Chapter 6)—had achieved limited successes but were too diffuse to produce a major impact. Thus, in a fresh effort to stimulate rural industry, the Government of India decided in 1962 to mount a new Rural Industries Projects Program (RIP) in some of the most "backward" areas. This program, though it has apparently had a measure of success, demonstrates how exceedingly difficult it is to stimulate small industry development in traditional rural areas where agriculture is relatively stagnant and the population is widely dispersed.

The Rural Industries Projects (RIP) Program

Objectives. The aim of the Rural Industries Projects Program was to foster the growth of very small rural businesses and off-farm employment by upgrading and modernizing the skills of traditional artisans and their sons, by training new entrants to the labor force, and by providing easy credit, common workshops and follow-up extension services for small entrepreneurs.

Structure. The program, as of late 1972, applies to forty-nine "project areas" embracing a population of about 20 million in more than 34,000 villages. It is administered by the state governments largely with funds and within general guidelines provided by the central government. Accordingly, different states chose different approaches. A few elected to send their trainees to existing training institutions, and at least one (Maharashtra) paid substantial fees to have them get in-plant training in larger industrial firms. But the great majority of states chose to establish new RIP training centers in which full-time courses are offered, usually of a full year's duration. Modest payments are made to participants to help cover living costs.

As an illustration of the diversity of potential rural occupations, these RIP centers provide facilities, for example, for machining and welding, carpentry, tanning, textile dyeing, wool carding, milk chilling, fruit preservations, pottery making, stone crushing and concrete mixing.

Performance. The official statistics of the RIP program's accomplishments are impressive. From 1965 to 1968, 418 new training centers and 161 common work facilities were created. By 1971 a total of nearly 40,000 artisans had received training, more than 20,000 "industrial units" had been assisted, and some 30,000 owners of small enterprises had received financial help through the special low-cost credit program. Some RIP projects created their own general engineering workshops and manufacturing facilities for such products as paints and varnishes, sprayers and dusters, footwear, woolens, and chalk. These were seen principally as training facilities rather than as serious money-making ventures.

The above statistics reflect a great deal of activity but do not tell the whole story. Serious problems have plagued the program, including inadequate funding and staffing, difficulties in recruiting trainees, underutilization of training facilities, high unit costs and, most fundamental of all, the powerful constraints on expanding small manufacturing businesses in a relatively stagnant agrarian economy.

The funding problem arises partly from the Indian government's general strategy of subsidizing the main costs of new national programs for a limited period (usually five years) and then, once programs are established, transferring financial responsibility to the state governments. While this is an effective way to promote innovations, the state governments have by now accumulated responsibility for such a variety of new programs launched in the past that they are unable to finance them adequately. Hence there is a tendency for new programs to start slumping after central financing is phased out. Cutbacks are made, salaries lag and become inadequate to attract and hold good staff, and such staff as there is becomes too thinly spread to get effective results. The RIP Program fell victim to such financial undernourishment once the peak of central government support had passed.

The RIP projects also suffered from the high costs of serving a widely dispersed rural clientele and from the reluctance of many members of that clientele to use the services offered, particularly the training and common facilities services. Established artisans were often unwilling to leave their work or to release their sons for a long stretch of training, either because they could not afford to or because they had greater faith in the traditional apprenticeship method of training. Thus the demand for training often proved disappointing and the new training centers became seriously underutilized. The 450 training centers existing in 1966-67, it appears, trained an average of only eleven people each the following year.

Partly because of this lack of demand and partly because of the shortage of state government funds, the number of centers fell to 250 by 1970-71 and was still declining. The average total number of persons trained per year in the RIP program as a whole declined from 7,200 during the first three years to 4,000 in the most recent four years.

The common workshop facilities have been similarly underutilized, apparently because it was difficult for many of the artisans to get to them. The number of such facilities was reduced from 161 in 1965-66 to 118 in 1970-71, and many of those that remained were still underutilized.

The low-cost credit feature of the RIP program proved more popular and possibly more effective than the other parts. For the first time a supply of credit was available to small rural artisans and entrepreneurs to help them buy tools and raw materials and to improve their shops. They grasped at the opportunity. Large numbers of small loans were disbursed, totaling Rs 135.1 million by 1972. But provisions for screening loan requests, projects and borrowers and for training the small borrowers in how to use credit properly and how to meet repayment schedules were quite inadequate. Hence the repayment record has been poor on the whole.

Appraisal. Still, this infusion of government funds (some of which became a subsidy instead of a loan) was doubtless an important stimulus to a larger investment in small industry and to rural employment as well. More recently these business loan activities have been largely taken over by banks—principally the State Bank of India—which are making major efforts to continue the flow of investment funds to small industries while at the same time tightening up the appraisal, disbursement and collection functions.

With central government support scheduled to be fully phased out by 1973-74, the existing RIP pilot projects appear to face a precarious future. Starting in 1973, however, the central government intends to launch and finance fifty-seven new pilot projects, but with important changes from the original RIP scheme. Whereas the first generation of pilot projects was confined to "backward" areas and to communities with populations not exceeding 15,000, the second generation projects will apparently be concentrated in larger rural hub-towns (possibly up to 50,000 population) which have more adequate infrastructures and can become "development growth points" for the surrounding area. This new strategy seems likely to reduce somewhat the various inherent handicaps of the initial RIP program.

The central government's earlier leadership in promoting small industry inspired some of the Indian state governments to make innovations of their own. One of the most interesting is the pioneering program in Ahmedabad, sponsored by three public development corporations in the State of Gujarat, beginning in 1970, to train aspiring entrepreneurs and help them get started in businss. This novel program, discussed below, soon prompted the State of Maharashtra to establish five similar centers of its own, and the Government of India to arrange for similar programs at three existing institutions, specifically to train unemployed engineers and technicians to become small manufacturers.

The Gujarat Training Program for New Entrepreneurs

Target group. To gain admission to the new Ahmadabad Center a candidate must have a serious desire to become an independent entrepreneur and a specific and plausible idea of what he wants to produce. Previous formal education is not a major criterion for entrance; roughly half of the first fifty-five participants had a technical diploma or college degree of some sort, but others had only primary or secondary schooling. Previous work experience is given more weight: all of the initial participants had at least one year and some had six years or more of work experience. A conscious effort was made to select a group with widely diversified work experience, on the theory that they could learn much from one another.

Content and methods. Classroom instruction in the twelve-week course takes place in the evening and deals with basic management skills. Much of the instruction is given by visiting experts—successful businessmen, government experts, management specialists and others, all of whom have been carefully briefed on what ground to cover. Trainees spend daytime hours on visits to various businesses, self-study and developing a "project" to start a business.

Attempts have been made in the course to provide for the development of "achievement motivation"—an individual and group technique for self-analysis and for developing human relations skills, originated by the Center for Research in Personality at Harvard University and previously tried out in some courses for businessmen in Bombay and other cities in India. The purpose of "achievement motivation" is to enable each participant to discover for himself whether he has the necessary qualities to become a successful entrepreneur and to strengthen these attributes through conscious effort.[12]

Performance. By late 1971 three groups of trainees had been through the new program, and the first had been out long enough to permit an initial evaluation. Of the first fifty-five participants, forty-seven had completed their project reports (though tardily in a number of cases); twenty-one of the projects had been submitted to financing institutions; and thirteen loans had already been granted. (Administrative problems in the lending institution had slowed the loan process.) More important, thirty-one of the participants had actually opened factories, more than half without financial aid. How well they would eventually do and how representative they were of participants yet to come remained, of course, a question that only the future could answer. But clearly this innovative entrepreneurial development program was off to an auspicious start.

The early returns from the Indian government program, modeled after the Ahmadabad Center but aimed at a different audience ("surplus" engineering graduates) were less reassuring. On the basis of preliminary indications, it was estimated that perhaps only 15 to 30 percent of the early trainees in this program would succeed in launching a business. There were also grounds for suspecting that there may not be a high correlation between formal technical education and success as an entrepreneur. But it was much too early, of course, to draw any firm conclusions.

This chapter has reviewed a wide diversity of programs for training rural and small-town artisans, craftsmen and small entrepreneurs, with a view to achieving balanced economic development and creating more employment. In common, these programs place their trust in systematic, institutionalized training as the best means of promoting mastery of the basic skills and knowledge required for particular occupations. In common also, they trust to the surrounding economy to absorb and make productive use of the skills they generate, however, there the similarities end. The programs differ widely in their specific objectives, in the characteristics of the target audiences, in course content and pedagogical methods, and in the extent to which the training activities are linked to and followed up by other support services.

Thailand's MTTS program and Senegal's Rural Artisan Training System, for example, are confined exclusively to training functions, whereas all of the Indian programs integrate training with other complementary services. The MTTS program provides mainly pre-employment skill training and the Gujarat program works with would-be entrepreneurs, whereas all the other programs aim primarily at upgrading the skills of people already employed or running a business. The Indian programs pay considerable attention to developing the managerial as well as technical skills required by entrepreneurs, but the programs in Thailand and Senegal, even though their trainees are or may

---

[12]David C. McClelland and David G. Winter, *Motivating Economic Achievement: Accelerating Economic Development through Psychological Training* (New York: The Free Press, 1971).

become small entrepreneurs as well as artisans, concentrate their efforts on technical skill training.

There are also wide differences in methods of financing and in the unit costs of these programs, as well as in their effectiveness and economic impact. And no one of these training models has yet been tested under enough variable conditions to prove its distinct superiority over the others. We shall return to these questions later.

6: THE SELF-HELP APPROACH
TO RURAL DEVELOPMENT

Most of the programs reviewed thus far were based on a relatively narrow view of rural development, seen through the eyes of one or another group of specialists. Most were also based on the implicit assumption that rural development could be initiated only by outside intervention and by the introduction—even the imposition—of modern production technologies.

The designers of the program reviewed in this chapter began with a wider concept of development and with different assumptions about how it can be induced.

- They saw rural development as involving a thoroughgoing transformation of all the economic, social, political and cultural institutions, processes and relationships in a rural society.
- They regarded as the main obstacles to such transformation the historically rooted fatalism, dependency and lack of self-confidence of traditional rural people; hence they believed that the first requirement was to initiate a broad educational process that would alter these attitudes, raise aspirations and self-confidence, and encourage individual and community initiatives for self-improvement.
- Further requirements, as they saw it, were to create greater political awareness and participation by villagers and greater community cooperation, through strengthening local democratic institutions and broadening the leadership base.
- They acknowledged the importance of modern expertise and other forms of assistance coming from the outside but were concerned that such help be in response to expressed local needs and desires—as part of an "enabling process"—rather than one-way intervention from the top down.

To put it differently, the proponents of the self-help approach to rural development base their strategy on a more humanistic and less technocratic theory of development. They respect the power of science and technology but put their basic faith in the adaptability of human beings. Simultaneously, they are trying to overcome an inherent difficulty of a community development approach: namely, that of meeting local needs that are in fact more broadly based than the articulated demands of the more affluent rural minority who are in a position to control such an approach. And for this they place heavy reliance on education—but a kind of education much broader, more subtle and more inner-directed than that associated with formal schooling. They have no fixed pedagogical models, dogmas or techniques, save the basic principles that learning comes from action, that development itself is educational, and that villagers learn best from teachers with the same background. Many proponents of this approach are deeply skeptical and critical of formal schooling, believing that it alienates young people more than it helps them adapt to their environment, and that it chains them to an orthodoxy more than it frees them to be themselves.

These proponents, however, do not reject the nonformal educational techniques of extension and training previously discussed. What they do reject are the authoritarian attitudes that so often accompany these techniques.

Although programs epitomizing the self-help approach spring from similar philosophies of development, they differ greatly in other respects.[1]

- India's *Community Development (CD) Program* and Senegal's *animation rurale* movement were both nationwide, government-sponsored efforts to arouse the development spirit and ambitions of rural people and to unleash their energies to help carry out national objectives and policies with the aid of official support services.
- The Philippine *Rural Reconstruction Movement* (PRRM), a voluntary effort which began in a limited geographic area in the Philippines and then spread to other developing nations, represents another design for bringing traditional peasants into a modern world primarily through educational means.
- Tanzania's *Cooperative Education* system, created and operated with the blessings of the central government, yet not a part of the official formal education system, assumed the mission of strengthening cooperatives—at all levels—as a basic economic and social institution for reshaping an agrarian society along the lines of African socialism.
- The *Comilla Project* in what is now Bangladesh was, by contrast, an unconventional and quasi-autonomous pilot experiment in a limited geographic area, alternately aided and frowned upon by official government agencies.
- *Acción Cultural Popular* (ACPO) in Colombia is in a class by itself as a nongovernmental, church-supported and nationwide educational service (making unusually extensive use of modern communications media), which seeks to transform the neglected and disadvantaged campesino into a "new Latin American man," inspired and equipped to pull himself up by the bootstraps.

Only three of these six programs are covered by ICED case studies (Tanzania, Senegal and Colombia). Extensive documentation on the others was examined, however, and two were briefly visited in the field (India and the Philippines). Efforts to develop a full case study of the Comilla Project were aborted by the troubled circumstances at the time.

The Community Development Approach

The term "community development" gained currency in pre-independence British Africa when colonial social welfare officers—later designated community development officers—sought to stimulate self-help actions in selected rural areas to improve health, nutrition, adult education and general community welfare. Social development was the main objective, not economic development.

India's massive Community Development Program, launched in 1952 soon after independence, gave the term a broader meaning, embracing both social

---

[1]The costs and financing of the programs summarized in this chapter are treated in Chapter 11.

and economic development objectives and wider range of activities. The Indian CD program was inspired by the social philosophies and earlier rural experiments of Gandhi and Tagore, but also by the necessity facing the Nehru government of beginning the gigantic task of modernizing rural India with a minimum of resources. A further inspiration was the outstanding Etawah pilot project which seemed to prove that rural people, given dynamic leadership and a modicum of help from the outside, could substantially improve their lives through their own constructive efforts.[2]

The Indian Community Development (CD) Program

The Community Development program began on a well-designed pilot scale with Ford Foundation assistance. With the pressure of rising popular expectations, it was hastily expanded to a national scale under the First Five-Year Development Plan (1952-56), before the lessons of the pilot experience had been digested.

At the same time a National Extension Service was launched with the intent of placing the expert services of government ministries in agriculture, health, educaion, public works, cooperatives and small industry—at the disposal of the community development effort and within reach of the rural people. Lacking the means to provide rural people with new supplies and equipment for improving agriculture, health, education and housing, the government resorted to a much lower-cost but massive program of technical assistance and popular nonformal education aimed at unleashing and guiding the constructive energies of the villagers themselves.

Organization and staffing. The organization and staffing of this program in the world's second-most populous nation is of particular interest, first because it established foundations for later rural development programs and, second, because it dramatizes the inherent difficulties of harnessing the resources of independently minded bureaucracies to create a unified rural development effort—a problem shared by virtually all developing nations.

Over the protest of various ministries, Prime Minister Nehru created a new Ministry of Community Development with extraordinary authority to draw upon and coordinate the specialized services of other ministries and to establish and oversee a nationwide organizational network, reaching down to the village level, for planning and executing community development actions.

Several organizational and staff innovations were adopted in order to bring the planning, coordination and implementation of community development actions as close as possible to the local level and to involve villagers themselves in the decision-making. Existing districts of each state were subdivided into several "blocks," each block embracing about 100 villages in an area up to 200 square miles, with a total population ranging from 70,000 to 100,000. Each district was equipped with a diversified team of specialists-from various ministries to backstop the field extension services, under the general supervision of the existing District Collector. Each block headquarters was staffed with a similar (though less high-level) team of specialists, and was headed by a Block Development Officer.

The key local agent was the multipurpose Village Level Worker (VLW)—a young man or woman high-school graduate, typically of rural origin, with two

[2] Albert Mayer, and associates. *Pilot Project India: The Story of Rural Development at Etawah, Uttar Pradesh* (Berkeley and Los Angeles, California: University of California Press, 1958).

years of specialized training and apprenticeship in the multiple aspects of community development, including agriculture, health, home economics, local self-help projects and saving schemes. The VLW lived in the village among the rural people and might serve as many as 10,000 people in ten villages, acting both as their agent to the government services and vice versa. For problems beyond his technical grasp he could turn for help to the specialists at the block or district levels.

A third important innocation, which resulted from a critical evaluation of the initial years of CD, was the three-tier *panchayat* (council) system, at the local, block and district levels. It was designed to give locally elected representatives a more important role in planning and executing community development actions in their area, and thereby strengthen the "spirit of self-help."[3]

Educational programs. The educational arrangements under the Community Development Program were practically all nonformal and nonstandardized. The VLWs, often in company with visiting specialists from the block or district level, served as general extension agents on a wide range of subjects. Often they visited farmers and their families in their homes or fields; at other times they met them at village meetings and discussion groups. They disseminated information and recommended practices coming from the block headquarters or above (concerning agriculture, health, sanitation, road building, well cleaning, etc.); organized campaigns and local projects; promoted traditional folk songs and dances; collected census data on people, livestock and crops—in short, they were all-purpose development stimulators, communicators and helpers at the village level.

Other educational activities were carried on through whatever voluntary groups existed or could be organized—cooperative societies, 4-H clubs, women and youth groups, all of which were actively encouraged by the VLWs in league with the local *panchayat*.

One of the priority targets in many villages was to build a primary school and teacher residence with local contributed labor. The new government-paid teacher was expected to work with adults as well as children.

The great variety of semieducational schemes and projects with which VLWs and the *panchayats* concerned themselves is illustrated by the ambitious program agenda for 1968 of the (block level) Medchal Panchayat Samiti near Hyderabad:

1968 Agenda—Medchal Panchayat Samiti

A. Agriculture
> Distribution of improved seeds
> Supply of fertilizers and pesticides
> Distribution of improved implements
> Promoting Japanese method of paddy cultivation
> Loan schemes—wells, cattle purchase, crop loans, electric motors
>   for pumps

---

[3]Government of India, Planning Commission, *Report of the Team for the Study of Community Projects and National Extension Service,* 3 Volumes (Delhi, 1957). The prestigious Balvantrai Mehta Committes which evaluated the evolving CD program concluded that it had thus far failed to foster a sufficient "self-help spirit" and that "democratic decentralization" and stronger organs of local self-government were needed.

Rural manpower program
Fruit development scheme
Intensive manuring scheme
Soil conservation scheme
Intensive vegetable cultivation scheme
Minor irrigation—restoration of tanks and wells, construction of small weirs and dams
Animal husbandry schemes—livestock census, artificial insemination, veterinary service
Fisheries—construction of fish farms, breeding and distribution

B. Roads
Construction of feeder roads, cross drainage, etc.

C. Health and Rural Sanitation
Health centers, family planning clinics
Drinking-water wells for schools and villages
Vaccination
Maternity centers
Applied nutrition program

D. Education
Provisions for teachers, buildings, school means, etc., for 115 primary schools
Pilot scheme for compulsory primary education
Adult literacy centers—one per village
Youth clubs
Libraries, provision of community radio sets

E. Women's Programs
Clubs
Tailor and dressmaking centers
Improvement in cooking and sanitation equipment

F. Small Industries
Survey of small industries and artisans
Provisions of workshops

G. Joint Action with Cooperatives
62 multipurpose; 8 milk supply; 5 fishermen's; 18 Toddy Tappers' Societies.[4]

Almost two decades after the CD program was launched, the evidence and testimony on its impact were mixed. Undeniably, CD had created in its early years a great surge of hope and enthusiasm among the rank and file of CD workers and villagers, brought an unprecedented infusion of new resources into the countryside, and inspired a large number of self-help projects. All over India, community schools and village halls were constructed, roads built and paved, water wells dug and protected, compost pits filled, school gardens and backyard vegetable patches planted, sewing classes and youth clubs opened. Moreover, a new image of the government as a source of help and service was

---

[4]Guy Hunter, *The Administration of Agricultural Development—Lessons from India* (London: Oxford University Press, 1970), pp. 49-50.

created and the villagers began to see that for the first time the agents of government were there to help them, not simply to demand taxes and enforce regulations. Another important achievement was the creation of the *panchayat* structure as an instrument of self-government and self-expression for the rural population.

Granting these positive accomplishments, it must also be said that after its first decade of operation the Community Development Program had not significantly altered the basic conditions of life in rural India. Abject poverty, malnutrition and ill-health, indebtedness, and above all, India's worsening food crisis had but one remedy—a larger production of wealth from the land. In the latter respect, the CD program admittedly had little impact. Apparently mainly on this score—on its failure to stimulate sizeable increases in production and income flows—many Indian observers (especially economists) declare Community Development a failure.

Such a production breakthrough, however, requires greatly improved supplies of chemical inputs along with improved technologies, not to mention adequate cost-price incentives. This combination of conditions was not present in India when Community Development was initiated. Had the CD effort coincided with these other essential factors it might well be heralded today as the great catalytic agent of rural development. But to have expected it to produce something like a Green Revolution all by itself was asking the impossible.

The "Animation Rurale" Approach

The *animation rurale* movement in Francophone Africa was, like Community Development, inspired by the conviction that the prerequisite to rural development was the awakening of rural people and their energies. Also *animation* was similarly conceived as a national movement calculated to implement broad national goals and plans. But in contrast to CD, *animation rurale* concentrated on the identification and systematic training of *animateurs,* who were to act in the villages as innovators and catalysts for change linking officialdom to the mass of rural people.[5]

Both Community Development and *animation rurale* —terms now somewhat tarnished—were fundamentally educational, political and sociological in character. Both generated enthusiasm for development among the rural people. But when the time was ripe to follow this with more substantive assistance, both programs floundered and fell victim to various rival bureaucratic aggressions.

It is impossible to evaluate their ultimate impact at this close range. Only future historians can judge whether, by the longer term and subtler calculus of the philosophers of social change, they will have precipitated the long process of freeing the rural masses from the psychological, intellectual and material constraints of their tradition-bound lives. Whatever the final judgment, both movements, cast against strikingly different cultural and colonial backgrounds, were definitely disturbing to the status quo.

---

[5]For a description of the *animation rurale* movement see Yves Goussault, "Rural 'Animation' and Popular Participation in French-Speaking Black Africa," *International Labour Review* 97, no. 6 (June 1968), pp. 525-550.

Animation Rurale in Senegal[6]

Background. A private French technical assistance society,[7] is credited with conceiving the idea of *animation rurale* and first trying it out in Morocco in the 1950s. The essence of *animation rurale*—an amalgam of sociological and political concepts with a dash of economics—was that village peasants should be stimulated by one of their own number to identify and articulate their needs for improvement, to take initiatives to help themselves, and to demand from their central government and its various technical services the kinds of help they needed to reinforce their efforts, consistent with national goals and plans. The key change agents in this process—the *animateurs*—would be farmers selected by their fellow villagers and given special training to serve as guide and stimulator for the village and also as liaison with outside sources of technical and material assistance.

Objectives. Transplanted to Senegal in 1959 with IRAM's help, *animation rural* was viewed politically as a means of "decolonizing" the inherited relationship between the central government bureaucracy and the rural masses, of spreading the "mystique of development," and of "mobilizing the rural masses" for collective grass-roots development initiatives. Far from being meant to inspire local pockets of political opposition to the dominant national party leadership, it was seen as a means of giving local political roots to that leadership, to help implement the national government's purposes and plans. It was seen also as a means of making the national bureaucratic services the servants rather than the overlords of the people

Organization. After *animation rurale* got under way, a constellation of institutions grew up around it to support a broad strategy for modernizing Senegalese farming methods, increasing agricultural production, achieving greater crop diversification, and establishing a larger development role for the rural population through rural cooperatives and decentralized planning. These other institutions included:[8]

    1. OCA (Office de Commercialisation Agricole), whose mission was to promote village cooperatives, distribute farm implements and fertilizer through the cooperatives, and exercise control over the peanut marketing operations jointly with the cooperatives.

    2. BSD (Banque Sénégalaise de Développement) to provide credit for financing the OCA operations and the cooperatives.

    3. Seven regional technical centers (Centres Régionaux de l'Assistance pour le Développement, CRAD) to provide storage and transportation services for the cooperatives, assist with their bookkeeping, and serve as liaison between local cooperatives and government agencies, including

---

[6]See Pierre Furter and Sven Grabe, *Senegal: Rural Vocational Training centers*, ICED Case Study No. 8 (unpublished). See also Edward G. Schumacher, "Bureaucracy, Party, and Rural Commercial Reform in Senegal: The Politics of Institutional Change, 1957-1968." (Ph.D. dissertation, Columbia University, 1970).

[7]Institut de Recherches et d'Application des Méthodes de Développement (IRAM).

[8]All these organizations survived the political crisis of 1962 and the subsequent government reorganization, though with changes in nomenclature and minor modifications of function. OCA after 1967 was OCAS (Office de Commercialisation du Sénégal); BSD was renamed BNDS (Banque Nationale de Développement du Sénégal) in 1964; and regional CRADS were reorganized into a more centralized organization 1966 under the title of ONCAD (Office National de Centres de l'Assistance pour le Développement). More extensive reorganization was in store for the early 1970s.

OCA and BSD. (The functions of CRAD were ultimately taken over by regional federations of cooperative societies.)

4. A network of Rural Expansion Centers (Centres d'Expansion Rurales, CER) to provide technical support to local *animateurs.*

In principle, each administrative subdivision (*arrondissement*) had its own center, containing a multipurpose technical support team made up of agents of the departments of cooperation, water and forests, fishery, animal husbandry, and rural housing. The CER teams (comparable to the block teams in the Indian CD program) were to work through the *animateurs* in providing civic education, technical training for agricultural improvement, counseling to new cooperatives, and other forms of help for rural development.

Methods. The *animateurs* were local farmers selected through consultation with the villagers. They were first given an intensive course in the Centres d'Animation Rurale (CAR) in general civic duties, the meaning of national planning, methods of cooperative management, and technical innovations in agriculture and animal husbandry. There were two of these training centers (one for men and one for women) in each *arrondissment,* a total of fifty-six by 1967.

On returning to their villages, the *animateurs* attempted, in consultation with other local people, to analyze village needs and problems, design local development actions, stimulate the peasants' awareness of their collective capacity for self-improvement, and facilitate the activities of technical agents of various government services. The *animateurs* returned to the training centers periodically for short (four to five days) consultation and training sessions. By 1967 a total force of some 7,000 *animateurs* was in action.

Reorganization. By 1967 *animation rurale* had not yet been built up to its full stature with the proposed network of training centers, backstopping technical terms and *animateurs* in every rural community, when the government went through another reorganization of the administrative structure for rural development. It was decided that specific technical services, rather than general educational and counseling services of the *animation* program, were more urgently needed by farmers. A new public technical assistance company (SODEVA) became the administrator of the agricultural extension service in the important agricultural regions, and *animation rurale* saw its activities reduced to cultural and social spheres of rural development.

Appraisal. There is little doubt that *animation rurale,* like the Indian CD movement, achieved considerable success in its first objective of stimulating rural people in behalf of development and creating a greater awareness of their own interests and capacity. The enthusiasm and esprit de corps of the *animation rurale* group inspired long-dormant rural areas.

But, as in India, inspiring villagers was not enough; sophisticated technical advice and more practical material help were necessary follow-ups. This is where the movement floundered. The ground design of interlocking support organizations, so logically conceived on paper, was never sufficiently realized. By the mid-1960s, *animation rurale* was getting more competition and criticism than cooperation from the various technical support organizations. Repeated efforts were made by the central government to rescue the flagging rural development effort through reorganization. New initiatives and different approaches were tried, in particular the SATEC scheme described in Chapter 3, which simply pushed aside *animation rurale* rather than joining forces with it.

In 1970, with production-oriented agencies having absorbed most of its oriiginal mandate, *animation rurale* was detached from the Ministry of Rural Economy and reorganized as *promotion humaine*— a cultural and educational program for youth under the Ministry of Youth and Sports.

There are wide differences of opinion among those who have tried to fathom and interpret the whole story of *animation rurale*. This much, however, seems clear. Senegal did not yet possess the supply of developed human talent and material resources, nor the planning and administrative capabilities, to translate this elaborate organizational design for rural development into suc-cessful action. Moreover, the efforts of the local farmers-*cum-animateurs* to transform the social, political and economic life of their villages were often no match for the powerful local traditional leaders.

IRAM's own critical evaluation reports to the Senegalese Government em-phasized the inadequacy of resources, the weaknesses of the regional planning and coordination machinery, and the lack of willingness or ability on the part of civil administrators to concert the energies of their respective departments in a cohesive attack on the problems of rural development.

Perhaps the simplest and most generous interpretation is that—in Senegal as elsewhere—the whole process of transforming rural life and institutions proved in practice to be a far larger and more complicated task than originally conceived.

Programs Involving Private Initiative

The self-help movements in India and Senegal were nationwide and govern-ment-directed, tied to national development plans and policies. More often, however, the self-help approach finds expression in geographically more limited programs, many sponsored by voluntary organizations. These voluntary programs have certain evident advantages over government-sponsored ones. For example, they have greater operational flexibility; they can recruit abler and more dedicated people, and often they can get better results at lower cost. But they also have certain built-in handicaps. Because of financial con-straints and uncertainties they are usually obliged to operate on a limited scale. Too often they decline sharply or disappear altogether, when funds dry up or when their architects leave the scene. In some circumstances they are also vulnerable to changes in government policies toward voluntary organizations, but even when the government takes a friendly attitude, ministries with programs of their own naturally prefer outside support funds to go into these.

These inherent advantages and disadvantages of voluntary programs apply to both formal and nonformal education, but they are especially important in rural self-help schemes, for their success depends heavily on the quality and continuity of the personalities operating at the local level. The Philippine Rural Reconstruction Program—one of the best known of the privately operated rural improvement efforts—demonstrates several of the foregoing points. Not all self-help programs include an emphasis on cooperatives or on the integra-tion of educational inputs with complementary factors. The program of Acción Cultural Popular (ACPO) in Colombia (also known as Radio Sutatenza) is a case in point. ACPO has, however, other unique features and a record of substantial accomplishment over two decades that make it a worthy candidate for ex-amination here. Among these unique features are its multimedia educational techniques for reaching rural audiences throughout the nation; its extensive use of local volunteers; and its record, as a voluntary agency, of earning much of its income through revenue-producing activities.

The Philippines Rural Reconstruction Movement (PRRM)[9]

Background. Conditions in rural areas of the Philippines in the early 1950s, especially in Central Luzon, were in a troubled state. Living conditions were wretched for many rural families, government services to help them were weak or nonexistent, and a number of areas had come under control of the anti-government Huk Balahak órganization, an underground, guerrilla-type movement generally considered to be Communist-inspired. Government officials, therefore, willingly gave their blessings and cooperation when Y.C. "Jimmy" Yen, a person of rare humanitarian and leadership qualities who had acquired rich experience in rural development work in prewar China, wanted to launch a rural reconstruction project in the Philippines. The Philippine Rural Reconstruction Movement (PRRM) was thus born in 1952 as a private philanthropic organization, and projects were started in a number of villages in the Nueva Ecija province in Luzon.

Objectives. The strategy of the program centered on rooting out what its founders considered the four fundamental obstacles to improving rural life — poverty, disease, illiteracy and civic inertia. They shaped the program — heavily educational in character — around four complementary themes:

1. *Livelihood:* Increasing rural production and income through scientific crop-production techniques for rice and secondary crops, modern livestock and poultry practices, and cottage industries; and organizing economic institutions such as consumers' and producers' cooperatives.

2. *Health:* Improving health services in the *barrios* (villages) through immunization against preventable disease, promoting the use of sanitary toilets, safeguarding drinking water, training auxiliary health workers, establishing rural health centers, improving home environment, and encouraging family planning.

3. *Education:* Promoting functional literacy and cultural development through literacy courses, drama, folk dances, folk songs and sports activities.

4. *Self-government:* Mobilizing the *barrio* people for self-expression and self-help through strengthening the Barrio Council (the village self-government body), establishing men's, women's and youth organizations, and conducting leadership training for selected members of the *barrios*.

Management and staff. As organized today, direction of the program is in the hands of the president of the PRRM and three directors in charge, respectively, of field operations, operational research and training, and administration. The technical and supervisory staff includes specialists in several pertinent fields (agricultural, health, cooperatives, community government, etc.) and field supervisors known as team captains and technical assistants. Local-level

---

[9]This report is based on a visit by an ICED team in October 1971 to the International Institute of Rural Reconstruction and extensive discussion with its Vice President for Training, Dr. Juan M. Flavier. For an earlier case study of PRRM see E. H. Valsan, *Community Development Programs and Rural Local Government* (New York: Praeger Publishers, 1970), Chapter 5, "Philippines Rural Reconstruction Movement: Case Study of San Leonardo, Nueva Ecija."

staff, who are backstopped by the technical specialists and supervisors, are called Rural Reconstruction Workers (RRWs) and are more or less the counterparts of India's VLWs and Senegal's *animateurs.*

As of late 1971 when an ICED team visited the project, the management, technical and supervisory personnel numbered about 100 and the Rural Reconstruction Workers about 200. They were concentrated mainly in fifty *barrios* in the Nueva Ecija Province with an approximate total population of 30,000.

The RRWs are the key to the program's effectiveness and hence of special interest. Young college graduates (both men and women), they are recruited for service (at low rates of pay) on the basis of their altruistic spirit and willingness to live and work with the *barrio* people. They undergo six months of intensive preservice training at a national training center in Nieves, San Leonardo. This training is designed to test their motivation, prepare them for a rugged life, and impart technical knowledge and techniques of human relations for application in the field. RRWs are brought back to the center twice a year for week-long inservice refresher training.

Financial support for the program comes from private contributions, both in the Philippines and abroad. Similar Rural Reconstruction Movements, it should be noted, have been initiated in Thailand, Colombia and Guatemala, with technical and financial help from the International Institute for Rural Reconstruction, located in the Philippines. The PRRM has its own headquarters, however, and operates independently of the International Institute.

Performance. It was not feasible for the ICED team in the time available to check directly on the effectiveness of the PRRM in a sample of rural areas, but the record of accomplishment, as evidenced by the following facts, has been impressive:

By demonstrating an effective methodology for promoting rural development, the PRRM inspired the creation (in 1956) of a somewhat similar governmental program known as the Presidential Arm for Community Development (PACD), and PRRM was asked to train staff for the government program on a contract basis

The staff of the PRRM, regarded by rural people as politically neutral and concerned only with helping them to improve their situation, has continued to function effectively in geographic areas where government representatives have been ineffective.

The PRRM's emphasis on strengthening local organizations as a means for self-expression and self-government encouraged the adoption of legislation for an elected Barrio Council in the national congress.

The PRRM cites the following as among the accomplishments for 1970: (1) an average income for farmers participating in producer cooperatives in Nueva Ecija barrios three time higher than the average for the province; (2) sales totaling one million pesos by fifty three consumer cooperatives; (3) distribution of 500,000 pesos in production credits by over 100 credit unions with 3,300 members; (4) income increases averaging 187 pesos for 261 families participating in a mushroom-growing project; (5) participation of nearly 18,000 *barrio* residents in various training activities.[10]

---

[10]"Philippine Rural Reconstruction Movement 1970-71." Manila, April 1971.

Appraisal. Within the confines of relatively limited geographic area, therefore, the PRRM appears to have had a discernible impact. PRRM officials point out, however, that the impact varies considerably according to the duration and continuity of the effort in a given *barrio,* the ability and enthusiasm of the RRW, and the peculiarities of the local situation.

Despite these accomplishments, the PRRM as of 1971 faced two serious problems (in addition to the perennial one of finding sufficient financial support). The first problem concerned the permanence of its impact—whether it was capable of creating a self-sustaining process of development that would continue when PRRM phased out of a given area. The experience thus far suggests that the answer is at best uncertain and perhaps negative. The Barrio Councils, cooperatives and other local organizations apparently require continuous encouragement, guidance and prodding by the RRW to maintain their effectiveness. The farmers and their families need continuing technical and other support—in agriculture, health, education, etc.—which the regular government services are often unequipped to take over from PRRM. Thus if PRRM, having once "opened up" a new area is obliged to stay with it more or less permanently, its capacity to move on to additional needy areas is seriously restricted.

The second problem concerns the recruitment of able and highly motivated college graduates to serve as RRWs. For whatever reasons, there has lately been a marked decline in the supply of volunteers meeting these specifications. PRRM has been forced to lower its standards and to accept a growing number of unemployed graduates whose main interest is in finding a job, even at low pay. Unless the enthusiasm and sense of dedication that characterized the earlier years of the program can somehow be restored, it would appear that PRRM's outlook is cloudy.

Acción Cultural Popular (ACPO)

Target group. Colombia's Acción Cultural Popular (ACPO), a Catholic church-supported but not church-managed organization,[11] began in 1947 as an educational radio station. It has since evolved into a multipurpose, multimedia educational system that operates all day and evening, with the entire rural population of Colombia—especially its most disadvantaged members—as the target audience.

Objectives. ACPO's objectives are:

to create motivation for development among *campesinos* and to integrate them into the mainstream of society through opportunities for self-impovement;

to stimulate economic progress by disseminating new agricultural technologies, promoting knowledge and understanding of economic institutions and practices, and inculcating a sense of the value of work;

to encourage participation in local and community organizations;

to foster spiritual development by helping the *campesino* to realize his ability to become an agent of social development, creating in him a critical consciousness of his world.

Educational content and methods. These ambitious objectives are pursued through an unusual combination of mass educational means and methods, in-

---

[11]Stephen F. Brumberg, *Acción Cultural Popular: Mass Media in the Service of Colombian Rural Development,* ICED Case Study No. 1 (Essex, Conn., April 1972).

cluding Colombia's largest nationwide radio network; a weekly newspaper (with the largest rural circulation); a series of high-volume, low-cost textbooks and well-illustrated supplementary reading materials; and written correspondence with groups of radio listeners. ACPO also operates two substantial training institutes for its field staff, runs a large modern printing plant, and produces recordings. These facilities not only serve ACPO's needs but earn substantial commercial revenues to help subsidize its educational activities.

Radio broadcasts are the mainstay of the ACPO program. Among its most popular programs are its regular news broadcasts (written to be easily understood by the uneducated *campesino* and to give him a sense of belonging to a larger community) and its early-morning light entertainment and information program geared to the interests of rural listeners.

Three systematic "courses"—for basic literacy and numeracy, for fundamental education and for formal primary school equivalence—are offered through the radio "school" with complementary printed materials. The first two courses are for groups organized in rural areas under a volunteer organizer or monitor. The third is for self-study.

The *cartillas* (textbooks), the *Biblioteca campesina* (the supplementary readers), and *El Campesino* (the weekly newspaper) essentially supplement and reinforce the radio lessons. All are especially edited for ease of comprehension by *campesinos*. Its "how-to-do-it" articles, for example, complete with diagrams and instructions, seem like an issue of *Popular Mechanics*.

ACPO also makes great use of educational campaigns designed to promote constructive action for self—and community—betterment and to demonstrate the practical utility of knowledge. Past projects have included, for example, tree planting and other conservation practices, kitchen gardens and better nutrition, health and hygiene, improvement of dwellings, participation in community organizations. Campaign themes, selected in advance, are publicized and developed through coordinated radio broadcasts, newspaper articles and ongoing courses. The local ACPO staff, the local parish organization formed to support ACPO activities, and the monitors of the radio classes work together to motivate the local residents to participate in the campaigns. (See Table 6.1.)

Correspondence with groups of listeners and individuals is used as a means of feedback by the program organizers.

Performance. ACPO's self-evaluation efforts are unusually extensive and candid. Not surprisingly, however, its quantitative accomplishments are much more fully documented than their qualitative dimensions and practical impact.

In 1968, the latest year for which full statistics were available, ACPO operated 22,200 radio schools (listening groups) for its "fundamental education" course, with a total enrollment of 167,000, of which 75,000 were illiterate. About 20,000 of the illiterates, it is claimed, learned to read and write by the end of the year. Another 92,000 attended the progressive course, of which 15,000 completed the course and passed a terminal examination. *El Campesino*, the weekly newspaper, sells about 70,000 copies per week and it is estimated that ten readers share the average copy. About 100,000 copies of the *campesino* books were sold in 1969.

Appraisal. The actual impact of these statistically impressive accomplishments is, of course, extremely difficult to evaluate. Several partial attempts to do so, including a limited field survey by ICED, suggest that ACPO radio school participants generally score higher than nonparticipants in scales measuring the "modernity" of one's attitudes: "innovativeness"; "integration" into society; average earnings; adoption of recommended health, agricultural and other practices; and participation in community organizations. There are marked differences in scores, however, for different communities suggesting the influence of such variables as economic conditions, the degree of support (or opposition) by the local priest, and related activities of other development agencies in the area.

There is also evidence that the ACPO program has had a differential effect on different rural subgroups in the same locality. For example, landowners (though with small holdings and generally functioning at the subsistence level) are more likely than the landless to adopt the innovations promoted by the radio schools. Very few landless peasants participated in the radio schools.

While ACPO has deliberately limited its sphere to educational and motivational activities, it has encouraged and assisted its participants to take advantage of useful services offered by government agencies and others—such as agricultural extension, credit, land reform assistance, and health clinics. There is good reason to believe that ACPO's educational efforts are more effective

Table 6.1
ACPO: Rural Improvement Campaign Projects Realized
in the Period 1954-1968

Category	No. of projects realized
Household improvement	93,440
New houses	39,271
Piped water	32,257
Latrines	50,457
Flower gardens	85,702
Trees planted	4,469,106
Vegetable gardens	108,058
Compost heaps	136,509
Vaccination of animals	99,977
Stables	29,078
Pig sties	37,507
Chicken coops	44,241
Bee hives	24,481
Spraying crops with insecticides	88,606
Neighborhood boards formed	18,397
Bridges constructed	6,635
Improvements to rural roads	37,348
Sports fields constructed	14,279
Musical groups formed	10,306
Rural theatre groups organized	14,121

SOURCE: *Los Campesinos Trabajan por el Desarrollo*. Bogota: Editorial Andes, 1971.

when they coincide with such complementary support services in a given area than when they are alone.

Self-Help Through Cooperatives

Farmer cooperatives were assigned a key economic, social and educational role in a high proportion of the self-help schemes studied by ICED. But unfortunately the record of success in the many efforts to implant Western-type cooperatives in developing countries, whether as part of a broader self-help scheme or simply on their own, is on the whole a discouraging one—with notable exceptions.

Various explanations are given for this poor record: for example, that the sociological setting was uncongenial; that the cooperatives under prevailing economic circumstances offered no significant advantages to farmers; that the central government or dominant political party was mainly interested in cooperatives a disguised form of rural tax system or as a device for building grassroots political support. But apparently the most serious and ubiquitous problem of new cooperatives has been the lack of education and training of cooperative members and functionaries in the principles, management and operation of such organizations. Too often the local members and member-directors have not really understood how a cooperative is supposed to work and what their own roles are in making it work. They have not known how to conduct meetings, establish policies and enforce them, audit accounts and oversee the work of hired functionaries. Hired functionaries, in turn, have been inadequately trained for their duties and have often acted against the interests of the members and the society's growth. All these deficiencies have bred distrust, inefficiency and failure. Clearly, a cardinal requirement for the success of any cooperative movement is an effective system for educating and training members and employees at every level, as well as government officials concerned with the supervision of cooperatives. The unique educational system that has evolved in Tanzania to meet these needs offers some useful lessons for others.

Tanzania's System for Cooperative Education[12]

Background. Cooperatives were given a central role in Tanzania's homegrown strategy for transforming her vast rural areas into a new type of African agrarian society based on socialist principles.[13] Soon after independence a decision was taken to displace private traders with a "single-channel marketing system" for agricultural products under a set of national marketing boards, with local cooperative "primary societies" and regional cooperative "unions" serving as the marketing agents. To meet the vast training needs created by these drastic policy innovations, Tanzania created a unique nonformal educational network expressly designed to train the members and functionaries of cooperatives at

---

[12]For fuller details see Sven Grabe, *The Cooperative Education System of Tanzania*, ICED Case Study No. 9 (Essex, Conn., April 1972).

[13]These *ujamaa* principles were enunciated in the Arusha Declaration of 1967, which stressed self-reliance by villagers and the cooperative organization of production and marketing. See *The Arusha Declaration and TANU's Policy on Socialism and Self-Reliance* (Dar es Salaam: Publicity Section, TANU, 1967).

every level in the principles and techniques of operating multipurpose cooperatives.

Organization. The vertical cooperative structure is based on nearly 1,800 "primary societies" at the local level, joined by "unions" at the regional level, with the Cooperative Union of Tanzania at the pinnacle. Though it is interlaced with government in various ways (Table 6.2), the cooperative movement has enjoyed substantial autonomy. Each primary society has its "member elite" (the more active members who promote its interests and are expected to educate the rank and file), its own governing committee, and one or two paid employees to handle its business and other affairs. These local employees are members of a professional cadre of career cooperative workers who serve the system at all levels. The system is supervised and aided by the Ministry of Agriculture, Food and Cooperatives, which employs a special staff for these purposes.

Some idea of the mammoth training needs for the effective growth and operation of this cooperative system—serving a potential clientele of some 12 million inhabitants in an area roughly twice the size of France—is suggested by the following tasks assigned to it by the national leaders:[14] (1) to transform the existing marketing cooperatives into production-oriented multipurpose societies; (2) to assist in all possible ways the formation and establishment of *ujamaa* villages; (3) to stimulate and promote an internal market system; (4) to organize and run regional wholesale and distribution trade, and at the local level the retail distribution of consumer and agricultural goods; (5) to improve the organization and administration of agricultural credit and the mobilization of rural savings.

In the early years after independence there were neither the facilities nor the time for careful training of the cooperative staff, committee chairmen and members, whose duties and responsibilities had been profoundly changed and broadened almost overnight. The urgent need for a greatly strengthened cooperative education program quickly became apparent. In the mid-1960s new institutions were created and old ones consolidated in an effort to meet the need.

Structure. This newly created cooperative educational system as it stood in 1971 consisted of three major parts, together serving four distinct clienteles:

> *The Cooperative College* at Moshi, which provides advanced training for cooperative staff personnel and selected government personnel, through a variety of full-time courses ranging from a few weeks to two full years of combined college and on-the-job training.

> *The Cooperative Education Center*, also at Moshi and closely allied to the College, which is responsible mainly for the initial training of cooperative functionaries, for the training of cooperative functionaries, for the training of local level society chairmen, committeemen and members, and for the general dissemination of information on cooperative principles and practices.

---

[14]"Notes on the Cooperative Movement in Tanzania," (Moshi, Tanzania: The Cooperative College, n.d.).

Table 6.2
The Co-operative Movement of Tanzania:
Its Organization and Relationship with Government

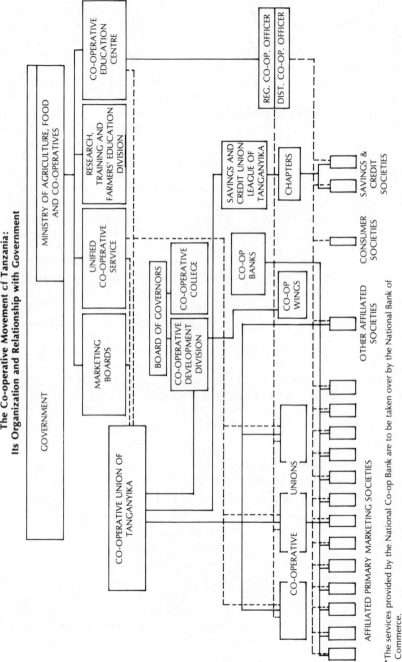

*The services provided by the National Co-op Bank are to be taken over by the National Bank of Commerce.

——— Lines of Organization   – – – – – Lines of Jurisdiction

The Cooperative Education Wings, eleven in number as of 1971, staffed by union and zonal education secretaries, which serve as oprerational arms of the Cooperative Education Center in the field.[15]

The College and the Center function jointly as a training department of the cooperative system, and their combined program is gradually being developed to meet the requirements of a career service. Admission to the College, where the highest level of training is given, is based on previous education and experience, including the successful completion of lower-level correspondence courses. The courses, largely technical and practical in content, are finely structured and rigorous. The longer programs—such as the two-year one for cooperative inspectors—involve extensive field apprenticeship under an experienced officer.

Educational content and methods. The education in the field of primary society secretaries, of the so-called member elite (the twenty to thirty most active members of each society, including the ten committeemen), and of the rural population at large, is of particular interest because of the innovative techniques employed.

The main technique thus far used for educating the public at large has been the campaign. Three campaign topics were selected for 1970: (1) the marketing of agricultural produce, (2) *ujamaa* in a cooperative society. The content, materials and logistics of these campaigns were prepared in advance by the Cooperative Education Center. Instructions and briefing materials were issued to the various people who were mobilized to conduct local meetings (union and zonal secretaries, officials of the TANU political party, etc.). Magazine articles, radio broadcasts, posters and simple information sheets were all used to publicize the meetings and the key messages. The meetings themselves, aimed at achieving wide participation, were the core of the campaign effort.

The longer-term and more basic training for the society secretaries and member elite, on the other hand, consists primarily of a series of correspondence courses on such subjects as: duties of the committee of a primary society; basic economics; elementary bookkeeping and cooperative accountancy; savings and credit societies. Society secretaries pursue these courses on their own and must complete a prescribed number before becoming qualified for work at the Cooperative College. Committee members and other member elite, on the other hand, take correspondence courses as a group. This procedure accustoms them to working together on cooperative matters and also enables the few literate members to share the learning experience with the nonliterate ones. ICED visitors were struck by the extensive and apparently effective use made of printed instructional materials in highly illiterate rural areas, thanks to this group method.

Appraisal. The impact of this cooperative education system is difficult to assess at this early stage, but the education is clearly having an effect. ICED visitors to village correspondence-discussion groups were questioned at length about how cooperatives worked elsewhere, and there was earnest interest in how cooperatives could be made to work better in Tanzania.

The dropout rates in various parts of the whole program are high, yet somewhat lower than the customary dropout rate for voluntary adult education

---

[15]A *zone* is an organizational grouping of several cooperative unions of local societies; several zones are covered by a wing.

programs. Popular interest has remained high. The 1,338 local correspondence groups that registered between January 1965 and December 1970 included more than 15,000 active members, or about one-third of the total target population for these courses. The 234 groups that had completed the four basic correspondence courses by the end of 1970 represented some 3,000 active members, or some 15 percent of all the committeemen in the cooperative movement of Tanzania.

Quantitatively at least, the program had reached a high proportion of the society secretaries by the end of 1970. More than half had completed a full cycle of training consisting of one correspondence course, a two-week regional seminar, and an eight-week course at the College. Moreover, short courses organized by the wings had covered most of the secretaries of primary societies in their respective regions. Little evidence yet exists, however, for assessing the qualitative impact of all this training.

Not surprisingly, mounting a novel educational effort of this cale and variety in the face of severe staff and other resource shortages has been accompanied by many problems. Among those that stood out in late 1971 were:

The content of the intructional materials: These tended to be too elementary for some of the learners, and sometimes carried an inappropriate Scandinavian bias because of the large role played by Scandinavian technical assistance experts in helping to prepare them.

Staff shortages: The qualified educational staff, especially at the wings, was too small and spread too thin. In order to visit each local society in their area at least once a year, the two education officers at each wing are obliged to do about 20,000 miles of hard driving—taking one-third or more of their time just getting from place to place. Available staff has been much too limited for conducting campaign meetings.

Slow progress on courses: Members and secretaries alike have progressed much more slowly than had been hoped in completing correspondence courses. And the rate of completion of courses throughout the system—even in the prestigious two-year program at the College—has been disappointingly low.

What is most important, however, about Tanzania's cooperative education system at this early stage is the simple fact that it has actually been established and has served such a large and scattered clientele in so short a time, making imaginative and unconventional use of a diversity of educational methods and media.[16]

---

[16]Since the completion of the case study, we have received the following information about the program:

By mid-1972, a total of 4,616 persons had attended courses at the Cooperative College in Moshi; of these, 855 were primary society staff, 526 union staff and 934 government staff attending regular courses. Another 2,301 had participated in short courses and seminars, including 182 participants from other countries. The number of participants in courses and seminars in 1971-72 academic year was 762.

A total of 10,244 individuals and 1,593 groups have enrolled for correspondence studies during 1965-1972. Of these, 2,750 individuals and 408 groups have received certificates after successful completion of their studies. An estimated 60 percent of the correspondence students dropped out during these years.

About 70,000 people attended film shows presented by the CEC wings and 12,800 attended one-day meetings in 1971.

A Grassroots Approach to Development

A quite different version of cooperative education is illustrated by the well-known Comilla project in the East Bengal wing of Pakistan, now Bangladesh. This experimental undertaking by the Academy of Rural Development at Comilla in 1959 aimed at providing an integrated attack on the obstacles to agricultural development in a selected *thana* — an administrative unit of about 100 square miles with more than 200,000 people, mostly subsistence farm families — by means of a planning and management structure in which the local residents, operating through cooperatives, would play a leading role.

The educational components of the Comilla experiment are of particuar interest because they involved an extension service in which much of the effort moved from the bottom up instead of from the top down. Starting with emphasis on boosting agricultural production, the educational structure that was established eventually provided a framework for a wider array of educational efforts serving a broad range of rural development needs.

The Comilla Project

Educational objectives. The *educational* innovation of the early Comilla project in Bangladesh[17] — it has many other features that we will not attempt to cover here — is that the village people chose one of their own number to serve as their educational liaison with outside sources of knowledge relevant to their needs (as *they* saw these needs). This was part of a broader set of procedures for the creation, governance and operation of local cooperatives, developed jointly over a period of time by the Academy of Rural Development and the villagers. Under this protocol villagers agreed to (1) organize themselves, choose a chairman and become a registered cooperative society; (2) hold weekly meetings, with compulsory attendance of all members; (3) select a man from the group and send him to the Academy once a week for training so that he could be the organizer and teacher of the group; (4) keep proper and complete records; (5) use supervised production credit; (6) adopt improved agricultural practices and skills; (7) make regular cah and in-kind savings deposits; (8) join the central cooperative association of the *thana*; and (9) hold regular member education sessions.

Structure. The village cooperatives thus became the prime agencies for agricultural improvement and rural education. The "organizer" and a similarly chosen "model farmer" became the key agricultural teachers in their own community, rather than an outside extension worker. These representatives regularly came to the Academy for training and received expert advice and assistance on problems identified through discussions in the village cooperative society. Later, when cooperatives became more organized and their operations more complex, the duties of organizer and model farmer were combined in a cooperative "manager," paid on an incentive-payment basis.

Later, as the need arose for a variety of common services for small local

[17]Materials on the Comilla project have been drawn from Arthur F. Raper, *Rural Development in Action: The Comprehensive Experiment in Comilla, East Pakistan* (Ithaca, New York: Cornell University Press, 1970); Earl M. Kulp, *Rural Devleopment Planning, Systems Analysis and Working Method* (New York: Praeger Publishers, 1970); draft proposal for an Integrated Rural Development Program in East Pakistan Prepared at the Academy; and personal observation and communication.

cooperative societies, two other organizations were formed: the Thana Central Cooperative Association (KTCCA), owned and managed by the village cooperatives, and the Thana Traraining and Development Center (TTDC). The KTCCA provided help in marketing of farm products, bulk purchasing of supplies, provision of machinery, production credit, storage and processing facilities, advice in water management, relatively advanced training in farm methods and, most important, coordination of development efforts and available services for all the neighboring villages. The KTCCA, being a larger organization with close links to both the participating villages and governmental and outside organizations, became an efficient channel for support services of many kinds from agencies—including even foreign aid agencies—that were not well equipped themselves to function at the village level.

Content and methods. The KTCCA provided skill training in response to specific needs. For example, schoolteachers and other literate villagers were trained to maintain the accounts of the village cooperatives. Young men from the village were trained as tractor drivers and irrigation pump operators. A machine shop was set up for repairing tractors and other equipment and for training mechanics.

The Thana Training and Development Center emerged initially to meet the needs for training, local development planning, and coordination for a new pilot rural public works program in the Comilla area. Because it was a convenient and efficient place for village leaders and cooperative managers to meet with one another and with representatives of ministries and outside organizations, the TTDC soon became the nerve center of development in the *thana* and helped to bring the educational functions of the various activities to a sharper focus. Arthur Raper notes that through the TTDS:

> The *educational processes* are facilitated by the physical location of government offices, with Academy personnel and advisors at one place, plus the gradual acceptance by the officials of a redefined role as teachers instead of desk-sitting issuers of directives and reports. Committees for training, extension and other functions, made up of civil officials, Academy instructors, KTCCA supervisors and advisors, establish procedures and assignments of responsibility that make possible a reasonably high degree of order out of what might otherwise be a chaotic mass of well-meaning but undirected effort. As time passed, the educational materials supporting the process were refined to include simple extension lesson plans, graphic material, booklets in English and Bengali, field observations, manual and other devices.[18]

Additional rural educational services, going well beyond agriculture *per se*, came to be provided through these same mechanisms and processes by the Academy, the TTDC and the Central Cooperative Society. They included, for example, the women's program, the family planning program, a pilot project for expansion of primary education by utilizing village mosques and their *imams*, a project to use nonmatriculated village women as primary teachers, and a project for improving physical facilities of rural schools by involving students, teachers and the community in planning and construction.

Appraisal. Up to the time of its disruption by the war of independence in late 1971, the Comilla project had a record of impressive accomplishments,

---

[18]A. Raper, p. 131.

along with some lingering problems and shortcomings. It had demonstrated a way to give local people and local-level public administration a larger voice and practical role in rural development, and a way of combining the rural services of distant government agencies—including education services—into a more cohesive and effective package.

Comilla had also shown that a two-way channel of educational communication between villagers and outside sources of knowledge and expertise—using as go-betweens teachers of their own choice in whom they had high confidence—can be more effective than the more familiar one-way, top-down extension model. The new Bangladesh Government is presently attempting to put these lessons to use on a nationwide scale.

Comilla, however, is not an unqualified success story, nor does it offer the full answer to the problems of rural development. In most villages no more than half the farmers have yet joined cooperatives or benefited directly from training programs. The greatest beneficiaries, as so often happens, have been the better-off farmers. For the smaller and poorer farmers or the landless farmhands, benefits were mostly in the form of new employment opportunities created by the rural works program and possibilities of intensive agriculture. The educational efforts that concentrated on agricultural production apparently had a sizeable effect, but other educational efforts—for example, in adult literacy and family planning—remained peripheral and poorly coordinated. No systematic effort was made to remedy the glaring educational deficiencies of the great bulk of out-of-school adolescents and young adults who had received little or no help from the formal educational system. In short, as good as it was, Comilla had only scratched the surface of the formidable problems of rural development.

It must also be recognized that the human and financial resources invested in the Comilla experimental area were substantially greater than the average for other areas in the country and could not be easily replicated for the whole country.[19] In addition to the normal government support for various services provided in rural areas, about 5 million rupees were spent between 1961 and 1968 in the *thana* for rural works programs, irrigation projects and rural electrification, or an average of about 3 rupees per head per year. The establishment and the operation of the Academy—its training and research service was meant for the whole province—cost about 20 million rupees for the years 1960 to 1968. Some of these resources, of course, can be charged off to research and development that yielded valuable lessons now available to other areas. But possibly the chief lesson is that significant rural development cannot be bought cheaply.

The self-help programs reviewed in this chapter differ widely in specific objectives, structure, management, staffing, methods, content and means of support. But they have a common—in contrast to most of the programs reviewed in previous chapters—a broader conception of rural development, including both social and economic criteria. They also share the underlying premise that rural transformation must and should be brought about primarily through

---

[19]Rural works programs and small-scale irrigation have been undertaken throughout the country, and Integrated Rural Development Program has been launched by the government to create the Thana Training and Development Center and eventually the cooperative structure in each *thana*. It is yet to be seen how effectively this expansion can be carried out and how the transplantation takes root in other areas.

transformation of the attitudes and behavior of rural people themselves. For this to happen, the argument runs, rural people must be given a large piece of the action; they should not simply be "programmed" to comply with plans and instruction devised by outsiders. They should have a large voice in diagnosing their own needs, in making decisions that affect their lives, and in managing their own destiny.

Self-help programs accordingly place heavy emphasis on nonformal education and on the creation and strengthening of local institutions, such as cooperatives, local councils, and voluntary discussion and action groups through which rural people can participate in collective decision-making and concerted local actions.

The philosophy of self-help and self-management is imbedded in a number of other programs otherwise classified in this report, particularly in certain of the integrated development programs to which we now turn our attention.

7: THE INTEGRATED APPROACH TO AGRICULTURAL DEVELOPMENT

There is a rapidly spreading consensus among agricultural experts, including many who have planning and decision-making responsibilities in international, bilateral and national agencies, in favor of a more comprehensive and integrated approach to agricultural development, in contrast to the piecemeal approaches earlier pursued by these same agencies.

The integrated approach is based on the premise that a combination of factors—not only the right technology and education but access to physical inputs and markets, and attractive prices—is essential to get agriculture moving. More and more observers have pointed up the need to create a balanced institutional and physical infrastructure in rural areas to provide the necessary transport, credit, input and marketing services, as well as the information and education services required for development.[1]

This systems view of agricultural development spread rapidly in the late 1960s and early 1970s and resulted in more comprehensive agricultural development projects. Four projects summarized in this chapter epitomize this recent trend—the Chilalo Agricultural Development Unit (CADU) Project in Ethiopia, the Programme on Agricultural Credit and Cooperation in Afghanistan (PACCA), the Puebla Project in Mexico, and the Lilongwe Land Development Programme in Malawi.

This integrated approach, however, is not entirely new. The above projects drew some of their inspiration from earlier experiences such as the Gezira project in the Sudan and the Intensive Agricultural District Program (IADP) in India, also considered in this chapter, as well as the Comilla project discussed in the previous chapter.

We are mainly interested here in the educational components of these integrated projects: in what they are, how they are organized and handled in relation to other components, how effective they have been, and what important problems they have encountered. But we need to remain aware that these educational elements are part of a more complex chemistry that includes many noneducational elements as well. It is the interaction among these various elements that constitutes the essence of an integrated program. Indeed, it is often difficult to differentiate the educational elements from the others, and harder still to segregate their particular costs and benefits from the whole.[2]

The six integrated agricultural projects reviewed in this chapter were inspired by quite different circumstances and designed by people with quite different backgrounds, objectives and preconceptions. The main architects of

---

[1]Arthur T. Mosher, *Creating a Progressive Rural Structure to Serve a Modern Agriculture* (N.Y.: Agricultural Development Council, Inc., July 1966). David Hapgood and Max Millikan, Eds. *No Easy Harvest: The Dilemma of Agriculture in Underdeveloped Countries* (Boston: Little, Brown & Co., 1967).

[2]The costs and financing of the programs summarized in this chapter are treated in Chapter 11.

the Gezira scheme were private entrepreneurs interested in profitable cotton production, though part of the profits was channeled, through profit-sharing, to the farmers and eventually into social development projects. India's IADP was conceived as a possible solution to the worsening food shortage and was largely government managed. The PACCA and CADU projects were inspired by a conviction born of Western experience that a more planned and integrated approach to agricultural production, using cooperatives as a central instrument, was the most effective way to release a traditional rural population from the bonds of subsistence agriculture, while at the same time enhancing social justice and the quality of family and community life. The designers of the Lilongwe project had similar aims but did not put emphasis on cooperatives.

Interestingly, the planners of all the above projects chose for their experiments high-potential agricultural areas where presumably the prospects for early success were at a maximum. The planners of the Puebla Project in Mexico, however, did quite the opposite. They purposely chose for their experimental effort an ecologically disadvantaged area, and within that area they chose as their clientele the smaller and poorer farmers who had shown the least inclination to be "progressive" in adopting innovations. If their experiment succeeded under these relatively adverse conditions, then perhaps its lessons could benefit vast numbers of similarly situated small farmers in rainfed maize-producing areas elsewhere in Mexico and Latin America.

All of these integrated projects made substantial provision for educational components, but there are striking differences among them. For example, PACCA used a high ratio of extension agents to farmers, whereas Puebla made very sparing use of its agents, seemingly with as good results. CADU, PACCA and Lilongwe deemed it necessary to do much of their own staff training, while the IADP in India and Puebla relied mainly on established educational institutions for staff training. Some of these projects made extensive and innovative use of new educational media, whereas others relied on very conventional ones. Some concentrated their educational efforts on "leader farmers," hoping for a multiplier effect, while others tried to spread their educational efforts more or less evenly over all farmers. All of them, however, knowingly or not, faced the problem of how to avoid widening the already large gap between the rich and the poor, the commercial and the subsistence, the progressive and the nonprogressive farmer. Moreover, all faced the risk of unwittingly generating adverse social and economic side-effects—"second-generation problems"—which tend to be more complicated the more "successful" the project is. Other significant similarities, differences and common problems will become evident in the fuller discussion of these integrated projects in this and later chapters. We will review them now, more or less in the order of their creation, taking the two oldest ones first—Gezira and the IADP.

From Economic Success to Social Development

The Gezira Scheme

The Gezira scheme in the Sudan is of special interest because in its evolution over several decades from a project with narrow economic objectives to one with somewhat broader social goals it underscores the point that economic improvement alone is insufficient to transform a rural society.[3] Gezira also demonstrates the feasibility of combining several ingredients under a single management structure for agricultural and rural development.

Initial objectives and methods. Briefly, the Gezira scheme was launched soon after World War I under British colonial auspices as a major irrigation project designed to expand production in a potentially profitable cotton-growing area in the Sudan, covering initially 100,000 acres and expanding eventually to about one million acres with 120,000 farm families.

The scheme was operated under a government franchise by a private syndicate under a tight regulatory system, with provision that 40 percent of the profits would go to farmers, 35 percent to the government, and 25 percent to the Sudan Plantations Syndicate. The syndicate's franchise was not renewed when it expired in 1950, and an autonomous board attached to the Ministry of Finance took over the management of the scheme. New profit-sharing ratios were introduced in the Gezira Scheme Act of 1960 and subsequent amendments: 49 percent of the net proceeds of the scheme were distributed among tenants, 36 percent went to the government, 10 percent to the Gezira Board, 3 percent to a Social Development Fund and 2 percent to the local government councils.

Land holdings were reapportioned so that each family ended up with about 30 acres to farm. The main problems then were to induce these peasant farmers to employ appropriate farming technologies (which were already known), to supply them with necessary inputs and to arrange for the marketing of their crops at satisfactory prices.

Under the tenancy agreements the Sudanese farmers were obligated "to cultivate in a proper manner according to the scheme of Crop Rotation . . . and . . . obey the reasonable orders of the Syndicate's officials."[4] Supervision was close: one inspector plus two junior officers for about every 15,000 acres, making a ratio of 170 tenants per officer.

Results and broadened objectives. By its own narrow economic criteria the scheme succeeded and all parties benefited, including the farmers. But the original simplistic assumption that, if their incomes rose, village people would be able to improve themselves in all other respects proved to be too narrow a concept of development. Government officials began to suspect that the objective of improved incomes should now be supplemented by broader social objectives and action, including a larger voice for village people in their own local affairs.

By 1940 it had become politically imperative to improve the quality of village and family life, to insure that rural people kept reasonably in step with the improving conditions of towns people, and to move toward "Sudanization." Gaitskell later observed, "We were experiencing phenomena shortly to

---

[3]The following information on Gezira is drawn mainly from two sources: (1) a paper prepared for the ICED in cooperation with the British Overseas Development Administration and the Institute of Education, University of London, by A.J. Loveridge, "A Survey of British Experience of Non-Formal Education for Rural and Agricultural Development in Developing Countries," and (2) Arthur Gaitskell's *Gezira A Story of Development in the Sudan* (London: Faber and Faber, 1959). For a recent description of the Gezira Scheme, see H.M.M. Khalil, "The Sudan Gezira Scheme Some Institutional and Administrative Aspects", *Journal of Administration Overseas* IX, no. 4 (October 1970), pp. 273-285.

[4]A. Gaitskell, *Gezira*, p. 340.

become general to the age, to deal with which . . . many territories set up community development departments."[5]

One of the first steps toward "Sudanization" was to give village representatives agricultural training to replace the syndicate's junior officers. Recognizing the vulnerability of a purely authoritarian approach to agricultural extension, the syndicate acknowledged that "it was essential to do more about practical agricultural education as a supplement to the mere giving of orders."[6] These newly trained village extension agents were put in place with no appreciable fall-off in production, contrary to the fears of some agricultural experts.

Subsequently, government departments stepped in with programs to strengthen schools, recreational services, local councils, adult education and other essentials for improved family and community life, in order to bring these elements of development into better balance with the improved cash incomes of the villagers. The Gezira scheme today continues to move toward the achievement of its new and broader social objectives.

Arthur Gaitskell, general manager for the Gezira scheme, suggested for the guidance of future developers the following principles which contributed to Gezira's success:

1. Renting of land at predevelopment rates, rather than expropriation;
2. Equitable distribution of the benefits;
3. Protection of tenants from creditors' claims on the land and prohibition of assignments by tenants;
4. Provision of funds from profits, after ensuring the economic viability of the undertaking, for "social development" of the region under a unified command but using other agencies as the instruments.[7]

This, as Gaitskell saw it, was the essence of the "integrated approach" — not merely combining the necessary elements to achieve *economic* growth, but combining economic growth with *equitable distribution* of the benefits and with *social* development.

In the Gezira case, however, social development *followed* economic growth, and economic growth was achieved under a tightly regulated, authoritarian management system. Whether this particular sequence will hold in all situations remains a critical question. The Indian experience sheds useful though not conclusive light on the question.

A Counterattack on Famine:
India's Intensive Agriculture District Program (IADP)

Background. The Community Development Program[8] that India launched soon after independence (see Chapter 6) had sought to achieve agricultural improvement and social uplift simultaneously. Whatever success it may have

---

[5]Ibid., p. 220.

[6]Ibid., p. 217.

[7]Ibid., pp. 356-357.

[8]ICED's information and evaluative evidence on India's Intensive Agricultural District Program was drawn from a variety of documents and publications, from discussions with knowledgeable participants and advisors, and from first-hand observations by ICED researchers in late 1971 (particularly in Tanjore District). A special paper on the educational aspects was prepared for ICED by Donald G. Green, *Relating Education and Training to Agricultural Development* ICED Background Paper No. 2. Green served as a training advisor to the IADP under the Ford Foundation.

attained on the social side, its impact on the production side was clearly disappointing. During the fifties India's food supply situation, exacerbated by rapid population growth, steadily worsened. Without heavy food imports from the West, the serious drought years of 1957-58 would have resulted in a disastrous famine.

Objectives. An international team of experts reporting to the Indian government warned in 1959 that this food crisis was not a temporary phenomenon; it would become worse, even in good monsoon years, unless vigorous corrective actions were taken.[9] Their recommended ten-point "package program," accepted in modified form by the government, became the basis for the Intensive Agricultural District Program, launched in 1960. The original ten points (not all adopted immediately) included: (1) adequate farm credit through strengthened cooperatives; (2) adequate supplies of fertilizers, pesticides, improved seeds, improved farm implements, and other essential production needs through strengthened service cooperatives; (3) price incentives to participating cultivators through assured price agreements for rice, wheat and millet, announced two years in advance; (4) marketing arrangements and services to enable cultivators to obtain the full market price for their marketed surplus; (5) intensive educational, technical and farm management assistance made available in every village and development block in the district; (6) participation of all interested cultivators, both large and small, in direct individual farm planning for increased production; (7) village planning for increased production and village improvement programs, strengthening of village organizations and leadership; (8) a public works program using local labor to undertake drainage, bunding, soil conservation, minor irrigation, building of approach roads and other development works contributing directly to increased production; (9) analysis and evaluation of the program from its inception; (10) coordination, on a priority basis, by village, block, district, state and center, of all resources essential to mount and carry out the program with maximum speed and effectiveness.[10]

Organization. The IADP was to be applied initially to one high-potential district in each of the then fifteen states of India. Each such district had a project director and a team of agricultural experts who, under the guidance of the chief civil administrator (the District Collector), were given extraordinary latitude to plan and implement an agricultural development program fitted to the district and to the resources available.

To implement these plans, the IADP districts were accorded a special priority on fertilizer, credit and other essential supplies (including the high-yielding wheat and rice varieties when they became available some years later). Intensified research services, soil testing laboratories and other similar facilities were also provided.

Educational components. On the education front, the normal quotas of district- and block-level agricultural officers and village level workers (to handle farmer contacts and other extension functions) were doubled in the IADP districts. Special agricultural information units were set up with their own printing presses; and All India Radio's Farm and Home Units were directed to give

[9]India, Ministry of Agriculture, Community Development and Cooperation, *India's Food Crisis and Steps to Meet It* (New Delhi, April 1959).

[10]India, Expert Committee on Assessment and Evaluation, *Modernising Indian Agriculture, Report on the Intensive Agricultural District Programme (1960-68)* Vol. I (New Delhi, 1969) pp. 3-4.

special attention to these districts. While the intensity of educational activities doubled, no basic changes in organization, methods or strategy were undertaken. Different functions and staffs for various educational parts of the program remained under the jurisdiction of several ministries.

The multipurpose village level workers (VLWs), who in the earlier Community Development Program had divided their time among a variety of community programs in addition to agriculture (e.g., health, nutrition, savings schemes, local projects, cultural activities), were now instructed to devote 80 percent of their time to agriculture under the guidance of block-level agricultural extension officers. (The VLWs remained at the same time under the jurisdiction of the State Ministries of Community Development.) In short, substantial educational components were provided for under the IADP, but the bureaucratic arrangements were rather untidy and hardly conducive to a well-coordinated effort.[11]

Performance. Various observers have since attempted to assess the effectiveness of the IADP in its first half-dozen years. The burden of the evidence suggests that during this period agricultural production in the fifteen IADP districts (allowing for their superior natural potential) was not significantly better than in many other districts.[12] However, the high-yielding varieties had not yet had their impact, the sharp rise in Indian fertilizer production had not yet occurred, the new irrigation projects were just beginning to be activated, and market-prices on the whole were still unfavorable. The recommended support price system had not been implemented and heavy U.S. grain shipments to India had been used to hold down prices to urban consumers, thus depressing incentives for Indian farmers to increase production.

In the late 1960s and early 1970s, however, when the above constraints on farm production were sharply reduced, Indian grain production improved dramatically, with most IADP districts taking a distinct lead over other districts. The adoption of the new varieties of wheat, rice, and millet spread much more rapidly in the IADP districts than in the country at large, as shown in Table 7.1. Wheat production in IADP districts reached an index of 340 in 1968-69 (from a base of 100 in 1958-61) against an index of 220 in non-IADP districts. In rice production the impact of new varieties came more slowly but the IADP districts maintained their initial lead over adjoining districts.[13]

By the time ICED researchers visited India in December 1971, the Green Revolution was in full swing in the higher potential districts and India's production of food grains was exceeding all expectations of a decade earlier—sharply reducing the need for imports. The main questions now were (1) whether and how rapidly the "revolution" could be spread to other areas including rainfed lands, to smaller farmers, and to those growing different food grains, (2) whether unforeseen disasters resulting from pests and diseases to which the new varieties were not resistant could be avoided, (3) whether farmers could adjust to lower market prices, resulting from improved supplies of major grain

---

[11]See D. Green, *Education and Training.*

[12]See Dorris D. Brown, *Agricultural Development in India's Districts,* Center for International Affairs Series (Cambridge, Mass.: Harvard University Press, 1971), for an evaluation of the IADP up to 1966.

[13]India, Ministry of Food, Agriculture, Community Development and Cooperation, *Modernising Indian Agriculture,* Appendices.

crops, by diversifying to other crops, and (4) whether research could keep pace with the rapidly expanding needs and demands of farmers.

One of the main questions ICED explored in India was how much of a contribution the educational components of the IADP—particularly the extension service—made to this dramatic breakthrough in Indian agriculture. The results of this inquiry are discussed in later chapters.

More Comprehensive Package Approaches

The IADP, along with the Comilla project and Israel's experience with integrated agricultural development, had a strong influence on the design of the CADU project in Ethiopia and on the decision of the Swedish bilateral aid agency (SIDA) to give it major and sustained support. From their own limited experiences with more or less piecemeal agricultural projects in Algeria and Tunisia, and from examining the experiences of others, Swedish aid authorities had concluded that a major push on agricultural development was a prerequisite to improving life in poor peasant societies and that a more comprehensive and coordinated approach was needed to get agriculture moving.[14] Ethiopia was selected for such an experimental approach from among several countries that had requested agricultural assistance from Sweden.

Chilalo Agricultural Development Unit (CADU)

Background. The Chilalo region in Ethiopia—the locus of the CADU project—was basically a traditional, static rural area.[15] Before 1968, when CADU was launched, scattered development efforts had produced little discernible change, except perhaps for the handful of larger, richer and more progressive farmers. The 650,000 hectares of arable land were still largely cultivated by traditional methods. The 800,000 cattle, goats and sheep were undernourished,

Table 7.1
Adoption of High-Yielding Grains in India—1966-68
Shown for Intensive Agricultural Districts
and for Country as a Whole

| Crops | Percentage of Crop Area Planted with High-Yielding Varieties | | | |
| | 1966-67 | | 1967-68 | |
	IADP Districts	Country as a Whole	IADP Districts	Country as a Whole
Rice	4.5	2.5	11.3	5.3
Wheat	7.2	4.3	56.1	18.4
Millet	3.3	1.3	7.9	3.7
Total	4.3	2.2	16.1	6.8

SOURCE: India, Expert Committee on Assessment and Evaluation, *Modernising Indian Agriculture: Report on the Intensive Agricultural District Programme (1960-68)*, Vol. I, Table V.

---

[14]Bengt Nekby, *CADU: An Ethiopian Experiment in Developing Peasant Farming* (Stockholm: Prisma Publishers, 1970).

[15]See Sven Grabe, *CADU: Ethiopia*, ICED Case Study No. 13, (unpublished).

diseased and often starved. Yields were low: a ton per acre of the main subsistence crops (wheat, rye and teff) and a couple of hundred liters per lactation period for each milk cow.

Of the total population of 400,000, 20,000 live in the one major town; an equal number inhabit smaller townships and market villages; the remaining 360,000 live in scattered homesteads flanking the one main road or further back on primitive trails. Illiteracy is close to 90 percent. About 13 percent of the children attend primary schools; there is but one higher secondary school, with 400 students, in the whole region. The landholding patterns—with sharecropping the dominant form—were not conducive to development incentives and still remain a problem. Except for a minority of large landholders, the bulk of farmers and tenants have less than ten hectares of land.

Planning. Preliminary surveys showed that the Chilalo region had great possibilities, but that development would require a fundamental recasting of the attitudes, practices and economic relationships in the district, including landholding patterns. Intensive agronomic, veterinarian, silvicultural, ecological, economic and social research was started once the Chilalo region was selected, and a plan of action was devised for a 13-year program (a three-year First Phase and two five-year phases thereafter).

Objectives. The goals of the project were: (1) to bring about economic and social development in the project area; (2) to give the local population an increased awareness of and responsibility for development work; (3) to verify methods of agricultural development; (4) to train Ethiopian staff for rural development work.

These objectives have gradually been elaborated in a series of more specific subgoals, including educational ones, linked to particular time phases and annual budgets and expressed, insofar as possible, in quantitative terms.

Target groups. CADU's clientele are all of the average and poorer farmers and tenants in the region. Richer farmers have been intentionally excluded as they are considered able to take care of themselves.

Development activities. The following operational tasks were set for the initial three-year phase (to which this summary mainly applies) and these largely determined the specific types of learning required by various subgroups in the population and by the project's own staff:

    1. Selection of better varieties for planting of crops, growing of trees and improving indigenous livestock;[16]

    2. Determination of optimal use of the various zones within the region for production of food and fodder crops, dairy products, meat and wood for fuel and construction;

    3. Development of implements and methods for more efficient cultivation, including optimal use of fertilizers, control of pests and weeds, and maintenance of healthy livestock;

    4. Establishment of an effective trading system for the supply of inputs and marketing of products, including local production and cleaning of seeds and, if possible, the production of lighter agricultural implements and other supplies for improved farming and home life;

---

[16]CADU does not undertake genetic research; its research is mainly in adaptive testing of varieties and crossbreeds developed elsewhere and in supporting ecological, economic and social explorations needed for project planning and evaluation.

5. Development of the physical and organizational infrastructure of the area (the regular government services would handle roads);

6. Exploration of methods for improving the health and nutrition of the population and for improving the quality of life, with emphasis on clean water supplies and more nutritious foods;

7. Provision of credit for the purchase of inputs in agricultural production;

8. A start in the development of a system of cooperatives.

The CADU management was given responsibility and authority by the central government to handle these tasks, though the ultimate aim is to transfer most functions from the project's centralized management to the farm cooperatives as soon as they are prepared to handle them.

Educational Activities. The foregoing tasks implied a variety of educational requirements, both for the project staff and for the local farm families. During the first three years the following training and extension activities were undertaken: (1) training of key Ethiopian staff (largely recruited from agricultural colleges and schools) for adaptive research, agricultural extension work, management of trade centers and other specialized tasks; (2) training (from scratch) of assistant extension agents, including girls for home extension work, from the local secondary school (grades 10-11); (3) preliminary training of leaders of cooperative societies; (4) training of selected model farmers in improved crop production methods and, in a few cases, in the care of cross-bred cattle; (5) extension services to participating farmers for establishing farm plans; appropriate combinations and application of fertilizer, seeds and other inputs; hygienic milk production; marketing of field crops and milk through the new system of collection and trade centers.

The teaching methods used are on the whole traditional, but with more than usual emphasis on practical on-the-job training under supervision.

Staff have been trained mostly through planned rotation of recruits to different job stations where they serve as counterparts or apprentices to experienced expatriate and Ethiopian staff. Basic training of younger staff recruited from the local secondary school involves a combination of classroom instruction in a special agricultural school run by the project, supervised work on experimental farms, and on-the-job training in extension.

Model farmers have been trained in short courses (approximately one month per annum) at the CADU experimental farm and are given intensive advice by field agents at their homesteads. Extension efforts are focused especially on model farmers, in the expectation that they will inform their neighbors. The home extension agents hold lecture courses and demonstrations in available facilities, mostly in homes of model farmers. Most of the teaching materials used in these various training and extension activities have been produced within the project.

The plan of operation for 1970-75 provides for a gradual enlargement of the education program to include: (1) special educational activities for youth through newly formed youth clubs; (2) expanded education for women, with emphasis on home economics; (3) more intensive cooperative education for members, officers and staff of the emergent cooperative societies; (4) the initiation of a diversified adult education program; (5) the retraining of evicted tenants and unemployed persons to become either craftsmen or small-scale manufacturers.

Structure and staff. For purposes of extension work and adult education, the CADU area has been subdivided into four development zones, each with ten extension areas containing approximately 1,700 farm families. The second-phase plan envisages a staff of thirty-nine members for each "zonal center," including one extension supervisor (head of the zone), ten extension agents, twenty assistant agents and one demonstration farm manager. One of the zonal centers to which the agricultural school will be attached will also serve as the overall project headquarters for educational activities.

At present, extension agents and their assistants are *multiple-function* field workers. They not only teach and assist farmers in applying new methods and practices but also assist in the credit program, participate in contract discussions between farmers and landlords, and act as general representatives for the project within their respective areas. According to the longer-term plan, these noneducational functions of field workers will gradually be transferred to the cooperatives now being formed. Simultaneously, the extension and training functions of field workers will be broadened to include further aspects of agriculture.

Thus the planned educational network, which is already partly in place, is a comprehensive one. If extension management and agricultural school training staff are included, this network will consist of at least 160 staff concerned with various educational activities, representing a ratio of one "educator" to about 440 farm families. Each of the forty local field agents will have responsibility for fifteen model farmers (a total of 600) with a ratio of one model farmer for every 115 farm families.

Facilities. Physical facilities for the CADU project as a whole, which are partially used for education, include: three large farms for experimentation, seed production and breeding of livestock; and central workshops, staff housing and other common facilities. For exclusively educational purposes there is already one agricultural school, and there may be a vocational center for training of youth and retraining of adults. In addition, each zonal center (and some subcenters) will have a fully equipped demonstration farm and special facilities for conducting short-term courses for farmers, women and youth, and for meetings of cooperative committees.

Appraisal. Thus far the main difficulties in implementing the CADU scheme have been basically political in nature. The exclusion of larger and richer farmers has inspired considerable opposition from them, as has the project management's insistence on land reform.[17]

Relations between the CADU management and the local administration have at times been strained. Other authorities have at times resented the priority enjoyed by CADU in resource allocations and staff recruitment. Arrangements for interministerial coordination have not, on the whole, averted such problems; nor apparently has the CADU area committee for coordination and planning been especially helpful in planning and implementing the project. Since representatives of the local authorities and of farmers were unac-

---

[17]Contrary to expectations, the Government of Ethiopia did not institute a national land reform scheme; hence the CADU management was obliged to take substitute action in its particular area to alter, standardize and record the legal relationships between landowners and tenants that were deemed necessary to increase production incentives, protect the interests of small tenants and avoid adverse social side-effects of agricultural improvement.

customed to working together for common causes, two separate committees had to be formed.

One of the major unresolved problems for the future is how ultimately to integrate the CADU operation into the regular national structure of governmental organization and rural services. CADU thus far has been relatively autonomous, with management and high-level technical functions largely in the hands of Swedish expatriates. How well the transfer takes place will be a crucial determinant of CADU's ultimate impact on the development of rural Ethiopia. A related question is whether self-sustaining local cooperatives which are planned to take over the local agricultural management can finance activities such as marketing credit-provision, road maintenance, construction of farm-roads, water supply, construction of clinics, etc., and support the present staff level with available local resources.

We turn now to PACCA, a project based on a concept and philosophy of development similar to CADU's. Though newer and smaller than CADU, PACCA's long-term goals are no less ambitious. Its basic aim is to develop on a pilot scale a methodology and practical pattern for an integrated approach to rural development that can eventually be spread throughout Afghanistan.

The Programme on Agricultural Credit and Cooperation (PACCA)

Background. The Programme on Agricultural Credit and Cooperation in Afghanistan (PACCA)[18] grew out of a mutual interest on the part of FAO and SIDA in developing cooperatives as a means of breaking agricultural credit bottlenecks and, more broadly, of making a more comprehensive and integrated approach to agricultural development in which farmers' own organizations would play a central role.[19] Afghanistan, whose government had sought help in strengthening its rural institutions, was chosen to try out this approach. There were no illusions that such an approach would be easy in the circumstances of one of the world's poorest, most isolated and least modernized countries. As the exploratory mission observed, "there are no easy successes to be won in Afghanistan. But methods that prove their value under such conditions must be assumed to have wide validity."[20]

After preliminary studies and planning, the project went into action in early 1969. SIDA was to be the main external funding agency and FAO the executing agency; the Government of Afghanistan would also make a sizeable contribution and would, among other things, enact a national law authorizing the establishment of cooperatives.

Strategy. The PACCA scheme was founded on five basic propositions:

1. In order to achieve agricultural development and improvement of farmers' lives, an integrated and coordinated combination of services should be provided to farmers.

2. Cooperatives can be the key organizational means for integrating and coordinating these services.

3. Provisions for training, credit and other aspects of the program should be integrated with the national system of agricultural institutions

---

[18]This summary is based on Manzoor Ahmed and Philip H. Coombs, *PACCA: Education in an Integrated Agricultural Program*, ICED Case Study No. 10 (Essex, Conn., June 1972).

[19]FAO, *Agricultural Credit Through Cooperatives and Other Institutions*, Agricultural Study No. 68 (Rome, 1965).

[20]FAO, *Report of the Agricultural Credit Mission to Afghanistan*, (Rome, 1967) p. 18.

and services so as not to isolate the program from the national agricultural production and development system.

4. The program should include ample training opportunities, not only for local personnel within the project but also for other national agricultural personnel.

5. Built-in evaluation procedures should be included in the program from the outset because of its experimental nature.

The project also rested on two important economic assumptions determined by the exploratory mission: first, that markets and prices for increased production in the selected pilot areas would be adequate to provide strong incentives for farmers to work for agricultural expansion; and second, that the resulting private and social benefits would outweigh the costs to all parties, including the external agencies.

The two pilot areas were (1) Koh-i-Daman, 35 km north of Kabul on the main highway to the USSR border and a major grape-producing area (over 40 percent of the national output) covering 45,000 hectares of partially irrigated land, with some 10,000 farmers; (2) Baghlan, north of the Hindu Kush mountains and 250 km from Kabul, covering about 5,000 farmers and 15,000 hectares of Afghanistan's most fertile and productive land (80 percent irrigated), largely devoted to the production of sugar beets and cotton, with wheat, fruit and other commodities as secondary crops.

These two areas had been selected because of their relatively high and immediate potential in contrast to most farming areas where subsistence farming predominated and access to markets was severely limited. Many farmers of Koh-i-Daman and Baghlan owned their own small plots; many had irrigated land, and they were skilled producers with experience in commercial farming. Moreover, it was considered technically feasible for them to achieve large and prompt increases in yields without having to learn drastically new practices—mainly by applying heavier dosages of fertilizer, with which most were already familiar, and by adopting other relatively minor innovations that would present no great problem once the farmers were convinced of their efficacy. They had good road access to the country's main market center in Kabul. The most apparent needs were to increase the supply of credit at reasonable rates and the flow of chemical inputs into the area, to improve the marketing arrangements, and to ensure favorable prices to the farmers.

Objectives. The basic goal of the PACCA project, however, was not simply to expand agricultural yields in these two areas but to introduce institutional innovations that would put local farmers much more in control of their own affairs and ultimately could be adopted throughout the country.

There were formidable constraints, however. The national agricultural extension system was still in the early stages of organization (six provinces covered and four more partially covered out of twenty-nine, as of 1967) and there were no facilities for training extension agents. Rugged terrain and poor transport limited domestic markets for agricultural produce, and the landlocked position of Afghanistan severely restricted its external markets for bulky produce. Socially, economically and politically the country still bore features of its feudal past; the newly modernized institutions of government, including the new legislature, were inexperienced and weak. Powerful vested interests could be expected to resist any major innovations that threatened their position. Government budget priorities neglected rural and agricultural development, and prevailing policies and procedures for agriculture and commerce tended to discourage rather than promote increased farm production.

Structure. The plan envisaged organizing the PACCA project around four newly created institutions: (1) a *Project Headquarters* in Kabul, closely associated with the Ministry of Agriculture; (2) two *Development Centers* (at Koh-i-Daman and at Baghlan) that would work directly with farmers in providing credit, physical inputs and educational services, as a temporary surrogate for the cooperatives to be developed; (3) a *central training institution* (the Institute of Cooperatives, Credit and Extension Training), located outside Kabul, which would concentrate on staff development both for the project itself and for the national credit and agricultural services.

Educational activities. The educational elements constitute a major part of the whole PACCA project and command a substantial portion of its total resources. The following main educational tasks were targeted for action in the First Phase, 1969-71 (see also Table 7.2):

1. *Training of extension supervisors* (graduates of the Faculty of Agriculture of the University) and credit officials of the Agricultural Bank, in two six-month preservice training courses at the central training institute;

2. *Training of cooperative supervisors and field extension agents* in two separate eighteen-month courses at the central training institute, including six months of practical work at the development centers and supervised apprenticeship in the field;

3. *Refresher courses for extension personnel;*

4. *Field extension services* to farmers in the Koh-i-Daman and Baghlan project areas, emanating from the two development centers;

5. *Training of farmers in credit use and cooperatives,* in group meetings at the development centers.

The extension methods, as near as an ICED research team could determine during its visit to the PACCA project in late 1971, were traditional and conservative, involving mainly tutorial instruction and demonstration for a relatively small number of farmers on their respective plots.

A functional literacy component, originally conceived as one of Unesco's regular pilot literacy projects, was incorporated into the PACCA project.

Staff. The staff provisions for PACCA's ambitious education program are relatively thin, as shown on Table 7.3. Of a total project staff of ninety-four (sixteen international and seventy-eight national), eighty-one were primarily engaged in training and extension, including eighteen at the central training institute and sixty-three based at the two development centers.

Performance. By the end of the initial three-year phase, PACCA had become a going concern, though not without birth pains. The headquarters establishment, the training institute and the two development centers at Koh-i-Daman and Baghlan were all in operation. Significant progress had already been made on most parts of the multifaceted education program, though various delays, particularly in the arrival of staff and equipment, had held actual performance substantially below the target levels.

The scale of extension activities was still small and involved a ratio of experts and extension workers to farmers that clearly would not be economically viable for long. In early 1970, 28 agents and advisors were working with 150 pilot farmers in Koh-i-Daman. By late 1971 a reported total of 600 farmers out of

Table 7.2
Schedule of Major Activities Planned for the First Three Years of PACCA (1969-71)

At Training Institute	Koh-i-Daman	Baghlan
	First Year	
1. An 18-month course for 25 extension agents. 2. An 18-month course for 10 cooperative supervisors and a 9-month course for 6 to 10 trainees from the Agricultural Bank. 3. A 6-month course for 10 students from the Faculty of Agriculture for training extension supervisors. 4. A preparatory course for officials involved in the two pilot projects.	1. Definition of the pilot area, its size and distribution; mapping. 2. Economic and social survey of the area as described in the program. 3. Starting extension activities for part of the pilot area. Outlining a research program. 4. Approaching some 500 farmers for grouping into cooperatives. Collection of raisins for building up member's share capital. Starting marketing operations on a limited scale. Providing short-term credit in kind for the next cultivation season.	Program not yet started.
	Second Year	1. Definition of the pilot area, its size and distribution. Establishment of the center. 2. Starting intensified extension activities for part of the pilot area. Concentrating on one crop (e.g., wheat). 3. Survey of potentialities for starting cooperatives. Examination of group behavior and leadership in villages. Consideration of location of societies. Approaching 200 farmers for creating the first local cooperatives. 4. Providing credit to individual farmers mainly in kind (improved seed, fertilizers, insecticides).
1. Completion of the first two 18-month courses. Starting two new ones. 2. A 6-month course for students from the Faculty of Agriculture. 3. A 1-month course for inservice training for extension agents and supervisors. 4. Short courses for cooperative personnel from the pilot area.	1. Expanding extension activities to reach other farmers. Taking up new cultivation problems to be solved by the research program. 2. Approaching 1,500 other farmers for creating local cooperatives. 3. Providing credit to farmers, making use of the best consolidated cooperatives. Otherwise, individual credits. 4. Starting regular training courses for "model farmers" and cooperative leaders.	
	Third Year	1. Expanding extension activities to other farmers and also other crops. Concentration on wheat and sugar beets. 2. Approaching 400 additional farmers for creation of more local credit societies. 3. Providing credit to farmers through the first established cooperative societies. 4. Starting regular training courses for "model farmers" and cooperative leaders.
1. See Previous Year.	1. Expanding extension, credit, and marketing activities. Approaching additional 2,000 farmers. 2. Starting provision of medium-term credit for farmers who joined the project the first year. 3. Starting a saving scheme among the farmers. 4. Extending training and education activities to farm women.	

SOURCE: "Plan of Operations."

Table 7.3
PACCA: Professional Staff
November 1971

International Staff (16)	National Staff (78)

A. Project Director's Office (Kabul) (13)

International Staff	National Staff
Project Adviser	Project Director
Administrative Officer	
Chief Technical Adviser (Functional Literacy)	Director (Functional Literacy)
Reading Materials Specialist (Functional Literacy)	Reading Materials Supervisors (4)
	Field Supervisors (2)
	Artist/Illustrator

B. Training Institute for Agricultural Cooperation, Credit and Extension (18)

International Staff	National Staff
Training Adviser	Institute Director
Coop./Credit Specialist	Coop./Credit Supervisors (3)
Extension Specialist	Extension Supervisors (2)
Agronomist	Agronomy Supervisors(2)
Rural Sociologist	Rural Sociology Superviser
Equipment Superintendent	Equipment Supervisor
Farm Management/Economist	Farm Management Supervisors (2)
Economist (Vacant)	

C. Koh-i-Daman Development Centre (44)

International Staff	National Staff
Team Leader	Centre Director
Extension/Rural Youth Specialist	Extension Supervisors(2)
	Extension Agents (Field) (24)
Viticulturist	Viticultural Supervisors
	Viticultural Agents (2)
Coop./Bookkeeping Instructor	Coop./Accounting Supervisor
	Coop./Accounting Agents (2)
	Cooperative Agents (4)
Marketing Specialist (Vacant)	Marketing Supervisors (2)

D. Baghlan Development Centre (19)

International Staff	National Staff
Team Leader	Centre Director
Extension/Rural Youth Specialist	Extension Supervisors
	Extension Agents (Field) (14)
	Farm Management Supervisor
Functional Literacy Specialist (Vacant)	

SOURCE: Project Adviser's Office, PACCA.

10,000 in that area had been "reached." In Baghlan, where activities got off to a later start, 4 extension agents were working with 29 farmers (out of 5,000); the 1971 plan called for more extension agents, to boost the number to 180.

The training institute had telescoped the four originally planned regular courses into only two, evidently due to shortages of both recruits and instructors. By the end of 1971, fifty-nine extension agents and cooperative advisors, twenty-four bank officials, and eight extension supervisors had completed training.

The part-time functional literacy program as of late 1971 was still developing appropriate materials geared to the needs and interests of PACCA participants.

It did not appear to have been significantly integrated as yet with the rest of the PACCA program. Two four-month *general* literacy courses, started before the literacy program became part of PACCA, had reportedly been attended by a total of some 700 villagers with about 5 out of every 6 completing the courses. (The explanation given for this unusually high completion rate was the strong support given by local Moslem religious leader.) There was no hard evidence, however, on the actual reading ability of those completing the course.

Significant gains in yields had been registered in the initial years of PACCA, but they were limited to a comparatively few participants for whom the development centers had been able to secure credit and inputs. The supply of credit was still far short of demand, due mainly to the cautious criteria of the Agricultural Bank.

Much more serious than credit, however, was the question of markets and prices. A relatively modest increase in grape deliveries to the New Delhi market had depressed the price below profitable levels for the Koh-i-Daman farmers. This caused PACCA managers to accelerate efforts to establish a high-quality local raisin industry that they could ship to international markets at profitable prices. The initial test shipments to Western Europe got an encouraging reception. The problem was to expand raisin processing and shipping capacity rapidly enough to keep step with expanding grape production.

Satisfactory markets and prices for sugar beets and cotton presented a more difficult problem. The more PACCA succeeded in raising production, the more quickly incentives to farmers would diminish unless certain major bottlenecks were broken. These included the monopolistic processing plants for cotton and sugar beets and the government's own agricultural pricing and international trade policies. Unless these economic impediments were removed, even the best of agricultural education efforts would come to naught.

A further problem was the government's failure to enact the promised authorizing legislation for cooperatives.[21] There was also growing doubt whether the cultural environment of Afghanistan was conducive to Western-type cooperatives, at least in the foreseeable future, and whether this particular type of farmer society was essential to the project's success. Evidence was building up that a more indigenous type of farmer society, compatible with local traditions, might serve the purpose better.

On the education front, three major requirements stood out that would have to be handled effectively in the second phase: (1) a more viable approach to extension; (2) a better system for training and recruiting personnel; (3) improvement in agricultural and social science research. These are examined in later chapters of this report.

One important lesson that emerges from the PACCA case is that a pilot project in a particular area of a nation—however skillfully planned and operated—cannot escape the strong influences and constraints that arise from *national* economic and social conditions and policies, and even from international market conditions over which the project managers have no control. It is like trying to run an isolated hothouse whose supply of heat and water is controlled by someone else. The first phase of the PACCA project brought these broader

---

[21]Since the time of ICED's visit to the project in 1971, a Cooperative Law was drawn up within the framework of the Afghan commercial code. The Cooperative Societies Regulations of Afghanistan which were the result became law in September 1972.

constraints and influences into sharper perspective. The success of the second phase will depend in no small degree on getting such constraints altered in appropriate ways.[22]

An Effort to Boost Production in Low Potential Areas

We move on from PACCA to another integrated project—the Puebla Project in Mexico—which has quite similar objectives and clienteles, yet employs strikingly different methods. Whereas PACCA has an extraordinarily high ratio of extension agents to farmers, the Puebla Project has a very low one. PACCA works primarily with individual farmers; Puebla works through natural groupings of local farmers, using their chairmen as liaison. PACCA found it necessary to erect an elaborate staff training system of its own; Puebla relies largely on a nearby agricultural college—to be sure, an unusually creative one—for most of its staff training. PACCA is only loosely connected with research; the prime initiative for Puebla came from an agricultural research institute, which has continued to play a close role in the project. In later analytical chapters we will attempt to draw some inferences from these differences. For the present, however, we turn to a brief look at the Puebla Project.

The Puebla Project

Stimulus for the Puebla Project in Mexico[23] grew out of a concern by researchers at the International Maize and Wheat Improvement Center (CIMMYT), near Mexico City, over the low rate of adoption of improved technology (including improved corn varieties) by small subsistence farmers in rainfed agriculture, in contrast to the high rates of adoption on larger farms and in more favored ecological regions. In cooperation with the state and national government and the nearby Agricultural College at Chapingo, CIMMYT researchers developed an experimental scheme to try to overcome obstacles that appeared to discourage such adoption, and they selected an area in the northeast part of the State of Puebla to try it out.

Conditions in that area closely resemble those confronting a great proportion of the poorer farmers in rainfed agriculture at high altitudes on the slopes and valleys of the Andes. Family farms are small, averaging little more than two hectares. The weather is fickle and the yields are generally low—1.5 tons per hectare was considered good. The seeds used are the traditional *criolla* maize, the principal food of the people living there. The farmers typically have little or

---

[22]The PACCA Project Adviser informed us in May 1973 that: "Phase I came to an end on 20 March 1972. External funding for the Phase II of PACCA had not been approved as of August 1972, six months after it was scheduled to start, because the passage of the Cooperative Law was a prerequisite required by SIDA before they would agree to finance Phase II. The Project was carried by bridging finance provided by SIDA until 20 March 1973. This allowed time for the preparation and passage of the prerequisite Cooperative Law. The Plan of Operation for Phase II was signed on 21 March 1973, following the adoption of a cooperative law. During the period of bridging finance, recruitment of new and replacement staff was stopped and the Project suffered a loss in development momentum, especially with regard to Cooperative Development in the field."

[23]This summary is based on field notes of an ICED research team and documentation furnished by the Puebla Project. It also draws on an unpublished article by Delbert T. Myren, "The Puebla Project: A Developmental Strategy for Low Income Farmers." (Paper delivered at the Seminar on Small Farmer Development Strategies, Columbus, Ohio, September 1971).

no working capital and are without access to production credit at reasonable rates. The farmers in Puebla, however, are somewhat better off than many other small Latin American farmers, in that they are occasionally able to find part-time wage employment on larger farms and in the nearby city. These small farmers received little help from the thinly spread government extension service, nor did the extension service by itself have much help to give them.

Objective. The aims of the Puebla Project were simple and straightforward: to develop a methodology for helping the 46,000 small subsistence farmers in this rainfed agricultural area—and ultimately those in similar areas—to improve both their nutrition and income by growing more food for consumption, fodder and sale.

Once support had been assured by the Rockefeller Foundation (which had also supported CIMMYT), the first steps taken (in 1967) toward mounting the project were to carry out research in the project area to define more precisely packages of production practices that should be recommended to farmers and to conduct a socioeconomic baseline survey of the population. These studies identified two main bottlenecks: the lack of credit and the lack of technical knowledge on the part of small farmers. Accordingly, the following operational tasks were set out: (1) to advise farmers on improved and tested practices for increased maize production; and (2) to help farmers secure credit (through established banking channels and other sources) for supplementary inputs required for using these improved practices. In 1972, another objective was added: to improve the nutrition of farm families by adding additional crops, particularly fruit and vegetables (a secondary priority).

Management. The general organization and staffing of the Puebla Project are surprisingly simple for an undertaking intended to break a poor population out of a subsistence economy. Its management staff is composed of a part-time director in Mexico City (who is also a professor and communications specialist at the Chapingo College of Agriculture) and a full-time field director in Puebla City. The administration of the project is handled by CIMMYT. The project team in Puebla is backstopped by researchers and other specialists at Chapingo College, at CIMMYT, and in the federal and state departments of agriculture.

Staff. The principal extension agents are bright, energetic and well-trained recent graduates from Chapingo and other agricultural colleges in Mexico. After participating in the Puebla Project for two to three years, they usually enter the Graduate College at Chapingo and pursue programs that augment their capacity to work effectively in rural development programs.[24] They meet regularly with scientists, evaluation specialists and the managers of the project to ensure a continuous appraisal of overall project operations and the work of individual agents and to make whatever adjustments seem indicated. To allow for such adjustments, the general planning of the project is kept flexible; there are no fixed production targets.

The project staff consists of the field director or coordinator, three agronomic research scientists, an evaluation specialist and five technical assistance specialists. In addition, several local farmers have been selected and trained to assist the professional staff.

---

[24]This and other novel features of the Chapingo program constitute a promising breakaway from the customary practices of most agricultural colleges in Latin America.

Content and methods. The agronomic research scientists develop recommendations on how best to grow maize (more recently, also beans and the maize-bean association) by conducting experiments at carefully located sites on farmers' fields throughout the project area. The evaluation specialist conducts socioeconomic studies to measure progress toward project objectives and to identify obstacles limiting farmer use of the new technology.

The technical assistance staff is deployed over five ecological zones within the total project area. Each zone has one well-qualified extension agent for approximately 10,000 farmers. His primary tasks are to (1) convince farmers that they could grow more maize; (2) acquaint them with the recommended "package of practices" for this purpose; (3) teach them how to use credit, including the importance of adhering to the recommended practices so as to ensure their ability to repay loans out of increased production; and (4) encourage the organization of local credit groups and serve as liaison, when necessary, between such groups and the banking system.

Each agent is backed up by an assistant whose main job is to organize film shows, group meetings, study tours to experiment stations and demonstration plots in the area, and other gatherings. The assistant also occasionally helps to expedite the delivery of fertilizer and other supplies to farmers when the regular channels are clogged.

The local credit groups constitute both the learning unit and the borrowing unit. The chairman, chosen by the group, is the principal liaison with the extension agent and the main coordinator and communicator of information to the other members. There are no hard rules on group size and no specified criteria for the selection of a chairman. Groups are formed largely on the basis of existing informal social organizations, with *compadre* ties as an essential element.

Facilities. The Puebla Project staff works out of their Puebla city office with a minimum of facilities. The main items are trucks equipped for film shows and for transporting farmers to meeting places and to strategically located demonstration fields used for verification trials and cared for by selected farmers.

Performance. Encouraging progress was made during the first three years of the Puebla Project. The first important discovery for the Puebla Project researchers was that under the difficult and capricious ecological conditions of the Puebla area, the *criolla* varieties generally proved superior to the new varieties of the National Agricultural Research Institute (INIA) and CIMMYT. This discovery highlighted the need for research directed at significant variations in ecological conditions from area to area, and for good two-way communication between researchers, farmers and extension workers.

Fortunately, the *criolla* varieties were very responsive to increased fertilization (a fact also known to the farmers). With proper treatment, yields could often be trebled. The problem was to create the conditions under which it would be economically and logistically feasible for the small farmers to apply such treatment.

In the fourth year of the project the sharply rising curve of farmer participation in credit units unexpectedly started to flatten out, with only a small fraction of the total potential participants yet having joined.[25] The project staff

---

[25]Project evaluators measure participation by the number of farmers joining credit groups. With the project just under way there were 103 participants in 1968. The number rose sharply to 2,561 in 1969 and sharply again to 4,833 in 1970. But in 1971 the rate of increase suddenly fell off, to a total of only 5,240.

were perplexed as to the reasons for the drop-off in participation and the narrowing gap between the average per-acre yield of participants and nonparticipants which had been dramatically large the first year but shrinking ever since.

The latter phenomenon could be at least partially explained by the narrow definition of "participant" (membership in a project credit group) by which progress was being measured. Although the evidence was far from complete, there were indications—including a rising curve of average yields by nonparticipating farmers—that a good number of these "nonparticipants" had in fact adopted the recommended practices without resort to borrowing through a credit group, suggesting that the Puebla Project was having a "halo" effect not included in its evaluation measurements. At the same time, evidently, a number of "late adopters" with lower production potentials were joining credit groups, causing the average yield curve of participants to decline. Thus the two curves, though still significantly apart, were coming closer together.

But this still did not explain why so many farmers were neither joining a credit group nor adopting the recommended practices (particularly the increased application of fertilizer, greater plant density and greater frequency of weeding). One plausible hypothesis advanced by ICED researchers was that many of the "nonresponding" farmers were discouraged by the opportunity costs involved in applying the recommended practices. These, the hypothesis runs, are mainly part-time farmers who earn cash wages in other employment. To apply the recommended practices would require them to devote 55 percent more hours to their own maize crops, particularly for increased weeding (unfortunately, weeds are as responsive as *criolla* maize to increased fertilizer). This extra cultivating time would be at the expense of their outside earnings.

A further hypothesis is that, particularly because of the unreliability of rainfall in the area, the recommended practices of the Puebla Project, as seen by many farmers, entailed a higher risk of serious financial loss than their conventional practices.

Whether or not the above "opportunity cost" and "risk" hypotheses hold in the Puebla case (which we suspect they do), they certainly are relevant to many other agricultural situations and appear to have been important blind spots in many well-intentioned but abortive efforts to encourage farmers to increase production.

Perhaps the most important lesson of this initial period was that agricultural experts who set out to help small farmers are well-advised to find out first of all what practical economic and related factors in the particular situation enter into the farmer's decision-making.

An Ambitious Development Effort in a Small Country

We close this chapter with a few highlights about the largest, most comprehensive and most complex integrated rural development scheme we ran across in this study—the Lilongwe Land Development Programme in Malawi—for which the World Bank made its first "integrated package" loan in 1968.[26]

While not the subject of a case study, Lilongwe is too important an undertaking to be entirely ignored in this report. The facts presented below are

---

[26]For a description of the Lilongwe Land Development project, see T.A. Blinkhorn, "Lilongwe: A Quiet Revolution," *Finance and Development* 8 no. 2 (1971), pp. 26-31.

drawn largely from documentation furnished to ICED by the World Bank and the project management, supplemented by discussions with some of its early advisors and a brief visit to the project by an ICED researcher in late 1971.

The Lilongwe Land Development Programme

The Lilongwe Land Development Programme in Malawi's Central Region encompasses more than 1.1 million acres of the country's richest agricultural land. It contains some 52,000 homesteads averaging five acres each, and a population of 350,000 out of a national total of some 4.5 million. Most farmers in the area, besides growing their own food, have long grown crops for sale—particularly maize, groundnuts and tobacco. Their production is limited not by available land but by the relatively primitive state of their hand-cultivation methods and other archaic production practices. The introduction of animal power (oxen) and of improved inputs and techniques could significantly increase their productivity.

Objectives. The immediate objective of the project is to boost agricultural output and to bring the farmers of this partially commercialized area more fully into a cash economy. Its ultimate goal is to promote rural development in a larger sense—to improve health services, local government, education of women and youth, and the general quality of life in the area.

Planning development activities. To move with dispatch in these directions, the project plan calls for both heavy capital investment and intensive technical assistance. Its components include credit and market facilities, soil conservation and water supply, road construction, a livestock program, and the development of an administrative and social infrastructure, including health and educational facilities. Of particular significance for our purposes is that this project includes the development of a large and diversified learning system designed to meet the educational needs of both the project staff and the local inhabitants.

It was recognized in advance that to apply the more advanced technologies envisaged by the project, all farmers would have to learn many new things— how, for example, to use improved seeds and fertilizers to increase yields, how to apply ridge and contour plowing to reduce erosion, how to rotate crops to save on fertilizer, how to build secure crop storage facilities to prevent losses through rodents and rot. Thus, if the investment in capital facilities were to pay off, a parallel investment would have to be made in human skills and knowledge—not only for the men but for their wives and children as well. It was further recognized that the investment in intensive staffing of the project, involving a wide variety of talents and functions, had to be accompanied by a corresponding investment in the education of the staff.

Management and staff. As Malawi's existing educational capabilities were clearly too limited to meet these needs, the project planners provided for their substantial expansion. Responsibility for directing the development and operation of a multifaceted "learning system" was put in the hands of a high-level program training officer, with authority to draw upon a wide assortment of project talent for educational contributions, to direct a central training institution, and to supervise a network of other training facilities.

In 1966 Malawi's total extension service had 614 members, of whom only 297 had been systematically trained as technical assistants. When the project was launched in 1968, there was an average of one extension worker to every 1,800 farm families. To get the project under way the short-term goal was to achieve a ratio of one extension worker to every 200 families in the Lilongwe area; the long-term plan called for one to every 600 to 800.

Two agricultural training institutions already existed in the project area—Bunda and Colby Colleges. These were well equipped to produce good extension agents and supervisors, but not enough of them. Together they were graduating 110 persons per year—mostly two-year certificate holders but also a number with three-year diplomas and a few with five-year degrees. Spurred by the needs of the new project, these institutions accelerated their ablest students, expanded their enrollments (with the Lilongwe project selecting and financing their recruits), and enlarged their capacity by annexing the facilities of a former Farmer Training Institute. By these efforts their combined output was expected to rise from 110 in 1968 to more than 250 in 1972.

But this was only a part of the story. The project's own staff training center by 1972 was offering a great variety of preservice and inservice orientation and refresher courses for many dozens of staff members at all levels. A farmer-training center was in full operation, offering one-week specialized courses for leading local farmers and their wives. Local educational centers were offering one-day programs for a larger number of farmers. A multimedia system was in operation, including daily broadcasts over a P.A. system, the production and wide dissemination of pamphlets, bulletins and other learning materials in the local language through the "extension aids" office, two "yellow vans" visiting several villages daily with puppet shows, films and pertinent announcements and instructions.

Problems. The overall design and performance of this elaborate "learning system" are impressive, but it is not without problems. The root of the problems, as seen by the energetic training officer, is that production-minded senior officers of the project undervalue the critical importance of training and too often give it a low priority relative to other components. In a comprehensive report on training requirements in 1972, he dismissed as "ludicrous" their claim that operational personnel could not be spared for training. Any field agent below the required standard, he insisted, "is doing more damage by being kept in the field than he is being taught or retaught at the Training Centre."[27]

The training officer also struck out against what he considered an excessive preoccupation of senior officers with short-range, cost-benefit tests applied to training matters:

"One is often confronted with the attitude that every activity must be economically justified. I do not agree that in the public service every little thing must be economical. Obviously expense must be the first consideration but in a developing country the long-term objective of a particular course of action must always be remembered and it is not always easy or necessary to measure human achievement in monetary terms. I am thinking particularly here of attitude towards the transport of farmers, for example, to the Residential Training Centre."[28]

---

[27]P.J. Allister, "Training Report: Lilongwe Land Development Programme". Mimeographed. (March 10, 1972), p. 2.

[28]Ibid., p. 2.

The Lilongwe training officer's candid criticism of senior officers, accompanied by a detailed catalogue of common-sense suggestions for strengthening the project's overall efficiency and effectiveness in a variety of ways, strikes us as convincing evidence of the project's good health.

Any authentic "integrated approach" inevitably involves tension, competition and a running debate among those responsible for its various components, reflecting their different professional backgrounds and viewpoints. The time to worry, perhaps, is when debate ceases and a "gentlemen's truce" creates an uneasy peace under which each band of specialists—educators and non-educators—is given unchallenged rule over its particular province.

8: A CRITIQUE OF AGRICULTURAL EDUCATION AND RESEARCH SYSTEMS

The five chapters of Part II—the main analytical section of the report—examine critically the evidence gathered from our case studies, field observations, interviews and pertinent documents, and attempts to arrive at some operationally useful conclusions and recommendations. Since the programs under review constitute but a fraction of the total of such programs, our general observations and conclusions must allow for many exceptions.

The division of topics by chapters is necessarily somewhat arbitrary. For example, the present chapter focuses on knowledge and skills directly applicable to agricultural production, whereas the next one deals with artisan, craft and other nonagricultural skills useful in rural areas. While this dichotomy has a certain basis in logic and in the present pattern of rural training programs, the important reality for educational planners to heed is that most rural famililies actually need a combination of *both* farming and nonfarming skills.

The remaining three analytical chapters focus on major issues that cut across all types of nonformal education: the quality of content and the different instructional methods, media and materials used (Chapter 10); questions concerning costs, resources and evaluation (Chapter 11); and finally, problems of planning, organization, management and staffing (Chapter 12).

The Context of Farmer Education

We turn now to our main interest in the present chapter—field-level farmer education programs, such as extension services and farmer training centers.[1] To appraise such programs properly they must be viewed in a larger context. First, they must be looked at as components of an overall *knowledge-generation and delivery system* whose mission is to help farmers and their families make the best of their opportunities. Second, they must be seen as part of an *agricultural development system* in each rural area involving, along with educational elements, a number of essential noneducational factors.

Determinants of Productivity

When we view these programs in this larger context it is evident that their *internal efficiency* (cost effectiveness) and *external productivity* (cost-benefit ratio) are determined not simply by what the programs do themselves, but by (1) the kinds of backstopping they get from other components of the agricultural knowledge system; (2) the ecological, economic, political and social characteristics and development potential of the particular agricultural

---

[1]Agriculture is defined broadly throughout this report to include not only the growing of crops but also poultry and animal husbandry, forestry and fishing. The term "farmer" is used loosely to cover all these activities.

zone in which they operate; (3) the characteristics of the farmers themselves and the relevance of the knowledge offered to their true interests and motivations; and (4) the presence or absence of complementary development factors (such as supplies of credit, water and chemical inputs, access to markets, and attractive incentives) and how well the educational inputs are geared to these.

For these reasons we are obliged in this chapter to look beyond the strict limits of farmer education programs at other key components of agricultural knowledge systems and at some of the noneducational factors that influence their productivity.[2]

Recent Growth and Future Tasks

It will be useful first to review briefly the recent evolution of agricultural knowledge systems in the developing world and the adequacy of these systems to cope with their future tasks.

Handicaps

In fairness it should be noted straight away that most of the programs and institutions discussed are young and immature and all of them have been burdened with severe handicaps not of their own making. In the allocation of resources, for example, most national development plans, their rhetoric to the contrary, have given low priority to agricultural and rural development generally, and in particular to agricultural education. Further, agricultural education of every sort, in trying to attract good teachers and students, has suffered from the low social esteem and financial reward attached to rural careers. Within the educational community at large, agricultural education has been given second class treatment, even though its basic mission is often more pertinent to national development than much of what is taught in the more prestigious urban academic schools and universities.

Quantitative Expansion

Notwithstanding these handicaps, impressive progress has been made over the past ten to fifteen years in establishing the basic infrastructures of agricultural knowledge systems. Practically all developing countries today have some sort of agricultural extension service, some have several and quite a few also have farmer-training centers. Many countries have made a start on building their own agricultural research capabilities; some—such as the Caribbean Commonwealth countries, India, Republic of Korea, Mexico, Nigeria, the Philippines and Uganda—have come an impressive distance in this respect. Meanwhile, agricultural vocational schools, institutes, colleges and universities have fairly exploded in number all over the developing world.[3] Whatever their han-

---

[2]Some farmer education programs include peripheral activities such as home economics instruction for rural women and special programs for rural youth, but to keep this chapter manageable we shall confine it largely to their central agricultural production concerns. Programs for rural women and youth are examined more closely in ICED's study sponsored by UNICEF.

[3]FAO reports reveal an increase in the number of higher agricultural education institutions in Asia by over 150 percent between 1957 and 1968, and an increase in Latin America from 15 to 151 such institutions between 1964 and 1969. FAO, *The State of Food and Agriculture 1972* (Rome, 1972), p. 125.

dicaps and shortcomings, the infrastructures now in place provide a much more solid base to build upon than existed earlier.

Future Requirements

Despite this dramatic growth—often virtually from scratch—most of these agricultural knowledge systems are no match whatever for the burdens thrust upon them by the agricultural production targets for the UN Second Development Decade. These targets call for a 4 percent annual growth in overall agricultural output (against an average of 2.8 percent achieved in the 1960s). This seemingly modest goal is in fact extremely ambitious. It implies roughly a doubling of the past rate at which farmers in the developing world have increased their productivity. More than half the previous increases in agricultural production came from new land brought under cultivation, whereas now, with the supply of reserve land sharply reduced—particularly in Asia and in much of Latin America—the bulk of new increments must be won by higher yields on existing farmland.

To get these higher yields, not only must many millions of farmers, large and small, have better supplies and better incentives, but they must also become better planners and managers of their farm businesses and must master a steady succession of improved technologies.[4] For all this to happen, there must be greatly intensified efforts in agricultural research and farmer education.

These expanded research and education efforts, moreover, must be directed particularly to *smaller* farmers, who need the most help and have been getting the least. If agricultural development officers, eager to meet assigned production targets in the quickest and easiest way, concentrate their attention mainly on the more progressive and affluent cultivators and on major export crops, the smaller farmers will again be left behind and already serious socioeconomic disparities will be compounded. To avoid this will require, in many countries, major reforms in land tenure arrangements and farm credit systems, and great strengthening of farmer associations and local self-government. While, in the short run, quick boosts in agricultural output can most readily be achieved from the larger and more sophisticated growers, in the longer run agricultural production can keep moving upward at a satisfactory rate only if smaller farmers—including many who are still bound to subsistence agriculture—step up their productivity.[5]

Gross Inadequacies

The gross inadequacy of existing agricultural knowledge systems for the tasks they now face is suggested by the figures in Table 8.1 comparing the number of field-level extension agents with the number of farm families in

---

[4]A. A. Johnson, *Indian Agriculture in the 1970s* (New Delhi: The Ford Foundation, August 1, 1970), discusses the areas of technological advance needed to implement a stronger agricultural development policy.

[5]Unfortunately, agriculture is already off to a poor start in meeting the production goals of the Second Development Decade. Due especially to bad weather conditions in most of Southeast Asia—and to civil conflicts in what was formerly East Pakistan—crops have suffered seriously and less than half the targeted increase in farm production for the developing world as a whole was achieved in 1971 and 1972. FAO, *The State of Food and Agriculture 1972*, Chapter I, foreword by A. H. Boerma; and U.S. Department of Agriculture estimates.

several developing countries for which data are available. In the late 1960s Mali, for instance, had only 111 extension workers to serve 936,444 farm families; Uganda had 125 for 1,432,200 farm families. In Latin America the ratio ranged from 1:1,057 (in Chile) to 1:15,679 (in Guatemala). India's statistical record of 1:828 looks quite favorable by comparison, but it is based on Village Level Workers, whose training in agriculture has been notoriously inadequate.

Table 8.1
Estimated Extension Workers and Farm Families
in Selected Countries,[1] 1971

	Farm Families	Extension Workers	Farm Families per Extension Worker
Mali[2]	936,444	111	8,436
Senegal[2]	448,333	206	2,176
Uganda[2]	1,432,200	125	11,458
Zambia	470,000	560	839
India[2]	53,594,242	64,720	828
Korea, Rep. of[3]	2,506,000	{ 3,628[4]	691[4]
		6,049[5]	414[5]
Argentina	1,074,883	239	4,497
Bolivia	571,600	70	8,165
Brazil	8,624,902	1,556[6]	5,543
Chile	389,206	368	1,057
Colombia	1,832,453	350	5,236
Costa Rica	140,000	37	3,784
El Salvador	351,090	61	5,756
Guatemala	627,170	40	15,679
Honduras	323,653	51	6,346
Mexico	4,585,461	514	9,452
Nicaragua	169,531	38	4,461
Peru	1,220,000	558	2,383
Venezuela	559,811	272	2,058

[1]The sample is heavily drawn from the Latin American region because of a recent study on the subject. Data on other countries of Africa, the Far East and the Near East were hardly comparable and were thretore not included. As far as possible, only extension personnel in direct contact with farmers were included.
[2]1967.
[3]1965. *The Economy of Korea,* Vol. 3, Seoul, 1966.
[4]Includes only general guidance workers (village level).
[5]Includes also subject specialists of agricultural extension (excluding provincial and national levels). Most are in direct contact with farmers.
[6]Includes veterinarians and other technical staff not directly dealing with agricultural extension.

SOURCE: Food and Agriculture Organization, *State of Food and Agriculture 1972* (Rome, 1972), p. 137, Table 3-4.

Another revealing indicator of inadequacy is that in many countries where 50 to 90 percent of the population depend on agriculture for a living only a small proportion of college and university students major in agriculture. In Asia the proportion in 1968 was only 3.5 percent; the figures for Africa and Latin America are similarly low. Yet many agricultural colleges, especially in Latin America, are having trouble filling their places because of their low drawing power in competition with "regular" colleges and universities.

These agricultural education and research systems will clearly require massive enlargement. But, for reasons presented later, it would be a serious mistake simply to expand the existing programs and institutions in their present condition. The foremost requirement now is to reform, reorient and strengthen them. Only then will heavy investments to enlarge existing programs be assured a good yield.

Functions and Components of an Agricultural Knowledge System

The basic mission of an agricultural knowledge system, as noted earlier, is to provide pertinent information, knowledge, skills and encouragement to farmers to help them take the fullest advantage of their opportunities—for the good of their families and communities and of general national development.

Such a system requires components which, together, perform five critical functions. The first three interconnected functions listed below are crucial to the system's basic mission as defined above. The fourth and fifth functions are essential to the effective operation of the system itself:

1. Identification of the knowledge needs of farmers. This is where the whole process must begin. It is a diversified and continuing function, since the knowledge needs of various types of farmers and farming areas differ widely and can change rapidly. The more effective the system is in meeting these needs, the more rapidly new knowledge needs arise.

2. Generation of knowledge to meet the identified needs. This function, taking its cues from the first, includes the creation of new knowledge through domestic research and the adaptation to local conditions of pertinent knowledge based on research and experience in other countries. It includes both social science and natural science research as applied to agriculture. New knowledge can be generated in the farmers' own fields as well as at remote research centers and experiment stations.

3. Dissemination and application of knowledge. To be useful to farmers, knowledge must be translated into their own terms, communicated to them through appropriate channels, and its practical application demonstrated. The complexity of the process ranges from the simple communication of timely information that requires no further explanation to much deeper and lasting learning. Knowledge can reach farmers through a great variety of channels, both official and unofficial.

4. Staff development. For the system to function effectively, its various specialized manpower needs must be met and there must be steady renewal and growth of staff competence in all its components. Both formal and nonformal as well as informal educational processes are generally involved in meeting these needs.

5. Management of the system. An agricultural knowledge system requires good management not only of each component but of the system as a whole. Management includes planning, coordination and continuing evaluation. It also includes the harmonization of education and research with complementary agricultural development factors, area by area, and the integration of educational plans and policies with broader rural development plans and strategies.

Whatever institutional means are chosen for performing the above key functions, it is essential—if the system is to perform efficiently and effectively over-all—that all the parts be kept in balance and attuned with one another and with the surrounding environment.

External Constraints

The system operates, as suggested earlier within a milieu of contraints over which its managers (at various levels) have little or no control. These include, for example, the pressure of population growth on the land; national development priorities; agricultural policies and budgetary allocations to agricultural education, tax and fiscal policies and the basic condition of the economy; the general social and economic status of agriculture as a career; land tenure arrangements; marketing policies and the state and prospects of domestic and international agricultural markets; the general political climate; related educational or supply functions under the jurisdiction of other ministries or authorities; the development potential and readiness of particular areas.[6]

Any of these conditions and constraints can help or hobble the system's performance. In India, for example, the establishment of support prices for major cereal grains in the latter half of the 1960s contributed greatly to the adoption of high-yielding seeds coming out of new research. In Afghanistan, government marketing policies have seriously handicapped the Programme on Agricultural Credit and Cooperation in Afghanistan (PACCA). The Ethiopian government's delay in instituting land reforms has created problems for the Chilalo Agricultural Development Unit (CADU) project.

Performance Criteria

The best vantage point from which to begin an evaluation of an agricultural knowledge system's performance is at the local level. Here—where the system makes direct contact with its main clients, the farmers—the various components and internal relationships meet their acid test. The test is how much usable knowledge gets through· to the farmers, and whether and how it affects their decisions and behavior, their productivity, and their income. All other criteria of performance are secondary. Regardless of how much or little its own inputs cost, or how well any particular components may appear to be performing, if the system's impact on local agricultural productivity and income are trivial, its cost-effectiveness and cost-benefit rating must be judged poor.

At the local level also, one can best observe the critical linkages and interplay between the outputs of the knowledge system and all of the other essential factors required for agricultural development. The system's productivity

---

[6]See Arthur T. Mosher, *Creating a Progressive Rural Structure to Serve a Modern Agriculture* (New York: Agricultural Development Council, Inc., 1969), which provides a broader systems view of the various essential infrastructures and services required by a modernizing agricultural society.

will be greatest when all the other factors are present; it can be virtually nil when they are not. In other words, education and research cannot precipitate or accelerate agricultural development all by themselves, but given favorable conditions they can make a large and critically important contribution. Twenty years of substantial investment in agricultural education in the Philippines, for example, showed little impact on overall production until improved seeds and fertilizer supplies and favorable price incentives came along in the mid-1960s. Only then did the earlier educational investments have a chance to start paying off.

From this brief sketch of the key parts and relationships of an agricultural knowledge system, we move now to an assessment of how such systems appear to be working in practice, judged by the evidence gathered in the study. Each of the five essential functions listed above will be examined in sequence.

Identification of Farmers' Knowledge Needs

Extension agents are not only the local communication and education arm of the knowledge system; they are also its local eyes and ears. Being in closest contact with farmers, they are in the best position to help diagnose the farmers' knowledge needs. If they cannot directly satisfy these needs from their own knowledge, they can relay problems back to a higher echelon for solution.

This, at least, is how the system is supposed to work, but often it does not—for several rrasons. One common reason is that in many situations extension workers are neither trained nor encouraged to diagnose the farmers' needs and to pass questions needing answers back to more knowledgeable experts and research centers. Local extension agents are often treated mainly as one-way messengers who pass along to farmers in their area a package of recommended practices which experts at a higher level have decided will fit the farmers' needs and opportunities, and they are expected to do their best to persuade farmers to adopt these practices.

Sometimes the recommended practices fit the situation, especially if a visiting expert has carefully diagnosed the local needs, but more often they are inappropriate and are rejected by the farmers because their needs and circumstances—especially the economic factors in their situation—have not been properly diagnosed.

Even if a bright extension agent, who knows his farmer clients well, succeeds in identifying an important knowledge need, the work may never get through to the researchers because of clogged or nonexistent channels of communication from extension to research. The researchers may be isolated from both the farmers and the extension service and choose their research priorities to fit their own predilection and interests.

Liaison of Research, Extension, and Farmers

The problems of identifying and responding to the knowledge needs of farmers are best handled when the research system reaches down to the farmer—when researchers are in close liaison with both the extension service and a good sample of farmers themselves. This favorable condition exists in the Republic of Korea, at least with respect to rice production (the priority concern of both research and extension). The Office of Rural Development's (ORD) research service as well as its extension service extends down to the local level in many areas through a network of experiment stations and intensive experimental rice production schemes. Even when the extension agents are not technically qualified to diagnose the farmers' more difficult problems and needs, better qualified researchers are close enough to help.

We witnessed what can happen when research experts and farmers get together—generally a rare event—on a visit to the lush rice-producing District of Tanjore in the South Indian State of Tamil Nadu. In a series of roadside seminars, farmers besieged with sharp technical questions a group of experts, including India's leading rice research expert, the Director-designate of the International Rice Research Institute (IRRI), and a Ford Foundation expert. In many instances, the experts had no ready answers but, having seen for themselves what the farmers needed, they promised to try to get answers.

Narrow Focus on Major Crops

Another major problem is the narrow focus of most agricultural research and extension services on major commercial crops and animal and forest products, to the neglect of other crops of great importance to many farmers. Farmers specializaing in a major crop such as rice or corn or wheat consider diversification when supplies of their main crop become more abundant and the market price starts softening. But at that point, though the farmers' needs for information may be clear, the one-commodity research centers and extension service that helped them boost rpoduction of their major commercial crop are likely to be poorly equipped to help them on alternative crops.

This concentration of research and farmer education on one or a few principal commercial crops puts subsistence farmers at a major disadvantage, for their main needs often run in other directions. They need help on improving the quality and output of nutritious family-consumption crops, which often are not sifnificant commercial crops. Relatively little research has been aimed at meeting these nees of subsistence farmers anywhere in the developing world.[7]

A third problem—perhaps the largest of all—has been the preoccupation of research and extension services with the purely technical aspects of agricultural production, to the serious neglect of other important knowledge needs of farmers and rural families.

Knowledge Needs of Small Farmers

Small farmers especially need help on becoming better planners and farm managers. For a subsistence farmer to become a successful commercial farmer he must first visualize his farm as an economic unit—a business—and not simply as a way of life. A retired pioneer of agricultural extension in East Africa told us that he now realized that extension services had approached the problem from the wrong angle. "Instead of selling technologies," he said, "we should have begun by teaching simple farm planning and management. Then

---

[7]The IBRD-FAO-UNDP Consultative Group on International Agricultural Research has recently taken the initiative, in cooperation with the Government of India, to establish in Hyderabad a new International Crops Research Institute for the Semi-Arid Tropics. The institute will concentrate its research on food legumes, various other subsistence crops, and animal husbandry needs of major importance to small farmers throughout the tropical belt extending across Asia, Africa and Central America.

the small farmers would have recognized the importance of improving their technologies."

Farmers also need to learn more about improving and maintaining their capital facilities—how, for example, to construct and repair buildings, dig compost pits, make and repair small tools, handle and care for draft animals. Many extension services and farmer training centers ignore these practical subjects. Often they also ignore sideline crops and activities with which farmers could earn extra income.

Even within their limited field of concentration—mainly the improvement of technologies for expanding production of one or two major commercial crops—farmer education and research services have often failed to diagnose adequately the diverse needs of different subgroups of farmers and different areas. They have inclined toward standardized "messages" on the false assumption that would fit the conditions of all types of farmers and areas.

The net effect has been that many needs have been misinterpreted or altogether neglected, particularly with respect to smaller farmers. Larger farmers, more competent to diagnose their own needs and in a position to bypass the local extension agent and go directly to the main sources of knowledge, have benefited far more from new research findings than their less fortunate small neighbors. This clearly is what happened in the Green Revolution districts of India and Pakistan.

Generation of Knowledge

Without a nourishing flow of pertinent knowledge, and the capacity to convey it effectively to farmers, an agricultural knowledge system is little more than a series of rituals. To maintain such a flow, a developing country requires a knowledge-generating process of its own. It cannot benefit fully from research done elsewhere—at international research centers such as IRRI—without research capacities of its own to adapt high-yielding varieties or other new production technologies to its own ecological and economic circumstances.[8]

Nor can a developing country train its own national cadre of agricultural research and production experts simply by sending them for advanced training to a more developed country that has very different agricultural conditions, or by instructing them in its own colleges and universities largely from textbooks written in other countries. While the findings of external research may be very helpful, there must also be a dynamic internal research process feeding into staff development and out to the farmers (whose improved productivity and welfare is the cardinal object of the whole effort).

Effective indigenous agricultural research is now going on in several countries—for example in India and the Philippines—and many additional major efforts to strengthen national research capacities are under way, as they are in

---

[8]Albert H. Moseman, ed., *National Agricultural Research Systems in Asia: Report of the Regional Seminar held at the India International Centre, New Delhi, India, March 8-13, 1971* (New York: Agricultural Development Council, Inc., 1971): "...in addition to these specialized 'International Research Centers' the continuous infusion of new technology for agricultural growth and development to meet future needs of the region must depend increasingly upon 'national capabilities' in agricultural research. This is necessary because of the many production problems which are nation-specific.

Indonesia and Sri Lanka (Ceylon).[9] Notwithstanding these encouraging examples, agricultural research is generally weak and inadequate in virtually all developing countries and, unless strengthened, the ability of farmer education programs to help farmers will continue to be seriously fettered.

Our study draws particular attention to the following actions needed with regard to research tied to agricultural development: (1) greatly increased investment in the expansion and strengthening of national research networks, reaching down to the farmer level; and (2) the strengthening of social science research on agricultural development and better integration of research efforts at all levels.

Need for Increased Investment in Research

The meagerness of present expenditures on agricultural research (and extension) is shown dramatically by the fitures in Table 8.2, drawn from an FAO review.[10] Total expenditures on agricultural research in the Asian developing countries—the most populous region of the world—were in 1966 barely over 10 percent of what the United States spent. This represented only one-tenth of one percent of their combined GDP from agriculture, as against 2.17 percent for the United States. Africa, with a much smaller total population and less severe food problem than in Asian countries, nevertheless had somewhat higher aggregate research outlays than did Asia. All of South and Central America combined spent one-fourth less than either Asia or Africa.

With such slim investments in research, and even less in extension (see columns 2, 4 and 6 in Table 8.2), it is little wonder that farmer education programs in all these regions have for the' most part yielded disappointing results.

There are, however, some notable exceptions which demonstrate the potency of concerted research efforts and the importance of extending national research networks to the farmers' own fields. In the two decades since independence, India has made a tremendous effort—considering its severe resource scarcities—to strengthen its agricultural research system. Dramatic results are now evident, at least in certain sub-areas and in some commodities.

The Tanjore District mentioned earlier is an example. In this rice-producing area the farmers themselves are part of the research process (which is quite exceptional). Selected farmers, under the guidance of government agricultural officers, are conducting adaptive research trials in portions of their own fields on experimental rice varieties not yet released for general use. Roadside posters marking these special plots provide neighboring farmers with all the pertinent data needed for making their own assessments: the name of the variety, the date it was planted, the type and amount of fertilizer applied, and when it will be harvested. Harvest day is a community educational event. Rice seeds are stripped and weighed at the roadside for all to witness. The spectator-farmers, many of them illiterate, rapidly calculate the cost-income ratios of the experimental crop and compare it with their own ratios for established varieties. If this economic ratio and other features of the new variety are clearly superior, they are ready to try it next season.

This explains why the Tanjore farmers bombarded the visiting research experts with sophisticated technical questions; they had become research-

---

[9]Ibid.
[10]FAO, *The State of Food and Agriculture 1972*, p. 149.

Table 8.2
Agricultural Research and Extension Investment in Selected Countries and Regions

	Estimated Expenditures per year Million U.S. dollars (1966)		Share of GDP originating in agriculture spent on Percent		Number of farms per	
	Research	Extension	Research	Extension	Senior Researcher	Extension worker
United States	388	178	2.17	0.99	346	555
Canada	60	26	1.62	1.05	321	167
Australia	51	(24)	2.98		126	...
New Zealand	6	5			159	160
Western Europe	200	130	0.88	0.62	1,605	822
Eastern Europe and USSR	200	(130)				
Mexico	2	0.3			4,550	6,320
Central America and Caribbean	4	3	0.11	0.52	4,270	3,407
South America	(24)	(18)	0.16	0.08	3,846	2,538
Africa[1]	47	(52)	0.49			
West Africa	10.3	(10)	0.11			
East Africa	17	(20.1)	1.20	1.80	19,143	801
Central Africa	1.7	(2)			6,179	
North Africa	18	(20)	0.68		6,050	
South Africa and Rhodesia	(7)	(5)				
Japan	62	36	1.24	0.72	1,131	433
Israel	6	4	2.67			
Asian Developing countries	42	(60)	0.10		16,700	1,038

SOURCE: FAO, *State of Food and Agriculture, 1972* (Rome: FAO) p. 149, from Evenson, R., "Economic factors in research and extension investment policy," *Proceedings of the Conference on Agricultural Research and Production in Africa, Addis Ababa, 1971.*

[1]Excluding South Africa and Rhodesia.

NOTE: ... not available.

minded because they were partners in research. Seeing a demonstration in their own or a neighbor's field is far more persuasive to farmers than seeing good results under the controlled conditions of a government experiment station—which the farmers doubt they can affored to match at home.

The unusual relationship between researchers and farmers in Tanjore cannot, of course, be duplicated everywhere because there are not enough researchers. But it should be standard practice (though it rarely is now) for researchers to leave their laboratories for frequent visits with sample farmers in their own fields, to listen to the farmers' questions and hypotheses, to observe production problems and results under normal (nonlaboratory) conditions, to take the farmers into their confidence—in short, to become direct parties to the extension and feedback process. For this to happen on a sufficient scale, however, there must be many more well-trained researchers and a new attitude on their part toward contact with farmers.

Need for Strengthening Social Science Research

ICED's field observations bear out a point made strongly by Carl Eicher with respect to Africa, and by FAO reports with respect to the entire developing world:[11] there is a serious imbalance and lack of integration between agronomic research and related social science research, both at the level of formulating national policies and plans and at the level of the farmer.

Eicher notes that the center of gravity in biological research on African agriculture is now located in Africa. Most of the related social science research, on the other hand, is still carries on by itinerant scholars from Western Europe and North America, and for that reason is frequently irrelevant.[12]

With few exceptions, the teaching and research programs of agricultural colleges and universities in all regions, and in-service training programs for extension personnel as well, are largely confined to the natural sciences and production technology. They are extremely deficient in agricultural economics (particularly small farm management), rural sociology and other social science aspects of agricultural development. This helps explain the frequent complaint of farmers that the new practices urged upon them by extension services made no practical economic sense from the farmers' point of view. The farmers are often better economists than the agricultural scientists and production experts who formulate these recommendations. Looking through narrow technical lenses, these experts generally pay too little attention to the implications of their recommendations for the farmer's costs,prices, risks and probable net earnings, and too little attention also to broader social and economic implications. As noted in a recent FAO document:

> It is only quite recently that the magnitude of the rural employment problem has alerted [agricultural] planners and scientists to the fact that a technology is needed which is not merely effective in its impact on output or quality but which is also socially and politically acceptable.[13]

Lester Brown's recitation of the "second generation" problems of India's Green Revolution makes it evident that social scientists need to be brought

---

[11]Ibid., pp. 126, 133.
[12]Carl Eicher, *Research on Agricultural Development in Five English-Speaking Countries in West Africa* (New York: Agricultural Development Council, Inc.; 1970).
[13]FAO, *The State of Food and Agriculture*, p. 146.

into the formulation of agricultural strategies.[14] Indeed, up and down the line, from the fashioning of national policies to the fashioning of recommendations to farmers in particular areas, there is great need for a multidisciplinary approach. The places for this to take root are in agricultural universities, ministries of agriculture, research centers, and extension services themselves.

The lack of sufficient attention to social science was evident in a few of our case studies. In the planning of PACCA, for example, too little weight was given to the serious marketing problems that participating farmers would encounter in disposing of their increased output, and too little study of the peculiar obstacles in that country to expanding credit supplies. (See Chapter 7.) In Senegal, when the market for groundnuts slumped, farmers who had faithfully followed the recommendations of SATEC (the Société d'aide technique et de coopération) found themselves saddled with debts they could not pay. Bitterly disillusioned, a good number of them are said to have withdrawn from the commercial production of groundnuts into subsistence farming. (See Chapter 3.)

One important factor frequently overlooked regarding new farming technologies is the increased labor inputs they often require. While this is highly advantageous in terms of generating rural employment, it can present serious problems for individual farmers at the peak points in the crop cycle. The Puebla Project's technical recommendations to small farmers implied a 60 percent increase in man-hours of effort per acre (mainly to eliminate the extra weeds nurtured by more fertilizer). The planners, though aware of this fact, did not investigate what its impact might be on the decisions of farmers, particularly those with part-time wage-earning jobs which they might have to forego in order to spend time weeding. Evidently a good many farmers figures out their options and opportunity costs, however, and decided that they could not afford the sacrifice.

The myth that farmers often reject the technical recommendations of extension services because they are irrationally conservative has by now been exploded, especially by the Green Revolution in Asia. Farmers reject technical recommendations that are, from their own overall and realistic point of view, impractical or unduly risky. But when a favorable set of conditions is created, they respond affirmatively.

The power of research should not, however, be exaggerated. Nor should the difficulties in putting good research findings to effective use be oversimplified. Journalistic accounts of the Asian Green Revolution, featuring the "miracle seeds" as a panacea, have encouraged the belief that further dramatic research breakthroughs are the cheap and simple answer to the Third World's agricultural problems. Nothing could be further from the truth. A close look at the anatomy of India's Green Revolution makes clear that the seeds fortunately came along at just the point when essential complementary factors, because of years of heavy investment and effort, were at last ripe for a major forward thrust in Indian agriculture. In particular, fertilizer production was up sharply, irrigation was greatly expanded, more credit was available, markets were strong,

---

[14]Lester Brown, *Seeds of Change: The Green Revolution and Development in the 1970s* (New York: Praeger Publishers, 1971).

and prices higher than in a long time. As Mosher comments, "It is the last essential item added that usually get the credit."[15]

While it may be hoped that further major research breakthroughs will occur, most of the increases in agricultural productivity are going to have to come from small, steady increments based partly on fuller and better application of existing technologies, partly on new research findings and largely on improvements in input supplies, credit, markets and prices.

It is worth noting that none of the substantial production increases per acre obtained thus far under the CADU, PACCA and Puebla projects came from research miracles. They resulted mainly from breaking critical bottlenecks in credit and transport and especially from the intensive application of fertilizer to existing types of seeds and plants.

Dissemination and Application of Knowledge

Assuming that the needs of farmers have been correctly identified (Function One) and that appropriate knowledge to respond to these needs has been assembled or freshly generated (Function Two), the next requirement is to complete the cycle by conveying this pertinent knowledge to the farmers and assisting them to assimilate and apply it (Function Three). This third function — essentially synonymous with farmer education — has been performed in the past in a variety of ways which, as we noted in Chapter 2, may be roughly grouped under four main approaches: (1) the autonomous extension approach, (2) the vocational training approach, (3) the self-help community development approach, and (4) the integrated agricultural development approach. In attempting to evaluate programs fitting these approaches, we have applied the following test questions:

How adequate and valid are the underlying concepts and philosophy of agricultural development, and how valid are the assumptions regarding this program's role in the process?

How clear and appropriate are the objectives, the priorities and the target audiences?

How efficiently are available resources being used to serve these objectives and purposes?

Shortcomings of Extension Services

There is no question that many agricultural extension programs — especially those operating independently of other services — were founded on a narrow vision of the objectives and process of agricultural education to promote mass development. Extension was seen mainly as a process of informing farmers about new technical practices and persuading them to adopt them. This process, in and of itself, was seen as capable of bringing about increased agricultural production. Increased production in turn was seen as the overriding objective and criterion of success of agricultural development. (E. B. Rice

---

[15]Arthur T. Mosher, *To Create a Modern Agriculture: Organization and Planning* (New York: Agricultural Development Council, Inc., 1971), p. 128.

ascribes essentially the foregoing narrow views to the U.S.-inspired "extensionist school" in Latin America; other well-informed observers have made similar criticisms of extension services in Africa and Asia.[16])

These are demonstrably myopic views of the agricultural development process, whether applied to extension or to farmer training center programs. In fairness, however, three observations should be added: first, this narrow outlook by no means characterizes all people engaged in agricultural extension and training; second, this narrow view is often reinforced by the extensionists' unfortunate bureaucratic isolation from other types of agricultural support services; and third, many other types of agricultural specialists are, in their own way, equally narrow and unrealistic in their perceptions of agricultural development.

We found it encouraging, however, that a strong intellectual tide is now running toward a broader, more integrated view and approach to agricultural development. This outlook is being given encouragement by the FAO, the World Bank, a number of bilateral agencies, and a growing number of individual observers and writers, particularly agricultural economists who have transcended the conventional confines of their discipline. It is also finding increasing expression in agricultural projects such as CADU, Lilongwe, PACCA and Puebla. (See Chapter 7.)

Another widespread characteristic of extension and farmer training programs, one found in some highly integrated projects as well, is an authoritarian attitude and stance of the sort that traditional teachers have taken toward their pupils—the "father knows best" and "you listen to me" attitude. It reflects the expert's view of the farmer—especially the small traditional farmer—as a simple ignorant fellow who does not know his own best interests and has to be treated as a child.

In contrast, most self-help community development-type programs start with the premise that rural people are just as intelligent as urban people, even if they are less "educated," and are basically just as capable of analyzing their own needs and solving their own problems as anyone else, if given the chance to do so and some encouragement.

As must be evident by now, our own views on the foregoing matters are that: (1) only a broad conception of the objectives and criteria of agricultural development is consistent with reality, and with the democratic and humanitarian goals and values espoused by the Member States of the United Nations; (2) only through the close integration of educational efforts with other factors of development can agricultural development be most effectively accelerated; (3) only by moving away as soon as possible from the "father knows best" approach and bending every effort to involve rural people in articulating their own needs and running their own affairs is there any hope of unleashing the massive human energies required to bring about broad-scale rural development. Educators, whose business is people, should be in the vanguard of this movement.

---

[16]See U.S. Agency for International Development, *Extension in the Andes. An Evaluation of Official U.S. Assistance to Agricultural Extension Services in Central and South America*. Prepared by E. B. Rice. AID Evaluation Paper, no. 3 (Washington, D.C., April 1971); also D. G. R. Belshaw, "Planning the 'Improvement Approach': Agricultural Extension and Research" (paper delivered at the Third East African Agricultural Economics Conference at the University College, Dar es Salaam, April 1967).

Objectives, Priorities, and Target Groups

Agricultural extension services vary greatly in the clarity of their objectives and priorities, though they are strikingly similar in the choice of target audiences to concentrate upon.

Those with the clearest picture of their objectives, priorities and daily tasks are generally extension agents associated with well-managed integrated projects such as CADU, Lilongwe, and (ealier) the Gezira scheme. This is because they are operating within a clearly defined framework from which their objectives and tasks can be readily derived.

Extension workers with the least clear notion of what they should be doing from day to day, how they should allot their time and to whom they should given first attention are generally those associated with autonomous extension services that are off on their own, without a local development plan to guide them and with no collaboration with complementary agricultural support services.

In both situations, however, there is a common tendency on the part of individual extension workers and the whole extension system to concentrate on the larger and more progressive farmers, who can expand production most quickly (if conditions are favorable). This is part of a broader syndrome of concentrating on those activities and audiences that will produce a good statistical record with which to impress the supervisor at the next level or to convince national policy and budget authorities that the extension service is performing well and merits more support.

These are understandable forms of behavior, but they often conflict with the broader long-run interests of rural development as well as with proclaimed egalitarian objectives. Production increases brought about by means that exacerbate rural unemployment and socioeconomic disparities may temporarily win plaudits but yield a bitter harvest of "second generation" problems that obstruct and undermine the whole rural development process. There are numerous instances, for example, where premature introduction of sophisticated labor-saving farm equipment has compounded rural unemployment problems. The social and political difficultires left in the wake of India's Green Revolution illustrate the point.

To direct extension efforts to the larger, more sophisticated farmers may well prove a wasteful strategy as well as a misguided one. The more sophisticated farmers hardly require the help or prodding of an extension agent to adopt an attractive new technology (such as new high-yielding seeds), accompanied by incentives and other favorable conditions. It would be more to the point to focus extension efforts on the less affluent and less sophisticated farmers who really do need help.

Concentrating on activities that can be measured statistically can result in a poor allocation of effort. For example, hasty "windshield visits" to fifty farmers might look statistically good in a weekly activity report, but helping ten farmers make better farm plans and become better farm managers, though a less measurable activity, would contribute much more to local development.

We see no solution to this problem of putting the production of statistics ahead of the production of real progress, except by ingenious changes in the pattern of bureaucratic incentives. If extension workers can earn equal merit by concentrating on the most productive activities, they would undoubtedly prefer this course.

As for clarifying the prime objectives and priority activities for farmer education efforts in any given situation, the only real answer lies in developing well-conceived local agricultural development plans that will provide farmer extension and training services with a clear road map to follow. Short of this, these services—right down to the last local agent—have no choice but to improvise as best they can, often with little result.

Another important issue concerns the differentiation of extension messages and techniques to fit the varying circumstances of different areas and different subgroups of farmers even in the same area. The SATEC (later the SODEVA) project in Senegal is one of the few cases we encountered where differential programs were designed for more progressive and less progressive farmers (though here again the more progressive farmers got the most intensive treatment). Most extension services, it appears, make no real program distrinctions for different clients; they tend to offer the same standard messages to all farmers and all areas, which is like offering the same size and color of suit to people of very different sizes and tasts.

Neglect of Women Farmers

Before leaving the question of target groups, it is important to stress the serious neglect of the rural female audience by agricultural extension services. True, many services include, as a sort of sideshow, "women's programs" focused on home economics and other household affairs. These efforts, however, overlook the major role women play in many rural societies in agricultural production, marketing and farm management. (See discussion of this point in Chapter 2.) Agriculture is a man's *and* woman's world in these societies, but agricultural extension is almost exclusively a man's world.

Correcting this unwholesome discrimination presents delicate and difficult problems, deeply rooted in the traditional sex roles and attitudes of these societies.[17] In many situations the solution would require women agricultural (*not* home economics) extension agents to help rural women increase their agricultural productivity and the quality of thier produce. It would probably also require special research attention, since in many places (in much of Africa, for example) women grow the family consumption crops while the men, in different fields, grow the commercial crops. In all events, this great lacuna in extension programs urgently needs serious attention, not merely good words and token actions.

Efficient Use of Resources

All that has just been said about clarity of objectives and priorities, choice of audiences and differential programs for different audiences has a major bearing on the efficiency and effectiveness of extension services. But there are additional factors that influence efficiency, relating especially to how extension agents spend their time.

One major cause of inefficiency is loading extension workers with extraneous tasks—clerical office work, record-keeping, collecting savings, gather-

---

[17]See Ester Boserup, *Women's Role in Economic Development* (New York: St. Martin's Press; London: George Allen and Unwin, 1970), especially footnote on p. 222; also J. E. Smithells, *Agricultural Extension Work Among Rural Women* (Reading, England: University of Reading, Agricultural Extension and Rural Development Centre, March 1972).

ing census data, etc.—which divert them from their central mission of assisting farmers. The Village Level Workers (VLWs) in India have a great miscellany of such duties. Officially, they are supposed to devote 90 percent of their time to agricultural extension, but actually they give only 50 to 60 percent because of the pressure of other tasks.[18] In the Republic of Korea, Office of Rural Development's (ORD) guidance workers, who are administratively responsible in part to county-level government officials, complain of being saddled with office chores having little or nothing to do with their agricultural duties. The same problem exists in many countries, the extension worker is all too often treated as a handy general chore boy.

Another factor that keeps extension workers from their priority duties is the lack of available transport—often a serious false economy. An extension worker in an area of widely dispersed farms can spend half or more of his time just getting from one farm to the next, by foot or bicycle; he may never get to the more distant ones. This is hardly a good use of his professional skills.

One of the most important issues of efficiency concerns the ratio of extension agents to farmers—a subject of much simplistic thinking. We will defer our discussion of this ratio however, to Chapter 11, in which we consider costs and benefits.

Toward Improving Dissemination

The discussion of the last several pages highlights the following specific ways in which the dissemination function could be strengthened and made more productive:

1. by broadening the training of extension personnel and broadening their perceptions of development, their recognition of the need to integrate education with other development factors, and the scope of farmer knowledge needs with which they should be concerned;

2. by replacing an authoritarian approach to farmers, where it exists, by a new emphasis on community self-analysis, self-help and self-determination;

3. by moving toward coherent development planning, area by area, and a much more integrated approach by all agricultural support services (making the objectives and priorities of extension and farmer training programs much clearer);

4. by giving much greater emphasis to helping subsistence farmers first to become better subsistence producers and then to begin the transition to successful commercial production;

5. by giving much greater emphasis to helping women become better farmers and farm managers in all those rural societies where women play a major role in agriculture;

6. by increasing the professional status and efficient use of local extension workers, in part by relieving them of nonprofessional chores and by increasing their mobility, hence the time they can spend productively with clients.

---

[18]Dorris D. Brown, *Agricultural Devleopment in India;s Districts* (Cambridge, Mass.: Harvard University Press, 1971.

Other steps required to improve the coverage, efficiency and productivity of agricultural knowledge-dissemination services are dealt with in later chapters.

Staff Development and Renewal

One of the most fundamental needs for improving farmer education programs concerns the initial education and the later in-service training of staff members. To function effectively, agricultural education systems must have a wide variety of well-trained, specialized manpower, with appropriate preparation at the secondary and tertiary level followed by continuous inservice training so that they can keep pace with new developments and grow on the job. The largest and in some ways most crucial category in such manpower, and generally the most neglected, is the local-level extension worker.

The staff development structure of most agriculture education systems includes a combination of formal educational institutions—agricultural vocational schools, colleges and universities—and an assortment of nonformal staff training centers.

Ideally, this whole staff development structure would be planned and operated as a coherent whole, providing a clear division of labor and mutual reinforcement among its parts. Research activities would be carefully interlaced with the staff development process at all point to ensure the quality and relevance of its content. The planning and periodic replanning of the whole structure would be based on as clear a projection as possible of the system's specialized manpower requirements for at least several years ahead (plus the manpower needs of other parts of the agricultural sector which some of the same institutions, especially the formal ones, are expected to fill).

The reality is a far cry from this ideal vision of how staff development should work. For example, we know of no country that has taken a unified view of the staff development structure of its agricultural knowledge system, or that has taken a comprehensive view and made projections of the system's specialized manpower requirements. We found, to the contrary, a marked fragmentation of efforts throughout the staff development structure, each element going its own way, judging its own performance and needs by its own parochial criteria, and scrambling with companion elements for a bigger share of available resources. Moreover, this fragmentation results from an approach that has prevailed not only in the developing countries but among and even within the various external assistance agencies that have sought to help them.

Formal Agricultural Training

The agricultural colleges and universities at the pinnacle of the structure are by far its most costly units and undoubtedly in many instances its least efficient and productive units. Evidence from all regions of the developing world produces a well-worn list of standard shortcomings of most of these institutions:[19] (1) the low quality and excessively academic character of their instruction and the lack of field practice; (2) their lack of contact with rural life and the everyday needs and problems of farmers; (3) the paucity of faculty and student

---

[19]See *Report: The World Conference on Agricultural Education and Training,* a symposium sponsored by ILO, Unesco, and FAO, Copenhagen, Denmark, July 17—August 8, 1970, Vol. II.

research, and the frequent irrelevance of such research as there is; (4) the neglect or total exclusion of agricultural economics, rural sociology and other social sciences in the curriculum and faculty; (5) their lack of attention to the needs of the extension services; (6) their heavy reliance on textbooks based on research and experience in greatly dissimilar foreign countries; (7) the lack of refresher courses for personnel already in the agricultural services; (8) the lack of real motivation in most of their students for careers in agriculture and rural areas, which is reflected in the high proportion of their graduates who escape immediately to nonagricultural employment.

A number of exceptions—or at least partial exceptions—come to mind, such as India's new agricultural universities and the agricultural colleges at Los Banos in the Philippines, at Makerere University in Uganda, and at Chapingo in Mexico. These and others like them are the pace-setters that have enjoyed stronger support and inspired leadership.

The seventeen agricultural colleges in the Republic of Korea, referred to in ICED's case study of ORD, can be presumed to be better off on the average than those in less economically advanced countries. But with the notable exception of the Seoul National University's Agricultural College at Suwon (much the strongest of the group), they manifest practically all of the shortcomings listed above. None of them, at the time of the ICED study, offered training in extension or was engaged in extension. These institutions were remote from farmers and rural life, and the abstract character of their instruction showed it.

These colleges have admitted few, if any, students from agricultural high schools; the highly acedemic screen they use in selecting students yields a harvest largely of applicants from urban academic secondary schools for whom agricultural education is likely to be a second or third choice. It is hardly surprising, therefore, that so few graduates choose agricultural careers: a Ministry of Education survey of 2,600 of their 1969 graduates revealed that only 300 had taken employment anywhere in the agricultural sector.

The Republic of Korea is somewhat atypical in that it has had relatively low unemployment in recent years and a booming modern urban economy that has been siphoning educated young people from rural areas. But from the spotty evidence available it appears that a high rate of abandonment of agriculture by graduates of agricultural secondary schools and colleges is a common phenomenon in most developing countries. Indonesia offers an exception; practically all agricultural college graduates there, we were told, are currently entering the agricultural extension service—and upgrading its quality. But these graduates do not have as good employment alernatives as the Korean ones.

Agricultural secondary schools—where they exist—are in the worst plight of all. They are often the only option for rural young people seeking a secondary education. Typically, these schools are not clear about what their purpose is, where they fit into the agricultural system and what they are preparing their students for. Their graduates are not wanted by the colleges, who consider them academically inferior, and they are often not qualified for middle-level technician posts in government agricultural services. In truth, they are usually unqualified for almost any position demanding reasonably high standards. These students have not been well taught, especially in the technical aspects of agriculture, because of the great difficulty these schools have in finding competent teachers and because their learning has taken place mostly in classrooms, with little if any agricultural practice.[20]

Preservice and In-service Training

Special preservice orientation and training for new recruits of extension services (particularly for those with only a secondary education) are typically provided in training centers run by a ministry of agriculture. It is also common, at least in principle, to provide for periodic refresher training of extension personnel. In exceptional cases there is advanced training for the best performers to qualify them for a higher grade and post.

There is strong reason to believe that frequent and good in-service training is a primary key to developing and maintaining a high level of competence and effectiveness in any extension program, regardless of what previous formal education its personnel have had. Arthur Mosher tells of an extension program at the Allahabad Agricultural Institute in India that recruited a mixed batch of young extension agents. Some had completed college, others high school only, and a third group had attended practical agricultural schools. All were given ten days of induction training, then sent out on the job and thereafter brought back for two days of in-service training every two weeks (later every three weeks). "By the third year...," Mosher reports, "there was no difference in the level of performance among the three groups . . . the in-service training had made up for what differences there were at the beginning."[21]

Other evidence confirms that investments in well-conceived in-service training programs pay high dividends. In-service training is doubly important in any situation where the technology and structure of agriculture is changing rapidly.

Yet for various reasons, judging from our evidence in several countries, in-service training for extension personnel is seriously neglected. When ORD's budget got tight, the length and frequency of in-service staff training programs were slashed. India's 60,000-odd Village Level Workers were originally supposed to get two months of refresher training every three years (which seems hardly too much), but in practice today they typically get this training about every six years. The VLWs were never really trained for agricultural extension originally, and they were not retrained for it after being converted to this role in the 1960s. Many now working in Green Revolution districts have had no refresher training in agriculture since the Green Revolution got started, yet they are supposed to be agents for spreading it.

The training officer of the Lilongwe Project in Malawi complained in a report that several of the project's production-minded senior officials often refused to release field workers for moderate amounts of inservice training even through, in his view, some field workers could do damage in the field without it.

---

[20]The Republic of Korea has 115 such three-year agricultural schools (grades 1-12). Total enrollments have stabilized at about 40,000 and the annual output of graduates is approximately 10,000. We could find little evidence of what had become of their graduates, except for a sample tracer study in 1968 (for one of the relatively stronger schools) which revealed that only 25 percent of recent graduates were engaged in any sort of agricultural work, and some of these were believed to be biding time on the family farm until a city job turned up.

[21]Arthur T. Mosher, Getting Agriculture Moving: Essentials for Development and Modernization (New York: Paaeger, 1966), p. 138.

We can only speculate about the reasons for such neglect of in-service training. With so few extension workers to go around, supervisors may be reluctant to pull them off the job, even for a short period. Another reason no doubt is that many in-service training programs have been weak and irrelevant: they have been too abstract, too detached from the realities of the circumstances in which extension agents work, and not sufficiently addressed to their real learning needs (a complaint heard from VLWs in India). A third likely reason is that many production-minded agricultural specialists do not really believe in the importance of training—other than formal training in colleges and universities. To them it is a waste to assign a talented and experienced agricultural officer (such as IRRI's trainees in the rice production course) to the training of others, and a waste to release the others from their daily tasks "just to hear some lectures."

Such reactions point up another problem; that in-service training has often been thought of, quite unnecessarily, as the complete withdrawal of the staff from the field for the duration of the course. Systematic efforts have rarely been made to reach extension agents with professional and technical advice and information in the field through regular correspondence, bulletins, radio broadcasts and other media. Yet such efforts would reinforce institution-based in-service training courses and partially compensate for the too infrequent and too short in-service courses.

Conclusions on Staff Development Structures

The main conclusions we draw from this general review of the staff development structures of agricultural knowledge systems are these:

1. Most *agricultural colleges* are serving their national agricultural knowledge system poorly and are yielding a low return on the relatively large resources invested in them. Some countries, such as the Republic of Korea, would undoubtedly be better served if they put the same resources into fewer but much better agricultural colleges, closely tied to the real needs of rural areas and to the personnel and research needs of all other components of the agricultural knowledge system and sector as a whole.

The long-run aim, we suggest, should be to develop one or more *rural universities* (depending on the size of the country) that would address their research and instructional programs to the gamut of rural development needs, not simply agriculture. Such universities would open much wider opportunities for able and motivated rural young people—girls as well as boys—to develop their potentialities for a wide variety of leadership roles in rural development.

2. The appropriateness of *agricultural vocational secondary schools* for developing countries needs to be critically reexamined. It is not at all clear that in their present form they are relevant or viable institutions. Possibly what is needed is a fresh conception of a rural secondary education, one that fits the needs, resources and life styles of rural societies and that is not simply a poor substitute for a traditional urban academic high school or misplaced imported mode.

3. Major efforts should be directed at strengthening *in-service training* for the career development of all who are engaged in educating and advising farmers and their families. In a later chapter we suggest the

possibility of multipurpose training centers that would serve the staff development needs not only 'of agricultural extension services but of all other rural services. Short of this, however, existing arrangements for the in-service training of agricultural extension officers should be overhauled and such officers should be released more frequently to receive pertinent refresher training from well-qualified instructors. Under-investment in such training impairs the productivity of all other investments in the system. New ways should be found to keep rural service personnel up-to-date and growing intellectually, for example, by using well-programmed radio-correspondence courses.

4. All staff development components of the system—colleges and universities, agricultural schools and inservice training programs—should be brought into close relationship with one another, with the research process, and above all with the rural communities they exist to serve.

Management of the System

We come finally to the fifth key function, which is in our judgment the vital heart of the matter and the place where corrective action is required first if all other efforts to improve agricultural education and research are to be the right actions and fully effective.

What we have been referring to in this chapter as agricultural knowledge systems were in fact never planned as systems nor do they behave today as systems. The various functional components examined in this chapter have a great propensity to go their own separate ways and not to act as responsible members of a system. The information flows, evaluative mechanisms and provisions for coordination that any well-functioning system requires are simply not there. As a consequence, the resources invested in these unsystematized components—inadequate as these resources have generally been—have yielded far poorer results than would have been possible and is still possible if only these systems would behave as systems.

There is no mystery about how and why all this happened. It was not primarily for lack of resources or lack of bureaucratic harmony. Fundamentally, it was for lack of an idea, lack of a unifying intellectual concept larger than the specialized concepts on which each and every one of the components was founded—an all-encompassing vision of what the basic social mission of agricultural education and research should be and of what different elements, in conjunction with one another, would be required in order to accomplish that mission.

It is true, of course, that bureaucratic divisions of responsibility for various elements of the system have exacerbated the problem. In the Republic of Korea, for example, the Ministry of Education is responsible for agricultural secondary schools and colleges, the Ministry of Agriculture (through ORD) is responsible for nonformal programs of in-service staff training, and various agencies under both ministries have a hand in research. Meanwhile, still other government organizations are responsible for for assorted complementary rural development factors and services (farmer credit, land use, irrigation, marketing, etc.) with which the agricultural knowledge system must be effectively coordinated at all levels if agricultural and rural development is to proceed efficiently.

The problem has been furthur compounded by divisions of responsibility among external agencies that assist individual countries in the matters. A ministry of education seeking help on agricultural secondary schools or colleges, or on rural social sciences, might well get in touch with various subdivisions of Unesco. But the ministry of agriculture in the same government, wanting to improve the extension service or agricultural research, would call on at least two different branches of FAO for help. Conceivably, four or five different types of specialists would be separately dispatched from these agencies to render advice, and each would examine the situation through the narrow lens of his particular specialty. One can even imagine four or five separate specialists arriving by chance on the same plane to work independently on different pieces of the agricultural knowledge system, and never crossing paths again until they meet once more at the airport on departure. This may seem a ridiculous illustration, but in retrospect it is no more so than the piecemeal approach by which ministries and external agencies—multilateral and bilateral—have pursued the building of agricultural knowledge systems in the past

Our preliminary conclusions on this matter of management are that the piecemeal approach to repairing and strengthening separate components of agricultural education and research should be promptly abandoned and a broader systems approach adopted in its place—by national governments and external agencies alike. Fortunately, the need for this more coherent approach has come to be recognized by a growing number of leaders in these governments and agencies.

Recommended System-wide Review

We suggest that each developing country—with or without outside help as it sees fit—undertake a comprehensive and dispassionate appraisal of its agricultural knowledge system. This effort should be led by one or more broad-gauged senior analysts who have no axe to grind either for or against any particular component, and should involve the participation and close cooperation of all interested government organizations.

Many of the specific questions to be answered in such a review have already been identified in this chapter. Their relative importance and urgency would be different in different situations. But a special concern in all situations should be how the system works at the delivery end and what difference it makes in the lives of the majority of the rural people. It would be necessary, especially where large numbers of subsistence farm families are involved, to look beyond agricultural education, narrowly defined, at the educational aspects of farm-related and nonfarm economic activities and at related activities affecting the general welfare of rural families.

Such a general review, we believe, could result in identifying a series of important steps that could be taken at various points within the system—and in the system's relationship with other elements of agricultural development—which could substantially improve its overall performance and productivity. These steps, once identified, would constitute a rational plan of action and an attractive basis for seeking such external assistance as might be needed.

One of the important outcomes of such a system-wide appraisal could be the establishment of more permanent arrangements to provide for continuing consultation among those resposible for the different components of the system, for regularized information flows and monitoring and evaluation services—all of which are essential to steady improvement of the system's overall efficiency and productivity.'

How External Agencies Can Help

We are confident that external assistance agencies, especially in cooperation with one another, could do much to encourage and assist interested countries to carry out the sort of system-wide appraisal suggested above, to implement some of the import action steps identified by the appraisal, and to establish the new habits and mechanisms requisite to a systems approach that would displace the old piecemeal approach.

External agencies could exert strong leadership toward a more unified and systematic approach to strengthening agricultural knowledge systems by abandoning the piecemeal approach themselves. Specifically, we suggest that hereafter such agencies give heavy preference to country proposals that have emerged from—and can be justified by—a system-wide review of the type suggested above, as distinct from ad hoc proposals formulated independently by a particular ministry, institution or program. Given the demonstrated disadvantages of the piecemeal approach and the scarcity of resources available for international assistance, it will become increasingly difficult for the trustees of such resources to justify deploying them in a fragmented manner.

To move from a piecemeal to a more unified approach, however, the various specialized assistance agencies will have to concert their efforts far more frequently and effectively than in the past, and they will have to destroy the remaining vestiges of unwholesome bureaucratic rivalries and myopic perspectives. Fortunately, the UN specialized agencies—in particular Unesco, FAO and ILO—have lately taken significant steps in this direction. But all would agree, we feel sure, that these steps, as promising and welcome as they are, constitute but a modest beginning. Far more remains to be done by way of joint planning and direct operational collaboration, not only at the headquarters level but, more importantly, at the field level where the action takes place and really matters.

9: A CRITIQUE OF TRAINING PROGRAMS FOR NONFARM RURAL SKILLS

Interest in skill training programs for off-farm employment in rural areas is mounting rapidly today as governments grow increasingly concerned with the urgent problems stemming from population pressures on limited land, rural unemployment and rural-to-urban migration. Though governments and external assistance agencies have long recognized the need to provide rural people (especially young people[1]) with occupational skills and to broaden the skills of rural artisans, craftsmen and small entrepreneurs,[2] such programs in the past generally received a low priority.

Clearly, even in relatively static rural areas many occupational skills are needed besides those used in farming, animal husbandry, fishing and forestry. And, as we have noted earlier, these other skills are needed by farmers as well as by nonfarm artisans, craftsmen and small entrepreneurs. Though for analytical purposes we shall treat nonfarm skill training programs in this chapter as a category separate from that of farmer education, in reality it is hard to draw such clear divisions.

We should also note at the outset that as rural development gets under way in any particular area—usually spurred in the first instance by a forward thrust in agriculture—demand increases for a wide range of goods and services and for new and more diverse kinds of skills. Thus, just as the farmers' requirements change and multiply in those areas undergoing dynamic changes in agriculture, so too do the requirements of whole rural communities when development achieves a momentum. These demands arise both in the villages and in nearby market centers and intermediate "hub-towns."

The rural hub-towns can in fact become critical growth-points in the widening process of rural development, given such favorable circumstances as well-conceived public policies and area development plans, essential economic and administrative infrastructures, and the necessary human skills and initiative. As connecting points between the villages and the metropolitan centers and outside world, they can become centers of commerce, manufacture, administration and culture.[3]

---

[1]For a survey of such youth programs see ICED's Report for UNICEF, *New Paths to Learning For Rural Children and Youth* (Essex, Conn., September 1973), Chapter IV, "The Present Pattern of Nonformal Education."

[2]John C. deWilde, *The Development of African Private Enterprise*, IBRD Report No. AW-31 (Washington, D.C., December 10, 1971).

[3]See Joseph Klatzmann, B.Y. Ilan, and Yair Levi, eds., *The Role of Group Action in the Industrialization of Rural Areas* (New York: Praeger, 1971), pp. 97-98 for a discussion of the historical and sociological features of rural market towns, and in the same volume, B.F. Hoselitz, "Types of and Location of Industries in Developing Countries," which discusses the rural labor force and the need for industry in this area. See also Eugene Staley and Richard Morse, *Modern Small Industry for Developing Countries* (New York: McGraw-Hill, 1965) for a discussion of the costs and benefits of decentralization policy; See E.A.J. Johnson, *The Organization of Space in Developing Countries* (Cambridge, Mass.: Harvard University Press, 1970), Chapters 6 and 7, and Raanan

The smaller villages also feel the effects of rising income flows and new demands. And these will stimulate the strengthening and diversification of smaller-scale nonfarm economic activities in villages themselves.

A strategy of rural development based on area planning and growth centers would include direct and indirect measures for the development of rural industry, ranging from the building of infrastructures to provisions for training and credit. It would recognize the interdependence of agricultural and off-farm economic activities within the framework of an all-round development plan for the area. It would also help gradually to eliminate the existing dualism between urban and rural economies and would place rural development efforts within the context of a process of unified national development.

Within this broader perspective, the present chapter seeks to extract useful lessons from the case studies on ways to generate the many kinds of nonfarm skills required to support and accelerate this dynamic process of rural development. Before examining the specific types of programs covered in the cases, however, we should point to some of the overall problems in the design of skill training programs, and particularly to several major differences between rural and urban situations that bear on their design.

A major cause of weaknesses in many rural skill training programs, we found, was that their architects had given too little attention to what kinds of skills were really needed in the rural situation, to the local social and economic context of the proposed new training project, to the special characteristics of the intended trainees, and to the educational processes already in being. In short, they focused too narrowly on the internal design and mechanics of their new training activity and not enough on the relationships it must have to other factors in the local environment in order to be most effective.[4]

Urban-Rural Differences

First, as noted earlier, the skills needed for survival and for earning a living in villages and rural towns often differ considerably from those needed in metropolitan areas, even when they wear the same label. The handyman village artisan (generally a part-time farmer as well) requires a variety of skills and much ingenuity in applying them. The urban industrial worker's skills are generally more specialized and sophisticated (as are the tools and equipment he works with); they are also narrower, more routine and often less readily transferable to other tasks. Too often rural training programs have followed the

---

Weitz, "Regional Planning as a Tool for Rural Development in Developing Countries," *Rural Development in a Changing World,* edited by R. Weitz (Cambridge, Mass.: MIT Press, 1971) for discussions of the importance of location and regional base planning for rural development; see Peter Kilby, "Hunting the Heffalump," in *Entrepreneurship and Economic Development,* edited by P. Kilby (New York: The Free Press, 1971), pp. 1-40, for a discussion of entrepreneurial development.

[4]Eugene Staley, in identifying procedures that national governments should follow in planning occupational education, states, ". . . the analysis of needs on which to build programs of occupational education and training must not be limited to national or even regional aggregates and averages. Just as important, even more important when it comes to planning specific programs, is analysis of needs in each *local* area to be served." *Planning Occupational Education and Training for Development* (New Delhi: Orient Longmans Ltd., 1970), p. 21.

urban pattern of concentrating on a single type of skill, defined in urban terms, when a cluster of skills would have been more appropriate.[5]

Second, rural employment structures and the manner in which they evolve as development takes place differ considerably from typical urban employment structures. Hence it is misleading to reason from the latter to the former in predicting the future pattern of skill demands in a particular rural area. It is also incorrect to assume that the skill demands are generally the same in all rural areas; actually they differ considerably with local tastes and conditions and with the stage of local development.[6] The only safe rule is to examine each local skill market and its future prospects before plunging into a new training program, and to keep a close eye on the market in order to adapt the training offerings to changing conditions.

Third, rural economies, more so than metropolitan ones, are characterized by large numbers of small enterprises in which technical and managerial roles are performed by the same small entrepreneur. This needs to be kept in mind in designing the content of rural skill training programs because many of the trainees may become—later if not immediately—self-employed artisans or employers of others. And in these capacities they will require not only improved technical skills but managerial skills as well. Moreover, given the fact that rural infrastructures for credit, procurement of materials and equipment, marketing, and so forth are much less developed than in major urban centers, the small rural artisan-entrepreneur may also need special support on some of these fronts if the investment made in training him is to pay off. Technical training programs that ignore these complementary needs and narrowly "stick to their own last" may easily end with a low benefit/cost ratio.

Fourth, there are much lower rates of school participation and completion in rural areas than in major urban centers. Since literacy is an important tool for applying many trade skills effectively and is indispensable for efficiently managing most enterprises, even small ones, rural training programs must be prepared to remedy serious deficiencies in basic education where necessary. We found an almost universal reluctance among managers of rural skill training programs to take on this extra educational burden. But in bypassing this issue they con-

---

[5]The planners of the Rural Artisan Training Centres in Senegal, having this point in mind, provided for three broad "streams"—for village-level metal workers, wood-workers and construction workers. Eventually, however, they found it desirable to give trainees in each stream at least some exposure to the skills of the other two. Pierre Furter and Sven Grabe, *Senegal: Rural Vocational Training Centres,* ICED Case Study No. 8, unpublished. In contrast, the courses of the Mobile Trade Training Schools in Thailand provide specialized training in a specific skill rather than in a combination of skills that a rural artisan may need.

Staley asserts that ". . . a basic aim of OET [occupational education and training] policy should be to produce reasonably *versatile* persons, able to learn new skills quickly and to transfer, with some retraining, from one specific job to another over a fairly broad range of jobs. This will minimize the losses to individuals and to society from wrong anticipations of future needs and will facilitate quick adjustment to the occupational changes sure to come with changing technology," *Planning Occupational Education,* p. 28.

[6]Social and Cultural factors also influence which occupational skills are learned and by which groups in rural communities. In parts of Thailand, for example, carpentry is traditionally practiced, we have been told, by persons of Chinese ethnic origin, and the skills are passed on from father to son in the family. Carpentry courses, therefore, have not been offered in most Mobile Trade Training Schools. Similarly, the caste system in India is in effect an occupation-specialization system, though its rigidities have been breaking down in recent years.

fine their services to the lucky minority who managed to get some effective schooling earlier, and impose a further disadvantage on those who did not.

Fifth, modernized urban economies have a greater capacity for absorbing all sorts of skills than do less developed rural economies. They also have a greater capacity for nurturing new skills, for converting unneeded ones to needed ones, and for developing more advanced skills on the job (especially in modern industries and other larger enterprises). Thus, to teach young rural people specialized skills for which there is no ready market in their own area results either in educational waste and personal frustration, or in sending them off to the city in search of a job.

Importance of Indigenous Training Systems

Finally, occupational skills in rural areas—even relatively "modern" areas— are largely acquired *informally* (e.g., from parents) and through an almost invisible but often highly efficient *network of nonformal indigenous training systems*. Indigenous training networks, such as traditional apprenticeship systems (not to be confused with European-type industrial apprenticeship schemes), are also important in urban centers, but mainly among the smaller craft and artisan enterprises. Archibald Callaway estimated that in 1964 some two million skilled workers were being trained in Nigeria through recognized apprenticeships. Callaway noted that:

> The vast apprenticeship training system began as part of a wider education process in which the indigenous societies of Nigeria passed on their cultural heritage from one generation to the next. ... Learning a craft often began with personal service to the master. Young boys would become house servants to a close relative, who would feed and clothe them, and after some years of promising usefulness would then gradually be introduced to the craft of the guardian. Crafts varied according to the area, but included mat making, carving of doors and figures for shrines, building of houses, leatherwork, blacksmithing and goldsmithing, making masquerades, weaving, pottery making. ... This indigenous apprenticeship system is central to any explanation of the emergence and growth of Nigeria's private enterprise economy.[7]

These indigenous nonformal skill training systems are not limited only to traditional techniques and products; they have often shown a lively response to new products and technologies requiring new types of skills. An ILO survey in three rural towns in Nigeria, which included interviews with 535 small businessmen employing a total of 811 apprentices, showed the highest average number of apprentices in firms engaged in motor-mechanics, metalwork, textiles and carpentry.[8]

In fact, the bulk of the supply of skilled manpower for meeting the overall technical skill requirements of industry, construction and service trades for the modernization of developing countries has been developed through in-

---

[7] Archibald Callaway, "Nigeria's Indigenous Education: The Apprentice System," *University of Ife Journal of African Studies*, I, No. 1 (July 1964), p. 63.

[8] "Apprenticeship in Nigeria—Traditional and New Trades," *CIRF Training for Progress*, VI, No. 1 (1967), pp. 17-18.

digenous training processes. Newer "modern" training programs in both urban and rural areas—mostly created within the past ten to fifteen years—have contributed only marginally to these purposes. Although the level and sophistication of the skills produced by some newer programs, and the broader educational base they often provide, have frequently been superior to much of the indigenous training, the numbers turned out by new programs have generally been small in comparison with the needs. And the costs—allowing for the inefficiencies and wastage—have often been so high as to be prohibitive on a greatly expanded scale.[9]

Logic would suggest that the first step toward trying to strengthen the skill-generating capacities of developing countries—above all in rural areas—should be to find out what indigenous processes are already there, and whether the best solution might not be to strengthen and reprogram them with more up-to-date content and improved skills rather than bypassing them in favor of new and more expensive models imported from industrialized countries. Indigenous training systems merit a great deal more study than they appear to have received and than we were able to give. But there is every reason to believe that a considerable step forward could be taken by increasing the systematic opportunities for training by enlarging support for these indigenous systems.

As we proceed now to examine a variety of training programs, it will be seen that these major differences between urban and rural situations have played an important role in the degree of success achieved by various programs, for those that took careful account of these differences had a greater chance for success.

Four Categories of Training Programs

At first glance, our case studies and other programs in this field gave the impression of a bewildering melange that defied any rational classification. On closer inspection, however, we found that for analytical purposes they could be usefully grouped—allowing for some inevitable overlap—into the following four main categories:[10]

1. *Programs to provide farm families with ancillary skills for home improvement and better farming, and for earning extra income through sideline activities.* These are illustrated by portions of the Office of Rural Development's (ORD) Rural Guidance Program in the Republic of Korea, by SENA's rural mobile training program, Promoción Profesional Popular Rural (PPP-R) in Colombia, and by Accion Cultural Popular's (ACPO) multimedia program for campesinos, also in Colombia.

2. *Programs to provide rural young people with employable skills for off-farm use.* Illustrative of this category are Thailand's Mobile Trade Training Schools (MTTS), Kenya's Village Polytechnic, the residential Diayagala Boys' Town School in Sri Lanka (Ceylon), Jamaica's Youth Camps, and a host of other occupationally oriented rural youth programs.[11]

---

[9]See International Labour Office, *Assessment of Pre-Vocational Training Projects Assisted by UNICEF and ILO* (E/ICEF/L. 1272 and E/ICEF/L. 1272/Add. 1), March 1969.

[10]The topics of staffing, costs and financing of these programs are treated in Chapters 11 and 12.

[11]The programs cited in Kenya, Sri Lanka and Jamaica are covered in ICED's case studies for UNICEF. Other pertinent examples can be found in James R. Sheffield and Victor P. Diejomaoh, *Non-Formal Education in African Development* (New York, N.Y.: African-American Institute, 1972).

3. *Programs to upgrade and broaden the skills of practicing artisans, craftsmen, and small entrepreneurs.* These are illustrated by the Rural Artisan Training Centers in Senegal, the Vocational Improvement Centres (VICs) in Nigeria, and a variety of more conventional training programs.

4. *Integrated training and support programs to promote small industry and other nonfarm rural enterprises.* The most extensive examples of this category are the programs in India, described briefly in Chapter 5. Many others exist, however, such as those in Africa described by deWilde.[12]

Ancillary Skills for Farm Families

Programs in this category are aimed essentially at improving the quality of rural family life and enabling farm families to earn extra income in their spare time. Judged by these objectives they are often worthwhile, even if they do not go to the heart of the rural employment and development problem.

Accion Cultural Popular in Colombia (ACPO), through its series of "campaigns," carried on through the coordinated use of its multimedia system and local volunteer agents, has built an impressive record of stimulating local self-help projects to improve family and community life. Many thousands of new houses have been built and home improvements made, flower and vegetable gardens planted, compost heaps started, piped water installed and latrines built, chicken coops and pigsties constructed, bridges erected, and so forth (see Table 6.1). ACPO's statistical claims for these projects seem well founded; the evidence is visible.[13]

The Office of Rural Development's (ORD) home and community improvement activities in the Republic of Korea (see Chapter 3) — conducted to a great extent through local clubs and volunteer leaders, and reinforced by specialized extension agents — have undoubtedly benefited many rural families. Of particular interest are ORD's special projects for increasing farm family incomes through off-season home manufacture of marketable products and the adoption of profitable agricultural sidelines. Participation has been high in the selected areas where these programs have operated, though to what extent the recommended practices have been adopted is unknown. Still, the basic idea is sound and worthy of serious consideration elsewhere.[14]

The main objective of SENA's rural mobile training program, Promoción Profesional Popular-Rural (PPP-R) (see Chapter 4) is to improve employment opportunities for the rural unemployed and underemployed and in so doing slow down rural-to-urban migration. But a number of its courses might be more accurately described as efforts to supplement the incomes and raise the living standards and quality of life of rural families basically wedded to the soil. This might apply, for example, to SENA's courses in first aid, home handicrafts, beekeeping, and raising rabbits and chickens as a sideline.

This rural program is still very young, in contrast to SENA's well-established urban industrial training program, and younger also than the ORD and ACPO programs discussed above, hence there is much less to go on in evaluating its

---

[12]deWilde, *The Development of African Private Enterprise.*

[13]See Stephen F. Brumberg, *Accion Cultural Popular: Mass Media in the Service of Colombian Rural Development,* ICED Case Study No. 1 (Essex, Conn., April 1972).

[14]See Manzoor Ahmed, *Farmer Education Program of the Office of Rural Development in the Republic of Korea,* ICED Case Study No. 5 (Essex, Conn., July 1972).

impact. (SENA itself is currently engaged in an extensive self-evaluation.) So far as the matters just discussed are concerned, its impact is probably not as great as ACPO's and ORD's: the PPP-R's roving rural instructors are often operating on their own, their courses unrelated to complementary rural services or local development plans, without reinforcement from mass media, local organizations, volunteer leaders, or other special support. Some of these problems will presumably be overcome in time.[15]

Many community development programs have also undertaken various activities to improve nonagricultural skills and to help generate off-farm employment. The Philippine Presidential Arm for Community Development (PACD), for example, by providing financial grants and technical advice and by helping to organize local groups for action, assisted *barrios* and individuals in *barrios* in such nonfarm economic activities as irrigation and related water control projects; construction and repair of community centers, schools, playgrounds, communal toilets, garbage disposals, compost pits; and also setting up cottage industries.[16]

There are no fixed formulas for programs to provide farm families with ancillary skills to improve their living conditions and win them extra income from sideline activities. Their target audiences are extremely wide and diverse, including in principle virtually all members of all rural families. The general methods and specific content of training in ancillary skills — as shown by the contrasting approaches to ACPO, ORD, SENA, and community development programs can be very diverse. Applying strict economic cost-benefit tests to such activities is virtually impossible. Moreover, some of the most important benefits often are not primarily economic in character — they are more social and political.

Equipping Rural Youth with Off-Farm Employable Skills

Confusing Diversity of Approaches

Providing technical training for young people in advance of actual employment has presented serious dilemmas for policymakers in developing countries. In no other sector of education did we encounter — wherever we went — such apparent confusion of objectives, contradictory approaches, duplication of effort, lack of coherent planning and coordination, and sometimes misplaced investment.[17]

---

[15]Stephen F. Brumberg, *Promoción Profesional Popular-Rural of SENA: A Mobile Skills Training Program for Rural Colombia,* ICED Case Study No. 2 (Essex, Conn., June 1972).

[16]International Labour Office, *Employment Problems and Policies in the Philippines* (Geneva, 1969), pp. 69-71.

[17]In Thailand, to take but one example, we found almost every imaginable type of technical training program, formal and nonformal, long-term and short-term, sponsored by more than a dozen different public and private agencies, with no sign of joint planning or coordination of effort. The Ministry of Education's Department of Vocational Education was the largest sponsor, with 121 vocational high schools (grades 11-13), 13 commercial and industrial schools (grades 11-13), 17 agricultural schools (grades 11-13); 11 technical schools (grades 11-13), the MTTS program and a short-term (5 months) polytechnical program, with aggregate enrollments exceeding 62,000 in 1967. A total of 359 private schools and centers were offering a vast variety of technical training courses ranging from one month to three years, with total 1967 enrollments of about 24,000. Numerous government ministries and agencies ran smaller programs relating to their particular specialties and clients. (See Manzoor Ahmed, *Mobile Trade Training Schools in Thailand,* ICED Case Study No. 6 (Essex, Conn., April 1972), pp. 72-76.

Among the main causes of this condition are the great variety of skills needed in modernizing societies, the numerous public and private agencies having interests and jurisdictional claims in the training field, the absence of any central mechanism for assessing overall skill needs and for planning actions to meet them, and not least of all, the competing doctrines, models, and advice of different external experts and specialized agencies that have worked with different domestic agencies. The situation has been further complicated by efforts to deemphasize highly academic schooling, especially at the secondary level, by introducing multipurpose schools combining academic and vocational streams and by creating single-purpose technical and vocational high schools within the formal education system.

Finally, this whole field has been heavily clouded by lingering popular prejudices against manual labor of any sort and by the skepticism and even hostility of many employers toward the training of their future workers outside their own businesses.

Record of Formal Vocational Programs

For the most part—allowing for exceptions—the formal education models have not provided a satisfactory solution. Their costs are too high to allow for more than a small fraction of young people to be served; they have had severe difficulties recruiting and holding good technical teachers in the face of competition from the private sector and other government agencies; the training they provide is often poorly adapted to market demands and to the practical needs of employers; their unchanging curriculums, methods, and equipment become increasingly ill-adapted to the dynamically changing requirements and working conditions of their environment; and frequently a high proportion of their graduates do not end up in jobs that effectively utilize their training. On the whole the record of formal vocational training at the secondary level bespeaks strong caution against an undiscriminating pursuit of this approach in the future, above all in rural areas.[18]

Record of Nonformal Programs

Various nonformal skill training programs for young people have been tried in most countries. Unconventional nonformal programs generally tend to be better adapted to realistic needs, have lower costs, and probably on average have better benefit/cost ratios than most formal training programs. Nevertheless they have important problems and limitations of their own, rooted often in organizational, administrative, and staffing difficulties.

For the most part these programs are small and raise serious questions of replicability on a large scale; many are restricted to young people who have completed primary school, thus leaving the great majority at a further disadvantage; sometimes the training they give (especially in rural areas) is not sufficiently linked to realistic job opportunities in the area and, like formal schools, they do not provide follow-up support to their trainees to help them apply their training and enlarge upon it.

---

[18]P.J. Foster, "The Vocational School Fallacy in Development Planning," in *Education and Economic Development*, ed. by C.A. Anderson and M.J. Bowman (Chicago: Aldine Publishing Co., 1964), pp. 142-166, and also in Unesco, *Readings in the Economics of Education* (Paris, 1968), pp. 614-633.

Potentialities of Nonformal Training Programs for Youth

In searching for better solutions to pre-employment training for rural young people, we examined a number of unconventional and innovative programs and found some useful leads.

The MTTS program in Thailand (see Chapter 6), with its part-time courses and low use of capital, seems a promising alternative to formal vocational schools in rural hub-towns. The Village Polytechnics in Kenya have much to commend them as a practical and flexible means of developing skills for local use, drawing on local talent and other local resources. The Jamaican Youth Camps—in their earlier incarnation—developed self-reliance and general competence in disadvantaged rural youth and equipped them with initial skills for successful entry into the working force. The Diyagala Boys' Town School in Sri Lanka—a largely self-supporting residential institution which combines general education and self-help with practical training in a diversity of rural skills— shows what extraordinary results are possible through unconventional means under dedicated and ingenious leadership. The multipurpose, multifaceted youth development program in Jombang District, Indonesia, is almost a textbook case of mobilizing local resources through local leadership and initiative to develop the knowledge and practical skills of boys and girls and to initiate them into the world of work with a positive sense of family and community responsibility.[19]

These and many other examples demonstrate the *potentialities* of nonformal approaches for equipping rural young people with usable occupational skills as they move toward full adulthood. These potentialities can be briefly summed up under three main points:

- Great flexibility in adapting to local needs, changing conditions and opportunities in the selection of what to teach and how to teach it and in combining learning with practical work.
- Freedom to adapt to the convenience of the trainees, for example, by scheduling part-time instruction that can be fitted to their workday and family obligations, and by devising limited learning units which trainees can master and accumulate at their own pace and convenience—dropping into and out of the learning process, then back in again, to suit their wishes and circumstances.
- Ability to harness local talents, facilities, and general support—and in the process generating a sense of community proprietorship and self-reliance—leading among other things to more economically viable training opportunities.

Causes of Low Effectiveness

Yet nonformal skill training programs for youth often fail to live up to their full potential. Three of the most important causes are: (1) *the inhibiting effects of traditionalism and uniformity,* (2) *failure to investigate sufficiently the needs and circumstances of the intended clientele,* and (3) *lack of follow-up support to trainees.*

---

[19]The Jamaican Youth Camps, the Diyagala Boys' Town Programme in Sri Lanka, and the multipurpose youth program in the Jombang district, Indonesia are the subjects of ICED case studies for UNICEF.

The deadening hand of traditionalism and uniformity is heaviest in nation-wide programs managed by a central bureaucracy, or where successful small pilot programs start to be replicated on a larger scale under the aegis of such a bureaucracy.

The MTTS program in Thailand, despite its evident virtues, seemed to us an unfortunate victim of such uniformity. An MTTS unit that moves into a new community selects the skills it will offer from a standardized national list and proceeds to teach each chosen skill in accordance with a standardized national syllabus. The duration of each course is uniform for each skill, regardless of differences in degree of difficulty or of what prior skills the individual trainees arrive with. Auto-repair, welding, hairdressing, electric wiring, tailoring and bar-bering get equal time. The most inhibiting constraint of all is that MTTS is sub-ject to the same Ministry of Education regulations on staff qualifications and reward structures that apply to formal technical schools. These regulations effectively bar the MTTS from using, for example, local master craftsmen as part-time instructors.

The Village Polytechnic in Kenya won international acclaim as a pragmatic, homegrown approach to helping rural young people acquire a diversity of skills they could use profitably in their own villages. The handful of early pilot models seemed so attractive that the government decided to expand the number through public subsidy and sought international funding for the pur-pose.[20] It remains to be seen, however, whether the vitality of the original idea can survive this official expansion. Some of the early admirers of the Village Polytechnic are deeply concerned that it will not. They fear—and believe they already see—an inexorable formalization of this highly flexible model for non-formal education.

There is no cause to believe that successful small-scale nonformal programs must *necessarily* become progressively formalized and standardized as they are expanded, but clearly there is always a strong risk of this happening. It is to be hoped that government bureaucracies, as well as international agencies, will learn how to nurture and enlarge programs such as the Village Polytechnic without stifling them in the process.

The second major inhibitor of success listed above—the failure of many nonformal training programs to relate to the realistic needs of their clients and environment—is a common ailment among all sorts of training programs, for-mal and nonformal, urban and rural. As we noted earlier, training experts, like other specialists, are prone to see their training activities in a narrow perspec-tive and to take it for granted that the training skills they propose to generate will become absorbed by the local economy.

An important flaw in the MTTS program and in a good number of other training programs was that no serious effort was undertaken to investigate the local skill market and its likely future needs before deciding what type of skill training to offer local youth. The full consequences of this blind approach are as yet unknown, but there is considerable circumstantial evidence that in the MTTS case it has resulted in underutilization of the training results and hence reduced benefits from the investment.

---

[20]See J. Anderson, *The Village Polytechnic Movement*, IDS/SRDP Evaluation Report No. 1 (Nairobi: Institute for Development Studies, University of Nairobi, August 1970), which discusses the development of the Village Polytechnic movement.

The most serious shortcoming of all is the third one mentioned earlier—the failure to conceive of a particular nonformal training program as but one in a series of steps required for the effective employment of rural young people.

In MTTS, for example, some of the trainees already had work experience and a part-time job. Their MTTS training might help them advance in that job, or it might help them find a better one. Others without a job presumably wanted to find one. Still others aspired to become self-employed, to set up their own small businesses if they could and eventually become employers. But MTTS had no regular provision for placing its trainees in appropriate jobs in the area, nor for offering them more advanced technical training later on as they needed it. There also appeared to be no provision—inside or outside MTTS—for rudimentary management training and counseling, help in getting credit, or for other necessary support services for those who wanted to become small entrepreneurs on their own (which, in a rural town or village, is a quite common goal for an able young person to have).

These various weaknesses, which are common to a great many skill training programs, are not fatal defects but rather promising points at which to improve them and thereby to boost their productivity. The managers of MTTS, we know, are already giving consideration to a number of such improvements.

Military Training for Civilian Use

In some developing countries the armed forces are instrumental in generating various kinds of employable skills and exerting an important modernizing influence for large numbers of young people, many of whom start out as illiterate recruits from rural areas. There are instances also where military services make important direct contributions to the improvement of civilian life in rural areas. It was not feasible for ICED to include any case studies of basic education and skill training programs conducted by military establishments in developing countries, but this is clearly an area that warrants further research. The medical education system and rural public health services run by the military in Mexico are reported to have made an outstanding contribution. The People's Liberation Army in the People's Republic of China is, of course, a unique example of large-scale and systematic use of the armed forces for civilian education, construction and other development activities throughout the country. The Education Corps in Iran offers the option to secondary school graduates to spend the period of their compulsory military service in teaching rural children and adults. In Peru, soldiers are trained in various occupational skills before mustering-out of the service to prepare them for their return to civilian life. Similar examples can be found in other countries, but it appears likely that the peacetime potentials of the military—so long as there has to be a military—for spreading useful civilian skills and services in rural areas are generally underestimated and inadequately utilized.[21]

Upgrading and Broadening the Skills of Artisans and Entrepreneurs

There are a large number of well-established and often quite successful programs for upgrading the skills of workers in modern industrial firms in urban areas. One thinks immediately, for example, of the industrial training programs

---

[21]See Hugh Hanning, *The Peaceful Uses of Military Forces* (New York: Praeger, 1967).

of SENA in Colombia,[22] INACAP in Chile,[23] and comparable semi-autonomous national training organizations in several other Latin American countries. Their effectiveness is partly explained by the close liaison they maintain with the employing firms whose workers they train, whose special levies support them and in whose plants they sometimes conduct their training.

Upgrading the skills of small-town workers, rural artisans and small entrepreneurs (often one and the same person), is a very different matter; it does not readily lend itself to the same training procedures, generally calls for greater versatility and follow-up, and often involves higher costs. Moreover, it is generally more difficult to secure the cooperation and participation of small employers and their employees.

Most of the shortcomings noted above regarding pre-employment skill training for rural youth apply as well to training programs for those already employed (or self-employed). Often the content is not well tailored to their needs, or the quality of instruction is poor, or the technical training is not supplemented by effective management training. In some instances, the training, however good, is not coupled with other essential support services required by small entrepreneurs, such as help in securing credit and raw materials and in marketing.

Full-Time versus Part-Time Training

The physical location and time schedule of training programs is a particularly critical matter in the case of employed persons. On the whole, full-time training programs for a period of several weeks or months, requiring a worker or entrepreneur to be absent from his place of work, have had great difficulty recruiting customers. This has been the case, for example, in India (see Chapter 5)[24] and in the Rural Artisan Training Centres in Senegal (see Chapter 5). Even to attract clients for part-time courses at the end of a day's work is not easy, especially before they are convinced that the benefits are worth the effort.

There are in these respects revealing contrasts between the Vocational Improvement Centres (VICs) in Nigeria (see Chapter 5)[25] and the rural training centers in Senegal. Their specific purposes, to be sure, are somewhat different: the VICs set out to upgrade the skills of technical workers in medium enterprises and government services in provincial towns and to strengthen small entrepreneurs, whereas Senegal's Rural Artisan Training Centres set out to create a village elite of self-employed young adult artisans who, it was hoped, would remain in their villages.

Most of the VICs have had little difficulty filling their part-time practical courses; in fact they have sometimes been heavily oversubscribed and many participants have enrolled in successive courses. The reasons for this appeal quite clearly are, first, that participants were not obliged to sustain heavy opportunity costs and risks in order to attend these evening and weekend courses and, second, that many found that the effort paid good dividends. In a

[22]See ILO, *Towards Full Employment: A Programme for Colombia,* Chapter 16, pp. 237-240.

[23]For a description and analysis of the activities of INACAP, see A-Agustin S., "Vocational Training in Chile," *International Labour Review,* XCV, No. 5 (May 1967), pp. 452-565.

[24]See also John C. deWilde, *Nonformal Education and the Development of Small Enterprise in India,* ICED Case Study No. 4 (Essex, Conn., January 1972).

[25]See also Clifford Gilpin and Sven Grabe, *Programs for Small Industry Entrepreneurs and Journeymen in Northern Nigeria,* ICED Case Study No. 7 (Essex, Conn., April 1972).

substantial proportion of cases this added training was rewarded by a grade promotion or by a firmer hold on the job they already held (particularly for those in government service).

By contrast, the young artisans-entrepreneurs in Senegal had to leave their businesses for about nine months—with all the risks and sacrifices entailed—in order to participate in the full-time residential program of one of the rural training centers. Many apparently considered it a poor gamble, and the facts later showed that they had a good point. A follow-up study revealed that many had not improved their economic situation as a result of the training, and quite a few testified that they had not been able to make great use of new skills they acquired.

A generally valid rule-of-thumb is: *the closer training is given to the point of actual employment and the more convenient it is made for the intended clients to attend, the better patronized and more effective it is likely to be.*[26]

Special Requirements of Entrepreneurs

Upgrading skills of small entrepreneurs, as distinct from those of hired employees, presents particularly complex problems. Typically, entrepreneurs need enrichment of both their technical skills and their management skills, but they are more likely to recognize the need for the former than the latter.[27] The experiences of programs in India and Nigeria show that luring small businessmen into courses for management improvement is often difficult, and teaching such courses effectively is even more difficult. Unusually qualified instructors are required—not university professors proficient in sophisticated systems and techniques of management for large modern firms, but rather persons well acquainted with the problems of running shoestring enterprises, who can communicate with small entrepreneurs in terms of the realities of their kinds of businesses. What can be usefully taught to a group in a classroom is relatively limited. The most effective teaching, and the kind that captures the small businessman's real interest, is that which takes place when a good advisor visits his shop and seeks out ways to improve his operation. But this again requires a relatively rare kind of teacher-advisor (in effect, a small-business extension agent) and can become a costly undertaking, particularly where the small firms to be visited are widely dispersed.[28]

---

[26]The Small Industry Extension Training Institute (SIET) in Hyderabad, India, has limited the length of several of its management courses to approximately three months. "This seems to be the best compromise, under Indian conditions, between the maximum time that a manager can be away from his unit and the minimum required for training to be effective." SIET, "Small Industry Extension Training Institute in India," in *Promotion of Small and Medium-Sized Firms in Developing Countries through Collective Actions*, comp. by the Organisation for Economic Cooperation and Development (Paris, 1969), p. 147.

[27]Peter Kilby identifies "thirteen roles or specific kinds of activities that the entrepreneur himself might have to perform for the successful operation of his enterprise." Among those mentioned are management of human relations within the firm, financial management, production management, and introduction of new production techniques and products. He notes that "the domain where performance [of entrepreneurs] is reported to be least satisfactory is that of technology and production management." "Hunting the Heffalump," pp. 27-30.

[28]S.K. Rau, in "Generalities on Problems of Assistance to Small and Medium-Sized Enterprises in Member Countries of the Asian Productivity Organization," in *Promotion of Small and Medium-Sized Firms in Developing Countries through Collective Actions*, compiled by the Organisation

Without such follow-up services, however, such as on-the-spot consultation, help in acquiring credit, and advisory services on raw materials procurement, marketing and the like, a training course for small entrepreneurs all by itself may prove a sterile exercise. Again, one of the serious problems encountered by the Senegal centers was that there was no provision for follow-up support services once their trainees had returned home—no way to help meet their credit needs, no way to advise them on practical problems in their own businesses, and no way to *continue* upgrading their knowledge and skills.

A single infusion of training, we conclude, however good it may be, is likely to be far less effective than a well-ordered succession of training experiences accompanied by other essential support services.

Training as Part of an Integrated Small Industries Program

The severe disabilities illustrated in previous pages can be averted only when training activities are viewed in a wider and more realistic context that includes the other essential factors affecting local employment and the dynamics of small business.

A more comprehensive, systems-type approach is well illustrated by India's program for promoting small industry, dealt with in one of our case studies (Chapter 5).[29] To the credit of India's planners, this broad-gauged program was adopted nearly two decades ago, well before the "integrated approach" to agricultural, rural and industrial development had gained wide approbation. The original objectives of what subsequently came to be known as SSIDO (Small-Scale Industrial Development Organization) bear repeating here because of their contemporary relevance: (1) to create immediate and substantial employment opportunities at relatively small capital cost; (2) to facilitate mobilization of capital and skills that might otherwise remain inadequately utilized; (3) to bring about integration of small-scale industries with the rural economy on the one hand and the large-scale industry on the other hand; (4) to improve the productivity of workers and the quality of small-scale industry products; and (5) to ensure equitable distribution of national income and balanced industrial development in different regions in order to provide the basis for a "decentralized" society.[30]

Conceptually, the initial vision of the program would be hard to improve upon today, even with benefit of hindsight. (The main component subsequently added—an important omission in the original plan—was a staff development and research center to support the whole operation.)

---

for Economic Cooperation and Development (Paris, 1969), pp. 114-116, discusses the role of "Consultants" (extension workers, industrial counselors, or advisors), who "help the firm to reorganize its own business operations and also give guidance to the business holders on methods for better daily operations. . . ." Other duties may include "giving Advisory Service on the loan applications, license and procedures, financial sources, availability of raw materials, marketing and sometimes even on the choice of business itself." He may also have to devote time to plant management or maintenance procedures.

[29]deWilde, *Nonformal Education and the Development of Small Enterprise in India.*

[30]Ibid., pp. 8-9.

Not surprisingly, many practical difficulties were encountered in implementing this complicated scheme, which tied a variety of training activities for entrepreneurs and their employees to a complex of related support services involving, for example, credit supplies, plant layout, product design, subcontracting with larger industries, help in procuring raw materials and equipment, central workshops for small businsses to share, marketing advice, and actual marketing of products. The surprising thing is not that there were many difficulties, stemming in large part from India's scarcity of resources and overburdened administrative system, but that the program held together, moved forward and apparently made a considerable contribution. The lessons that India paid heavily for—in particular the expensive lessons learned in the later Rural Industries Projects (RIP) Program, created to counterbalance the urban bias of the original SSIDO program—are now available gratis to other developing countries. Some of the most important of these lessons are included in the following section of conclusions from our review of training programs for nonfarm skills.

Conclusions

Needed: A Broad and Systematic Perspective

Widespread generation of a great variety of nonfarm skills is an obvious essential for rural development. But new and improved skills cannot by themselves create jobs or bring about development; other favorable factors must also be present. Thus, a systems perspective, similar to that discussed in Chapter 8 with regard to farmer education, is required for the effective planning, operation and evaluation of nonfarm skill training programs.

Training programs aimed at creating "marketable" skills that will facilitate economic development and increase employment in any area must be closely tied to the actual and prospective market conditions and skill needs of that area, if such programs are to engender substantial benefits in relation to their costs. Moreover, they must be closely tied to whatever other support services are needed by those with newly acquired or improved skills in order to put their skills to most effective use. Such services might include assistance in obtaining credit, raw materials or subcontracts, help on product design and marketing, and follow-up training as it is needed. In short, skill training programs—just as farmer education programs—cannot be designed or successfully operated in a socioeconomic vacuum, without close regard to related factors in the environment.

Most Promising Areas

The most favorable opportunities for skill training programs are in areas already on the move economically, especially where development is being guided by a well-conceived integrated development plan for a natural market area, embracing the rural hub-towns within the area and the surrounding countryside, and where such a plan is strongly reinforced by compatible public policies and government actions.

In such conditions, the pattern of skill needs is clearer and a cogent strategy for skill training can be devised much more reliably than in areas lacking development plans and strategies.

While there is a place for mobile skill training programs that reach out to small remote villages, the main focus of nonfarm skill training programs, we believe, should be in the rural hub-towns, for here is where the main opportunities lie for generating new employment for both the rural unemployed and the underemployed.

Strategies for Areas of Low Promise

Special emphasis should be given to ancillary skill training in rural areas of low development potential and where there is little hope for change. Efforts at training in marketable skills and for promoting small industry could be costly, ineffective and wasteful in such areas, whereas supplementary skills directly tied to upgrading subsistence living could bring some measure of improvement and more hope to the people in these backward areas. Mobile training programs may sometimes be a good solution in such areas.

If such programs are to be successful, however, they must adhere to the following precepts which, though applicable to other kinds of nonformal education programs and to other types of areas, are especially important here:

1. The skills to be taught, and the place and scheduling of such activities, must be carefully fitted to the convenience, felt needs and motivations of the target audience and to their environmental circumstances. The best way to achieve this—a way too seldom followed—is to consult at length with the potential trainees and listen to their views before making any program decisions. Only in this way will it be *their* program, not just what uninformed outsiders thought would be "good for them."

2. The skills taught and practices recommended must be not only technically sound but physically and economically feasible for them to apply in their particular circumstances.

3. The methods of training used must fit the vocabulary and learning styles of the audience. Classroom-type lectures are likely to fail. The discussion method, practical demonstrations and trial-and-error practice exercises by the participants themselves are most likely to succeed.

4. The training activity should not be a one-shot affair, but rather one in a continuing series of learning experiences, organized if possible by local groups using local volunteer leaders in key roles. The skills and content should be broken down into successive units which most members of the audience can easily digest and keep pace with; they should not be overwhelmed with an indigestible mass of facts and abstractions.

5. The objectives of the training should be clearly defined from the outset, which will permit continuous evaluation to serve as a guide to program adjustments and improvements.

These seemingly obvious, common-sense guidelines bear repeating here, for our findings suggest that they are more often violated than observed.

Rural Youth Training Programs

Alternative solutions should be carefully explored and weighed before any particular educational model is decided upon for youth training. In particular, *high-cost, full-time formal vocational training programs should be approached very cautiously and adopted only when there are clearly no better alternatives available.* Usually, we suspect, there will be.

In general, part-time training programs for youth, sandwiched with part-time work, are preferable to full-time, highly institutionalized programs, particularly if there are provisions—as there should be—for continuous training opportunities. Among other advantages, part-time training at nearby centers can be combined with apprenticeships, which permits such programs to be integrated with indigenous training processes.

Special attention should be given to determining in advance the degree of specialization and sophistication of skills and the appropriate mix of skills—sometimes combining on-farm and off-farm activities—that would enable a trainee to obtain employment in rural areas or become a successful rural artisan or entrepreneur. No standard model can be applied everywhere, because the appropriate mixture of skills and the degree of specialization would vary for each rural area, even within the same country, and would change over time as development efforts begin to produce results.

Skill training services for young people should be closely tied to and coordinated with other support services in order to help them get successfully established in the world of work. An able and promising young man or woman, for example, who performs well in a training program and wants to start a business, should have access to sound advice, to help in securing credit, to further special training and to other needed follow-up support.

Except for the minority of rural young people who already have a solid base of general education, and perhaps even for them, skill training programs should include wherever possible general education—including literacy—that is relevant and organically tied to the skills and occupations for which they are being trained. For older youth and young adults who may become small entrepreneurs, a few essential skills of management should also be included, if not in the same program then in a readily available follow-up course.

Much greater consideration should be given to the creation of useful training for girls, beyond the usual household skills. On this point MTTS has set an excellent example; half of its participants are girls, learning skills which, though useful in the home, can also be applied in gainful employment.

Skill Programs for Practicing Artisans and Entrepreneurs

Programs for upgrading the skills of artisan-entrepreneurs are likely to have the highest immediate payoff to participants in income terms since they are already employed, are likely to have a clearer idea of what they need and want to learn, and can immediately apply the learning they acquire.

If such programs are to be well patronized, however, they must not only offer clearly relevant training from the participants' point of view, but also arrange the time, place and duration of training activities to minimize the opportunity costs imposed on participants.

Programs of this type can have a strong multiplier effect in two particular circumstances: first, when they focus on upgrading and broadening the skills and knowledge of key trainers in indigenous training programs and, second, when they focus on new and unfamiliar skills for which a fresh demand will soon be arising as the result of some major project or new development in the area.

Training Components of Capital Projects

One of the potential opportunities and major necessities in the skill training field is the inclusion of appropriate training components within the plans for major development projects. Such training should be aimed at creating the skills and understanding essential not only for constructing and operating such projects but especially for ensuring the effective *utilization* of the new service or product. This applies, for example, to power, irrigation, transportation and industrial projects as well as to more diversified, integrated development schemes for a particular region. The planning for such training should begin with the planning of the capital facilities themselves and not be left as an afterthought. Critical skill shortages—and lack of understanding and appropriate skills on the part of *users*—can become serious bottlenecks and ruin the cost-benefit record of otherwise well-conceived capital projects.

Integrated Programs to Promote Small Industries

From the rich and lengthy experience of India and from that of Nigeria and other countries which have sought to spur the growth of small and medium-sized nonfarm enterprises as essential to rural development, we draw the following conclusions:

1. Programs of this sort are far more viable and effective when they are centered in rural hub-towns as key growth points for rural development, rather than being dispersed in sparsely settled village areas. Moreover, they can be significantly productive in relation to their costs only in areas where other essential factors for rural development are also present and a dynamic upward movement of agriculture is taking place. They should be conceived of as part of a strategy for *accelerating* a development process that already has some momentum; not as a means of creating such momentum from scratch.

2. The most serious constraint on the effectiveness of such integrated programs is likely to be the availability of competent staff, especially those involved in counseling small businessmen on their practical problems of management. There is no easy solution for this problem. Adequate incentives have to be provided to attract and retain competent personnel, sometimes transgressing the limits of what the civil service structure permits. More use should be made of part-time personnel, and greater attention paid to the possibilities of servicing groups of clients organized in cooperatives or similar institutions instead of dealing with individuals.

3. Credit supply is likely to be as crucial a factor as training in small enterprises and industries. But the sound management of credit systems for small enterprises, at least for some time, is bound to involve higher administrative costs than can be covered by ordinary interest charges and will therefore require public subsidy. The efficacy of such subsidies, and of related training activities as well, should properly be assessed in terms of longer-range social and economic benefits, including contributions to employment-generation and to bringing a whole area alive; they should not be judged simply in narrow terms of the short-range incremental earnings accruing to individual trainees and borrowers.

4. Training programs for smaller entrepreneurs and their employees

are most effective when tailored to the needs and conditions of particular categories of manufacture, service trades and the like, rather than attempting to cover very diverse enterprises with dissimilar learning needs.

5. Smallness should not be promoted as a virtue in itself; special care should be taken to avoid placing size limitations on program participation that fall below the minimum scale for efficient operation in particular industries. The objective should be to help small employers not only to operate more efficiently and profitably but also to become larger employers of personnel from rural areas.

6. Finally and most fundamentally, training programs and related support services designed to spur the growth of nonfarm enterprises and employment in rural hub-towns and the surrounding area will have greatest effectiveness when they are made an integral part of a broader development strategy and package of actions aimed at the balanced overall development of such an area.

10: IMPROVING THE TECHNOLOGIES OF NONFORMAL EDUCATION

Educational technology is often thought of mainly in terms of the "hardware" of new and sophisticated media—films, radio, television; and, more recently, computers and communication satellites. But this narrow view creates distorted perspectives and often misplaced emphasis. We therefore use educational technology very broadly in this study to include *all* the various means and methods, old as well as new, that can assist an educational process to accomplish desired learning results.

Thus defined, educational technology includes not only such "hardware" as chalk and blackboards, scissors and paste, pencils and paper, printed materials, film projectors, and radio and television equipment, but also the methods of organizing and using these items as components of an integrated teaching-learning "system." Moreover, the techniques, for creating appropriate "software" (content) to accompany such hardware is also an important, and often neglected, aspect of educational technology. Only by viewing educational technologies in these broader terms and in the specific context of where and for what purposes they are to be used is it possible to discuss them rationally and to make sound decisions on which ones to use.

This study's interest in educational technologies arises from two self-evident propositions. First, the cost-effectiveness of any nonformal education program is determined not only by what it has to teach but by the means it employs to teach it. Second, and by extension, the ability of any developing country to meet the learning needs of its rural population depends not only on the resources it can spare for the purpose but on the availability and efficient use of educational technologies that are both low cost and educationally effective. Applying these propositions to the rural areas and educational programs observed in this study, we are led to the following basic conclusions:

First, nonformal education, taken as a whole, has an extraordinary capacity—much greater than formal education—to use an almost infinite variety of educational technologies. In principle, it should be in the vanguard of harnessing low-cost technologies in new ways and serve as a laboratory for developing innovations useful to formal education.

Second, while we found many instances of the creative use of educational technologies (some are cited later in this chapter), it is our overall impression that nonformal education as a whole has tended (like formal education) to cling to traditional, costly and inefficient instructional means and methods, failing to take sufficient advantage of the alternative technologies available. Thus there are abundant opportunities for increasing the cost-effectiveness of existing programs through improving their technologies.

Third, a major cause of economic bottlenecks to expanding nonformal education is the over-reliance on face-to-face instruction of learners by teachers. The least used educational resources—which could do much to break these bottlenecks—are print materials, radio and the enormous capacity of people to learn for themselves when given access to good self-instruction materials.

Fourth, the cardinal emphasis in seeking to improve technologies for education in poor rural areas should be on promoting the ingenious use of effective, *low-cost technologies that already exist,* not on introducing sophisticated new media that are beyond the economic grasp of poor countries for a long time to come. To encourage pipe dreams of dramatic educational breakthroughs involving advanced technologies such as computerized instruction and satellite television can only lead to disappointment and in slowing progress.[1]

This chapter, drawing upon evidence gathered in the study, first presents several interesting examples of the imaginative use of low-cost technologies used in nonformal education in rural areas. Second, it identifies several major factors that influence success or failure and which therefore should be taken into account in planning and organizing technologies for nonformal education. Finally, it recommends several concrete ways in which improvements could be made, starting immediately.[2]

Examples of the Imaginative Use of Low-Cost Educational Technologies

The examples sketched below illustrate how ingenious combinations of nonformal education technologies have been used or are now being used to pursue a variety of objectives. They are presented not as success stories or as specific models for others to follow, but rather to illustrate the wide range of possibilities available and to stimulate further imaginative thinking.

Using Mass Media in Campaigns

Two of our cases show dramatically how mass media can be used effectively, in conjunction with other means, to motivate rural people for specific action projects. As we shall see, the campaign—usually with a short-term, specific objective—lends itself well to the use of broadcast, film and print media that can reach large numbers of people, including many illiterates, at a low unit cost.

The Ghana Cocoa Campaign (1953-56). In Ghana in the mid-fifties a serious blight had forced the destruction of many diseased cocoa trees; new trees were being planted but they too would become blighted unless systematically sprayed. But the Department of Agriculture's extension service was having no luck persuading farmers to buy sprayers and to use them systematically. After a year of unsuccessful efforts, the agriculturalists turned for help to the adult educators in the Department of Social Welfare and Community Development.

Together they devised a multimedia educational attack on the problem. Films and filmstrips were used to show the importance and methods of pest and disease control; a handbook and discussion sheets were supplied to field

---

[1]Research and development of such new technologies should certainly go forward on an experimental scale where it can be afforded. But to imply that they promise viable solutions for poor countries within this century would simply nurture distracting illusions.

[2]The cost aspects of educational technologies are treated more specifically in Chapter 11.

workers and pamphlets to farmers; a series of multicolor posters and radio recordings of an amusing "high-life" song proclaiming the virtues of spraying cocoa plants were widely distributed. Specially trained field teams from both departments visited all the cocoa districts, performing "village drama," giving demonstrations, holding discussions, and distributing posters and pamphlets. Meanwhile, the high-life jingle played incessantly wherever there was a radio and soon became a popular tune.[3]

In fact, as one of the participants later commented, it was a case of "overkill." The inventory of sprayers was soon sold out and farmers who were left without one protested bitterly against the government.[4]

ACPO's campaigns. Another striking example of the effective use of a multimedia system for promoting action in rural communities is ACPO's yearly succession of campaigns in Colombia for projects to improve the health and welfare of rural families. All of its media and personnel are prepared well in advance for an intensive, coordinated attack on one target at a time in accordance with a set timetable. To illustrate just a few of the many projects carried out, these campaigns—according to ACPO's estimates—have resulted in 40,000 new houses, 50,000 new latrines and 6,000 new bridges being built, in 100,000 animals being vaccinated, and in 4,000,000 trees being planted. (See Table 6.1 in Chapter 6, p. 79, for list of specific campaigns and estimated results.)

The Mastery of Complex Ideas by Illiterates

The above examples from Ghana and Colombia reveal the great potential of mass media—especially when used in combination to reinforce one another—for reaching, motivating and instructing large numbers of people to take specific kinds of constructive action. The next two examples involve more difficult educational tasks; namely, helping illiterate peasants to grasp relatively complex ideas and information requiring a sustained learning effort over a considerable period of time. The first case belies the popular notion that written instructional materials cannot be used with illiterate populations; the second proves that education can be fun.

Tanzania's radio correspondence groups. In Tanzania, following independence, the government promoted rural cooperative societies for production, marketing and allied economic tasks. For these societies to succeed, it became imperative to educate the local members and directors in the management and effective supervision of cooperatives and in the whole range of socioeconomic purposes and principles of the cooperative movement. Though most of the

---

[3]J.A. Seago, "The Use of Media in Non-Formal Education for Rural Development: A Report on British Experience," mimeographed (Reading, England: Agricultural Extension and Rural Development Centre, May 1972), pp. 16-19. Paper commissioned by the Overseas Development Administration for ICED.

[4]There were two interesting sidelights to this case. The first was the discovery that the farmers' decision on capital investments of this importance were usually made only on the advice of more "modern" members of rural families residing in the city, who were presumed to have greater financial wisdom. The regular agricultural extension service had overlooked this strategic urban audience, but the high-life records and other mass media messages reached them with good effect. The second was the discovery—thanks to an efficient feedback mechanism—that the original recommendations for spraying were scientifically incorrect. As a consequence, all of the media messages had to be reprogrammed and reproduced.

village-level members were illiterate, a series of courses was designed for study groups, using printed text materials and correspondence units, reinforced by related radio broadcasts. Each of these study groups has at least one literate member who reads the questions posed by each correspondence unit and the related text, then writes the answers formulated by the group and sends them to the correspondence center for review. Available recorded evidence plus limited direct observation by an ICED researcher indicate that this unique program is getting useful results, in spite of inevitable difficulties.

Radio-discussion groups, incidentally, have been used for nonformal education in a variety of contexts.[5] In India, radio forums promote better farming practices and community improvement programs.[6] In the People's Republic of China as well, extensive use has been made of radio-group discussions and nonformal teaching.[7] But the rapid spread of low-cost transistor radios among rural families, we were told in several countries, has lately reduced the drawing power of radio-discussion groups. People can now stay home and listen to the radio. In some places farmers even plow their fields with transistors slung over their shoulders. This trend, however, opens up wide new possibilities for using radio as an educational medium.

Ecuador: experimental games. In Ecuador, the Ministry of Education and a team from the University of Massachusetts, acting on the premise that education can be enjoyable and spontaneous, have designed low-cost games as educational media for compesinos in rural areas.[8] One purpose of these games is to promote literacy and numeracy; but an even more important purpose is to provide disadvantaged rural people, young and old, with a better understanding of the processes and institutions around them, how they operate and impinge on the life of the community and individual, and what compesinos can do to improve their lives by modifying these institutions and processes and using them more effectively.

The game of "Hacienda," for example, modeled after the popular game of "Monopoly," is basically a board game, with some elements of role playing. The players' object is to make use of the opportunities offered to them by society. The board squares are filled with various institutions of the *campo:* the church, bank, jail, school, center for adult education, savings and credit co-ops, and so forth.[9]

These inexpensive, often home-made, games are played by neighbors gathered in a common building, a home or the marketplace. Though the games are designed by the technical team, they are often modified on the spot by the players themselves to fit local circumstances. Often a game goes on for hours, generating great amusement and wild enthusiasm as well as serious discussion

---

[5]James R. Sheffield, *Education in the Republic of Kenya* (Washington, D.C.: U.S. Government Printing Office, 1971), p. 35.

[6]Wilbur Schramm, "Ten Years of the Radio Rural Form," in *New Educational Media in Action— Case Studies for Planners, vol. I,* comp. by IIEP (Paris: Unesco/IIEP, 1967), pp. 107-134.

[7]Hsiang-po Lee, *Education for Rural Development in the People's Republic of China,* ICED Background Paper No. 3 (Essex, Conn., June 1972).

[8]See David Evans and James Hoxeng, *The Ecuador Project,* Technical Note No. 1 (Amherst, Mass.: School of Education, University of Massachusetts, 1972), which gives the background of the project and its basic philosophy.

[9]James Hoxeng, *Hacienda,* Technical Note No. 3 (Amherst, Mass.: School of Education, University of Massachusetts, 1972), pp. 3-4.

and debate. Preliminary indications of impact are encouraging, but a fuller judgment awaits the findings of a systematic evaluation now under way.[10]

This experiment underscores again the unlimited possibilities for stimulating learning by building on people's motivations and utilizing their unbounded capacity to learn for themselves.

Educational aids for extension workers. As we saw earlier, agricultural extension services are faced with various complicated educational tasks in trying to help farmers improve their methods and welfare. But we also saw that most extension services rely largely on traditional and costly methods—mainly on direct personal contacts between extension agents and farmers. Because of the limited number of extension agents (see Chapter 11, p. 187 on ratios of agents to farmers) and the great demands on their time, this means that only a small minority of farmers can usually be reached effectively. The problem for most countries is therefore how to multiply the effects of extension by low-cost means. The answer necessarily lies in using some sort of multimedia system in which face-to-face communication by extension workers is supplemented and reinforced by additional means of communication.

The ORD in South Korea. In the Republic of Korea, the Office of Rural Development (see Chapter 3) adapted this multimedia approach, using—in addition to extension workers—farm radio broadcasts, films, posters, bulletins and a farm journal. Though little systematic effort has been made to determine the impact of these media, or even to find out who is listening to the broadcasts and how they feel about them, such evidence as we could gather suggests that they have had significant influence. Undoubtedly, they would now be having much more impact if budget cuts had not, for example, curtailed the production of new and more up-to-date films designed to take farmers the next step forward.[11]

The Puebla Project in Mexico. The Puebla Project in Mexico (see Chapter 7, pp. 105-108) has made good use of a film unit that shows small farmers improved techniques of corn planting and how to use credit. These films have apparently been popular and effective.[12]

Experiences in India. A Coordinated Farmer Training Program in India, for relatively high-potential districts outside those in the Intensive Agricultural District Program (described in Chapter 7, pp. 92-95), includes a combination of radio-discussion groups, farmer training centers, national demonstration fields, and functional literacy courses. Although coordinating these components has been a big problem, the program has made rapid headway in some districts.

Perhaps the most striking example we saw of the imaginative use of a local multimedia system of farmer education was that referred to earlier in the Tanjore District in South India. (See Chapter 7, pp. 92-95). The able and energetic District Agricultural Officer and his staff, taking account of the latest technical developments and changing market conditions, lay out a specific plan of action and recommended practices for each crop season, week by week, to corre-

---

[10]See also the following publications from the School of Education, University of Massachusetts, Amherst: W.A. Smith, *Concientizacao and Simulation/Games*, Technical Note No. 2; J. Gunter, *Market Rummy*, Technical Note No. 4; J. Gunter, *Ashton-Warner Literacy Method*, Technical Note No. 5; J. Gunter, *Letter Dice*, Technical Note No. 6.

[11]Manzoor Ahmed, *Farmer Education Program of the Office of Rural Development in the Republic of Korea*, ICED Case Study No. 5 (Essex, Conn., July 1972).

[12]ICED field notes.

spond to each phase of the crop cycle. All educational activities are guided and harmonized by this plan and all available media, methods and channels of communication are mobilized to get the story across—including radio, newspapers, bulletins, traveling exhibits, posters, and visits by local extension agents (Village Level Workers or VLWs) and agricultural officers from higher levels. Strong efforts are also made to get effective feedback from the farmers to modify the plan as needed.

It should be noted, however, that Tanjore is an unusually dynamic district, caught up in the Green Revolution, with farmers who value new and useful information. It is much easier to run an effective multimedia extension system when agriculture is on the move, when farmers are literally demanding new knowledge, and where there is a research system to generate it.

Using retailers and farmers as extension agents. Important additional sources of useful knowledge for farmers in some countries are the manufacturers and local distributors of farm supplies and equipment. Many manufacturers of fertilizers and insecticides, for example, do considerable research on their products and on how best to use them. Such information, conveyed through their distributors, who are often progressive cultivators themselves, can be of considerable value to farmers (though they need to guard against being oversold on a particular commercial product).

Often the most important source of new knowledge for farmers is their neighbors, who communicate and demonstrate new and desirable practices. A former Minister of Agriculture in India, who was instrumental in launching India's integrated drive in the 1960s for increased agricultural production, told us that "the best extension agents we have in India are the farmers themselves." Farmers often accept the advice of trusted and respected neighbors more than the word of government agricultural officers.

Some extension services consciously try to take maximum advantage of this neighbor-teach-neighbor propensity. CADU, for example, does much of its extension work through selected leader-farmers. The Puebla project can afford to have relatively few (but well-trained) extension agents because much of the teaching is done through the chairmen of self-formed credit groups. ORD has put great effort into training local volunteer leaders who serve in effect as an arm of the extension system.

Local sociological conditions and human relations do not always favor this sort of horizontal spread of useful knowledge through progressive farmers. Working through leading farmers sometimes serves to increase their already strong advantage over their less fortunate neighbors and to exacerbate large disparities between rich and poor. CADU found it necessary to drop some of its leader-farmers on these grounds. But in many situations, using selected farmers as extension surrogates is preferable to spreading a limited number of official extension agents too thinly to be effective.

Providing Skill Training in Remote Areas

Extension services are accustomed to meeting their clients where they live and work, but this is not the style of most other occupational programs. Vocational skill training is usually performed in a central facility equipped with classrooms and workshops to which trainees come for part-time instruction. This is feasible in densely populated towns and cities where trainees do not have to travel far to reach the instructional center, but is often impracticable in sparsely populated rural districts.

Senegal's solution. One alternative—the one chosen by Senegal—is to set up residential training centers (RTCs) to which trainees come for a substantial period of full-time instruction. But as Senegal's experience demonstrates, the high opportunity costs to the trainees of leaving their homes and businesses for a long period are a major handicap to this solution.[13] Moreover, the high capital and operating costs per trainee preclude the nationwide expansion of this pilot scheme.

SENA's solution. Another solution—used by SENA in Colombia—is to bring the trainers to the trainees, or at least within easy reach of them. As SENA's experience shows, this approach also presents special problems, among them the difficulties of transporting essential tools, equipment and materials over rugged terrain to remote rural areas; getting the local program well organized in advance of the instructor's arrival so that he knows what courses are to be taught and can start right in; following up with further training in each area within a reasonable period; and recruiting training experts who are willing to spend much of their time away from home under hard conditions.[14]

No doubt the above problems encountered by SENA help explain why we found so few examples of truly mobile rural training services. But problems or not, if rural people are to learn new and useful skills which they cannot readily acquire in their local environment. the only practical solution is for the instructors to come to them. The convenience of the learners must take precedence over the convenience of the teachers, though teachers who assume these arduous responsibilities should be rewarded accordingly.

Multimedia education packages. In the Philippines we ran across an unusual organization—the Social Communications Center (SCC)—that specializes in creating multimedia educational "packages" for government agencies and other organizations under contract, particularly for use in rural areas. Like ACPO in Colombia, SCC is a privately operated communications organization with its own printing, broadcasting, film and other facilities, and its own creative staff (its full-time staff numbers about 250). Its educational packages are built around selected themes, such as cooperatives, family health, responsible parenthood, land reform, trade union practices, and civic duties. By late 1971, SCC had produced, for example, over 1,200 theme-oriented radio dramas (in four different local dialects) that were broadcast over more than 100 radio stations. It had also produced large numbers of related posters, booklets, comic strips and other materials supporting the same basic themes.[15]

The foregoing illustrations by no means exhaust the great number and combination of methods and media currently being used in nonformal rural educa-

---

[13]P. Furter and S. Grabe, *Senegal: Rural Vocational Training Centers,* ICED Case Study (unpublished).

[14]Stephen Brumberg, *Promoción Profesional Popular-Rural of SENA: A Mobile Skills Training Program for Rural Colombia,* ICED Case Study No. 2 (Essex, Conn., June 1972).

[15]In addition to its contract work, SCC has its own constituency, served by three attractively produced periodicals with high educational and social content: (1) *NOW,* a fortnightly publication in English for school children (circulation 50,000); (2) *Philippine Digest,* a monthly magazine in English aimed at more educated urban readers (circulation 25,000), and (3) *Ang Tao,* a monthly journal in Tagalog for poorly educated rural families (circulation 122,000). Like ACPO, SCC does commercial printing to help earn its own way.

tion. But they demonstrate two basic truths: first, that countries need not rely on the promise of future technological breakthroughs in order to devise effective solutions to the problems now at hand; second, that no one type or combination of technologies is "best" for all nonformal educational purposes, but rather each situation calls for its own solution.

The programs referred to above and numerous others reviewed by the study also provide many useful do's and don'ts that can be useful in planning the use of educational technologies and their organizational problems. We turn now to a discussion of some of the do's and don'ts arising out of the reviewed programs.

Suggestions for Planning New Technologies

The introduction of any basic technological change or innovation in an educational program is likely to be more complicated than expected and to pose a number of problems. A great deal can be gained by anticipating these problems and taking steps to avoid some of them in advance and to surmount others as they arise.

A Problem-Solving Approach

Experience has shown repeatedly that one of the main causes of failure with new educational technologies has been an inability to put first things first—in other words, starting with a technology that someone was anxious to use rather than with an important educational problem that needed solving. As one observer noted, "Many developing countries had imported such 'hardware' as radio stations, television and filmmobiles and those responsible for education were expected to use them. Very often no consideration was given to what use they might be put and 'software' was usually lacking."[16]

Ethiopia's example. Ethiopia illustrates the point, though many other countries have been through a similar experience. Since 1954, communication programs in Ethiopia, assisted by the United Kingdom and the United States, have been making intermittent efforts to use radio, television and other audiovisual aids to advance education. But a review mission that visited Ethiopia in 1971 to appraise a new proposal for establishing a nationwide radio-TV network for educational use had to begin its task by helping various government agencies interested in popular education to arrive at a consensus (apparently for the first time) on what the specific educational purposes and objectives of such a network would be.[17]

To avoid such abortive efforts, planning must begin by identifying some important educational needs that cannot be met by conventional means, then clearly defining the learning objectives to be sought,[18] the characteristics of the audiences to be served, and the built-in constraints that must be taken into

---

[16]J.A. Seago, "The Use of Media in Non-Formal Education," p. 40.

[17]Center for Educational Development Overseas, "Development of Educational Mass Media in Ethiopia—A Report by the CEDO Survey Team," mimeographed (London, 1972).

[18]As Helen Coppen notes, "Whatever programme of educational activity is undertaken by a Ministry some change in behaviour is envisaged and these changes should be clearly enunciated. There should be a specific, explicitly formulated series of objectives, not just a vague generalization about 'education of youth' ..." "Educational Media for the Development of Rural Education," Document CRE (70) A/4 (London, September 1969), paper prepared for the Commonwealth Conference on Education in Rural Areas, Legon, Ghana, 1970, p. 5. Mimeographed.

account in designing a solution. Only then is it the time to consider which technology or combination of technologies is likely to produce the best results at the least cost. However elementary and obvious this procedure may seem, it is, astonishingly, rarely followed.[19]

Choosing and Combining Technologies

Different nonformal programs, as we saw earlier, call for quite different types and combinations of educational technology, according to differences in their clienteles and learning objectives and in the conditions under which they operate. The best combination of methods, materials and media to serve illiterate subsistence farmers, for example, is likely to be substantially different than that for literate larger farmers in the same area. And the most appropriate techniques for training rural artisans are bound to differ from those appropriate for a broad-scale rural health program. The particular strengths and limitations of each medium must be considered in designing and using any multimedia system. We attempted in our case study of ACPO to analyze the different combinations of media used for different program objectives and the relative importance of each medium in each of these uses. The results of this analysis are shown in Table 10.1, drawn from the case study. It will be seen, for example, that radio broadcasts play a primary role in pursuing learning objectives relating to health, economic understanding and spirituality, but only a secondary role with respect to literacy and numeracy, where printed materials play the leading role.

Another important point for planning—one often overlooked—is that the choice of educational technologies is greatly affected by whether the information and knowledge to be delivered have relevance and utility for a mass audience spread over a wide geographic area; or whether, conversely, they must be tailored to the special needs and conditions of each locality, or each subgroup of learners. The latter applies, for example, where there are important linguistic, ecological, social and economic differences between rural areas and between subgroups in the same area. Such differences are abundant in rural areas of developing countries and impose serious limitations on the utility of low-cost mass media such as radio. Well-programmed nationwide educational broadcasts, printed bulletins and the like can be highly effective for some purposes, but in many cases the information and knowledge required must be of a specific local character and hence must be generated at subnational levels. Thus, for example, an agricultural extension program that deals with content ranging from local-specific to nationally applicable requires a combination of educational technologies capable of handling all gradations.

Returning for a moment to an earlier point, we should caution against the temptation to treat a technology—such as radio or television—as an autonomous teaching-learning system that can do the whole job by itself. Sometimes it can, but rarely. For best results it must usually be teamed up with other components to make up an integrated teaching-learning system.

ACPO began mainly with educational radio broadcasts but soon found it desirable to add a variety of printed materials integrated with the broadcasts.

---

[19]See Wilbur Schramm, Philip H. Coombs, Frederick Kahnert, and Jack Lyle, *The New Media: Memo to Educational Planners* (Paris: Unesco/IIEP, 1967), pp. 162-164, for a discussion of a system approach to planning media programs.

When the producers of the popular and successful *Sesame Street* television program for preschool children in the United States took on the ambitious task of teaching reading through *The Electric Company,* they added much printed material whose content is closely geared to the TV broadcasts. To cite a quite different example, India's rural radio forum surely would not have been as effective without being tied to well-organized local listening and discussion groups that could convert ideas into local action projects.

A Checklist of Essential Preparatory Steps

Another major cause of past difficulties for educational innovations—particularly those involving radio or TV broadcasting—has been the compulsion to rush into action before all the critical components of the system have been adequately prepared. The reasons for rushing are, of course, understandable; once agreement is reached to use a new technology, pressure soon builds up from all sides to get under way quickly and start showing results. But the consequences of undue haste can be disastrous.

Table 10.1
Relevance of Media Employed in the Delivery of
Information According to Educational Objectives
of ACPO

Medium	Educational Objectives				
	Health	Literacy	Arithmetic	Economic	Spirituality
Radio					
Programming:					
Courses	A	B	B	A	A
Informal	C	X	X	B	B
General	X	X	X	X	C
News	C	X	X	C	C
Textbooks	A	A	A	A	A
Book Series	B	B	X	B	B
Newspaper					
Sections:					
Information	C	B	X	C	C
Recreation	C	B	X	C	C
Knowledge	B	B	B	B	B
Supplements	B	B	B	B	B
Correspondence	C	C	X	C	C
Recordings	C	X	X	C	C
Campaigns	B	X	C	B	B
Local Personnel					
(personal contact)	C	B	B	B	B

Key: A Highly Relevant   C Minor Relevance
      B Relevant   X Little or No Relevance

SOURCE: Table prepared by ICED in collaboration with H. Bernal, director of planning and programming for Acción Cultural Popular (ACPO).

Based on lessons from our case studies and other sources, we suggest the following checklist of preparatory measures that should be taken before putting any major technological innovation into action:

1. First and foremost, the careful preparation and pretesting of program content (the "software").

2. Preparation of the users on the receiving end—particularly teachers or group organizers—to accept the new educational service and to use it effectively.

3. Adequate provision for repair and maintenance of equipment, continuity of power supply, and efficient alert system for spotting breakdowns.[20]

4. Provision for efficient intrasystem communication to facilitate, for example, feedback of pertinent evidence and opinions from users to producers, sending out advance notices and advice to the field on upcoming programs, timely delivery of coordinated learning materials to reception points, and flow back of reports and correspondence to the center.

5. Creation of public understanding of the new program: what the plans are, why they have been adopted, what results are hoped for, how it will affect children and/or adults, when things will start happening, how people can help.

6. Contingency planning for success: every significant educational experiment needs not only a well-conceived short- and middle-range plan of operation to carry through the experimental phase, but also a longer-range contingency plan in the event the experiment succeeds. Technologies that may be feasible on a pilot scale, particularly with substantial temporary help from the outside, are sometimes not feasible for a developing country to replicate on a larger scale with its own resources.[21]

Suggestions for Organizing New Technologies

These requisites for effectively planning and preparing any major new venture in educational technology imply important, and often quite complex, organizational and personnel requirements. How these requirements are dealt with can make or break an innovative effort. Some of our case studies and other evidence shed light on these matters and suggest a few lessons on how to handle them.

Staff requirements. The first essential is good teamwork—often interagency teamwork—to harmonize the various specialized competencies usually re-

---

[20]In one developing country that rushed into a classroom TV experiment, involving over 100 scattered schools, it was discovered by a visiting consultant after the programs had been on the air quite some time that 90 percent of the classroom TV sets were not working. In most instances it was simply because they were not tuned properly—no one had thought to show the teachers how. Nor had any feedback alert system been set up to warn of things going wrong on the receiving end. Meantime, a great deal of program effort and TV time had been wasted.

[21]It is entirely possible for an ingenious pilot scheme involving new educational technology to succeed brilliantly, only to discover that, for economic or other reasons, it cannot be expanded on a large scale to benefit more areas and people. For example, many small education broadcast experiments are given a small allotment of "free" radio or TV time by stations for a limited period. But if the experiment succeeds, far more broadcast time would be needed to expand the service, perhaps even requiring one or more full channels exclusively for educational use. In any event, the whole cost structure of a program changes enormously when it moves from a limited pilot scale to full scale and could well become prohibitive.

quired. For a relatively uncomplicated innovation—say, the introduction of programmed instructional materials into MTTS (actually under consideration)—a mixed team of only three or four competent and energetic persons might suffice, at least to get through the initial phase.[22] One member of this team would have to have a good mastery of the subject, another would need to be a competent "programmer," and a third could handle reproduction and distribution.

However, in a more complex program that employs a variety of media and serves a wide and diversified clientele—such as ACPO and ORD—a considerable number of functions must be performed, each requiring special abilities. Typically, they would include:

Overall design of the delivery system requires skilled educational system designers aided by various communications specialists.

Overall management of the system requires skilled and knowledgeable administrators who see the system as a system and keep its various components functioning harmoniously.

Determination of knowledge needs requires field researchers knowledgeable in the social sciences to diagnose in advance, and continuously thereafter, the needs and characteristics of the intended audience, so that the system can deliver pertinent and useful knowledge.

Provision of knowledge to fit the needs requires experts in the particular subject fields, including researchers who can develop answers where they do not exist.

Translation of knowledge into comprehensible forms requires skilled communicators in the type of media used, generally including writers sensitive to the interests, vocabulary and learning styles of the particular audience; artists and layout specialists to prepare illustrations and print materials; executive editors and producers (for film or radio or TV) competent to orchestrate all the elements into an interesting, unified and effective presentation.

Transmission of the program to users requires cameramen, audio engineers and various other types of technical personnel, depending on the media used.

Maintenance and troubleshooting requires good expediters, engineers and others qualified to ensure proper maintenance and functioning of all essential equipment, delivery of materials on schedule, and feedback of reactions from receiving points to the production centers, in order to keep the system operating well.

Operations research and·evaluation requires persons mainly trained in social sciences to keep constant check on all aspects of the system's performance and effectiveness, and to identify ways to improve it.

No one of the above items can be neglected; if the system is to function effectively each must be well performed and all must be well coordinated.[23]

---

[22]One authority has estimated, as a rough rule of thumb, that one hour of programmed learning material requires about 100 hours of preparation time.

[23]Sometimes the same person or group can perform more than one function. The system designers, for example, might also serve as evaluators; subject matter experts might also serve as writers or broadcasters (provided they are lucid writers or speakers for the particular type of audience).

Interagency collaboration. The root of the organization problem is that few, if any, ministries or agencies responsible for one or another aspect of rural education combine all the required special talents in their own staff. If an individual agency tries to do the whole job by itself the results are likely to be ineffective. But if, on the other hand, each agency (especially in a small or medium-sized country) sets out to acquire a full complement of professional skills and its own total delivery system, this is certain to lead to great expense, duplication and waste, and even then the results may be mediocre and the impact limited.

In most situations it makes the best sense for specialized subject agencies with rural education responsibilities to seek the help of the central information agency or any other well-equipped communications organization on functions they cannot readily perform themselves. Beyond this, it makes sense for various education agencies to collaborate closely with each other in the preparation, scheduling and delivery of their messages to the rural population.

Large organizations such as ACPO and ORD that pursue a wide range of rural educational objectives are partial exceptions to the above general rules. In effect, they constitute general communication agencies and diversified subject matter agencies rolled into one. Yet, even ACPO has found it desirable to draw on various specialized government agencies—ministries of health and agriculture for instance—for help on substantive knowledge in order to avoid the expense of creating its own full complement of subject matter experts and to insure that the knowledge it disseminates is accurate and useful.

The problems of coordinating activities of different agencies—of achieving a smoothly functioning interagency team—are often more complex in government operated multimedia systems than in voluntary agencies such as ACPO. It is especially difficult, as many of our observations testify, to get subject matter specialists and communications specialists and their respective agencies to collaborate effectively. In one district we visited, for example, an agricultural specialist from the university and an information specialist from the government information agency were each responsible for separate radio programs for farmers in the area. Even though they had neighboring offices they never consulted together in an effort to coordinate the content of their programs. The farmers, of course, were the losers.

In another country we visited, a relatively small one, a bilateral assistance agency had gone to considerable expense to help develop a well-staffed and -equipped common information center that could assist all the specialized government agencies to get their stories across to the public. It was a good idea but it did not work. Each specialized agency proceeded to collect its own staff of communications experts, and the new information center—with a much better trained staff—ended up servicing only the Ministry of Information within whose jurisdiction it came.

If such professional jealousies and bureaucratic obstacles can be overcome, however, there are enormous opportunities in virtually every developing country, based on *existing* facilities and talent, to improve educational delivery systems to the benefit of both rural and urban people.

Indonesia's example. Indonesia illustrates such an opportunity. There the Ministry of Agriculture's Extension Department is in process of creating an impressive network of Agricultural Information Centers to supply each rural province with specially tailored radio programs, printed materials and films to fit different local needs throughout the country. The first such center to get into operation, at Surabaya, is evidently getting a warm reception from rural families in the area. At the time of an ICED visit to Indonesia, however, the content of the programs was limited to matters within the Ministry of Agriculture's field of competence. Yet it seemed clear that this same well-devised and well-operated knowledge delivery system could also convey other useful knowledge to the same rural audiences—for example, on health and nutrition, child care and family planning, home improvements, sideline jobs for farmers, and even school equivalency programs for young people. Whether this actually happens, of course, will depend not only on the agriculture ministry but also on the willingness of other specialized ministries to collaborate with it in using these facilities.

Senegal's interministerial approach. Senegal has found an effective way to ensure the efficient sharing of radio facilities by different government agencies to support rural development. An Inter-Ministerial Commission on Education Broadcasts—created by presidential decree and composed of ministers concerned with various aspects of rural development—defines the roles of broadcasting in the context of the national development plan, provides guidance on program content, and prevents multiplication of rival and parallel communication to rural audiences. A second structure, the Educational Broadcasting Service, brings together the broadcast technicians and content experts from various ministries and serves as a day-to-day executing organ of the Commission. This body, also not tied to any one ministry, leads to a broad rural development perspective instead of a narrow departmental approach.[24]

There is no one formula for combining the talents of media experts, subject-matter experts and educational specialists from different agencies; each country must work out its own solution. But unless and until such solutions are found and put in force, the mass media will remain a major wasted asset for serving the learning needs of the vast and growing rural populations of developing countries.

Practical Paths to Improvement

Our findings make clear that any developing country anxious to achieve a massive strengthening of nonformal education in rural areas must, among other things, overhaul the educational technologies of existing programs extensively and innovate on a large scale.

While new resources will certainly be required, the most immediate need is to use more fully and effectively the substantial expertise and facilities that virtually all developing countries already possess for strengthening educational technologies. As they move forward, many will need special external assistance to break important bottlenecks such as shortages of newsprint, equipment, and certain crucial types of personnel. Some will be ready for help also in

[24]Michel Bourgeois, "Radio at the Service of Rural Development: The Senegalese Experience of Educational Broadcasting," IIEP/S28/4. Paper read at the Seminar on Planning Out-of-School Education for Development, December 1971, at the International Institute for Educational Planning. Mimeographed.

mounting major experiments and new programs.[25] To avoid the pitfalls of a hit-or-miss approach, they will also need a well thought out strategy and set of objectives to guide the whole effort.

An Initial Inventory

A sound way to begin, we suggest, is by making a rough-and-ready inventory of (1) the types of educational technologies being used in present nonformal programs and any significant innovations contemplated; (2) existing talents, facilities and special capabilities possessed by various governmental, academic, voluntary and commercial organizations that might be more fully utilized for nonformal education; (3) major bottlenecks that inhibit the fuller use of these assets and (4) any measures already taken to facilitate the coordination, sharing and better use of technology resources for nonformal education.[26]

This inventory could be carried out in a number of ways. One would be to create a temporary task force drawn from a few public and private agencies with competencies germane to the inventory. The inventory would not have to be detailed and exhaustive; a rough perspective would do. Refinements could be added later as needed. A full-time task force under good leadership and with high level support could complete the job in six months or so.

Several advantages could come from such an inventory and the process of producing it. It could stimulate wide interest and fresh thinking about nonformal education and educational technology; it would probably reveal surprisingly large assets that could be used to support nonformal education; it could encourage more permanent mechanisms for mobilizing these assets and highlight promising opportunities for immediate constructive action; it could identify a rational set of requests for external assistance to help break critical bottlenecks. Not least, this inventory would provide a sound foundation for building an effective strategy to guide future plans and actions regarding educational technologies.

Building a Strategy

A good strategy articulates a clear set of objectives and the basic means for moving toward them. While each country must formulate its own strategy, we suggest that all will be well advised to give serious consideration to the following points of emphasis:
  • Greatly increased reliance on self-instruction; less on face-to-face teacher to learner methods.

---

[25]It is noteworthy that in 1969, per capita consumption of newsprint in most countries of Asia and Africa was less than one kilogram per year, in contrast to 43.9 kg. in the United States and 17.3 kg. in Japan. In the same year, newspaper circulation per 1,000 people was 11 in Africa, 16 in South Asia, 65 in Latin America, 299 in North America, and 321 in the USSR. Unesco, *Statistical Yearbook 1970* (Paris, 1971) Table 7.1 and p. 686. Production of newsprint and other paper is a serious problem for tropical countries due to lack of good pulp materials. We are told that it is technically and economically feasible, however, to use tropical reeds, bamboo, rice stalk and other tropical materials for paper pulp, provided the local market is large enough to justify the investment. Where this is the case, a much enlarged use of print materials for educational purposes would improve the economic feasibility of local paper production and also economize on foreign exchange.

[26]This educational technology inventory could be made a subdivision of a more comprehensive "sizing up exercise" of the type discussed in *New Paths to Learning*, Chapter VI.

- A greatly enlarged supply of learning aids, especially print materials and radio programming.
- More attention to creating good educational software for both print and electronic media.
- Greater collaboration among organizations in creating and transmitting high quality educational content.
- Expanded use of market places, and other popular meeting grounds, and of traditional forms of folk entertainment for educational purposes.
- A major effort to enrich rural learning environments for the purpose of *informal* education.

These interconnected objectives could be the guides for immediate decisions and form the frame of a coherent, longer-term strategy for extending the reach and effectiveness of nonformal education by improving its technologies. We will comment briefly on some of these points below.

Fostering Self-Instruction

The heavy reliance of rural education programs on face-to-face oral instructions has absorbed the bulk of resources in staff costs—leaving little or nothing for other aids to learning—and caused them to become the main bottleneck to expanding learning opportunities. Even literacy programs have been deprived of relevant reading materials. The effect has been to reduce the productivity of teachers and the learning of the learners. It has also wasted the greatest educational resource of all—the extraordinary capacity of motivated people to learn on their own when given easy access to the stuff of learning.

Another misallocation of scarce education resources that has thwarted the expansion of learning has been the excessive emphasis on mass media hardware to the neglect of the vital software.

In all these cases of misplaced emphasis, little can be accomplished simply by using more resources to do more of the same. The key to improvement is to redeploy the resources, devoting a larger share to the creation of relevant and attractive educational programs and materials from which people can learn a great deal more for themselves.

Improving educational software takes special talents. These can best be mobilized in developing countries by forming more partnerships between the operators of education programs, competent subject matter specialists, and experts in communication. Sometimes all three sets of skills exist in the same organization, but more often they must be drawn together from different organizations—university departments, research institutes, information ministries, and specialized operating agencies. Granted it is seldom easy to put good teams together from different organizations; unless a supreme effort is made, talents will be wasted and education will suffer.

Knowledge-generating centers—universities, research institutions, agricultural field stations—are in a unique position to help strengthen rural education by joining forces more closely with extension services and by helping to create authoritative "learning packages" for wide use. In Chapter IV, for example, we noted that the International Rice Research Institute supplies its trainees with lecture notes and other learning materials which they can use for training others on returning home. At relatively little extra cost an organization such as IRRI might go a step further and create fuller integrated "learning kits" that could be used much more widely by extension services throughout the rice-producing areas of Asia. Such kits might include carefully programmed text materials, organized by successive learning units, that explained in lucid terms the scientific principles of rice production, the proper methods to use with new varieties, crop protection techniques and so forth, accompanied by film strips, photographs, and other illustrations. They might also include suggestions for conducting local tests and experiments, and even some radio scripts that could be adapted for local use.

Prepackaged learning kits of this sort, with room for local inserts and modifications, could be used for a variety of learning needs—health and sanitation, for example, or managing small farms, growing nutritious family crops, making improved clothing and housing, organizing and operating cooperative societies. If widely used, the unit cost per learner of high quality materials could be kept to a modest level.

This is clearly demonstrated by ACPO's accomplishments in Colombia and the work of the Social Communications Center in the Philippines. It is impossible to measure accurately ACPO's total audience, much less its educational impact, but certainly the number of *campesinos* deriving substantial benefits runs into many thousands. Yet ACPO's total expenditures (in 1972) were only about $4 million (U.S.)—a tiny fraction of what Colombia spends annually on formal schooling.

Joint Use of Educational Delivery Systems

Numerous opportunities exist to strengthen rural education through sharing common facilities and personnel by different programs serving clienteles in the same area. The propensity of such programs to want their own autonomous delivery system from top to bottom—to "go it alone"—has resulted not only in fragmentation confusing to the public but in higher costs and poorer results.[27] A cluster of programs aimed at improving different aspects of rural family life—health, nutrition, sanitation, home repairs, backyard gardens, child care, family planning, odd job income, consumer economics—might well develop a larger and more enthusiastic audience and do them more good if they consolidated their efforts, invested much more in good software and staff training, and developed a stronger common delivery system.

Wherever a good multimedia delivery system exists or is being developed for the purposes of one ministry—as in the case of the new Agricultural Information Centers in Indonesia—the chances are that the same delivery system could also serve the rural education objectives of some other ministries as well. Senegal's coordinated use of radio broadcast facilities and a common program staff for serving a variety of rural education objectives is a good example of what can be done.

---

[27] At the time of our field work, for example, a new wave of family planning programs was breaking on the rural scene almost everywhere we went. Most were following the familiar piecemeal approach, despite its proven wastefulness. In one Asian country an international official had given up trying to keep track of new family planning programs—they were multiplying too fast. One observer commented wryly that birth control programs should begin with family planning themselves.

Enriching Rural Learning Environments

The point was made earlier that much more human learning goes on *outside* organized educational programs than within them, through *informal* education. But people in remote rural communities can only learn what is there to be learned. Investments in enriching their environments with new things to learn could reap a larger payoff on investments made, for example, in primary schooling, adult literacy programs, and other organized educational efforts.

We have been struck repeatedly by the efforts made to teach people to read through literacy programs, and the lack of efforts to create a steady flow of simple and pertinent reading matter for new literates. Great investments are made in radio broadcast and receiving equipment and rural people are spending more and more time listening, but mostly to entertainment programs for urban audiences.

Anyone who grew up a generation or two ago in a rural area of the United States can testify to the profound informal educational influences exerted by such institutions as the Sears-Roebuck catalogue, *Popular Mechanics* magazine, the daily radio Farm and Home Hour, and the county newspaper. While we do not suggest that these same institutions be applied to other countries, the basic techniques they employed are widely applicable.

Most developing countries have tried various rural media separately—radio, filmmobiles, local newspapers, and so forth at one time or another. But so far as we know, there has rarely if ever been a concerted, systematic, and prolonged effort to tie them all together and to program them appropriately in a massive effort to saturate rural environments with the "stuff of learning."

It would be a worthwhile investment—in terms of both educational results and important research lessons—to undertake some large-scale informal education experiments of this sort in a few selected rural areas of the developing world. Such experiments would need to be carefully prepared, designed, operated, and evaluated, and would need to be kept up over a period of at least a decade to determine the full impact. The lessons learned might dispel a good many educational myths and open up some radically new and more effective approaches to educating rural populations.

Among the educational media used in such broad experiments should be various forms of indigenous folk entertainment. The Ghana cocoa spraying campaign made effective use of folk drama and "high life" jingles; puppets have been used in some places as effective "teachers." Bowers has emphasized the great potentialities of market places as educational forums.[28] Rural people trek to market not only to buy and sell goods but for social recreation, to exchange news, to see interesting things and people, to pick up interesting ideas. Films, exhibits, contests, and the like, combining entertainment and education, can find receptive audiences in the market place.

Summing Up

This brief review of educational technologies has shown both a dark side and bright side of the picture. On the dark side, nonformal education programs

---

[28]See John Bowers, *The Use and Production of Media in Nonformal Adult Education,* ICED Background Paper No. 6 (Essex, Connecticut, July 1972).

have tended to cling to traditional modes of face-to-face instruction resulting in high costs and reduced effectiveness. The lack of learning aids for self-instruction and the dominance of hardware over software has dampened the effectiveness and narrowed the reach of such programs.

But the bright side—illustrated by some of our case studies—reveals innumerable opportunities to strengthen nonformal education through new combinations of media and greater use of creative talents to produce richer and more effective program content.

Progress lies largely in finding *low-cost combinations of technologies* suitable to each type of program and situation, and in finding ways to combine the talents and facilities of different agencies in a more unified and creative effort. The difficulties should not be underestimated, but the gains can be large and reasonably rapid. There are many ways by which external agencies can help, not by encouraging dreams of great technological breakthroughs that will produce educational miracles—there are no such breakthroughs in the offing that can be afforded on a large scale in poor rural areas—but by helping countries to design and implement systems of low-cost, effective technologies.

11: THE ECONOMICS OF NONFORMAL EDUCATION

The "economics of nonformal education" was a virtually nonexistent subject when this study began in 1971. The improved techniques for analyzing the costs, finances and benefits of *formal* education had only limited applicability to the far more diversified programs of nonformal education. The sparse literature on such programs had almost no data on costs and finance, not to mention efficiency and productivity.[1]

The Key Questions and Definitions

Thus, we set out to uncover whatever data and clues we could that might help answer the following questions:
- Would a large-scale expansion of nonformal rural education be economically feasible in developing countries? Where could the resources come from?
- What are the costs and cost structures for different types of nonformal education? How do they compare with the costs of formal education?
- What are the potential cost advantages of nonformal education, and what are the main opportunities for economies?
- Is it feasible to apply efficiency and productivity tests (cost-effectiveness and cost-benefit analysis) to such programs? What operational purposes could be served by such analysis?

Although the data we were able to find exceeded our expectations and shed useful light on these questions, they were incomplete and often imprecise. Hence this chapter should be seen as only an initial foray into the economics of nonformal education—one that we hope will open the field for others to explore further.

It became important in looking at the *costs* of nonformal education to distinguish between *financial costs* (as recorded, for example, in budgetary accounts) and *real economic costs* (including opportunity costs). Since many nonformal programs make extensive use of borrowed facilities, volunteer help, and contributed materials and services, their real costs often exceed their recorded financial costs by a wide margin.

In assessing the *benefits* of such programs it is important to look beyond the *direct economic* benefits (as reflected, for example, in incremental production and income). In many situations the *indirect economic* benefits and various *noneconomic* benefits, both private and social, may be even more important than the direct economic benefits. These noneconomic benefits should not be

---

[1]Frederick H. Harbison has noted: "Probably no country has ever made a complete inventory of all nonformal learning programs conducted by its many public and private agencies; there are no reliable estimates of either capital or recurrent expenditures allocated to them." *Human Resources as the Wealth of Nations* (New York: Oxford University Press, 1973).

lightly dismissed simply because they do not readily lend themselves to statistical measurement with present tools of the social sciences.

We will use the term *cost-effectiveness* here to refer to the relationship between the costs incurred in a given educational activity and the immediate learning results attained (such as occupational skills acquired or competency in literacy). We will use *cost-benefit* (or benefit-cost) to mean the relationship between costs incurred (investment) and the cumulative benefits (both economic and noneconomic) that accrue over time as a consequence of knowledge and skills gained through an educational activity. Cost-effectiveness, thus defined, reflects the *internal efficiency* of a program, whereas the cost-benefit relationship reflects its external productivity.

Practical Problems of
Data Collection and Analysis

Scarcity of data. So that others may know what to expect, we begin by noting some of the typical problems we encountered in probing the economic aspects of various nonformal education programs. As expected, we found a paucity of usable cost data, little "cost consciousness" on the part of many program managers, and few efforts to trace the subsequent record of former students and trainees.[2] It was usually necessary to splice bits and pieces of evidence together and to take substantial statistical leaps in order to arrive at a picture and assessment of finances, costs and benefits.

There were some exceptions, however, particularly among our selected cases. The managers of the Acción Cultural Popular (ACPO) and National Apprenticeship Service (SENA) programs in Colombia[3] are quite cost-conscious and are becoming increasingly cost-benefit minded. Thus the budgetary and operating accounts in these cases were relatively orderly and illuminating. Evidence of impact was, not surprisingly, much more meager but was being strengthened. The managers of the Chilalo Agricultural Development Unit (CADU) in Ethiopia were much concerned with both costs and results, and with laying out a path by which the CADU project would in the not too distant future become self-sustaining, using domestic resources alone.[4] In Tanzania, similar cost and finance planning was going on for the transition of the Cooperative Education system from heavy external assistance to full reliance on domestic personnel and financial resources.[5]

By contrast, there was considerably less ready evidence on costs and results, and less apparent concern with these matters, in the cases of the Office of Rural Development (ORD) in the Republic of Korea, the International Rice

---

[2] These problems also exist in formal education, but they are compounded in nonformal education, where programs are usually far less standardized, regular accounts are rare, and financing and management are often highly improvised.

[3] See Dr. Stephen F. Brumberg, *Acción Cultural Popular: Mass Media in the Service of Colombian Rural Development,* ICED Case Study No. 1 (Essex, Conn., April 19720, pp. 85-91; and *Promocion Profesional Popular-Rural of SENA: A Mobile Skills Training Program for Rural Colombia,* ICED Case Study No. 2 (Essex, Conn., June 1972), pp. 27-32.

[4] Based on ICED field notes by Sven Grabe for an unpublished case study; documentation provided by the project management, and Bengt Nekby, *CADU: An Ethiopian Experiment in Developing Peasant Farming* (Stockholm: Prisma Publishers, 1971).

[5] Sven Grabe, *The Cooperative Education System of Tanzania,* ICED Case Study No. 9 (Essex, Conn., June 1972), pp. 54-71.

Research Institute (IRRI) in the Philippines, and the Mobile Trade Training Schools (MTTS) in Thailand. Perhaps it was more than coincidence that we also found in these cases some fairly evident potential ways to improve their productivity.

In general, independent extension services and skill training programs seemed least concerned with cost analysis and with assessing benefits, while integrated development projects, where extension and training are integral parts of a coherent package, seemed most concerned.[6] This correlation was certainly no accident. People who think in terms of integrated projects are likely also to think in terms of cost-benefit relationships, for this is basically what the case for integration is all about.

Because there was usually so little to go on in judging the practical impact of programs on their clients, ICED undertook limited field surveys in connection with the studies of ACPO and SENA in Colombia, IRRI, the Vocational Improvement Centres (VICs) in Nigeria, and ORD.[7]

These efforts—limited as they were and had to be—yielded useful, if inconclusive, evidence on impact (see the case study reports for details[8]). These exercises also revealed the sizeable practical difficulties of measuring, or even defining and identifying, the kinds of benefits that flow from different types of nonformal education programs. But most important, they demonstrated that it does not take a massive and expensive field study to get a fairly good idea of what is happening on the receiving end of a nonformal education program. *We suggest, therefore, that it would be most worthwhile for programs themselves to do more sample drillings of the kind ICED attempted. Modest efforts invested in keeping relatively simple but systematic financial and cost accounts would also pay large dividends.*

Methodological problems. Three particularly important methodological problems should be highlighted. The first, already noted, is that of accounting for "hidden costs" in a nonformal education program: such resources as volunteer labor, "free" radio time, borrowed facilities, and opportunity costs for trainees. Items such as these never show up in the budget and operating accounts; yet they are usually a real cost to somebody and are important in producing results.

Another is the problem of unscrambling joint costs for joint products. In an agricultural knowledge system, for example, the *combined* costs and activities of all the different functional components produce the ultimate impact on

---

[6]One exception to the general lack of concern with assessing benefits in training programs is the rural training centers in Senegal. ILO arranged a tracer study of former trainees of the artisan training centers. What the study revealed was not altogether reassuring, but it is certainly better to discover unpleasant truths in time to take remedial action than to proceed under the delusion that so long as the program is operating satisfactorily its ultimate results must be good.

[7]Subsequently, ICED arranged a follow-up study of participants in Upper Volta's rural education system in connection with a study for UNICEF, but at this writing the results are not yet in.

[8]See footnotes 3, 4 and 5, above. Other case studies with details on field surveys are: Manzoor Ahmed and Philip H. Coombs, *Training Extension Leaders at the International Rice Research Institute,* ICED Case Study No. 12 (Essex, Conn., June 1972), pp. 27-30; Clifford Gilpin and Sven Grabe, *Programs for Small Industry Entrepreneurs and Journeymen in Northern Nigeria,* ICED Case Study No. 7, (Essex, Conn., April 1972), pp. 44-45, 61-62, Manzoor Ahmed, *Farmer Education Program of the Office of Rural Development in the Republic of Korea,* ICED Case Study No. 5 (Essex, Conn., July 1972), pp. 56-59.

farmer behavior, not simply the costs and actions at the final delivery end of the system.

Finally, there is the parallel problem of isolating the influence of noneducational factors on the productivity of the educational inputs—and vice versa. How, for example, does one apportion the credit for a Green Revolution among all the essential factors that produce it, including not only research and education investments over a long period but also investments in fertilizer production capacity, irrigation projects, road networks, and price supports?

We have cited these various practical difficulties not to show how impossible such analysis is, or because we have any tidy solutions to offer, but simply to emphasize that nonformal education programs function in a seamless web of interacting development factors that cannot easily be disaggregated for statistical measurement. For most purposes, the benefits of such disaggregation exercises (if indeed they can be done at all with any validity) are not likely to be worth the effort, at least in being useful for decision-making. The imbalances and maladjustments one so often observes in nonformal education programs and in their relationships to other factors are so conspicuous and gross that they hardly need to be measured with calipers in order to identify steps that can be taken to improve their performance substantially. If, for example, three-quarters of the trainees turned out by a skill training program have not found jobs to use their new skills, it takes no rate-of-return analysis to know that the wrong skills are being offered.[9] Or if an agricultural extension service is having no discernible impact on the learning and practices of farmers in an area, there is a fairly obvious checklist of possible deficiencies that should be investigated.

We turn now to the first side of the input-output equation to find out where the resources for nonformal education programs have been coming from and how they might be enlarged.

Sources of Support for the Sample Cases

Table 11.1 provides a rough picture of the sources of financial support for eleven of our cases (and in some instances, the sources when the program was just getting started). These cases, it should be emphasized, differ greatly in character, in their history and in their stage of development: The established ones (such as ORD, MTTS, ACPO and the Nigerian VICs) have a quite different pattern of financial sources today than in their initial development phase (generally with less external help and more domestic support now). Newer programs still in their developmental stage (such as CADU, the Programme on Agricultural Credit and Cooperation in Afghanistan (PACCA), and the Puebla Project in Mexico) have a much higher external aid component and a smaller domestic one. Ten years from now, if they survive, these programs may be nourished almost entirely by domestic resources.

The alphabetical ratings on Table 11.1 are only approximations of the relative contribution of various sources to these programs and reflect the best rough judgment we could make from the available evidence.

---

[9]This is not to deny that the trainees may nevertheless have acquired some useful learning, but such hit-or-miss programming is hardly the desirable approach to skill training. Accidental byproducts rarely justify educational expenditures unless the intended objective is well served.

Table 11.1
Sources of Finance for Nonformal Education Programs

Programs/Type of Cost	Natl. Govt.	Regional/Local Govt.	Public/Private Orgs.	External Aid Agencies	Fees[2]	Income[3]	Other
CADU							
Capital	B			A			
Operating	C			A		B	
Initial Development				A			
IRRI							
Capital				A			
Operating				A	B		
Initial Development				A			
ORD							
Capital	B	A		C			
Operating	A	B					
Initial Development				A			
PACCA							
Capital	A			B			
Operating	A			B			
Initial Development				A			
PUEBLA							
Capital				A			
Operating	B			A			
Initial Development				A			
MTTS							
Capital				A			
Operating	A			A	B		
Initial Development				A			
SENA							
Capital			A				
Operating			A				
Initial Development							
VICs (Nigeria)							
Capital		B		A			C
Operating		A		B			
Initial Development				A			
ACPO							
Capital	B			C		A	
Operating			B			A	
Initial Development							
Tanzania Cooperative Education							
Capital				A	B		C
Operating	B			A	C		
Initial Development				A			
Upper Volta							
Capital				B			A
Operating	A					B	
Initial Development							

[1] The rating scale, A, B and C, indicates the sources of finance in order of magnitude:

    A = *Source contributed most of the finances*
    B = *Source contributed significant share of the finances*
    C = *Source contributed relatively minor share of the finances*

The contribution rating represents the general situation in the recent past, c. 1970-71. Older programs such as ORD and SENA had substantial external assistance in the past. External assistance for other programs such as Upper Volta Rural Education and Nigerian VICs has been phasing out.

[2] Fees from participants in program of their sponsors.

[3] Income from products, services and investments.

[4] Contribution of local community in the case of Upper Volta and borrowed facilities in other cases.

Role of External Assistance

What stands out most strikingly in this table is the important role played by external assistance in almost all of the cases, especially with respect to capital items and initial development costs. To some extent this may reflect a bias in our sample, but a similar pattern was evident in the bulk of other nonformal education programs we looked at (excluding indigenous training systems) that have been created in the past ten to fifteen years.

One could infer from the above observations that governments of developing countries—with notable exceptions as India and Brazil—have not been very enthusiastic about initiating or extending nonformal education programs on their own; they have put their trust and money mainly in *formal* education, probably in part because that is what their people most valued and demanded. Yet in many of the same countries there appears to have been a sizeable, spontaneous growth of nongovernmental *indigenous* training programs—private responses to new needs, technologies and opportunities. This phenomenon has been almost totally without the support, or even the awareness, of outside assistance agencies; they are essentially self-supporting training systems.

Important differences in contribution of external assistance. There are important differences in the role played by external assistance in the different programs shown on Table 11.1 and in others we reviewed. At the one extreme, for example, IRRI and the International Maize and Wheat Improvement Center (CIMMYT), which supports the Puebla Project, have been almost wholly financed from outside sources and probably will continue to be, because they are *international* research agencies dedicated to helping many countries. At the other extreme, the Nigerian VICs have been almost fully weaned from dependence on foreign assistance and are being continued and enlarged with domestic (largely governmental) support. Similarly, the small-scale industry program (SSIDO) and related training programs in India (not shown on the table), which had relatively little outside help even at the start, have for years been entirely supported by the central and state governments. In most of our cases, external agencies provided capital facilities at the start and shared operating costs with the host country. This is the case, for example, with CADU, Tanzania's Cooperative Education system, and ORD. PACCA, in contrast, was provided its land and capital facilities mainly by the Government of Afghanistan. In almost all cases, initial development costs—apart from capital facilities—have been largely underwritten by external agencies.

Problems generated by external assistance. There can be little doubt that without the intervention of various external agencies—voluntary as well as official ones—many of today's nonformal education programs in developing countries would not exist, or would be much weaker. This heavy involvement of outside agencies, however, is not without serious problems.[10]

One problem is that outside agencies, by taking a narrow outlook confined to their own particular interests and specialties, have contributed to the fragmentation of rural education efforts. No agency has taken the lead in trying to tie the pieces together into a more rational and effective whole.

---

[10]For a discussion of the problem of U.S. foreign aid, see Edgar Owens and Robert Shaw, *Development Reconsidered: Bridging the Gap Between Government and People* (Lexington, Mass.: D.C. Heath and Company, 1972).

A second problem is that outside agencies, wishing to stretch their limited resources as far as possible, have tended to concentrate on generating "pilot projects" of limited scale and duration, in the hope that they would soon take root and be broadly replicated with local resources. But few such pilot projects seem to work this way. Many decline or disappear altogether when foreign assistance is phased out, often because they were ill-conceived and not subjected to adequate feasibility tests before being launched. All over the developing world there are graveyards of abortive pilot projects long since forgotten by those who first inspired them (who often are too busy with the next crop of pilots to conduct revealing post-mortems on their earlier attempts; hence old errors are often repeated).

Fortunately, some of our cases—the Nigerian VICs, for instance—that began as pilots were soundly conceived and have endured and grown. But most of the surviving older programs we studied did not start out as pilot schemes; they were designed from the outset as full-scale systems (ORD is an example) and were given sufficient initial support to become viable on the basis of domestic support.

There is certainly an important place for well-designed, genuine experiments on a pilot scale, aimed at learning how to solve basic problems that hitherto have defied solution in many countries (CADU and Puebla are such experiments). But there seems little justification for miscellaneous pilot projects unless they are soundly conceived as the first step toward a larger program whose long-term viability has been rigorously assessed in advance. Even then, they should be launched only if the external sponsoring agency is prepared to stay with the project long enough to see it to fruition, which is likely to be ten years or more.

Yet another problem associated with heavy dependence on external assistance is what might be called "the overbuilding syndrome"—the construction of externally funded facilities that are too elaborate for the host country to duplicate or even maintain on its own. This can lead not only to frustration and ultimate waste of resources but also to dissatisfaction among teachers, students and others who did not have the luck to occupy the impressive new facility and must use instead more modest facilities that reflect the country's pocketbook. This overbuilding phenomenon has been most evident thus far in formal education, but there is now some danger of its spreading to nonformal education.[11]

Potential Domestic Sources of Support

A major question for the future is what resources of their own—financial and nonfinancial—developing countries can muster to support a massive expansion of rural nonformal education. Our selected programs provided some useful clues. Collectively, they demonstrate the following main potential forms and sources of domestic support for nonformal education:

Regular government revenues, channeled through the budgets of a variety of national, state and local agencies. This applies especially to

---

[11]It already has in at least one case—Upper Volta's rural education system. Many villages have contributed land and built their own facilities at an average cost to the government of about U.S. $1,000. But other villages have externally aided models costing ten times as much. The discrepancy has hardly engendered popular support for the program in the deprived communities.

programs that are nationwide or of special concern to the central government. Examples include (1) ORD, whose research and extension services are financed by a combination of national, provincial and county government allocations; (2) VICs in Nigeria, now financed mainly by state governments; and (3) MTTS, financed (in addition to U.S. assistance) through a division of Thailand's Ministry of Education.

Diversion of resources from formal education, particularly newly available incremental funds, in situations where—all things considered—it appears that these funds will add more to the general welfare through nonformal than formal education. Such diversion of funds from formal schools is bound, of course, to create controversy among different groups of educators, as it did, for example, in the case of Upper Volta's unconventional rural education centers.

Special government levies, imposed exclusively for educational use. SENA, for example, is largely supported by a special payroll levy on all larger employers (including government agencies), reserved exclusively for SENA's use. Similar arrangements exist in several other Latin American countries (e.g., Chile, Venezuela, Brazil).

Local government and community contributions. Upper Volta's rural education system, for example, works on a local base: communities are challenged to build a school if they wish the central government to provide for its operation. Kenya's Village Polytechnics depend heavily on community self-help efforts.[12]

Borrowed facilities. Several of our selected programs hold down their capital costs by borrowing unused local facilities or by occupying active facilities after hours. They include, for example, Nigeria's VICs, MTTS and SENA.

Redeployment of existing communication resources. Countries determined to give a high priority to educating their rural populations can harness and redeploy resources, such as mass media facilities and communication talents, now being used for less important purposes. (India and Indonesia are doing this.)

Volunteer help. This is perhaps the most important nonbudgetary resource. It not only contributes economically but also helps to weave nonformal education programs into the fabric of local communities. ORD has some 100,000 local volunteer leaders (trained by ORD) who in effect are integral members of the extension service. ACPO in Colombia has no paid local staff; it relies exclusively at the village level on volunteer organizers. Tanzania's Cooperative Education system similarly relies mainly on unpaid local volunteers to carry out its local activities.

Self-support. In some nonformal programs the participants help build facilities, produce food for consumption, and prepare other needed services for themselves. The artisan participants in Senegal's rural artisan training centers (RATC) helped to build facilities for the centers. So did the early participants in Jamaica's youth camps. Students in the Boys'

---

[12]The *harambee* secondary schools in Kenya are also an interesting example of self-help efforts and have long depended on the community to raise sufficient funds for their operation. J.E. Anderson, *Education for Self Reliance—The Impact of Self Help,* Discussion Paper No. 67 (Nairobi, Kenya: Institute for Development Studies, University College, Sept. 1968).

Town School in Sri Lanka produce most of what they eat and perform the most necessary services at the school, thus making the institution largely self-supporting.

Earning income by selling services and products. In addition to servicing its own program needs, ACPO uses its modern printing plant and record-making equipment for commercial work. These earnings, plus revenues from the sale of ACPO's weekly newspaper, low-priced books and other materials for rural participants, finance better than two-thirds of ACPO's total costs—the rest coming from government and private contributions and endowment earnings. The Social Communications Center in the Philippines finances the bulk of its program activities in much the same way.

Fees from participants. A number of programs collect moderate fees from participants—Thailand's MTTS and Kenya's Farmer Training Centers (FTC) are examples—which not only helps to offset costs but also gives participants a stake in the program.

Every developing country already possesses many of the foregoing actual and potential resources to support rural nonformal education. The crux of the problem is to create the national will and popular elan—with top political leaders setting the tone and government bureaus setting the example—which are indispensable to unleashing and redeploying these financial, human and physical resources for a massive attack on rural education needs.

Cost Characteristics of Nonformal Education

One of our aims was to determine the typical characteristics of cost structures for different categories of nonformal education programs—the ratio of capital costs to recurrent costs, for example, and the role of staff costs in operating costs. We were interested also in the evolution of cost structures as programs moved from their initial development phase to "normal" operations.

Samples of the kinds of evidence obtained on these questions are included in Appendix Table 1, showing operating cost data, and Appendix Table 2, showing capital investment data, for twelve of our cases. On the basis of this and other evidence the following generalizations can be made:

1. Most nonformal education programs have a low capital cost component (lower usually than that for formal education programs), and a proportionately high operating cost component in which staff costs dominate.

2. Agricultural extension services are typically low users of capital and high users of staff. Mobile skill training programs are also low-capital, high-staff cost activities. Farmer training centers have a somewhat higher capital factor. The heaviest capital users are full-time, institutionalized skill training programs. As a general rule, the more a nonformal program resembles its counterpart in formal education, the higher its capital costs—the more so if it is a residential program.

3. The unit costs of a new program are considerably higher in its developmental stage than later on, because of the one-time-only starting up costs.

4. Programs that put most of their resources into staff costs, with only negligible amounts going to instructional materials and other learning aids, are likely to have low educational efficiency.

183

5. Nonformal education programs have wide scope for holding down capital costs by using borrowed or low-rent facilities in spare hours, and for holding down operating costs by using volunteers and part-time paid professionals.

6. There are many unexploited opportunities for nonformal education programs to increase their cost-effectiveness and benefit/cost ratios by internal program adjustments, by adopting new technologies, and by collaborating closely with formal education and with other nonformal programs serving the same geographic area.

In later sections of this chapter evidence will be presented to substantiate these general conclusions, and also to show some significant variations.

Comparative Costs of Nonformal and Formal Education

Nonformal education has a number of *potential* cost advantages over formal education programs with comparable educational objectives. But it should never be taken for granted that these advantages will be realized in practice. Poorly conceived or badly run nonformal programs can have extravagently high unit costs accompanied by poor results. In other situations, the unit costs may be low in an absolute sense but high in relation to what is achieved. An important rule to remember at all times is that *there is little virtue in low costs as such; what counts is a high ratio of desired results to costs.*

It is rarely if ever possible to make a valid, full-fledged cost-effectiveness comparison between formal and nonformal education programs, mainly because of the substantial differences that usually exist between their program content, clienteles and learning outputs. There are frequently major differences, for example, in the maturity and motivations of the students, in the subjects taught and the amount of time spent on them, in the quality of the inputs and in other major variables. Nevertheless, valuable lessons for improving both modes of education, and for deciding when it is better to use one rather than the other in particular situations, can be derived from certain comparisons, bearing in mind the precautions that must be taken in interpreting the results. We found three instances in which such comparisons are illuminating.

Nigeria's VICs. In Nigeria a government trade certificate is required for employment in certain posts. The normal way to acquire one is by attending a three-year formal vocational high school. A number of VIC trainees, however, some with little formal education, passed the test after one year of part-time training (ten hours per week). The average recurrent cost per student enrolled (including dropouts) in a formal trade school was U.S. $930 per year ($2,790 for the full three years), whereas the cost per student enrolled in one VIC we examined was $104 per year. If all the costs were charged only to those trainees who passed the government trade test, the cost would have been $467 per successful trainee. (Presumably, however, the other trainees benefited even though they did not take or pass the test.) Capital costs (not included in the above figures) are much higher for vocational schools than for VICs, which used borrowed facilities.

In interpreting these figures it should be remembered that the VIC trainees are somewhat older and more experienced on the average; that the curriculum is much narrower; and that where VICs use regular trade school facilities and teachers after hours, they have to pay only marginal costs that are well below the full average costs that the regular school program must bear. Granting all this, the VICs are obviously a more efficient way to produce trade certificate holders from among their particular clientele than sending them to full-time schools. Moreover, the results of comparison, while not conclusive, are sufficiently striking to warrant a serious reexamination of the assumptions, practices and viability of the full-time formal trade school approach.

Thailand's MTTS. In Thailand, a successful MTTS trainee with six months of part-time training (300 hours of instruction) costs the program about U.S. $100, whereas the operating cost per student enrolled in a formal vocational secondary school is approximately $300 for one full-time year of instruction. The difference between the two, per hour of instruction, is not very great, though if the higher capital costs and higher dropout rates of formal schools were added in, the difference would substantially favor MTTS.

The larger issue, however, is not the unit cost per hour but how many formal vocational schools Thailand can afford and whether less costly, part-time training courses might better serve the nation's overall skill requirements. From the limited evidence it would appear that the burden of proof is on the proponents of formal vocational schools.

Upper Volta's rural schools. Finally, there is the interesting case of Upper Volta's rural education system, which seeks to give rural adolescents, in the span of three full-time years, the equivalent of four years of regular primary schooling plus technical training in agricultural and related rural skills. The annual recurrent cost per student in the unconventional rural schools averages 5,500 CFA fr. (16,500 CFA fr. for three years) against 12,200 CFA fr. per year for regular primary students (48,800 CFA fr. for four years).

While great economic advantage seemingly lies with these unconventional rural schools, the big question is how much, comparatively, do students in the two systems learn and retain and how does it affect their later performance. An evaluation of the rural schools undertaken for ICED (under its UNICEF study) should help answer this question.

Cost Factors in Agricultural Extension

This study has revealed the extreme difficulty of ascertaining the true costs of any agricultural extension service and the even greater difficulty of making valid cost comparisons between different projects and countries. It has also cast doubt on the appropriateness of using standardized ratios of extension workers to farmers as primary criteria in planning or evaluating specific extension programs. In examining the cases we were able to identify a series of critical variables, apart from this ratio, that ought to be considered in planning or evaluating any farmer education program—variables that strongly influence costs and results and that differ greatly from one situation to another.

Limitations of extension ratios. Most agricultural extension specialists have regarded the ratio of extension workers to farmers as the primary, if not exclusive, determinant of the quality and effectiveness of any extension service and have been inclined to use budget increments to improve the existing ratio as the first order of priority. These ratios have been used not only as the key factor in planning extension services but also as an indicator of the adequacy of existing programs and as a basis for making international comparisons.

This simplistic approach is unsound. Undeniably it is important to consider the extension ratio in designing and costing an extension service, but to treat it in isolation from a great many other important factors and variables can be highly misleading and damaging.[13] Comparisons of these ratios internationally can be especially treacherous.

Determinants of extension ratios. Examination of our selected cases has shown the following variables to be of critical importance in determining the most appropriate ratio within the resources available in any given situation, or in assessing the efficacy of an existing ratio:

1. *The prime objectives and focus of action* of the particular extension program. These may range from promoting a well-defined package of practices relating to a single crop; to introducing basic changes in agricultural practices, crop patterns and farm economy; to supporting overall rural development goals, including agricultural improvement. Obviously, different objectives call for different strategies for deployment of field staff and different criteria for assessing their performance.

2. *The characteristics of the farmers to be served* and the nature of their needs. There is a vast difference, for example, between helping sophisticated commercial farmers increase their output and helping small subsistence farmers become commercial farmers—the latter generally requiring much heavier extension inputs.

3. *The caliber of the extension agents*—their background and training, general knowledge, and expertise; their motivation and enthusiasm; their attitude toward their work and their farmer clients; the extent to which they are kept up-to-date by in-service training.

4. *The time available to extension agents* for direct contacts with farmers, which depends on the geographic dispersion of their clients, the physical mobility of the agents, and the extent to which agents are burdened with ancillary clerical and other chores. Many local extension agents actually have less than half their time available for their priority extension duties.

5. *The extent to which various infrastructures exist*—for staff development, credit, input supplies, marketing, transportation, etc. (If these are weak or nonexistent, the burdens and costs of extension per client will be much heavier relative to results attained.)

6. *The inherent ecological potential and state of development of the area,* including its existing dynamic. An area with low potential and dynamic requires different and much larger extension inputs to obtain substantial results than a high potential, high dynamic area.

7. *The nature and strength of technical backstopping support given to local agents* from higher echelons—including research directed at local farmer needs and frequent visits by district and subdistrict level agricultural officers.

---

[13]Professional educators have made a similar fetish of the pupil-teacher ratio, viewing it as the most critical variable in determining the quality and effectiveness of education, despite the fact that most research studies have shown this not to be true. Putting the teachers (rather than the learners) at center stage in planning and evaluating educational processes has subordinated other important variables and blinded educators to alternative technologies. The result is that teachers and learners alike have been deprived of valuable educational tools that could help them both do a better job.

8. *The existence of unofficial communication channels* through which farmers acquire useful knowledge, apart from official extension agents, such as sales agents for commercial input manufacturers, radio and newspapers, neighboring progressive farmers, agents of credit organizations, and so on.

9. *The type of extension approach:* the technologies used (e.g., audiovisual aids, self-instructional materials and mass media used to supplement field-level agents) and the general strategies employed (e.g., demonstrations and other group methods as against individual contacts; working through master farmers or other key leaders as against direct contact with all farmers).

10. *The extent of decentralization:* if an extension worker is really well qualified to give advice, the less he has to refer back to higher authorities before giving advice and the more efficient he can become in concentrating on the farmers' problems.

Variables of these kinds lie behind the highly diverse extension ratios shown in Table 11.2 for different extension services and integrated agricultural development programs reviewed by our study. (Some of the ratios shown are necessarily rough estimates.) The main point is that these ratios cannot be compared or interpreted without knowledge of the particular circumstances.[14]

Table 11.2
Illustrative Ratios of Farm Families
to Extension Agents

Country/Program	Farm Families per Field Level Extension Agent
Ethiopia/CADU (1971)	1,725:1
Malawi/Lilongwe	
Short-Term Goal — 1970	200:1
Long-Term Goal	600:1 to 800:1
Afghanistan/PACCA	
Baghlan/Koh-i-Daman Area (1971)	21:1
Long-Term Goal	70:1
India (1967)	
National Average	828:1
Intensive Districts	600:1
Republic of Korea/ORD (1970)	425:1
Mexico/Puebla (1971)	1,048:1

[14]It would be foolish to conclude, for example, that the extension service operating in the Baghlan area of Afghanistan—showing in 1971 a ratio of one agent per 21 participant farmers—must be many times stronger and more effective than Puebla's extension service which had only one field agent for every 1,048 farmers participating in the project (in 1971). Similarly, it would be incorrect to conclude that extension services in the Intensive Agricultural Development Districts in India, where there is an average of one Village Level Worker for every 600 farm families, are several times stronger and more effective than that in the CADU area of Ethiopia, where there are (or will be) about one extension worker for 1,700 farm families.

One final point should be added as a partial qualifier of what has been said. The aggregate extension ratio for a nationwide extension service *can* be a useful planning datum when used with caution, insofar as the differing variables for different sub-areas tend to cancel out; but to insist on the same ratio for every area is likely to be unsound.

A Comparative Analysis of Three Integrated Projects

The reasons behind the great differences in these ratios, as well as critical factors that affect extension costs, can be illustrated by a brief comparison of three integrated development projects—PACCA, Puebla and CADU.[15]

Objectives and clienteles. First, their *objectives* are quite different. CADU's are the most ambitious, including not only the improvement of agricultural technology, productivity and incomes but also a fundamental transformation of the economic and agricultural structure, social institutions and human relationships in the area. Hence a good portion of CADU's efforts are directed at building new infrastructures—particularly farmer cooperatives, an efficient marketing network, a credit system and a reformed land tenure system (all of which involve educational requirements).[16]

PACCA's stated longer-range objectives are ambitious along similar lines. But thus far the project has concentrated mainly on boosting the production of a limited number of farmers (although a start has also been made on forming farmer associations and opening up new marketing opportunities).[17]

Puebla's central objective is the most clean-cut and narrow of the three: to help small, backward farmers in rainfed areas to increase their maize production and thus their incomes and standard of living.[18]

Second, the *clienteles* of the three projects, though they may seem superficially similar, are quite different. PACCA's present clientele consists mainly of farmers in two of Afghanistan's highest potential ecological zones. These farmers have had long experience in commercial farming and are generally acquainted with the use of fertilizer (the major factor in PACCA's recommended new practices).

CADU's farmers are for the most part small subsistence growers, situated on relatively good land but with poor access even to internal markets. Only a minority has done much commercial farming. The others need to learn how to use modern inputs and credits and to manage a farm as an economic unit.

Puebla's farmers, by Mexican standards, are just as poor, and their ecological conditions are less favorable than those in the PACCA and CADU areas. On the other hand, their country as a whole is much more modernized than Afghanistan and Ethiopia, both of which still retain strong feudal features.

---

[15]See Chapter 7 for brief descriptions of these projects, and Appendix tables for data on their costs and staffing patterns.

[16]Bengt Nekby, *CADU: An Ethiopian Experiment in Developing Peasant Farming* (Stockholm: Prisma Publishers, 1971).

[17]Manzoor Ahmed and Philip H. Coombs, *PACCA: Education in an Integrated Agricultural Program,* ICED Case Study No. 10 (Essex, Conn., June 1972).

[18]Delbert T. Myren, "The Puebla Project: A Developmental Strategy for Low Income Farmers." Prepared for the Seminar on Small Farmer Development Strategies, Columbus, Ohio, September 1971.

Staffing. Third, there are differences in *staffing,* resulting in part from differences in the existing educational infrastructures in the three areas and in the availability of trained manpower for extension work and other agricultural services required by these integrated projects. PACCA and CADU, faced with very weak national educational infrastructures (which are located almost exclusively in the main urban centers) have been obliged to invest heavily in creating their own training facilities and processes to develop needed local staff, in sending local people abroad for training, and in expensive foreign technical personnel pending the build-up of corps of competent local personnel.

Puebla, by contrast, was in the fortunate position of being able to obtain good manpower and other backstopping from two strong institutions nearby—the National Agricultural College at Chapingo and CIMMYT, and other Mexican agricultural colleges as well. Thus, Puebla's staff development costs and dependence on foreign technical personnel have been minimal. For the same reasons, Puebla's capital requirements have been minimal.[19]

Other infrastructures. Puebla was also relatively well off in having access to well-established credit, input supply, transport and marketing systems. To be sure, much of the project's efforts have been devoted to getting its marginal subsistence farmers tied into these established systems (a major aspect of the project), but at least the systems were there to tie into. Both CADU and PACCA, in contrast, were faced with weak or virtually nonexistent infrastructures of this sort and practically had to invent some of them.

Different extension approaches. The three projects adopted radically different approaches to reaching individual farmers, and therein lies much of the explanation for the great differences in their costs.

PACCA chose the simplest, most traditional and most costly approach—face-to-face work with individual farmers on a one-to-one tutorial basis, interspersed with occasional group meetings at the area centers. No modern communications technology, audiovisual aids or self-instructional materials were used (except to a limited extent at the staff training center, which works very much like a conventional agricultural college though with more field experience). Using these traditional methods, by late 1971 (near the end of the third year) twenty-eight PACCA agents and advisors had worked directly with only 600 "pilot" farmers out of a total of 10,000 farmers in the Koh-i-Daman area. In the Baghlan area at that time fourteen extension agents were working with only 300 farmers out of 5,000. The eventual goal of the project's opera-

---

[19]CADU's initial three-year net budget (deducting project revenues) totaled 13.8 million Ethiopian dollars, or about U.S. $5.8 million. This breaks down to 57 percent investment costs (including land, buildings, equipment and animals) and 43 percent operating costs. Expatriate staff costs took 23.2 percent of the whole budget and over 50 percent of the operating budget whereas Ethiopian staff (high- and middle-level) represented only 4.8 percent of the total budget and about 8 percent of total operating costs. (See Appendix Tables 1, 2).

PACCA's planned budget for the initial three years totaled U.S. $2.4 million (one-fourth) capital costs and three-fourths operating costs). Expatriate personnel accounted for 54.9 percent of the total (including capital) and local personnel for only 5.5 percent. Most expatriate personnel were for staff training and extension work. (See Appendix Table 4).

Puebla's direct costs for the first four years totaled $506,105 (capital costs were minimal). The bulk (52 percent) was for personnel costs, but we estimate (in the absence of direct data) that probably only one-third or at most one-half of total personnel costs were for field-level extension personnel. (See Tables in Appendix).

tional plan was to stabilize at a ratio of one agent per seventy farmers (which seems impossible for a country like Afghanistan to afford).[20]

CADU chose an extension approach with a built-in multiplier effect. It makes much use of selected model farmers as unofficial extension workers (they are given a month of training each year at CADU's experimental farm). Under this arrangement, as the system evolves each of forty CADU field agents will (by 1975) be responsible for keeping in close touch with fifteen model farmers, each of whom in turn will serve as demonstrator and communicator for 115 farm families (making a ratio of one extension agent for every 1,725 farm families). Apart from this unique arrangement, however, CADU's extension methods appear to be conventional ones.

Puebla's extension approach combines the multiplier principle used by CADU (a well-qualified extension agent works closely with chairmen of credit groups) with group meetings, study tours to experiment stations, demonstration plots and the use of mass media (radio, film showings, etc.). Puebla's small number of agents spend little time visiting individual cultivators; they concentrate on groups and group leaders and on breaking bottlenecks in the flow of credit and physical inputs and in marketing channels.

The above examples demonstrate why there is no magic in any particular extension ratio or any one "best" extension staffing or cost model. Ideally, such services should be tailored to fit the objectives, clients and all other major variables of each situation. And to keep costs down, the most efficient possible extension methods should be chosen, consistent with getting the job done well in the circumstances.

Costs of extension services. As mentioned earlier, it is nearly impossible to segregate the local-level extension service costs from closely related costs at other levels. In any event, such segregated costs have limited meaning or utility. What matters most are the extension *system's* costs, including those of training, supervision, expert backstopping, broadcasts and instructional materials production, as well as the local agent costs.

The projected 1975 costs of *all* the educational components combined in the CADU project are estimated at U.S. $210,000, including depreciation on buildings and equipment (ICED's estimate based on CADU data). This is equivalent to an average annual cost of about $3 per family in the CADU area—not simply for agricultural extension *per se*, but for continuous staff training, several adult education programs, and skill training for those displaced from the land through consolidation of small, uneconomic parcels. Considering the breadth of CADU's educational objectives and activities, these costs appear very moderate.

If Puebla's *total* 1970 expenditures (c. U.S. $203,000) are divided by the number of participating farmers that year (4,833), the average cost per farmer works out to $42. It seems evident, however, that the project is having a large spillover effect on many nonparticipating farmers, judging from the significant rise in their output per acre. Thus the true average cost per benefiting farmer is probably well below $42. Puebla's staff and budget will remain relatively constant through 1975; if by then a large number of additional farmers have bene-

---

[20]We are told by project staff that there has been considerable "spillover effect" and that extension efforts may have benefited, in some form, about three times the number of pilot farmers reached directly.

fited, then the actual average cost could easily fall to $10 or less. (Puebla's projected total costs for 1975, divided by *all* farmers in the area, bring the average cost per farmer down to $6).

PACCA's 1971 estimated operating budget of $660,000, divided by the *total number* of farmers (15,000) in the two operating areas combined, averages $44 per farmer. But if it is divided only by the farmers who had been directly "reached" by late 1971 (about 900) the average cost per farmer would be over $700. In reality this figure would probably be lower because there is evidence of some spillover effect on other farmers. In fairness it should be added that PACCA (like CADU and Puebla) is still in a relatively early development stage and thus is burdened with many one-time-only costs (especially heavy costs for international experts).

Benefits from Agricultural Extension Services

Potentially, a wide variety of benefits—social and private, economic and noneconomic—can be generated by agricultural extension services. But, for a variety of reasons, these benefits are sometimes not realized.

Latin American examples. In his evaluation of thirteen Latin American extension services assisted by the U.S. Agency for International Development over a period of thirty years, E.B. Rice concluded that by and large these services had contributed insignificantly to increasing production, mainly because of their divorce from other essential agricultural support services and the lack of research backstopping. But, viewing the situation through a wider lens, he concluded that these malfunctioning services could at least be credited with the following probable benefits:

> The extension services have provided a training ground for professional agriculturists in the public and private sectors.
>
> They have partially converted government bureaucracies to a new appreciation of the farmer and of their responsibilities to him.
>
> They have improved the quality of life for many communities, farm wives and rural youth.
>
> They have contributed in a small way to the raising of farm productivity and cash income.
>
> They form a substantial organizational infrastructure that links the farmer with the government, all the way from Guatemala to Chile. And this infrastructure could become the backbone of the structure for rural development in the region.[21]

Our own impression is that most general autonomous agricultural extension

---

[21]E.B. Rice, *Extension in the Andes: An Evaluation of Official U.S. Assistance to Agricultural Extension Services in Central and South America,* A.I.D. Evaluation Paper No. 3 (Washington, D.C.: April 1971).

services, similar in form and behavior to those studied by Rice, have a very low cost-benefit score. Others share this view.[22]

The ORD example. Properly conceived and managed, however, and given a favorable set of other circumstances, a general extension service can have a good pay-off. This, we would judge, was the case with ORD during the 1960s.

No cost-benefit appraisal, to our knowledge, has ever been made of ORD, but there seems little doubt that even in strictly economic terms (ignoring other benefits that have undoubtedly been produced) ORD's guidance program deserves some share of the credit for the impressive 4.2 percent average annual increase in the Republic of Korea's agricultural production during the 1960s—the bulk of which came from increased yield per acre. And ORD deserves special credit for the considerable diversification of agriculture that has occurred, involving much sharper production increases in such items as poultry and eggs, fruit and fresh vegetables. Sweeping land reform—which gave the great majority of South Korean farm families their own modest holdings, requiring them to become efficient farm managers and giving them greater incentive to raise production—created conditions in which a broad-gauged extension service was especially needed and certainly could be highly productive.

Thus, despite the several shortcomings we pointed to earlier in ORD's guidance program and in the Republic of Korea's overall agricultural knowledge system, ORD has probably had a quite favorable benefit/cost ratio. It undoubtedly could be even higher if some of the notable deficiencies in the present system were remedied.

To take a different type of situation—the early Gezira scheme, in which the extension system played a critical role—there can be no doubt that it paid off well for the company, the farmers and the government, and that the extension activities contributed importantly to its success.

It seems safe to conclude that the extension components of any well-conceived, economically sound and tightly managed commodity production scheme are likely to have a high benefit/cost ratio (so long as market prices remain favorable, as they did not in the case of SATEC in Senegal). But schemes of this sort that concentrate narrowly on the production of a single commercial crop provide no assurance—as the initial Gezira scheme demonstrated—that the higher production and income they create will promote other important social, political and humanistic goals of rural development.

A Green Revolution example. The question of how much the extension services contributed to India's Green Revolution, and more broadly to rural development in India, is a particularly perplexing one. We would hazard the following general judgments. First, there can be little doubt that the organizational and personnel structure created by India's earlier Community Development Program, and the greater sense of self-confidence, self-government and

---

[22]"In countries where such [agricultural] institutions and services are properly organized, they easily repay their costs many times over from increased national production and specifically pay for themselves through increased tax revenues on the higher production base providing, of course, the country has a reasonably good taxation system. The point to be noted is that many existing agricultural institutions and field services systems are not increasing farm income at all and there is no rational justification for spending anything to continue them, unless they can be built up where they can help to realize increased gross national product from agriculture." FAO, *Provisional Indicative World Plan for Agricultural Development,* Vol. II (Rome: 1970), p. 40.

ties to the rest of the nation which it inspired in many Indian villagers, created very useful foundations for India's later more concerted agricultural development efforts (particularly the Intensive Agricultural Districts Program).

It seems doubtful, however, that the activities of the Village Level Workers in their new agricultural extension role in the late 1960s were significant in precipitating the Green Revolution. As technical diagnosticians of local agricultural knowledge needs and providers of knowledge to fill these needs, they were simply too poorly qualified to be very effective. This is not to deny that they benefited village life in other important respects or that they were frequently useful expediters in getting input supplies and other essentials to the farmers.

If one takes a broad view of India's agricultural knowledge-generating and dissemination system, including the research centers and experiment stations and the more qualified agricultural experts posted at the block and district level, then it seems fair to conclude that the system as a whole did contribute significantly to the dramatic increases in production in certain areas. The larger and more progressive farmers could use the system on their own above the village level where the sources of new knowledge were concentrated, and they brought home new answers to their questions which they put to profitable use.

But this haphazard process of knowledge dissemination gave India's agricultural knowledge system an unwitting bias that exacerbated existing social inequities. The smaller farmers, especially the subsistence farmers, got left behind.

Benefits of integrated projects. It would be premature to pass anything but the most tentative judgment on the cost-benefit prospects of the newer integrated development projects—Puebla, PACCA and CADU. The most important point is that these particular projects should not be judged solely—or at this stage even primarily—by their immediate impact on production and income, but rather by their broader and longer term objectives. These are, moreover, experimental projects to test out new approaches and to generate new knowledge that will be useful to many other countries. Therefore, to judge them solely or even primarily by a narrow and short-term economic cost-benefit calculation would be to ignore their larger purpose. However, their impact on production and income and their general economic viability remain important questions that must be examined carefully.

In this respect, CADU appears to be showing good progress at this stage, especially considering the many difficulties inherent in its context and the great complexity of the scheme. By 1970 the number of participating farm families had risen to 4,667, considerably exceeding the target of 1,375. Most other curves were also moving up briskly by then—loans, purchases of improved seeds and fertilizer, hectare yields, and income to the project from seed multiplication and trade centers (which had already begun to turn a net profit). CADU management is optimistic that by the end of 1975 the whole operation will become self-supporting (escept for the educational elements) and that the new cooperatives will be nearly ready to take over. The one cloud on the horizon is a possible drop in the domestic wheat price as CADU's production mounts from 10,000 quintals (2,200,000 lbs.) in 1970/71 to a projected 200,000 quintals (44,000,000 lbs.) by 1974/75.

The *Puebla Project* got off to a strong start between 1968 and 1970; the number of participants rose from 103 to 4,833, and their combined production rose from 304 tons, worth U.S. $22,861, to 33,647 tons, worth $2,530,254. Average yields per hectare for participants exceeded the control group average by about 40 percent.

As noted earlier, however, an unexplained slow-down in the rate of new participation in 1971 signaled possible unforeseen difficulties for Puebla. The fickle weather in the area is always another potential source of trouble. On the other hand, if CIMMYT succeeds in developing new hybrid maize varieties suitable to Puebla conditions and with substantially higher yields than the traditional *criolla* varieties, progress could greatly accelerate.

A set of calculations for the Puebla Project—using a range of alternative assumptions on interest rates, prices and input costs—show benefit/cost ratios ranging from 1.13 in the poorest combination of circumstances to 2.88 in the best. (See Appendix Table 7.)

PACCA's progress thus far has been more spotty and its ultimate economic viability is still open to question. PACCA's experience dramatizes how an integrated project confined to limited areas of a country can find itself severely handicapped by national institutions and policies beyond its control. Serious bottlenecks in credit (due to the conservative policies of the National Agricultural Bank), in marketing (due in part to incompatible national policies), and in the supply of well-qualified local candidates for staff positions (due to limitations of agricultural educational institutions) will continue to plague PACCA until and unless they are broken.

On the brighter side, the project made an important breakthrough by demonstrating that there is a broad international market for top-quality Afghan grapes. Significant progress has also been made in developing good local extension personnel and in laying the foundations for effective farmer organizations, both of which can have lasting value. According to more recent reports from the PACCA project, some headway is also being made in easing the credit bottleneck.

All three of these integrated projects may yield important lessons helpful in devising new and more effective ways to meet the needs of subsistence farm families throughout the developing world. But the truth must be faced that programs which are genuinely effective in helping subsistence families and reducing poverty will almost certainly have unattractive economic benefit/cost ratios measured in the narrow conventional manner. Most will have to be heavily subsidized by more fortunate areas and individuals in the country until they can get on their own feet, which in many cases will be a long time. A broader sort of cost-benefit measure will have to be applied, one that is addressed to the real issue: whether the social costs of *not* subsidizing these backward areas and subsistence families will be greater than the costs of subsidizing them.

Costs and Benefits of Rural Training Programs

This section examines the costs and benefits of six models of rural training programs about which much information has already been given:[23] (1) the Farmer Training Centres, FTCs, in Kenya; (2) SENA's mobile rural training program, PPP-R, in Colombia; (3) IRRI's rice production training program in the

---

[23]See Chapters 4, 5, 8 and 9, and the case studies.

Philippines; (4) the MTTS program in Thailand; (5) Nigeria's VICs, and (6) Senegal's training centers for artisans and farmers, RTCs.

All these programs (unlike agricultural extension programs) provide systematic skill training—for either farming or nonfarming occupations—for a sustained period (one week to ten months) for participants at a training facility. There the similarity ends; their objectives and clienteles, the skills they teach and how they teach them, the nature of their facilities and the duration of their courses all differ greatly. As a consequence, so do their costs and benefits.

Despite their diversity, however, it is useful to examine them as a group in order to identify some of the main variables that strongly influence their unit costs and the factors that condition their benefits.

In all but one of these cases we concluded that the program was basically sound and useful, but in four cases we identified ways in which their benefit/cost ratio could be substantially improved. In the case of the rural training centers in Senegal, though the training itself was good and resulted in some positive benefits, we questioned whether in a relatively poor developing country this approach could be economically viable on a broader scale and, even if it were, whether it would be as advantageous as several possible alternatives.

Major cost determinants. The principal variables influencing costs in these six training programs were:

> *Type of facilities*—whether permanent or borrowed, and investment cost per place.
> *Type of equipment*—investment cost per trainee.
> *Residential or nonresidential.*
> *Utilization of capacity*—full or partial.
> *Type of staff*—qualifications; full-time or part-time; domestic and foreign; staff salary levels.
> *Staff/Trainee ratio.*
> *Duration of course.*

Variations in unit costs. Table 11.3 compares the six sample training programs according to these important variables and shows our estimate of unit costs per trainee wherever it has been possible to make at least a rough one. (We experimented with converting the unit costs of different programs to some common denominator, such as a full-time week equivalent, in order to permit direct comparisons. While this is arithmetically possible, we concluded that such statistical manipulation would overstrain the fragile data and could result in unsound and unfair interpretations.)

Senegal's centers and IRRI have high costs per trainee, mainly because they have expensive permanent facilities and equipment; their courses are full-time, residential and relatively long in duration (six months and nine months respectively); they use full-time, relatively highly paid professional staffs (including expatriate members); and their ratio of trainees to instructors is low.

One significant difference between the two programs should be noted. IRRI's training program was created as an adjunct of IRRI's research program; hence it benefits economically and qualitatively by being able to draw upon IRRI's central administrative services, research staff (for occasional teaching), experimental plots and general facilities. The only incremental costs required were to add to the training program one special training building, extra dormitory space and a small training staff. (SENA's rural training program similarly benefits from being a new appendage of a larger, well-established training organization.)

Senegal's rural training centers, in contrast, had no ongoing organization to draw upon; they started from scratch as separate entities and were required to provide all of their own facilities, staff and administrative services.

At the low end of the cost scale (relative to hours of instruction) are Nigeria's VICs and SENA's mobile rural training programs. The main reasons for their low unit costs are evident. Neither has permanent facilities (they use borrowed ones by and large), their programs are nonresidential and part-time, their ratio of trainees to instructors is higher than IRRI's or the rural training centers in Senegal, and their total instructional hours are fewer. The VICs have the further advantage (unlike SENA) of using mainly well-qualified part-time staff.

Kenya's FTCs and Thailand's MTTS occupy the middle portion of the cost scale, though for somewhat different reasons. The FTCs have high cost elements: their own permanent facilities and equipment, a full-time professional staff, and full-time residential courses. Moreover, some of the FTCs are seriously underutilized, thus forcing up both capital and operating costs per trainee. What keeps these costs from being higher per trainee is mainly the short duration of their courses (one to two weeks); otherwise they would rival the high costs of the nine-month farmer and artisan training centers in Senegal.

Table 11.3
Comparison of Key Cost Determinants of Six Training Programs

	Senegal RTC	IRRI Extension Training	Kenya FTC	Thailand MTTS	Nigeria VIC	Colombia SENA/ PPP-R
Facilities						
Permanent (P)	P	P	P			
Borrowed (B)				B	B	B
Staff						
Full-time (FT)	FT	FT	FT	FT		FT
Part-time (PT)					PT	
Staff per center	3(3)[1]	(7)[1]	4	8	10	1
Staff Cost	High	High	Medium	Medium	Low	Low
Course Features						
Residential (R)	R	R	R			
Non-residential (NR)				NR	NR	NR
Duration	9 mos	6 mos	1-2 wks	5 mos (15 hrs/week)	10 mos (10 hrs/week)	40-120 hrs
Number of trainees per staff member	7	5	10	25	10	21
Cost per trainee per course[2] (in U.S.$)	$648-828	$3,249[3]	$30	$130	$104	$20[4]
Opportunity cost to trainee or employer	High	High	Medium	Low	Low	Low

[1]Numbers within parentheses are for international staff.
[2]Per trainee costs include amortization of capital except for Nigerian VIC and SENA/PPP-R. Only the operating costs are given for these two cases.
[3]Includes international travel costs for trainees.
[4]Unit cost for regular courses excluding migrant workers.

SOURCE: ICED estimates from project data.

196

MTTS has relatively low costs per trainee mainly because it generally uses borrowed or low-cost rented facilities, is nonresidential, and operates two shifts per day. But MTTS does have some high cost elements: a full-time, relatively highly paid staff, a comparatively low trainee/instructor ratio (averaging 12 to 1 per session, or 24 to 1 per day), and strikingly high costs (about 30 percent of total operating costs) for consumable materials.

Another important cost, not shown in the budget, enters into three of these programs: the opportunity costs to the trainees or their employers. For the Senegal training centers and IRRI these costs are very high (roughly equivalent to the full-time earnings of the trainee for the length of the training period). For the FTC in Kenya as well, there is considerable opportunity cost for the trainees. In contrast, these opportunity costs are virtually nil for the MTTS, VIC and SENA programs since they are scheduled so as not to interfere with the trainee's normal working hours.

Cost-reducing possibilities. There are a number of ways to reduce the unit costs of some of these programs without serious damage to their effectiveness. IRRI's course, for example, could probably be shortened somewhat without serious loss (participants complain that six months is needlessly long), and more short-term specialized courses could be conducted during the six months or more each year when the long course is not being given, thereby using staff and facilities more intensively.

Kenya's FTCs would be less expensive (and undoubtedly more productive) if they were converted to or combined with multipurpose training centers that could use facilities and staff more fully and enable each type of course to draw on a wider range of talent for instruction.

Thailand's MTTS program could reduce staff costs considerably by hiring local master craftsmen as part-time instructors for certain courses (as the VICs have done), and by investing in well-devised self-instructional materials (there are none at present). MTTS might also get better learning results for the resources invested by varying the length of courses for different skills, and by enabling each trainee to build on the skills and knowledge he arrives with and to proceed from there at his own pace (in part by using well-programmed self-instructional units).

SENA, we suspect, might also improve its cost-effectiveness and make its available resources go further by using master craftsmen in an area as part-time instructors, where possible. It could improve its benefit-cost ratio if it is able to link in with other rural development schemes and agencies in more areas, rather than being obliged to go it alone.

In summary, the following cost-reducing possibilities warrant exploration in any skill training program:

Converting from full-time to part-time programs, combining work and training and scheduling sessions to fit the convenience of trainees.

Making fuller use of expensive facilities and equipment.

Using available facilities where possible, rather than building new ones.

Sharing facilities, by different types of specialized programs.

Using competent artisans, craftsmen, farmers and others with special skills and knowledge as part-time instructors (providing them first with orientation in good teaching methods).

Placing more emphasis on self-instructional materials so that trainees can learn more on their own and proceed at their own pace.

Replacing expensive expatriate staff as quickly as possible by giving initial priority to the training of competent local instructors and administrators.

Improving benefits. The cost side of the equation standing alone has little meaning or utility, except for judging a program's general economic feasibility. Regardless of how attractive the program may seem, if the country cannot afford it on a sufficient scale to be effective it is not a realistic option.

To appraise the general efficacy of a program, its costs must be compared with the learning results (internal efficiency) and with the economic and other benefits accruing to the trainees and society from these learning results.

We had great difficulty finding hard evidence on the actual training results of these programs and especially on subsequent benefits. But we did gather enough clues, including some from our sample field surveys, to form a general judgment concerning the efficiency and benefits and how they might be improved.

IRRI's unrealized benefits. It was clear in the case of IRRI, for example, that the training itself was excellent but that as much as two-thirds or more of it was wasted because only a fraction of the trainees had returned home and trained other extension personnel—the central object of the program. In a few situations, however, such as Sri Lanka, Indonesia and one district of India, where concerted efforts were being made to strengthen extension services for rice farmers, the IRRI training was reported of great value. A tightening up of IRRI's recruitment and selection procedures—to gain greater guarantees that its trainees would be assigned upon returning home to posts that would utilize their new training effectively—could drastically improve the benefit-cost ratio of the program. (IRRI was in the process of taking such steps at the time of the ICED visit.)

Senegal's RTCs—a mixed record. An ILO follow-up study of the artisan trainees of Senegal's training centers revealed that though some former trainees had increased their earnings (presumably as a result of their training), many had not, and a substantial number were not getting a chance to apply much of what they had learned. Partly as a consequence of these findings, adjustments were made in the programs. (Among the six training programs under review this is the only case where a systematic effort had been made to check on former trainees.)

Kenya FTCs—another mixed picture. Several small and partial studies were made a number of years ago to investigate what useful impact Kenya's FTCs were having. (See Chapter 4.) Taken together, these studies suggested that many of the farmer participants had improved their practices and incomes and some had passed along useful ideas and information to their neighbors. But there is cause to believe that many who attended the FTCs were more progressive and productive farmers to begin with; hence it is difficult to know how much credit should be given to their FTC training. Moreover, there is also the disturbing fact that the popularity of the FTCs has declined rather sharply among farmers and their wives in recent years, strongly suggesting that from *their* point of view the benefit/cost ratio did not warrant the opportunity costs and modest cash fees involved in attending an FTC. Thus major improvement in the content and methods of FTC programs—taking careful account of the felt needs of farmers and their wives—seems strongly indicated.

MTTS—three common flaws. Thailand's MTTS program, judging from a limited follow-up study of its former trainees by an independent organization, appears to be getting some useful results for at least a portion of its trainees (see Chapter 5). But the same study suggested that substantial numbers were not getting any significant income benefit from their training (though about half were girls, and undoubtedly a high proportion of them were getting significant domestic benefits).

The MTTS program demonstrates three important flaws common to many skill training programs (probably the great majority). First, the program has been established in specific market areas without prior exploration of what types of training were most needed and offered the most promising employment opportunities. Second, no systematic effort has been made to monitor former trainees to ascertain whether and how they are actually using their new training and with what results, and to use these findings to correct shortcomings in the program (as ILO sought to do in Senegal). Third, skill training has been viewed in isolation from related development activities in the area and from other types of follow-up support services that trainees may require to realize the fullest advantage from their training, such as help in securing credit to start or expand their own enterprise, follow up advanced technical training, and useful entrepreneurial training, management counseling, etc. All three of these flaws are susceptible of correction, which clearly would improve the benefit/cost ratio.

VICs' results. The Nigerian VICs are undoubtedly producing significant benefits for their trainees, many of whom have earned promotions or improved their qualifications and job tenure. One of the best indications is that the number of applicants for training continues to exceed the available places. (See Chapter 5.) Again, the VICs could undoubtedly improve their benefit/cost ratio by putting some moderate effort into checking up regularly on a representative sample of their former trainees and adjusting their recruitment policies and program offerings in light of the findings. Practically the only hard evidence on benefits we were able to obtain was that collected in the field by our own survey (which, though useful, was far from sufficient).

SENA's uneven benefits. The latter comment applies also to SENA's rural program, the PPP-R, but we were assured that SENA would soon initiate efforts to evaluate impact. Our own limited survey in two contrasting SENA service areas (see Chapter 4 and the case study for details of the survey) left little doubt that the training was useful to many participants, but distinctly more so in one area than the other. The survey also indicated—and this we considered particularly significant—that the results were considerably better in areas where SENA was collaborating closely with one or more other agencies, supplying well-defined and clearly needed training inputs for a more broadly planned local development program. When the roving SENA instructors had to go it alone because no other agencies had done local development planning, which unfortunately was often the case, the results were less impressive. SENA's managers are aware of this and are endeavoring to correct it.

A summing up. Most training programs can improve their impact and hence their benefit/cost ratio by:

- Investigating local employment market conditions before deciding what skills to teach.

- Checking regularly on what use their former trainees are making of their training and how it is benefiting them and, if the record is unsatisfactory, finding out why and taking corrective action.

- Linking their training activities wherever possible with local development plans and with complementary activities of other agencies.
- Offering follow-up training for those who need and want it, and trying to harmonize their training efforts with credit and advisory services for small entrepreneurs and with such other support services as may be required to strengthen and accelerate the growth of small industry and other small enterprises.

Costs and Benefits of Educational Technologies

The inclusion of appropriate and well-programmed mass media—including print materials—as integral elements of rural learning programs could probably result in much improved cost-effectiveness and benefit/cost ratios in many cases. Unfortunately, there is little evidence to prove the point, mainly because there are so few such programs to examine.

The ACPO example. One excellent example of such a program is ACPO in Colombia. Earlier in this report (see Chapters 6 and 10) we summarized the evidence on the impact of ACPO's various programs, which is apparently considerable. There is no way to measure these economic and noneconomic results, however, and match them against the corresponding costs to get a clear benefit/cost ratio. But if it were possible, the ratios would undoubtedly be quite favorable, particularly compared with more conventional ways for attaining comparable results. That this voluntary program has survived and continued to grow for some twenty-five years is impressive testimony to the value its clients attach to it.

ACPO is by far the most capital-intensive and talent-intensive of all our cases. An inventory of ACPO's main facilities is shown on the comparative capital cost table appended to this report. Unfortunately, we cannot put a monetary value of them, partly because many of the items were contributed. Clearly such a figure, if available, would amount to several millions of U.S. dollars. On an amortized basis, capital costs would contribute a considerable fraction of the unit costs per learner (if unit costs could be calculated).

The projected operating costs of ACPO for 1972 are summarized below.

Anticipated operating expenses (U.S.$) for 1972:

Radio programs	$ 580,000
Cultural Division	676,000
Publishing	966,000
Newspaper	338,000
Administration and maintenance	870,000
Regional activities	725,000
Total	$4,155,000

Although it is a sizeable program for its type, ACPO's annual expenditures are modest in comparison with Colombia's formal education expenditures or even SENA's total expenditures (on its urban as well as its rural training programs). Unlike most formal and nonformal education programs, ACPO puts a large share of its operating funds into the preparation of good program content, relying on volunteers to staff its multimedia system at the local level. This seems a critically important procedure that others would do well to note.

Tanzania's cooperative education system. Tanzania's Cooperative Education system is the other one of our cases that depends heavily on mass media technologies, especially radio, correspondence and numerous print materials. We have a fair idea of the financial costs of this activity: the central facilities cost some $650,000; operating costs totaled nearly $300,000 for 1969/70 (excluding heavy costs of expatriate staff); and projected operating costs for 1972/73 total nearly $500,000 (including replacement of expatriates with local personnel). Beyond this, however, important locally built facilities and contributed manpower are used in the program. (See Appendix Tables.)

The benefits side of the equation is exceedingly misty, even as to the number of participants making effective use of these educational services. The Five-Year Cooperative Education Plan (1969-74) provides for 7,000 to 7,500 trainee-weeks in addition to seminars and conferences in the Cooperative College for over 1,500 cooperative staff, and some educational service for all of the 1.8 million farming families in Tanzania.

In practice, however, the numbers actually using the educational services are considerably lower. (See Chapter 6.) And the impact of the program on the operation of the cooperative system is not too clear. Our direct observation and other evidence from internal assessment in the program indicate that persons who have been exposed to the education program have a higher knowledge and understanding of the cooperative system than others. But it has also been observed that a cooperative's performance does not necessarily depend on the education of its staff and committeemen. While this may be partly due to the weaknesses in the education program, it is equally likely to be the consequence of the general "structural" conditions in the society that determine how effectively the cooperative system can function and that can limit the impact of cooperative education.

On the whole, despite its shortcomings, the program has, through its combination of media and various methods, reached large numbers of people, including those in poor rural areas with high illiteracy, and clearly suggests possibilities for such efforts in similar rural situations.

ORD. As previously noted, ORD's multimedia system has a high potential but is in need of reinvigoration by stronger programming inputs. This could produce substantially larger benefits from the resources already tied up in communications staff and facilities.

Need for large-scale experimentation. This whole field of new educational media and technologies, as emphasized in Chapter 10, is an inviting one for large-scale experimentation and development. Until this happens, questions of costs and benefits will remain largely unanswered. The basic point to be recognized is that the media and other technologies should not be thought of merely as elements to be tacked on to traditional teaching-learning systems to enrich their content and make them work a little better. New technologies, particularly new media, should be thought of primarily as potential means for answering learning needs that are totally beyond the pedagogical and economic reach of conventional educational technologies.

Provisional Answers to Key Questions

This review of the sources of support, costs and benefits of nonformal education for rural development has, we hope, made it clear that the economics of nonformal education must be viewed in a much wider perspective than that ordinarily applied to the costing and appraisal of individual projects for budgetary and external assistance purposes. Any massive attack on the urgent rural learning needs of developing nations through nonformal and informal as well as formal educational means must harness vast resources beyond those recorded in conventional financial accounts.

Moreover, the costs and benefits that must be considered in any such efforts far transcend the limits of conventional cost-benefit calculations. If rural development is to be conceived—as it must be—in terms of much broader social and human goals than are measureable by statistics of aggregate agricultural production and income, and in terms of critically important non-economic as well as direct income benefits to individuals and families, then it follows that measures of social costs and social benefits, and noneconomic private benefits, must be devised and brought to bear on the making of strategies, plans and decisions. To employ only a narrow economic calculus blind to many of the most fundamental human values involved in broad-gauged rural development is to run the risk of distorting and defeating these values rather than advancing them. It remains a major challenge to social scientists to develop through research and experimentation a much more adequate and workable set of indicators and methodologies for assessing these broader private and social benefits.

We close this chapter by venturing some answers to three of the key questions posed at the start. We wish to emphasize, however, the provisional nature of these answers and the importance of further investigation by many others.

First, would a large-scale expansion of nonformal rural education be economically feasible in developing countries?

To this our answer is definitely yes—*provided that the political conditions are favorable.* Developing countries, even the poorest, could mobilize the necessary resources—including many unconventional, partially hidden and poorly utilized ones they already possess—to support a steady and sizeable enlargement of nonformal (and informal) educational opportunities over the next two decades in order to meet the important learning needs of their rural people.

If sufficient importance were attached to this purpose by the governments and the people alike, these countries could harness all sorts of existing professional talent and institutional strength; educational, communication and other facilities; and, above all, much voluntary help. In carrying out such an effort they could make effective use of large amounts of carefully tailored external assistance, but the leadership and initiative and the bulk of the needed resources would have to come largely from within.

Second, what are the potential cost advantages of nonformal education?

The inherent flexibility and unconventionality of nonformal education—its freedom to be different, to improvise and to adapt to an endless variety of circumstances and opportunities—give it many *potential* cost advantages over formal education. But these advantages do not arise automatically; they must be continually sought out and exploited. The risks of missing out on these low-cost potentialities are especially great in large programs subjected to standardized national rules and other homogenizing influences of large bureaucracies.

Third, is it feasible to apply cost-effectiveness and cost-benefit analysis to nonformal education and, if so, what operational purposes would such analysis serve?

Again our answer is affirmative. Such analysis is not only feasible (as our case studies have shown) but absolutely essential to any rational diagnosis, planning or evaluation in the field of nonformal education. True, it is rarely possible to make rate-of-return calculations that have much real meaning or validity; but such calculations are only one very limited and specialized application of the general logic of cost-benefit analysis. What is basically important in attempting to examine any nonformal education program in its socioeconomic context is to *think of the relationships between resource costs incurred and results attained,* including both immediate and longer-term results, and both economic and noneconomic benefits. While these can never be fully or precisely measured or even fully defined and identified, it is generally possible, by asking the right questions, to obtain enough relevant indicative evidence to form reasonable judgments.

Analyses and judgments of this kind can be very helpful to planners and decision-makers in deciding: (1) whether a proposed pilot or experimental program, if successful, would be economically feasible to replicate on a larger scale; (2) whether a proposed program, even if economically possible, would be a worthwhile investment; (3) which of various alternative educational approaches to particular objectives would probably be the most efficient and effective; and (4) what steps could be taken to improve the efficiency or productivity of ongoing nonformal education activities.

It is evident from the foregoing review of the economics of nonformal education that the financing, costs, efficiency and productivity of such activities are closely tied to the manner in which they are planned, organized, managed and staffed. The next chapter explores these important matters.

12: PLANNING, ORGANIZATION, MANAGEMENT, AND STAFFING

Of all the problems that bedevil nonformal education programs, the most complex and often the most resistant to remedy are those associated with the planning and management of such programs. The variety of factors involved—organizational structures and chains of command, degrees of latitude for making decisions at different levels, geographic diversity, personnel structures and rules, integration and coordination with other development activities—all these are so tightly interwoven that they cannot realistically be segregated even for analytical purposes.

These organizational matters have cropped up repeatedly in earlier chapters of this report in a host of connections. Our aim here is to bring these points and additional ones together and to suggest ways to alleviate these ubiguitous problems.

Comparative Organizational Features of the Cases

One of the most visible features of the field of nonformal education is the great diversity of organizations and organizational approaches to dealing with different programs. In this aspect, nonformal education contrasts sharply with formal education's relatively uniform organization and centralized administration. We have attempted in Table 12.1 to portray this diversity in twenty-one programs covered by the study,[1] particularly with regard to such features as the nature of their organizational structures and sponsorship, their geographic coverage, the manner and extent to which their educational services are integrated with other educational and noneducational activities, and the types of personnel systems they use.

Differing organizational structures. Some programs, for example, have hierarchical structures with many levels—India's Intensive Agricultural District Program (IADP) is an extreme example of this.[2] On the other hand, programs such as that of the International Rice Research Institute (IRRI), Nigeria's Vocational Improvement Centres (VICs) and Senegal's Rural Training Centres (RTCs) have simple one- or two-tier structures.

Variations in autonomy. Some programs have a high degree of autonomy in planning their own activities, making basic program and operational decisions, and conducting their day-to-day activities. This applies, for example, to Acción Cultural Popular (ACPO) (because of its private character); it also applies to the Republic of Korea's Office of Rural Development (ORD) and Tanzania's Cooperative Education system, both of which have liberal mandates to run their own affairs though they are under the broad supervision of a regular min-

---

[1]Most of these programs are treated in separate case studies. (See list in Appendix.)
[2]Donald G. Green, "Training for Indian Agricultural Development: Challenge of the 1970s," mimeographed (New Delhi, India: The Ford Foundation, September 1970).

istry. Other nationally sponsored programs have considerably less autonomy. The Mobile Trade Training Schools (MTTS) program in Thailand is closely controlled, right down to the procurement of supplies by individual units of MTTS (which often wait for lengthy periods and make special trips to Bangkok to get needed items).

All of the tightly knit integrated development programs applying to limited geographic areas—such as those discussed in Chapter 7: Gezira Cotton Scheme in the Sudan, Lilongwe Land Development Programme in Malawi, Chilalo Agricultural Development Unit (CADU) in Ethiopia, Programme on Agricultural Credit and Cooperation in Afghanistan (PACCA), and Puebla in Mexico—also enjoy a high degree of independence from national bureaucratic structures, giving them unusual flexibility. The educational components within these projects do not operate autonomously but fall under the jurisdiction of the project managers.

Nationwide versus specific area programs. In contrast to those programs mentioned above with limited geographic focus, others serve, at least in principle, a nationwide area and clientele; among such programs are ACPO, ORD, India's Community Development Program, *animation rurale* in Senegal, and Promoción Profesional Popular-Rural (PPP-R), the National Apprenticeship Service's (SENA) rural training program in Colombia.

Extent of integration. One of the most important variations is the degree to which programs are closely linked to or actually integrated with complementary agricultural and rural development services in each area. Most of the skill training programs—such as the MTTS in Thailand, SENA's PPP-R, and the rural artisan and farmer training centers in Senegal—have virtually no connections with other development services. Among the exceptions to this rule are the small entrepreneur training activities in India, which are part of an integrated package of services for the same clientele.

Many agricultural extension services operate without organic links or close collaboration with credit, input and marketing services handled by other organizations. Most Latin American extension services are of this type and so, to a considerable extent, is ORD.

At the opposite end of the scale are, of course, such integrated projects as CADU, Comilla, PACCA and Puebla, in which extension services are fully meshed with virtually all complementary services for agricultural development.

Personnel systems. There is a corresponding diversity in personnel systems and practices. As a general rule, staffs of government-run programs (such as ORD, India's IADP, and MTTS) are tied into the civil service system. SENA is a notable exception; though technically a public agency, its unusual autonomy enables it to have its own career service and salary structure. In a project such as PACCA (for which FAO is the executing agency), international civil service rules and salary structures enter importantly.

As a relatively large private organization, ACPO has its own career structure. A number of other programs follow ad hoc staffing practices, as do the VICs in Nigeria (whose staff is composed largely of part-time employees) and IRRI and Puebla, which are not bound to any fixed salary and career service structures.

Criteria for Assessing Alternative Organization Arrangements

No one of these organizational patterns and modes of operating nonformal education is inherently superior to the others; each has its own value so long

Table 12.1
Comparative Analysis of Organizational Features of Selected Nonformal Education Programs[1]

	Total No.	AGRICULTURAL TRAINING/EXTENSION					NONFARM SKILLS			
		ORD Rep. Korea	SATEC Senegal	FTC Kenya	IRRI Phillipines	SENA/PPP-R Colombia	MTTS Thailand	VICs Nigeria	RTCs Senegal	SSII Ind
Type of Organization:										
Semi-autonomous public	9	X	X			X				
Regular govt. dept.	9			X			X	X	X	X
Nongovt., nonprofit	2									
Autonomous international	1				X					
No. of organizational layers		3	3	2	1	3	2	2	2	4
Geographic Coverage:										
Multinational	1				X					
National (in principle)	12	X		X		X	X	X	X	X
Selected Areas	8		X							
Degree of Integration or Coordination with Complementary Services:										
Largely self-contained, combination of essential services	3									
Combination of/coordination with multiple services	8		X							X
Little or no combination of/ coordination with services	10	X		X	X	X	X	X	X	
Personnel System:										
Part of civil service	13	X		X			X		X	2
Own career structure	6		X		X	X				
Ad hoc staffing	2									
International staff (used as regular staff)	9		X		X				X	

[1]See Table 1.1 for official name of each program.

	SELF-HELP				INTEGRATED				
Anim. Rurale Senegal	PRRM Philippines	Coop. Educ. Tanzania	Comilla Bangladesh	ACPO Colombia	IADP India	CADU Ethiopia	PACCA Afghanistan	Puebla Mexico	Lilongwe Malawi
		X	X			X	X	X	X
X					X				
	X			X					
3	2	3	2	3	5	3	3	2	3
X		X		X					
	X		X		X	X	X	X	X
						X	X		X
	X		X		X			X	
X		X		X					
X		X	X		X		X		X
	X					X		X	
	X								
X		X				X	X		X

207

as the most appropriate features are chosen for each purpose. There is certainly a place, for example, for tightly managed integrated development schemes applying to selected areas, but since the whole of a country cannot be blanketed with them, somewhat looser and less intensive nationwide programs must serve all the uncovered areas.

It would be absurd to try, for the sake of tidy organization charts, to impose some nonolithic pattern on all types of nonformal education. To do so would dry up many sources of initiative, competence and resources for nonformal education; each kind of arrangement, as we shall try to show below, has its own peculiar advantages and limitations and its own set of problems. These deserve careful consideration in designing or revamping any program.

The tests we have applied in assessing each of these alternative organizational features and arrangements are these:

- Does it facilitate effective planning and evaluation?
- Does it contribute, in the program's implementation, to flexibility and adaptability to individual areas, clienteles and changing conditions?
- Is it compatible with serving the needs of the whole population and the need for sustained socioeconomic development?
- Does it facilitate the recruitment, retention and efficient utilization of competent staff members?
- Does it encourage coordination with complementary services and the efficient joint use of resources?

In the sections that follow we attempt to extract from the cases various lessons regarding these questions, though we should warn at the outset that they do not yield answers applicable to all situations.

Before entering this discussion it is also important to call attention to the frequently harsh limitations on the administrative capabilities of developing countries, which vary greatly in this respect according to their heritage and level of development. If these limitations are not taken into careful account in designing programs, high hopes may be dashed because too great a burden has been imposed on fragile administrative structures and the limited talent available.[3]

Diagnosis and Planning

Need for national development strategies. Ideally, any nonformal education program aimed at promoting rural development should be planned within a framework of well-conceived national and rural development strategies, policies and priorities, adapted and elaborated to fit each area.[4] Without such a framework to guide them, the designers of educational programs must either devise their own strategies and priorities and improvise as best they can, or ig-

---

[3]"It is easy to suppose that, having made a correct diagnosis of the farmers' situation and attitudes, it is simply a matter of choosing the correct administrative tool. But this neglects the fact that society itself has not a total armory of tools to choose from. In some stages of a developing society, to call for a large, efficient, honest and well-coordinated bureaucracy is to ask for the moon; in some, to allocate a major function to private enterprise or Cooperatives may be equally futile; in some, to expect anything but self-interest and faction from local party-political activity may be to court disaster." Guy Hunter, The Administration of Agricultural Development: Lessons from India (London: Oxford University Press, 1970), p. 10.
[4]See Arthur T. Mosher, To Create a Modern Agriculture: Organization and Planning (New York: Agricultural Development Council, Inc., 1971), Chapter 8.

nore the matter and proceed blindly. Unfortunately, what one often finds in rural areas is several such program architects working independently on different objectives and assumptions with no reference to any general strategy or to each other's designs. The net result is bound to be educational chaos.

Though national plans often speak of strategies and policies for rural development, little progress has been made in most countries in actually fashioning realistic and internally consistent frameworks, not only for planning nonformal education but also for planning all other pertinent rural development efforts.

The best approximations to such frameworks are found in those relatively few special cases, such as CADU and Lilongwe, where a substantial amount of broad planning was done for a selected area prior to launching an integrated development scheme. But suffer from the lack of national perspective.

Even in the absence of clear-cut and consistent national strategy and policy frameworks, it is still possible and worthwhile to take a rational and comprehensive planning approach to the development of individual areas, especially if a watchful eye is kept on likely exogenous constraints and if local area planners are given sufficient latitude by higher authorities to tailor programs to local peculiarities.

Steps in planning. Planning nonformal educational programs in such a local context, we suggest, should start with the following sequence of steps:

1. diagnosis of the general features, potentialities and present state of development of the area;

2. diagnosis of the special characteristics and realistic needs and interests of potential educational audiences;

3. a clear definition of learning objectives, including relative priorities and proper time sequence, and the learning clienteles to be served;

4. identification of other pertinent educational activities planned or under way in the same area, and at levels above it, with which the new program should be appropriately related;

5. similar identification of relevant noneducational factors, services and broader development schemes and objectives applying to the same area, with which the new educational activity should also be properly related in order to make a maximum contribution to development;

6. identification of built-in social, economic, institutional, administrative or political factors that might either help or hamper the new program's performance;

7. identification of national policies and priorities that would affect the new program's performance.

Until these basic diagnostic steps have been taken it would be premature to decide what educational solution best fits the situation. Before fastening on any particular educational model, the merits of possible alternatives should be examined and weighed, including stringent testing of their short-term and long-term economic viability. Whatever design is finally chosen, it should include provisions for continuous evaluation that will feed back prompt signals when anything is going wrong and provide reliable clues for modifying the original design as conditions warrant.

The above step-by-step prescription for the initial planning of nonformal education programs in relation to other educational and noneducational factors in the same rural area may appear at first to violate our earlier injunction against overestimating and overburdening the administrative capabilities of developing countries. But these steps can and should be taken regardless of how strong or real these capabilities may be. To ignore any one of these steps or, worse still, to pass over the diagnostic stage and prescribe a particular educational model on the untested assumption that it will fit the situation, is a sure route to trouble. From the evidence and our observations we have concluded that wherever nonformal education programs have encountered serious trouble, it is almost invariably traceable, at least in part, to poor initial planning or no real planning at all.

Routes to trouble. The question is not *whether* the diagnostic steps outline above should be taken but rather *how* they can best be taken in particular circumstances. Elaborate fact-finding expeditions and sophisticated analytical methods are not essential, though obviously the more information there is and the more exacting the analysis the more useful and trustworthy the results are likely to be. Basically, it is more a matter of asking the right common-sense questions and of viewing the situation in a broad, systematic and analytical manner.

Good examples of planning. In CADU and Puebla, for example, the program planners undertook unusually extensive preparations (including a series of socioeconomic baseline studies) to gain an understanding of the local people and conditions before attempting to lay out specific action plans. And, knowing that some important factors were bound to elude their diagnosis or be misinterpreted and that unforeseeable developments would inevitably arise, they made provision for monitoring and assessing the program's performance and impact as it moved ahead, retaining wide latitude for making necessary adjustments.[5]

From what we know of its origins, the Comilla project was evidently planned intelligently and carefully by persons who took a broad view and were thoroughly familiar with the local scene. The project had an interesting genesis. Foreign experts had originally come up with a design to be applied simultaneously in experimental areas of East and West Pakistan. Their design was accepted and tried in West Pakistan, but with undistinguished results. But local leaders in East Pakistan (now Bangladesh) rejected the plan. They fashioned, after several years of experimentation and systematic study of local circumstances, a totally different design, based on a different philosophy, broader vision and better local understanding. This home-grown model became the Comilla Project, which has earned international acclaim as a novel and effective approach to integrated rural development.[6]

---

[5]The Puebla planners, for example, found that CIMMYT's hybrid corn varieties were poorly adapted to a high-altitude rainfed land, and so quickly switched the project's focus back to traditional *criolla* varieties of the area. Meanwhile, they initiated new research to develop higher-yielding hybrids compatible with these special ecological conditions.

CADU's planners wrongly estimated the impact their new milk collecting and marketing scheme would have on the nutrition of rural children. When their monitoring system picked up the disturbing fact that, with an easy and profitable new marketing mechanism available, subsistence farmers were sending the whole of the meager daily milk production to market, leaving none for their own babies and young children, CADU managers promptly suspended the premature milk marketing scheme until the scrawny cows could be bred up to being better milk producers.

[6]See Manzoor Ahmed, *Education for Rural Development In East Bengal*, ICED Background Paper No. 1 (Essex, Conn., April 1972), and Harvey M. Choldin, "An Organizational Analysis of Rural Development Projects at Comilla, East Pakistan," *Economic Development and Cultural Change*, Vol. 20, No. 4 (July 1972), pp. 671-690, for recent analysis of the Comilla project.

Granting the narrowness of its objectives, the Gezira Scheme must also be rated a well-planned operation. All the key factors requisite to boosting cotton production and agricultural income in the chosen area were carefully considered in advance: what technologies would be best, what local farmers would need to learn, how the inputs would be delivered, how the increased cotton production would be marketed, how the gains would be shared, and how the whole operation would be managed and monitored daily. Before the scheme was promoted to the farmers, its agronomic and economic feasibility was carefully tested and then demonstrated to them to their satisfaction.

Examples of blind spots in planning. For every well-planned program or project, however, there have been many ill-planned and unplanned ones. Several of our cases fall between these extremes; they were well-planned in some respects but had serious blind spots in others. The basic design of Thailand's MTTS, for example, was sound and innovative, but too little attention was given to the marketability of the skills that would be produced or to the follow-up training and other support services that trainees might require to benefit fully from their initial training.

India's Rural Industries Projects (RIP) program was well conceived, but two fundamental facts were overlooked: first, the high cost of providing a broad package of training and other support services to small entrepreneurs who were scattered over a wide rural area with poor transport; and second, the extremely meager benefits of such a program undertaken in poverty-stricken rural areas that had not yet achieved a strong agricultural momentum.

The planners of PACCA recognized the whole chain of factors that would condition the project's success—availability of credit, inputs and markets, for example—but they did not probe these factors sufficiently to discover that they would quickly arise to plague the project. Now did they examine sufficiently the longer-term economic feasibility of the extension techniques that were built into the design.

Requisite conditions for good planning. The key question here is what conditions favor good planning and what conditions militate against it? We conclude from analysis of our cases and other programs that good planning is most likely to be done—

- Where the planners, whatever their specialities originally, are broad-visioned, system-minded observers who look for all the factors and relationships likely to exert an important influence on the functioning and productivity of an educational program. Generally these qualities would lead to an appreciation of the merits of an integrated approach as against a piecemeal approach along specialized lines.

- Where the planners are not intellectually constrained by limited doctrines and conventional models espoused by their employing agency and are not inhibited from looking beyond the specialized jurisdiction of their agency.

- Where the planners are free from heavy pressure to get a project quickly into action and have reasonable time to explore the situation adequately, to seek out its inherent assets and obstacles, and to examine thoughtfully the comparative merits, limitations and feasibility of alternative educational approaches to the defined objectives.

- Where the planners are allowed and encouraged to pay as much attention to the longer-range implications of a proposed scheme as they do to preparing a short-range "work plan" or "plan of operation" that will win approval at headquarters.

- Where there is a strong spirit of cooperation and mutual understanding and interest among the staffs and leaders of the various ministries and agencies (both public and private) concerned with rural development.

Bureaucratic obstacles to good planning. These conditions, unfortunately, are often absent in the planning of programs. Unhappily, the official jurisdictional lines that divide the specialized United Nations agencies as well as the various specialized bureaus within the larger bilateral aid agencies, and the lines that similarly divide the various domestic ministries in developing countries, do not conform to the realities of the problems that need solving in rural areas. This cardinal fact, as much as anything else, has militated strongly against sound program planning in the developing world and in the agencies themselves.[7]

In this respect, as some of our cases demonstrate, private foundations and smaller bilateral aid agencies have distinct advantages because they are in a position to take a more flexible, multidisciplinary approach and to allow ample time for careful investigation and planning. We found a significant contrast, for example, between the lengthy and meticulous preparations made for the CADU project in Ethiopia, supported and directly staffed by the Swedish International Development Authority (SIDA), and the less thorough initial investigation and planning done for the PACCA project in Afghanistan, which is also financially supported by SIDA but executed by FAO.

The extensive preparations made for the Puebla Project in Mexico—including the socioeconomic baseline study—undoubtedly reflect the less pressured, more flexible and longer-range approach that is often possible with private foundation funding.

Domestic ministries and large international and bilateral government aid agencies with specialized manadates and bureaus are not, of course, inherently incapable of sound planning. But to do so they must alter some deeply ingrained notions, attitudes and behavior patterns. In the end, much hinges on the personalities involved, in the countries themselves and in the external agencies.

We returned from our field work convinced that there must be profound changes in what have become conventional approaches to external assistance, on the part of internal as well as external agencies, if the whole enterprise of international cooperation and assistance under today's altered conditions is to foster better planning and lead to maximum long-range development benefits.

Encouraging trends. Some promising signs of change are, however, already evident in the behavior, particularly, of the United Nations agencies. Interagency cooperation mechanisms between ILO, Unesco and FAO—three agencies most concerned with rural education and development—have been established to promote closer coordination and the adoption of common ap-

---

[7]United Nations, *A Study of the Capacity of the United Nations Development System* (Geneva, 1969).

proaches to development assistance. The UNDP country programming method, initiated in 1971, is an attempt to fit external assistance to the framework of overall priorities and goals of each country as spelled out in its own national development plans. In the course of this study, we found in all U.N. and other assistance agencies a high degree of sensitivity to inadequacies and receptivity to suggestions for change.

Flexibility and Decentralization

While in theory nonformal education has greater flexibility and adaptability than formal education, this inherent advantage is often poorly exploited.

Rigidity in large programs. As a general rule—there are notable exceptions—programs tied to large government bureaucracies have a strong tendency to become homogenized, rigidified and standardized for different areas and clienteles that require differentiated treatement. Thus, for example, the skills taught by MTTS in each area are drawn from a standardized national list and each course is taught from a standard syllabus for the same length of time. Much the same has been true of SENA's mobile rural training program (though, in principle, instructors have leeway to vary content to match local situations).

There is also considerable uniformity in the teaching programs and methods of Kenya's Farmer Training Centres (FTCs). Many agricultural extension services give essentially the same "message"—the same recommended package of practices—to all farmers in an area, disregarding important differences in their situation and needs.

These rigidities are also manifested in the setting of quantifiable targets for all areas, which has often led to poor implementation of program objectives, particularly when the emphasis is on the generation of favorable statistics rather than on the fulfillment of actual needs of people.

Decentralization essential. Closely linked with program flexibility is the degree of decentralization of authority and responsibility that can be permitted to ensure that large programs are adapted to local needs and can harness local support. But political constraints often dictate the degree of autonomy that can be devolved onto local government, regional boards and councils. Yet it would appear that without such devolution of authority, including a larger measure of local financial control, the essential need for local adaptation of large programs would be impossible to fulfill.

A number of Indian programs appear highly standardized on the surface—especially with respect to organizational structure, staffing patterns, budgets and methods—but they allow considerable discretion for local adaptation. This was true, for example, of the Community Development Program and the Intensive Agricultural District Program (IADP). The primary key to this flexibility has been the increasing decentralization of detailed planning and decision-making authority to the district level and the subdivision of Indian state districts into smaller "blocks."[8]

Building up adequate personnel and institutional capacities at the regional and local level is clearly the necessary condition for fashioning and operating educational programs that are suitable to local conditions and form an essential

---

[8]See S. C. Jain, *Community Development and Panchayati Raj in India* (London and New York: Allied Publishers, 1967), Part Four.

part of the local overall development effort. No generally applicable model for decentralization can be suggested. In India, for instance, considerable differences exist among states in the authority and responsibilities of the district government body (*Zilla Parishad*) and the district civil administrator (Collectoreputy Commissioner) with respect to development planning and coordination of development services by various departments. Similar variations exist in the case of block-level administration and local government organization (Panchayat Council).[9]

One practical approach to decentralization and improving the capabilities of local personnel is the establishment of district or sub-district *multipurpose development centers* and affiliated *local training and development centers* to provide educational and management support to all development activities in the area. Examples and prospects of such centers are cited later in this chapter.

Generally, there is more flexibility in integrated development projects where most of the components come under the full and direct control of the same management, as in the case of Puebla, CADU and PACCA. The greatest flexibility of all, naturally, is found in programs run by a single-tier institution such as IRRI, or in larger autonomous private organizations such as ACPO.

We conclude that there is no compelling reason why nationwide, governmentally operated programs cannot be highly adaptable to local conditions, though admittedly this requires a high measure of organizational decentralization and the development of strong lower-echelon staffs competent to exercise such latitude wisely.

Domestic Staffing Problems

The competence, spirit and common sense of the leadership and staff of nonformal education programs are invariably among the most important determinants of their success. A correlate, however, is that to recruit, retain and utilize good staff generally comprise the most formidable problems confronting such programs. There are many reasons for this. Sometimes it reflects a basic national shortage of well-developed manpower in various categories. More often it reflects idiosyncracies of civil service salary structures and promotion procedures. And often it reflects handicaps imposed by the formal education system.

Impact of civil service systems. Of the twenty-one programs shown in Table 12.1, eighteen are directly tied to national or state governments. Of these, thirteen are tied to civil service systems and, in most instances, civil service rules and rigidities are an important element in their staffing problems. This is not a condemnation of civil service systems as such (governments probably could not operate effectively without them); it simply suggests that such systems need to operate with greater flexibility and to use their power instrumentally wherever possible to help implement programs and to boost their efficiency and effectiveness. In most places this would call for substantial changes and innovations in the existing civil service rules, procedures and attitudes.

The extreme difficulty that ORD has lately encountered in recruiting and retaining well-qualified local extension workers (the annual turnover, we were

---

[9]G. Hunter, *Administration of Agricultural Development*, Chapter 3, "Administrative Coordination."

told, is very high) seems directly traceable to defects in the government personnel system. The same agricultural college graduate can earn twice as much teaching in an agricultural secondary school as he can as an extension worker under much harder conditions. The prospects for career advancement are very low for extension workers, unless they shift to another government service (as many do).

Agricultural officers in Kenya's extension service consider that an assignment to teach in an FTC may prejudice their chances for advancement, and this hardly makes them enthusiastic teachers.

India's civil service rules and salary structures have made it increasingly difficult to recruit and hold the rare types of persons competent to train and give practical advice to small inudstrialists and other entrepreneurs.

Thailand's MTTS program is saddled with the same Ministry of Education staff qualification requirements as apply to formal technical schools; this cuts the MTTS program off from other available talent pools and considerably enlarges its costs.

The vertical promotion rules of practically all civil services, whereby good performance at one level is rewarded by promotion to a higher one, have become a major obstacle to decentralizing planning, decision-making and initiative to lower echelons of government—a fundamental necessity for the effective administration of rural development. It should be possible to promote those persons working at the local level (i.e., in a geographic subdivision) who have a special flair for combining good practical planning with good implementation, and still allow them to keep working at the local level. But usually promotion means moving from the field to a desk job at a higher level. Without changes in this tradition it will be impossible to build strong cadres of competent people at those levels where they are now especially needed.

We appreciate the great difficulties involved in effecting major innovations in civil service systems and are aware of many past recommendations for such changes that have yet to be implemented. But the fact remains that until appropriate changes are made many rural development programs and their educational components will be seriously hobbled.

Incompatibility of urban schooling and rural manpower needs. Formal educational institutions also impose major handicaps on rural nonformal education programs, especially because of their dominant urban orientation. An able and motivated rural young person, for whom a career as a rural extension agent would be a big step up, has far less chance of becoming one than has an urban secondary school graduate in the lowest quarter of his class whose least ambition is to enter a rural career. Moreover, as we have seen, the agricultural colleges—with notable exceptions—do not equip their students for practical work in the countryside.

CADU's solution to this problem has been to recruit promising young people from a nearby small-town secondary school in the area and give them special training (a combination of classroom instruction and practical apprenticeship within the project) over an extended period.

PACCA, on the other hand, relies on the urban-oriented secondary system and on an urban agricultural college to supply candidates for its own higher training center for future extension workers. In so doing it largely rules out the possibility of recruiting and training able and well-motivated young people with rural backgrounds for careers in PACCA and the national agricultural service. Even those who come from rural areas, once they pass the secondary stage, set thier sights on urban careers and are likely to leave for an urban job at the first good opportunity. PACCA would probably do better if it recruited bright, mature and ambitious rural young people who are literate and well informed about rural life. It could then give them several years of career development training, combining general and specialized education with apprenticeship under experienced staff and increasingly responsible service in the field. Under such an arrangement, in a few years time these young people would undoubtedly make up a stable, competent and satisfied extenstion staff.

So long as agricultural and rural development services generally depend on academically oriented urban schools and colleges for their middle- and higher-level manpower, the whole enterprise of rural development will be thwarted and so will rural young people.

Toward a rural learning syytem. A radical new approach to developing leadership and competent manpower is needed. This new approach, as we visualize it, would involve the creation of a first-class rural education system specifically designed to promote among rural young people—girls as well as boys—the understanding, skills and above all the dedication and enthusiasm essential to accelerating rural development.

We have no detailed model to propose because we believe that each country must fashion its own, making the best possible use of existing institutions that could be transforemed to serve new purposes. However, a newly designed rural education system should not be simply a rural version of the present urban formal edcuation system. It should combine formal and nonformal components, allowing for easy transfer from one to the other, and provide alternative routes to advancement, starting from elementary learning and culminating in an open-ended rural university with socially oriented objectives. It should be relevant to the realities of its participatns' lives and needs, flexible and adaptive to changing needs, and accessible to motivated learners of any age or sex. It should not be intellectually second-class; it should have its own standards of excellence geared to its different purposes and clienteles and to the circumstances of its society. It should aspire to teach all children and as many adults as possible to read materials pertinent to their lives, at a functionally effective level. But such a rural education system should also turn out first-rate agronomists, economists, sociologists, public health specialists and development planners and administrators, all professionally and psychologically equipped to apply their talents in rural settings. It should also produce people with those technical skills that can directly improve the quality of life in the village—people who can direct the building of roads and bridges, assure a safe water supply, keeepthe electric water pump in steady operation, teach how to clean teeth to avoid gum damage, provide simple medical services, and so forth.

Where better can these professional abilities be developed than in the very rural milieu in which they are meant to be used? And why should the underlying assumption of every national education system be that its main strengths, from primary school upward, must inevitably be centered in the cities and that the ultimate in social justice is to prepare rural youngsters well enough in the early grades to give them a fighting chance to escape to the academic urban system? Why should not rural areas, where the great majority of young people will be born and live out their lives for several generations to come, have their own centers of educational excellence, fashioned to their own needs and to transformation of their rural society into a better place to live?[10]

No such rural learning system yet exists, but there is now considerable experience throughout the developing world that could offer useful lessons to countries wanting to move in this direction. A host of nonformal educational programs might find a useful place in such a broadly conceived rural learning system. There come to mind, for example, the Village Polytechnics of Kenya, the Diyagala Boys' Town school in Sri Lanka, Cuba's new schools-in-the-countryside,[11] the rurally oriented new agricultural universities in India, and the educational activities of the communes and People's Universities in the People's Republic of China.[12]

Use of volunteers. The possibility of harnessing the services of local volunteers and other personnel who are already living in the rural areas is a special advantage that nonformal education programs can exploit. We have noted that the agricultural extension program of ORD and the multimedia rural education program of ACPO make extensive use of local volunteers to augment the activities of the regular program staff at the village level. The rural primary school teachers form a potential reservoir of personnel who with guidance and supervision could play a useful role in nonformal educational programs in their own areas. They could also act as analysts and leaders of opinion in the rural scene and help in the articulation of village needs. And, finally, they could lead in bringing constructive change to the primary schools themselves.

The potential advantages of using local volunteers and other personnel (paid or unpaid) are several: (a) the impact of resources and personnel devoted to a program can be multiplied by using volunteers from the local community to assist in the educational effort as a model farmer, for example, or as a monitor of a radio listening group or an organizer of a youth or women's club; (b) a sense of involvement and participation in the educational program is generated in the local community by closely associating some of its members with the program; (c) the social and psychological acceptability of the educational messages is enhanced when the "opinion leaders" of the community are the educational agents for the program; (d) the use of local personnel can pave the way for changing the personnel structure in a program to allow a shift toward a smaller group of better paid and more qualified specialists and technicians in the field, while community people are enlisted for the simpler and less technical educational tasks.

---

[10]Nicholas Bennett, "A Scheme for Improving the Quality of Rural Life through Community Centered Education," mimeographed (paper prepared for a course given at CIDOC, Cuernavaca, Mexico, January 1973), discusses the parameters of a rural education system.

[11]Arthur Gillette, "Cuba's School in the Countryside: An Innovative Hybrid," in *Training for Agriculture: Annual Review of Selected Developments* (Rome: Food and Agriculture Organization, 1972), pp. 52-55.

[12]Hsiang-po Lee, *Education for Rural Development in the People's Republic of China*, ICED Background Paper No. 3 (Essex, Conn., June 1972), especially Chapters II and VI.

International Staffing Problems

We turn now from domestic staffing problems to international ones, which are often no less difficult.

In the course of our field work we heard many complaints from external agencies that developing countries often failed to assign their ablest people as counterparts to take over assisted projects as soon as possible from foreign experts. We heard at least as many (diplomatically expressed) complaints from developing country officials about foreign experts: too many were being sent; they stayed too long or did not stay long enough, and absorbed too much of the budget; their high salaries and life-styles were a troublesome contrast to those of their local counterparts. Most serious, however, the officials observed that in more and more cases the caliber of the experts being sent was no better than that of the country's own improved experts, and they could ill-afford to assign their best people as counterparts to such outside experts.

Changing needs for external personnel. In several countries, highly placed officials—speaking both candidly and gratefully—stressed that as conditions had changed, so had the nature of their needs. A typical statement was:

> Don't misunderstand, we appreciate the help we have received and we still need help. But we don't need the kind we are getting. We are now in a better position than earlier to make our own decisions and manage our own programs. We need fewer but better experts, usually for briefer periods, to advise us on specific problems—people who are highly competent and who at the same time have the sensitivity to understand us and our society.

The needs and circumstances, of course, vary greatly according to each country's state of development and high-level manpower supply. But it is clear that the priority need of all of them now is for greater *quality* of technical assistance, not simply a greater *quantity* of experts.

The "counterpart" problem. One important reason why new projects aided from the outside fail to recruit the ablest local manpower in developing countries is that many such projects, particularly innovative ones, have such a short guaranteed life-expectancy. For understandable reasons, external agencies are typically unwilling or legally unable to make commitments for more than a few years at a time. But it is often an inordinate career risk for an able and rising young civil servant to leave his secure post in an old-line bureau or ministry to become involved in a new and perhaps controversial project whose long-term future is highly uncertain. Even if he does a first-rate job, he may be forgotten and bypassed for promotion or even become tarred by criticisms of the project.

Another reason in some cases is that in the country's scale of priorities the project seems relatively less important than it does to the external agency, at least in terms of assigning scarce administrative talent to it. While it is true that the high-level manpower pool in most of these countries has improved and expanded greatly over the past decade, it is also true (as it is everywhere) that the need for top caliber manpower constantly outstrips the supply.

Recruitment delays and staff turnover. New projects that are heavily staffed with outside experts in their initial phase—such as PACCA and CADU—have a special crop of problems. One is the inevitable lag in the recruitment and arrival of experts for various posts; this, in turn, reduces the effectiveness of those experts, both foreign and domestic, who are already on the job. Another problem is the limited tour of duty of most expatriate experts (usually two years) and thus the need to replace them, just as they have become thoroughly familiar with the situation, with successors who must start again from scratch.

Cultural diversity: asset and liability. Another problem is the wide diversity of cultural backgrounds of the experts who are sent. While this has great virtue from some points of view, it can create difficulties—as it did in PACCA, for example—when it comes to establishing a new staff training institution with a viable educational philosophy and a coherent and relevant curriculum. Experts of different national backgrounds often have very different and conflicting views on such matters, and some unworkable compromises can result.

Having the foreign experts come from the same developed country—the case with CADU and Tanzania's Cooperative Education system—helps to provide greater project coherence and continuity. But this monoculture approach has its own problems, one of the most serious being the tendency of experts from the same country to impose, inappropriately, their own country's solutions, styles and forms on the host country, often to a greater degree than they may realize.

There is no easy or widely applicable solution to these problems in rural development and education programs with significant technical assistance components. We have noted the problems encountered in the course of our field work merely to emphasize the need for international agencies to be especially sensitive to them and to recognize that quick and spectacular results are difficult to attain in technical assistance for rural education.

Basic Requirements for Better Integration

A central theme in this report has been the need for better integration, at all levels, between different rural education activities and between such activities and related noneducational development activities and services.

The crippling fragmentation we have so often noted results mainly from the following factors: (1) the narrow conception that various specialists and their respective specialized agencies have of rural development and of how the process works; (2) the compulsion of every organization to want to run its own program without interference from others; (3) the time and trouble it takes to establish communication and cooperation, the geographic and other obstacles that separate the parties, and the pressures of everyday business that even with the best of intentions weigh against working out cooperative arrangements or implementing those agreed to.

A step-by-step process. Moving toward better integration—given the deep-rooted nature of these forces of fragmentation—must be seen as a gradual, step-by-step process. To attempt to achieve some theoreticaly ideal pattern of integration in a single leap would be unrealistic and probably self-defeating. What is most important at the outset is to create conditions favorable to getting the process started and to establishing as quickly as feasible those *minimum* linkages, exchanges and limited forms of collaboration that are mandatory for averting the egregrious penalties of excessive fragmentation.

In some situations sizeable advances can be achieved simply by informal exchanges of information and ideas among the interested parties, consultation on future plans, and an honest search for possible modes of cooperation. Other situations will be ripe for establishing more formal and systematic modes and mechanisms of coordination and collaboration. In certain instances it may be both desirable and feasible to effect an outright merger under a unified management of previously isolated activities. Clearly, there is no one formula or prototype to fit all situations; each must be sized up in its own terms and dealt with pragmatically as circumstances dictate and permit.

Sharing a broad conception of development. Nevertheless, certain principles apply as a general rule in all situations. As suggested earlier, the first and most fundmental requirement for achieving better integration of effort is for all parties concerned to arrive at a clearer understanding of why a piecemeal approach is so self-defeating and why closer integration is absolutely essential for getting the best results. They all need to share a larger conception of the whole, of how each part fits in, and of how these parts must reinforce one another in order to accelerate agricultural and rural development.

Without such a broader conception of the whole, genuinely understood and shared by all, no number of interagency coordinating committee meetings is likely to improve the situation. On the contrary, such meetings may actually worsen it by dividing up the territory and defining the jurisdictional rights of each agency even more sharply than before.

Necessary information flows. A second basic requirement is to establish certain minimum essential information flows, contributed to and shared by all the interested parties, which will place in clearer perspective the progress being made on various fronts, the gaps, duplications and malajustments that beg for corrective action, and the previously hidden opportunities that merit fresh attention.

Broad participation. A third essential requirement is that *all* parties whose operations and interests are in question be brought into the process in meaningful ways so that they can contribute positively to the deliberations and later feel they have a stake in the decisions made. At the national level, for example, real integration of rural development efforts cannot be achieved by a national planning body alone, though it can contribute importantly by fashioning a general framework and basic guidelines for the various operating agencies to follow. But to translate these guidelines into practical action, day-to-day harmonizing of detailed policies and operational plans is needed among all agencies directly involved in rural development through programs concerning, for example, education and culture, agriculture, labor, health, natural resources, transportation, industry and trade. By whatever means this harmonizing is accomplished, it is absolutely essential to an efficient and effective overall effort.

Physical proximity. Finally, there is nothing more conducive to good coordination and integration—especially in the field, where it matters most—than having the concerned parties in close physical proximity so that they can communicate easily and form personal ties. Physical proximity also gives the clients of service agencies easier and more convenient access to all of them; it can save resources through the sharing of common facilities and services; it can tie training more closely to operational realities (another much needed kind of integration); and it can improve the quality of programs, especially educational programs, by providing a broader range of talent to draw upon.

Multipurpose Training and Development Centers

The latter point about the advantages of physical proximity leads us to a specific suggestion regarding multipurpose training and development centers. As it is based especially on the earlier experiences of the Comilla project in Bangladesh and on innovations currently shaping up in Kenya, it is useful to relate the background of these two ventures.

The Kenya proposal. By the mid-1960s Kenya had twenty-seven Farmer Training Centres under the supervision of the Ministry of Agriculture (see Chapter 4) and, in addition, many other residential rural training centers sponsored by other ministries, churches and local governments. For lack of overall planning and coordination, these centers were unevenly distributed in relation to the rural population (some areas had too little capacity and others too much) and many were being inefficiently used. A Kenya government policy paper, dated January 21, 1969, observed that:

> generally unco-ordinated and therfore uneconomic dupliatory provision of extension services and training has developed throughout the country . . .
> These single line developments have led to a multiplicity of training centers at District level, an inadequate career structure for staff, difficulties in integrating training to development needs and difficulties in comprehensive planning.[13]

The newly established Board of Adult Education, whose members included representatives of the principal ministries and voluntary agencies involved in these fragmented training and extension programs, came to the conclusion that these largely single-purpose centers should be consolidated into multipurpose centers, which could also house the field headquarters of various related rural services.[14]

This proposal for multipurpose District Development Centres envisaged a series of educational and training "wings" at each center—for agriculture, community development, adult education, youth cooperatives, health, and trades. In charge of each center there would be a principal and vice-principal, "who must be of high caliber, capable of taking a broad overview of all kinds of extension work and training requirements." These two top managers would be supplied by the Board of Adult Education and the Ministry of Agriculture respectively; the specialized wings would be financed and staffed by the relevant ministries.

In this manner each center would contain a larger, stronger and more versatile staff then the old single-line centers—a staff that could be deployed by the principal as needed for various courses. Moreover, he could schedule courses so as to keep the center operating at high capacity. The placement of the district operating headquarters for various government services within the same compound would insure closer interplay between training activities and field operations.

---

[13]Roy C. Prosser, "The Development and Organization of Adult Education in Kenya with special reference to African Rural Development, 1945-1970, Ph.D. dissertation (University of Edinburgh, 1971).
[14]See Kenya, *Adult Education in Kenya (A Historical Perspective) Decadal Report, 1960-1970* (Nairobi, Kenya: Board of Adult Education, 1971), which describes the development of the various multipurpose centers.

The Kenya proposal also envisaged the district-level centers as backstopping facilities for a network of more modest multipurpose, local (nonresidential) training centers to which rural families would have easy access every day.

The proposal won government approval and Kenya's first two new multipurpose District Development Centres are now being implemented (with assistance from the World Bank and British and Norwegian bilateral aid).[15]

The Comilla Project's centers. The Comilla Project's Thana Development Centers (see Chapter 6) operated on much the same principles as Kenya's new centers. All the different training activities and rural services (credit, agricultural inputs, health, etc.) were centered in one place where they could interact with one another and be convenient to their clients. The locally selected agents went to the centers regularly to acquire special knowledge and services on behalf of the people of their villages.

There is an important point to be noted about the geographic service areas of such centers. The service area of the new Kenya centers will generally correspond to the political lines of existing districts. The Comilla Thana Development Centers served the equivalent of a subdistrict, which brought them even closer to the villagers. While it is always difficult to depart from established political jurisdictions, the ideal service area for such a rural development center would be the natural market area surrounding a principal market town. The services of the center could thus be geared to a variety of production, distribution, transportation, and marketing needs of the rural areas. And market areas also provide more logical bases for development planning.

Interestingly, the Provisional Indicative World Plan for Agricultural Development advocated a model rather similar to those of Kenya and Comilla for much broader adoption. It envisaged Agricultural Development Centres, located in or near the main market towns of rural areas. The Centre would be:

> ....a focal point within the rural community from which all agricultural development programmes and activities sponsored or assisted by the government are managed and carried to local farm people. Often this Centre can and should be incorporated into a larger and more comprehensive Rural Development Centre which deals with all aspects of rural development in addition to agriculture.[16]

We believe that the concept of multipurpose rural development centers, backstopping a network of corresponding local multipurpose service centers, would be applicable (with appropriate adaptation) and useful to a great many developing countries. It would certainly give a strong spur to the integration of rural training efforts with one another and with operational rural support services. More than that, it could become the hub for planning integrated development suited to each area and for managing the implementation of such plans.

---

[15]Interestingly, though it was not provided for in the original proposal, the Ministry of Information volunteered to locate a new district radio facility at one of the new centers, thus placing this mass medium at the disposal of all the rural educational services.

[16]FAO, *Provisional Indicative World Plan for Agricultural Development* (Rome, 1970), Vol. II, Chapter 10, p. 388.

The Discrimination Dilemma

No choice is more difficult for political leaders of developing countries than deciding whether, on the one hand, to spread the meager resources of an educational or other development program thinly across the whole nation to give at least the appearance of equal treatment to all areas (but with little prospect of having a major impact anywhere), or whether, on the other hand, to concentrate the bulk of available resources, at least initially, on a limited number of more promising areas and clienteles, thereby enhancing the likelihood of achieving a substantial impact at the price of overt discrimination.

Sometimes a compromise is adopted which differentiates between different categories of areas, or between different sets of clients in the same area. India, as of 1971, had three sets of agricultural districts: the IADP districts with the highest potential in each state, the IAAP (Intensive Agricultural Area Program) areas with the next highest potential, and all the others. The amount of attention and support they get corresponds directly with their agricultural production potential.

SATEC (and later SODEVA) in Senegal divided farmers into three categories, giving the most intensive help to the most progressive ones and the least to the weakest. By applying these kinds of differentiation there is something for everyone, at least in principle, but not equal treatment for all.

National versus area coverage. Of the twenty-one programs included in Table 12.1, twelve are conceived of as being nationwide in application, in the sense that they have not been restricted to selected areas for preferential treatment but are intended in principle to serve the entire country. Many such nationwide programs, of course, especially the younger ones, are not yet available to all areas equally but are striving to become so. SENA, MTTS, the Kenya FTCs and Cooperative Education in Tanzania are examples; their coverage is wide but not yet total. ORD and ACPO on the other hand already claim quite full (even if not equally intensive) coverage.

India has managed to achieve a wide geographical spread of certain nationwide programs (Community Development, SSIDO and RIP, for example). This has been accomplished by subsidizing state governments for a period of time to establish and operate new nationally conceived programs within the framework of general guidelines and limitations set by the central government (with the expectation that help from the cnetral government will eventually be phased out.[17]

Seven other cases shown in Table 12.1[18] all involve integrated agricultural development projects in selected geographic areas which by design are receiving preferential treatment. Various justifications are given for concentration in selected areas.

First, it is argued that there are not enough resources to achieve a major impact everywhere at once; therefore, it is best to concentrate substantial resoruces in a few particularly promising areas in order to get agriculture mov-

---

[17]This is the same "leverage" strategy generally followed by foundations and aid agencies. In principle it makes good sense, but it founders when the recipients become overcommitted financially to new programs, burdening local resources.

[18]The two cases not discussed in this section are IRRI, because it is multinational, and the Nigerian VICs, which is a borderline case.

ing vigorously. Eventually the benefits will spread to other areas, it is argued, particularly as the same or a similar approach is extended. (India's IADP and Senegal's SATEC were founded on this rationale.)

It is also argued that because the integrated approach is new, it is only feasible to try it out in one or two areas at first. The experience gained and the new institutions established would later benefit all areas of the country and possibly other countries as well. (This was the rationale, for example, of Comilla, PACCA, CADU and Puebla.)

Finally, such a strategy may be adopted because the area is the most profitable to exploit for private gain. This was the rationale behind the early Gezira Scheme, which later added broader social objectives.

There is little hard evidence or analysis thus far either to prove or disprove the hypothesis that by concentrating resources initially on selected high potential rural areas substantial benefits will spread reasonably soon to other areas. The question warrants further research, especially in the green revolution countries of Southeast Asia.

The basic conflict, at least in the short run, between increasing equity and increasing productivity and economic growth remains exceedingly difficult to resolve satisfactorily, in both philosophical and practical terms. Even programs conceived in the most egalitarian terms generally turn out to benefit the "haves" the most and to widen the gap with the "have-nots." When attractive new opportunities are available—such as increased supplies of low-cost credit, new high-yielding seeds, improved marketing facilities, valuable new knowledge and learning opportunities—those who know best how to take advantage of them, or can better afford the risks of innovating, or know how to manipulate local power, almost invariably are the first to respond and to get still further out front.[19]

No one of the cases we examined has yet found a practical solution to this dilemma, though some (especially India's Community Development Program, Comilla, CADU and Tanzania's Cooperative Education) have made a concerted effort to do so.

The long-range viability of a rural educational program and its capacity for contributing to sustained socioeconomic development hinge on how these problems of geographical limitation and equity are solved—whether the program can be successfully extended beyond the initial trial area and whether it can affect the large masses of disadvantaged people rather than a small elite.

Organizing to Help Small Farmers

As we have seen, agricultural production programs, including their educational components, almost invariably end up helping the well-off farmers the most and widening further the already large gap between the rich and the

---

[19]"A recent study of income distribution patterns in more than 40 developing countries estimates that at the beginning of the First Development Decade the average share in the national income of the richest 20% of the people was 56% but the share of the poorest 60% of the people was only 26%. . . . . preliminary indications are that this severely distorted income distribution is not only continuing, but in many countries may be growing worse. The poor are sharing only to a very limited extent in the benefits of growth." Robert S. McNamara, *Address to the United Nations Conference on Trade and Development, Santiago, Chile, April 14, 1972* (Washington, D.C.: International Bank for Reconstruction and Development, 1972), p. 5.

poor. What might be done to reverse this trend—to start narrowing the gap by giving subsistance families a good start upward?

To attempt to treat this question in full would take us well beyond the boundaries of this study, particularly into such complex issues as population control, land reform, and the strengthening and democratization of local political processes and institutions. Without strong policies and decisive action on these fundamental matters, all other efforts to release subsistence families from the bonds of poverty can at best be only superficial palliatives.

This said, we must confine our attention here to what might be done to help disadvantaged small farmers and their families by way of education and related support services.

The first step, we suggest, is to recognize that experienced and progressive commercial farmers require a great deal less help to move ahead than do smaller farmers with few resources and little, if any, experience with more modern technology, credit and commercial markets. The larger, more progressive farmers can learn and do much by themselves; what the government can most usefully do for them is to create attractive opportunities, mainly by breaking political bottlenecks.

The smaller farmers need far more help just to get moving, and especially to cross that great divide between the subsistence sector they are now locked into and the modernizing commercial sector. They are also far more numerous. Someone must intercede from the outside on their behalf if they are to get off dead center.[20]

To assume that an infusion of education alone will propel these small subsistence farmers forward would be naive. Educational infusions are vitally important, but they must be ssen as elements of a broader and more complex solution and must be planned in this wider context.

What governments can do. What poorer farmers need the most—assuming that they have a decent piece of land to work—and what governmets are best adapted to given them, are five basic kinds of help:

1. *Engineering help in building basic physical infrastructures,* in particular (depending on the conditions) roads, improved water supplies, and land clearing;

2. *Technical advice and knowledge* bearing on farm planning and management and agricultural production;

3. *Economic and logistical help* in securing credit and inputs and in marketing their output;

---

[20]"[The subsistence sector] is the far larger sector consisting of a mass of small, often fragmented holdings, whether worked by owners or tenants or share-croppers, which characterizes up to half of the cultivated area and three-quarters of the farmers in most countries in Asia and tropical Africa.

"The peculiar difficulty in developing this sector is that it seems to need a great deal of outside intervention. The farmers are often illiterate, often dominated by a 'subsistence' attitude to farming—they therefore need help from outside. They have difficulties with landlord systems or customary systems and with fragmentation—these difficulties can only be overcome from outside. The individual holdings at present provide too small and difficult a market for commercial suppliers of fertilizer or chemicals or tools—credit, supplies, and equipment have to be deliberately organized for them. Often ignorant of the movements of markets and prices, and powerless as individuals to influence them, their efforts to increase production may be regarded only by financial losses—again some organization and some regulation from outside is needed." G. Hunter, *Administration of Agricultural Development,* pp.12-13.

4. *Social services* (including education) to improve the quality of their family and community life, particularly with respect to health, sanitation, nuturition, housing, clothing and common community services such as clean drinking water, good drainage and an all-purpose community center.

5. *Management services* to help groups of farmers, especially smaller ones, to orchestrate the above elements into a dynamic process.

Importance of management services. A cause as well as a symptom of rural underdevelopment is that the facilities for provision of services and supplies are absent, inadequate or do not function effectively. But even when the provisions are made, they cannot be made to function adequately and effectively without a mechanism for management, coordination and adaptation at the local level.

It is in this matter of management where the larger farmers have a crucial advantage. The extreme examples would be agricultural estates and industrial and agricultural units, which are essentially tight-knit management systems from top to bottom. But any large and efficient farm is managed on the same basic principles—as a production "system." Small farms, especially subsistence farms, are not treated by their occupants as production units; they are seen as a way of life.

Governments in varying degrees have been providing the first four kinds of needed help listed above—engineering, technical, economic and social services—but rarely have they even tried to provide the fifth: management services. In the absence of any integrated, a systematic view of the farmers' overall situation, each rural support service has been viewed as an independent factor and each organization has gone its own way. The need for management services to tie them together has rarely even been recognized.

How might such management services be rendered to small farmers? One would like to think they could provide their own, by banding together in cooperatives or other local associations. But experience suggests otherwise, at least at the early stage. Cooperatives urged by outsiders have been notoriously unsuccessful in such situations. They are premature until the small farmers develop an economic momentum and have more to cooperate about, and even then cooperatives often run too much against the local sociological grain to succeed.

Governments have sometimes thought they were supplying the management ingredient by prescribing all sorts of targets for an area and the detailed practices that every farmer should follow. But this too has generally proved unsuccessful. A government can prescribe certain kinds of targets for *itself*—those within its own control fo fulfill, such as building a major irrigation system or a road network. But when the fulfilment of its targets depends on the unpredictable individual decisions and behavior of a host of small farmers (not to mention the weather), government ennters a never-never land.

A great deal of bureaucratic energy has been wasted setting unreal targets and collecting statistics about them in what Professor V. M. Dandekar describes as "a make-believe world" in which:

> . . . agricultural officers and the Extension workers under them [run] around with targets of agricultural production, crop by crop, targets of areas to be sown with improved seed, targets of areas to be brought under new minor irrigation, targets of green manuring

and targets of compost pits to be dug. In all these cases the officers ... know full well that what they can do in the matter of achieving these targets is extremely limited, and final decisions lie with the farmers.[21]

Guy Hunter suggests,[22] and we agree, that what is needed is not a *prescriptive* approach but an *enabling* approach whereby various management services, located within easy each of farmers (perhaps at a multipurpose rural development center in a nearby market town), would respond to their specific requests for help. Such a management service would not prescribe or in any sense act as a regulatory agency or an enforcer of government dictates and targets. Rather, it would offer encouragement and aid to small farmers. It could for example, help them get credit or input deliveries on schedule or help them organize the marketing of their produce. It would also, when the time was ripe, help them organize their own association to deal with some of these needs. If tied to a realistic development plan for the area the management service could also help them interpret its implications for their own situation.

Again, there are precedents that would offer useful lessons to countries desiring to move toward the provision of management services to small farmers. Comilla is especially instructive; it set out to play a light-handed but effective management role for villagers while they were working up to managing more for themselves. CADU is now following in the same path, providing centralized management services while simultaneously endeavoring to help new cooperative societies into being which, when they are strong enough, can take over the management functions now performed by CADU.

It is worth noting that the distinguishing feature common to various integrated development projects is that they attempt to fill this management vacuum at the local level. Each of them has established a management structure for the local development program, whether its focus is on agriculture or broader rural development.

Management services for small farmers, combined with the development of participatory institutions, could help them break away from subsistence life and give them a chance to move into the modernizing agricultural world. We therefore consider this to be an extremely vital approach that warrants much more attention and resources.

A political voice for the weak. The long-range solution to the problem of making rural education and development programs service the needs of the disadvantaged majority, rather than a relatively privileged few, will lie in a deliberate policy of organizing the political voice of the poor, encouraging them to take their rightful place in the local power structure, and ensuring their participation and involvement in the decisions which affect their welfare. Local institutions such as farmers' associations, cooperatives, irrigation groups and village councils can become the means for the small farmers and tenants to organize themselves for voicing their own needs and priorities and for progressively taking over the management of their affairs. But this can happen only with painstaking efforts on the part of planners and promoters of rural development programs, supported by appropriate national policies, to prevent these bodies from being captured by the articulate and privileged minority.

---

[21]Quoted by G. Hunter, *The Administration of Agricultural Development*, pp. 62-63.
[22]Ibid.

A Summing Up

This chapter has shown that the problems of planning and managing nonformal education are inseparable from similar problems associated with all other aspects of agricultural and rural development. Thus the conclusions below necessarily cut a wide swath across all of these aspects, not simply education.

What is called for fundamentally—in education and in all other programs aimed at rural development—is the abandonment of the previous piecemeal approach in favor of a systematically planned and integrated approach, in which educational elements become closely inerwoven with all related development factors and programs in each rural area.

For this to happen, four basic measures are required:

1. All organizations concerned (external as well as internal) must find ways to collaborate much more closely, guided by a broad view of rural development that transcends their particular specialities.

2. Each country needs to evolve a coherent national strategy for rural development and to overhaul any of its national policies (applying, for example, to agriculture, land, water, trade, prices and fiscal affairs) that are incompatible with the goals of their rural development strategy.

3. Within this national framework, development plans can be tailor-made for each rural area, adapted to its particular potentialities and constraints.

4. To design and implement such specific area development plans requires a greater decentralization of authority, including more latitude in financial control, to district and subdistrict levels, a corresponding buildup of competent administrative and expert staff at these levels, and strengthening mechanisms wherby local people can participate in the whole process of planning, decision-making and implementation.

The planning of nonformal education should take place within the foregoing context and be an integral part of it. By and large, the concepts and methods conventionally employed in planning *formal* education—which have emphasized the linear expansion of existing educational models and have dealt mainly in standardized national aggregates—have little utility for planning nonformal education, which must be much more flexible, localized and integrated with other development factors. Nonformal education cannot be treated as a separate sector (nor should formal education continue to be treated in this way).

The planning of particular rural education programs should begin by getting answers to several basic questions concerning critical features of the area and the population to be served, and by defining clearly the general purposes, specific learning objectives and the audience(s) to be aimed at. *Only then* should decisions be made regarding the most appropriate educational means and methods for meeting these needs and circumstances. Programs should be creatively designed to fit each situation. There should be an end to importing preconceived educational models into areas where the needs and circumstances have not even been diagnosed.

Useful integrated planning is possible even in the least developed areas, where reliable statistical data are sparse and where sophisticated methods of analysis are inapplicable. What counts most is not the amount of data available (though obviously the more the better) or the sophistication of the methods used, but the breadth of vision of the planners and their capacity for viewing *systematically* all of the key factors and relationships in any given situation.

The effectiveness of nonformal education—and of all other rural development programs—hinges critically on the ability to recruit, retain and utilize efficiently the types of staff required. There is wide scope for improvement here. Much could be accomplished, for example, through overhauling civil service structures and practices to make them a positive instrument for rural development instead of a major deterrent, which many now are. Much fuller use could also be made of local organizations, volunteers and part-time paid personnel outside the official career service.

Fundamentally, however, meeting the manpower and knowledge needs for accelerated, broad rural development requires a radically new approach to formal and nonformal education in rural areas. We recommended that large-scale efforts be undertaken (in a few selected countries and areas to begin with, and involving massive and long-term external assistance) to develop flexible, coherent and comprehensive *rural learning systems* that are directed at facilitating the transformation and avancement of rural societies and economies in all respects, and at opening up diversified and continuing learning opportunities for all subgroups in the rural population, irrespective of age or sex or previous educational attainment.

Initial priority in building such systems should go to the creation of those types of skills, knowledge and attitudes most urgently required for the improved planning and acceleration of all-round rural development. Such a system, we suggest, should include a diversity of means for spreading basic education to meet the minimum essential learning needs of all rural young people,[23] and should culminate in a new type of open-ended *rural university*, which will service as a knowledge-generating center for rural development. The design of such rural learning systems, making maximum use of existing facilities and processes, should be initiated in several countries at an early date.

The integration of planning and of operations in specific rural areas and the attainment of important economies can be greatly facilitated by bringing major training programs and the field headquarters of various rural programs into closer physical proximity, so that they can share common facilities, services, ideas and information. With this in view, we recommend the creation wherever feasible of *multipurpose rural development centers* connected to networks of modest local development and learning centers.

Finally, there is a great need to rectify the serious imbalance that has grown up in most rural programs (but especially in those for agricultural development) between the pursuit of production objectives and the pursuit of broader social objectives. In particular, well-conceived and massive efforts and urgently needed to help the great majority of poorer rural families to break loose from subsistence into the cash economy of a modernizing agriculture.

This will require a combination of support programs—for building basic physical infrastructures, for providing technical advice and knowledge on agricultural production and related matters, for helping *small* farmers acquire credit and inputs and market their produce, and for providing social services to

---

[23]See discussion of these minimum essential learning needs in ICED's report prepared for Unicef, *New Paths to Learning: For Rural Children and Youth* (Essex, Conn., September 1973).

impove the quality and level of family and community life. In addition to these types of help, small farmers need access to flexible and adaptable *management services* to assist them to organize and orchestrate the development factors around them into a dynamic, forward-moving process. They also need encouragement and support, through appropriate national policies and effective government interventions, in building up local democratic institutions and learning how to use them to take control of their own affairs. Such management services and participatory institutions for small farmers represent a frontier that calls for concerted and creative new efforts.

13: A FINAL RECAPITULATION
AND COMMENTARY

This closing chapter weaves together the main themes, conclusions and recommendations of the report and adds some final reflections. Specific conclusions concerning individual programs and particular topics are to be found in the preceding chapters; here we shall attempt to highlight the broader findings of this study.

Purpose and Scope

The study set out to examine the experiences—good and bad—of a diversified sample of nonformal education programs in hopes of shedding light on urgent questions being asked by developing country authorities and officials of external assistance agencies. For example, how can nonformal education promote rural development? Can it help fill the great gaps left by formal schools and help schools transform themselves? Can poor countries afford a sizeable expansion of nonformal education? How can nonformal education best be planned and evaluated? How can such operational issues as organization, staffing, facilities and educational technologies best be dealt with? What are the next steps developing countries might take, and in what manner can external agencies help?

In search of answers to these questions, ICED researchers examined, mostly at first hand and with considerable help from others, some twenty-five selected cases of nonformal education scattered throughout the developing world. Many additional programs were also reviewed, though more cursorily, through documentation or on brief side trips. The sample was highly diversified but not fully representative in a statistical sense. Cases were chosen largely because of unique features and the lessons they appeared to offer others.

Although a wealth of data was gathered, it fell far short of an analyst's ideal. Nevertheless, when this evidence was subjected to comparative examination it permitted us to draw many inferences and more solidly based conclusions relevant to a wide range of nonformal education programs and rural situations.

Almost any generalizations about such a complex and diversified field must allow, of course, for important exceptions. And though the study has succeeded in providing useful partial answers to the above questions, its limitations should also be noted. For practical reasons it was necessary to restrict the scope of the study to rural areas and more specifically to nonformal education programs aimed at improving rural productivity and employment. Its main focus was on educational services for farmers, rural artisans, craftsmen and small entrepreneurs. This leaves much important territory still to be examined, such as programs for adult literacy, improving family health, nutrition and housing, family planning and child care, not to mention educational programs to meet urban needs.[1]

Basic Concepts and Perspectives

The study's first task was to fashion some basic concepts and an analytical frame that would place the subject in broad perspective and guide the work of the case studies. This involved answering two fundamental but elusive questions: What is nonformal education, and what is rural development?

The literature proved of little help on these questions and thus we were forced to improvise some answers of our own. The problem was not simply to devise a dictionary definition; it was the profoundly more difficult task of trying to discover the real nature of nonformal education and of rural development, and to understand the relationship between the two. It was a problem of discovering ways to think more clearly, rationally and realistically about these matters—which is obviously the first essential for good planning and decision-making.

That there is a need for clearer and broader thinking is beyond dispute. The great majority of rural programs observed by the study—both educational and noneducational—were obviously founded on very narrow perceptions of rural development and the role of education, as seen through the lens of one or another specialty. These limited specialized views, more than anything else, explain the piecemeal approach that has so generally been made to rural development by various agencies, national and international, and the wasteful fragmentation that has resulted.

As we draw to the end of this study, therefore, we find ourselves hoping that, if it has accomplished nothing more, it will help practitioners in their own particular settings to think more clearly about nonformal education, its potentialities and limitations, and to view it more systematically in a wider context.

The View of Education

In contrast to the view that equates education to schooling, the study adopted a view that equates it broadly with *learning*—regardless of where or when the learning occurs (see Chapter 1). This *functional* view of education, contrasting with the structural and institutional view generally taken by educational planners and administrators, provides a radically different perspective. It underscores the important fact, for example, that education (learning) is inherently a lifelong process, starting in infancy and continuing throughout adulthood. It makes clear also that the great bulk of any person's total lifetime education is acquired *outside* schools (formal education) and outside other *organized* educational processes (nonformal education). People learn primarily from day-to-day experiences and from the multitude of educative forces in their environment—from family and neighbors, work and play, religious activities, the marketplace, newspapers, books, broadcasts and other media. For

---

[1]It has been possible, fortunately, for ICED to address attention to perhaps the most serious problem—the massive and much neglected learning needs of out-of-school rural children and youth—in a companion study to the present one, sponsored by UNICEF. ICED's first report on the UNICEF study—*New Paths to Learning for Rural Children and Youth*—is available (see References). A second report is scheduled for 1974.

purposes of the study, we called this important mode of learning *informal* education (not to be confused with *nonformal*). Formal and nonformal education, viewed in this broad context, supplement informal education—they are designed to facilitate certain valued types of learning, by both children and adults, that cannot as readily be acquired from the local environment in the normal course of daily life.

What we mean in this study by *nonformal* education is simply any organized activity with educational purposes carried on *outside* the highly structured framework of formal education systems as they exist today. Nonformal education, it should be stressed, is not a "system" of interrelated parts like formal education. Rather it is a bewildering assortment of separate educational activities, generally having little connection with each other. They are not contained within any sharply defined institutional structure or bound together by age restrictions, time schedules and sequences, curriculum boundaries, academic "standards," examinations, credits, degrees, and so forth. For precisely this reason, because it is *not* a coherent and unified system, nonformal education—at least potentially, and to a great extent actually—has a far wider scope and greater versatility, diversity and adaptability than formal education enjoys at present. Nonformal education has extraordinary freedom and latitude to serve people of any age or background in virtually any kind of learning they desire. It can have a multiplicity of auspices and sources of support, assume an almost infinite variety of forms, use all sorts of staff and pedagogical methods, operate at different times and places and for varying lengths of time. It can, in short, be totally pragmatic.

Along with the many advantages of nonformal education, however, go some important handicaps—not the least being the strong competitive disadvantages of nonformal education vis-à-vis formal education in terms of social prestige, access to good jobs and access to the public treasury. Beyond this, there often are many other obstacles in the way of nonformal education—political, bureaucratic, logistical, and others.

The above three basic modes of education—informal, formal and nonformal—are not watertight compartments. They overlap in places, occasionally turning up in hybrid forms. Most important, they interact with, supplement, and reinforce one another in a great variety of ways. Any nation that sets out to build a "lifelong learning system" to provide its whole population with a wide array of useful learning options at all ages would certainly make heavy use of all three of these educational modes, establishing strong links and a rational division of labor between them.

Obviously, the concepts and methodologies conventionally used today for planning formal education would be wholly inadequate for planning a lifelong educational system. Indeed, in this study we found them to be of little help in planning nonformal education. We also found the notion of education as a separate "sector" to be more of a deterrent than a help in making education—of any sort—an effective instrument of general development. This point becomes clearer as we look at the nature of rural development.

The View of Rural Development

The study adopted an equally broad and dynamic view of rural development, its goals and criteria, and the process by which it takes place. While admittedly a very sketchy view of a highly complex process that warrants much more study, the study has the virtue of demonstrating how narrow, simplistic and unrealistic are the views of rural development that underlie most rural education and other programs, and of providing a more rational basis for talking about the better integration of such programs with development.

This conception (see Chapter 2) visualizes the basic goals of rural development as being much broader than increased agricultural production and economic growth in the narrow sense. They also include more equitable distribution of income and land, increased rural employment, improved health, housing, education and general living conditions for *all* rural people, a larger voice for rural people in running their own affairs, greater integration of rural and urban areas, and a narrowing of the social and economic gap between them. In brief, this wider vision equates rural development with the thoroughgoing transformation of rural institutions, processes and human relationships, requiring a vigorous and forthright attack on rural poverty and social injustice.

Although these are long-term and difficult goals that can be achieved only gradually, even now they can provide a practical framework for rural development strategies and useful guidelines for all sorts of specific program plans, decisions and actions affecting rural areas.

Defining the *goals* of rural development, of course, is not enough; the *process* by which it occurs must also be reasonably clear to permit the design of programs that can effectively accelerate it. The process of development obviously differs greatly in detail from one rural area to another. But for our present purposes it can be envisaged everywhere as a gradually unfolding process, which once it gets started is characterized by an increasing diversification and specialization of economic activities requiring new divisions of labor. The implications for education are many: in order to fuel this unfolding process with appropriate human energies, more and more people must acquire more and more new kinds of skills and knowledge, as well as new attitudes and aspirations. Even a modest effort to classify some of the kinds of skills and knowledge needed (see Chapter 2) makes it abundantly clear that formal education can at best handle only a fractional part of the needs. Informal and nonformal education must handle the rest.

The above wide-angle views of education and rural development were of immeasurable value to the case studies in revealing more clearly the relationships and interactions between particular educational activities and their economic and social context, in identifying critical weaknesses as well as strengths of such programs, and in determining what types of action are needed to improve their performance. This broader "systems view," we are convinced, can be of major value in planning and evaluating nonformal education in any situation, mainly by forcing attention to be given to the most critical internal and external relationships of such programs and by prompting the right questions to be asked. We shall return to these points later on.

Three Basic Conclusions

Before coming to more specific findings and recommendations, it is useful to introduce three broad conclusions of the study; they provide grounds for encouragement but also call for some words of caution.

First, nonformal education — of the right kinds in the right places, properly tied to complementary efforts — is an indispensable and potent instrument of rural development.

Second, even the poorest of countries — given a favorable political climate and determination by its leaders and people to build a better future — should be able to mobilize the resources and human energies for a considerable expansion of nonformal education in rural areas.

Third, developing countries can forge ahead more quickly in nonformal education if given critical types of help from the outside. There is no shortage of ways for external agencies to assist strategically, but to do so with greatest effect they will be required to alter considerably their past policies, doctrines and modes of operation.

These are encouraging conclusions, but we hasten to emphasize that nonformal education is not a panacea for the problems of rural development nor for the ills of malfunctioning formal education systems.

Nonformal education can certainly make important contributions to rural development and can help formal schools to innovate and become more efficient, relevant and productive. But all this will require time, patience, and persistent effort. There are no dramatic shortcuts and important obstacles must be overcome. To make a new fad of nonformal education would slow its progress and cripple its potential. This is a real and present danger to be guarded against, and a point on which international agencies would be well advised to impose self-restraint and provide judicious counsel.

We would also caution against viewing nonformal education only from the vantage point of formal education. It should not be seen as a menacing competitor of the formal system, or as an expedient substitute until formal schools can be adequately expanded, or as some would have it, as a welcome means for doing away altogether with formal education. All of these are myopic and often unhelpful ways of viewing nonformal education; they obscure what should be the most fundamental consideration — the needs of the learners.

Central Themes

Three basic conclusions recur as themes throughout this report: the need for greater *integration* of nonformal education programs, greater *decentralization*, and greater *equity*. Because of their relevance to all situations and to all types of nonformal education, we shall introduce these themes here before coming to particulars.

The Need for Greater Integration

Integration, as we use the term here, does not imply the consolidation of functions in one organization; it simply means linking related elements together so that their collective impact and accomplishments will be greater than if they acted separately. Integration in this sense is the opposite of fragmentation, which, as we have seen, has been one of the greatest handicaps not only to nonformal education but also to most other rural development efforts.

The first point to be stressed is that education, *in combination with other essential factors,* is a necessary and often highly productive element of rural development; but *all by itself* neither education nor any other single factor can create or accelerate development. The key requirement, therefore, is to link each nonformal education program effectively with related development and educational activities.

Generally, nonformal education programs, to perform at their best, need to be well integrated *horizontally*—with both complementary educational activities and noneducational factors in the same geographic area—and also well integrated *vertically*, with organizations and activities at higher levels capable of nourishing and backstopping local educational efforts.

Thus, for example, local agricultural extension services and farmer training centers, as our case studies show, are much more productive when they are harmonized with other local support services (e.g., credit, input supplies and marketing services) and when they are effectively backstopped by agricultural colleges and research centers at higher levels. Viewed in these terms there is little doubt that the educational components of integrated agricultural projects such as CADU in Ethiopia, Puebla in Mexico and Lilongwe in Malawi enjoy higher cost-effectiveness than do most autonomous extension services.

The same principles of integration apply equally to other special fields. It was evident, for example, that the programs we examined offering training in production and management skills for small entrepreneurs got better results when their trainees also had access to credit supplies and to follow-up advisory and assistance services (e.g., on marketing, product design, raw materials procurement, plant layout, and quality control). We saw repeatedly that the generation of new skills without regard to whether there was a market for them in the area, and without regard to whether complementary services were available, often resulted in waste and disappointment.

To take a different example: there are many instances where a half dozen or more different agencies are operating in the same rural area, all trying, quite independently of one another, to improve the lives of the same rural families and each working on a different angle—home economics, child care, nutrition, family planning, literacy. In such cases even a modest dose of integration (e.g., joint meetings, the sharing of communications facilities, or consultation to insure better coordination of "messages") could help them all to do a better job.

As a practical matter, better integration of the kinds we suggest is a step-by-step process that moves ahead as the advantages of closer collaboration and the disadvantages of fragmentation become more widely recognized. Often the process can be initiated more easily at the field level, where people are closer to one another and to the realities of rural development, than in the national capital where even the simplest steps toward cooperation sometimes balloon into great bureaucratic issues. This fact of life brings us directly to the second central conclusion of the report.

The Need for Decentralization

Because of the great variations among rural areas—in their development potential and present stage, their resources and the pattern of economic activities, and so forth—no single development formula and no fixed package of educational services can possibly fit them all. Therefore, national plans must be translated into more detailed development plans appropriate to each area, and nationwide educational programs must similarly be adapted to the needs and conditions of each locality and population group.

For this to happen, however, substantial responsibility and latitude for planning, decision-making and program operations must be entrusted to lower echelons, and there must be sufficient personnel and other strengths at these levels to exercise such authority intelligently and forcefully.

We observed in the course of the study a few situations where these conditions obtained—the Tanjore District in India, for example, and the Jombang District in Indonesia. They were heartening demonstrations of what can happen when strong initiatives are taken at lower levels, and in sharp contrast to other situations we observed where, for lack of able leadership or of a clear "green light" from above, fragmentation still prevailed and development activities seemed stultified.

Again, of course, everything cannot be changed overnight or at the same pace everywhere. Decentralization, like integration, is at best a gradual process. But it *can* move faster if the necessity for it is recognized and if determined efforts are made to prepare the groundwork for it.

One important requirement is the redeployment of more development talent to the field—to critical action fronts—and substantial changes in civil service structures and promotion policies to make this possible.

Another basic requirement—one in which external agencies can be helpful—is a strong effort to develop improved techniques for subnational planning and administration and to train a larger number of subnational planners/implementers. Subnational planning calls for quite different methods and personnel qualities than does national planning.

For purposes of planning and coordinating nonformal education services and getting them tied effectively to other development activities, a new breed of broad-gauged, system-minded analysts is needed who are sufficiently conversant with various types of education and various facets of rural development to be able to see them clearly in relationship to one another.

The most fundamental reason why greater decentralization is important—why a greater measure of local initiative, planning and decision-making should not only be tolerated by the central government but also positively encouraged—is that, in our view, this is the *only* way to unleash the enormous latent resources, human energies and enthusiasm that are the absolute essentials for effective rural development.

The Need for Greater Equity

Most of the rural development programs we observed, including education programs, disproportionately benefit those who are already better off and seriously neglect the most disadvantaged, thereby widening the socio-economic gaps within rural areas.

This, we appreciate, is difficult to avoid. When a poor country is struggling, for example, to achieve quick increases in food and fiber production, it is naturally inclined to concentrate on those areas and farmers most likely to respond rapidly to new credit and input supplies, new technologies and improved incentives. Even where this is not a conscious policy, it is to be expected that those with the most assets, initiative and know-how will be the first to take advantage of any new opportunities, be they agricultural, educational or some other type.

But the changes involved in agricultural and rural development, while they produce many benefits, often involve heavy social costs and there is a strong tendency for these costs to be borne by the least fortunate while the benefits accrue largely to the most fortunate. An obvious example of this effect may be seen in the results of farm mechanization, which though often responsible for increases in productivity and income for the (generally) large farmer, brings unemployment to the sharecropper or tenant farmer on whom production once depended. This effect can, and often does, lead to a socially and politically intolerable situation whose consequences become highly counterproductive for development.

There are no cheap and easy solutions to this dilemma. Various palliatives have been tried, such as mass literacy programs and the spread of primary schooling, but without notable success. The only feasible strategy, it would seem, is to try to strike a better balance between short-range and long-range objectives, between immediate and longer-term production increases, between urgently needed immediate efforts that are bound to benefit initially the less needy and other kinds of efforts aimed squarely at attacking rural poverty and social injustice.

Nonformal education is *one* of the essential weapons to be used in such an attack, for knowledge is power and power follows the distribution of knowledge. But potent knowledge must be founded on new, relevant research—aimed, for example, at solving problems and opening new opportunities for millions of subsistence farmers and their families. This research must be not only in agronomy but also in the health sciences and the social sciences.

Yet new knowledge and new skills, though vitally important, are still not enough. There must be new and special flows of credit and agricultural inputs to which the disadvantaged have fair and genuine access; new work and income opportunities both on and off the land; better health, education and general welfare services. In many situations there must also be new access to productive land on fair and equitable terms, this being the *sine qua non* for steadily raising agricultural output in the longer run and for promoting all the other basic goals of rural development cited earlier.

From this brief discussion of central themes we move on to more specific findings and recommendations of the report pertaining, for example, to agricultural education, rural skill training, and promotion of small enterprises, and to a number of basic operational issues that cut across all categories of nonformal education.

Strengthening and Spreading Agricultural Knowledge

The study devoted more attention to agricultural education than to any other topic because of its complex dimensions and central importance to rural development everywhere (see Chapter 8). Actually, it is artificial to separate agricultural education and training from all other kinds, since farming people need skills and knowledge far beyond what is required for working the land. But in fact agricultural education is largely segregated—institutionally, professionally and organizationally—from other fields of learning; hence we are forced to start with this reality and contemplate eventual change.

The Need for a Systemwide View

Agricultural schools and colleges, research institutions, information centers, extension services, and training centers constitute what is tantamount to a knowledge-generation and delivery system whose primary mission is to change the behavior of farmers by helping them to take fuller advantage of their opportunities.

Most developing countries by now have, at least in elemental form, the basic components of such a system. The difficulty, however, is that these components do not behave as members of a system. Created in piecemeal fashion, the elements of the system continue to operate piecemeal, an outcome largely of the division of jurisdiction among different ministries (and different international agencies and their subdivisions) over the various parts of the system. There is no one locus of responsibility for viewing the system as a whole, for planning its future and keeping its parts in reasonable balance, or for monitoring its overall performance in relation to its mission and taking initiatives to improve it.

> *Recommendation:* In order to make all the components of an agricultural knowledge system, and the system as a whole, more efficient and productive rather quickly and better planned in the future, governments of developing countries, with appropriate help from external agencies, should undertake a comprehensive and dispassionate critical evaluation of them in a system-wide framework and thereafter make provision for keeping them under surveillance as systems.

Since this kind of comprehensive review has never been attempted so far as we know, it would seem advisable to test it out first in a few interested and willing countries in close cooperation with three or four concerned international agencies. The practical lessons learned in these trial runs—and no doubt there would be many useful ones—could then be compiled and circulated for the benefit of other countries.

Several important advantages could result from this system-wide review. It would create a fresh dialogue among key members of the system, helping them to see more clearly one another's needs and how they might better assist one another in meeting them. It would bring the realistic needs and problems of farmers into sharper focus and enable those responsible for each of the components to see more clearly how they could contribute better to meeting them. Not the least important, it could identify the critical points throughout the system where improvements were most urgently needed, thus providing a soundly conceived package of requests for external assistance agencies to respond to (in contrast to sporadic, uncoordinated requests for help from individual components of the system).

Improving Agricultural Extension

Agricultural extension services were a particular focus of the study's concern. Throughout the developing world, it must be said, they are a poor match for the enormous tasks they will be called upon to perform in coming years. Not only are they ill-financed, far too small and inadequately backstopped by research and staff development services from above, but many also suffer severely from self-inflicted shortcomings. To a greater or lesser degree, most extension services:

- go it alone, with insufficient cooperation with complementary services;
- operate haphazardly with neither priorities nor plans;
- spread themselves too thinly to be effective;
- concentrate their efforts on larger producers and major commercial crops while neglecting smaller farmers and the local crops of key importance to subsistence families;
- spend little effort diagnosing the differing needs of their client farmers, and instead hand out standardized recommendations that many of these clients find impractical and useless;
- depress the productivity of their field agents by neglecting their inservice and refresher training, burdening them with distracting chores, providing them inadequate transport, and failing to reinforce them with mass media and other communication supports.

Deserving special mention and emphasis is these services' striking neglect of girls and women *as agriculturalists;* typically, girls and women are trained, if at all, only for their roles as homemakers.

Recommendations: All these shortcomings, where they exist, are susceptible of remedy, given the necessary resources, time and determination. But first consideration, in addition to stronger general financial support and backstopping (discussed later), should be given to the following steps for improvement:

1) Increased integration of agricultural extension activities with complementary support services in every area, tied in with whatever local development plans and priorities exist.

2) Increased professional status and more effective use of extension workers: (a) by more frequent and relevant inservice training, (b) by removing low priority, nonprofessional chores, (c) by providing salaries and emoluments commensurate with their duties and qualifications, and with other civil service salaries, (d) by providing career advancement opportunities equivalent to those of other services.

3) More attention to diagnosing needs of various subgroups of farmers (including women and subsistence farmers) and to shaping differential services, recommendations, and information to fit these needs.

4) Adoption of multimedia educational technologies, including well-programmed print materials and broadcasts, to supplement extension workers and to reach a far larger number of farmers with pertinent knowledge.

5) Expansion of services, and creation of new ones where necessary, to serve (a) girls and women on an equal basis with men where they perform important roles in agricultural production, management, and marketing, and (b) subsistence farm families whose needs differ substantially from those of larger commercial farmers.

Generating Better Agricultural Knowledge

Without a nourishing flow of new knowledge useful to farmers, field-level farmer education services are impotent. While international research institutes can be very helpful in providing new knowledge, without knowledge-generating and adapting capacities of their own, developing countries are severely handicapped. Some countries, such as India, The Philippines and the Republic of Korea, have built substantial research networks of their own; most have not.

Even where research capacities exist, they tend to be detached from the priority needs and problems of farmers and therefore direct their efforts at the wrong targets. Moreover, different specialized branches of research are not integrated. The greatest weakness of all is that biological research, focussed almost exclusively on improving physical production, is not matched by social science research on factors that ultimately determine whether the results of biological research are actually feasible and profitable for farmers to use.

Recommendations: Well-directed investments to strengthen national agricultural research networks can produce a very high yield by raising the productivity of the entire knowledge delivery system. Such investments should be directed especially at:

1) strengthening social science research for agricultural development;

2) adapting international and other outside research results and technologies to local conditions;

3) balancing and integrating various specialized branches of biological research to yield packages of recommendations fitting the practical needs of various subgroups of farmers; and

4) tying the research process more closely to extension and staff development processes.

Transforming Agricultural Schools and Colleges

Agricultural colleges and universities have, in principle, primary responsibility for the preparation and career growth of personnel for agricultural knowledge systems. In addition, they are supposed to be important knowledge-generating centers.

Some perform these functions well, but hard evidence and testimony from throughout the developing world show that most do not, that their costs are high for what they contribute and the quality is low (see Chapters 8 and 11). The shortcomings are almost universal. A high proportion of these institutions, with notable exceptions, are marked by (1) the low quality and excessively academic character of their instruction and heavy dependence on foreign textbooks of dubious relevance to the country; (2) a lack of practical field experience for their students; (3) a paucity of research activities and irrelevance of that which there is; (4) the neglect or total exclusion of agricultural economics, rural sociology, and other pertinent social sciences from the curriculum and faculty; (5) an indifference to the training and research needs of the extension service and to the need for refresher courses for agricultural services generally; and (6) an especially disturbing and costly feature, the lack of background and real motivation of many of their urban-schooled students for agricultural or rural careers, reflected in the high proportion (often well above 50 percent) of their graduates who promptly escape to jobs unrelated to agriculture.

These points are not made in criticism of the administrators or faculty of such institutions, who are devoted and hard-working. The shortcomings reflect fundamental derangements in the institutions and their operational philosophies and assumptions. Basically, they need reorientation *away* from the traditions, rituals and attitudes of urban-based higher education and *toward* the real agricultural development needs and problems of their countries. They need to become instrumentalities of broad *rural* development, not simply agricultural development in the narrow technical and production sense. And they need to recruit students and faculty who are enthusiastically committed to the transformation of their country's rural societies.

In most developing countries where agricultural vocational schools exist, they are foreign transplants and serious misfits. Though often more expensive than urban academic secondary schools, their quality is typically much poorer and they suffer from serious staff problems, excessively theoretical instruction, and most importantly from great uncertainty as to what their real function is and how they are meant to fit into the overall agricultural system.

Recommendations:

1. In most developing countries, agricultural colleges should not be expanded or replicated in their present form. The first priority is to reorient and transform them; free them from the hypnotic and distorting influences of urban institutions; broaden their curriculum and alter the character of their student intake; tie them more directly and closely to the realities of rural life; strengthen their research and make it more relevant; help them to respond more fully and effectively to the practical manpower and knowledge needs of the nation's agricultural development system; and build them into prime instruments for transforming rural life. Some countries would no doubt be better off with fewer but better agricultural colleges.

2. The appropriateness of agricultural secondary schools needs to be critically reexamined in all developing countries where they exist. They should either be given a clearly defined, useful and feasible role and built up to fill it well, or they should be transformed to serve other more viable roles. Until such a reexamination is made, it would seem unwise — allowing for exceptional situations — to invest additional resources in them.

3. External agencies that have played a major role in the past in creating and shaping these agricultural colleges and secondary schools have a special obligation at this point to assist in reorienting, transforming and strengthening them for a more productive future.

Finally, we stress again that the full pay-off on any sort of agricultural education can be realized only when the education is teamed up with a combination of other essential factors and structures for development within the frame of a well-conceived strategy and plan for moving agriculture forward in a particular area. It is not feasible, or even necessary, to blanket whole countries with intensive integrated schemes such as Comilla, CADU, PACCA, Lilongwe or Puebla. But these innovative programs clearly demonstrate the superiority of a more integrated approach to development over the old piecemeal approach. The principles of integration can be applied anywhere in a host of ways. All who are involved in agricultural education and research of any sort or level, or in any other type of agricultural support service, should examine each situation through a wide-angle lens in search of ways to enhance the effectiveness of their own activities by linking them more closely with all related ones.

Generating Skills for
Off-Farm Occupations

The state of the art of designing rural training programs for off-farm employment is still in its infancy. This has been a neglected field; most of the attention and resources—domestic and international—have gone to urban skill training programs, especially for industry, and the rural training programs that do exist are often modeled, inappropriately, on urban programs (see Chapter 9).

First, there are important differences between rural and urban areas that call for different kinds of training—differences in the types of skills needed, the characteristics of the clienteles, and in the learning environments. Rural training programs designed by urban specialists are likely to be unsuccessful, except perhaps in encouraging the trainees to migrate to the city.

> *Recommendation:* Before any major push is made to create new rural training schemes, a quick but intensive investigation should be made of the types and combinations of skills typically needed in rural areas, how they differ from urban skills, how rural employment structures and skill demands evolve under development, and how these skills are now being generated and used in rural settings.

Second, most occupational skills in both urban and rural areas of developing countries, even skills associated with relatively new and advanced technologies, are generated by *indigenous* training systems—apprenticeships and the like—which have largely escaped the notice of Western training specialists, who think in terms of more structured and "modern" programs. Though these indigenous sytems often lack quality and sophistication, they have wide and firm local connections, are closely tied to active employment, and are much less costly than most Western training models. They deserve more attention than they have been given.

> *Recommendation:* Indigenous training systems should be carefully investigated to determine whether and in what circumstances it would make more sense to build up these foundations rather than to create *de novo* expensive Western-type training programs that have no local roots and that will be unable to meet more than a small part of the need for many years to come.

We would add a special caution about vocational high schools. These have been established mainly in larger urban centers thus far, but heavy pressure could well build up to spread them to rural centers. This, we are convinced, would be a great mistake. There are bound to be better fitting, far less costly and more effective alternatives. Even in larger cities vocational schools have a dubious record; there is every reason to suspect that they would earn a worse one in rural areas.

Third, most of the skill training schemes we observed had a serious common flaw: they tacitly assumed that whatever skills they produced would automatically be absorbed and put to good use by the local economy. Often this assumption proved to be at least partially false, as in the case, for example, of the MTTS program in Thailand.

A further hidden assumption in most cases is that skill training by itself can launch a young person into a successful career or help a more experienced employed adult to take the next big step.

We found, however, that skill training often fails to benefit the trainee significantly—particularly in the case of self-employed artisans and craftsmen who want to start a small enterprise or expand the one they have—unless it is followed up with other needed services such as credit, advice on product design, plant lay-out, marketing, and other management problems. In short, like agricultural extension, skill training for off-farm occupations needs to be viewed in a system framework and tied into complementary services to achieve results. Training all by itself cannot create employment or inspire development—but it can help enormously when other essential components are present.

> *Recommendation:* We would urge designers and managers of skill training programs, *before* deciding what skills to teach or what educational model to adopt, first to take a hard look at the people and the market to be served to ensure that the skills are needed and that the people they expect to develop will have good prospects of employment in that area; and second, to ascertain whether adequate follow-up support services are available for their trainees—especially if they are aspiring entrepreneurs—and if not, what measures might be taken to remedy the gaps.

A final basic point goes well beyond skill training to the larger issue or rural development strategies and planning. There is a crucial role that market towns and provincial centers—what we have called rural hub-towns—can and must play in the all-around development of rural areas. While new skills are widely needed in the smaller villages, it is primarily in the hub-towns that more skills and many new kinds of skills—for repair and maintenance services, small manufacture, banking, retailing and wholesaling, construction and the like—will be needed and must be generated.

If countries *as a whole* are to be successfully developed in reasonably balanced fashion, there must be a new emphasis not only on agriculture but on rural hub-towns. Techniques for planning and implementing the development of these hub-towns as vital centers of natural market areas urgently need to be devised and tested. Only when such plans exist and are in motion will there be a really adequate basis for developing strong and well-fitting skill-generation systems in rural areas.

Improving Educational Technologies

Our thoughts on this subject will disappoint those who dream of great breakthroughs in educational technologies involving satellites, computerized instruction and such, that will enable the deprived rural areas of the world to be saturated almost overnight with rich learning opportunities. Such bold ideas seem infeasible, at least for this century. Not only would these sophisticated technologies be economically impossible on a large scale for poor rural areas (they would be less so for densely populated and more affluent cities), but there would also be the inherent limitations on the kinds of program content they could handle, not to mention the myriad of organizational, logistical and personnel problems that would have to be solved (and which have scarcely been solved for the educational use of films, radio and printed materials). All these sobering considerations prompted us to consider less flamboyant means to enhance rural learning opportunities (see Chapters 10 and 11).

Clearly, great improvements in the use of technologies are essential to the expansion and increased effectiveness of nonformal education. These improvements can and must be achieved, mainly by drawing upon the rich and diversified inventory of technologies already available to education, most of which are grossly underutilized. A further imperative is that whatever combination of technologies is used, it must combine low unit costs with educational effectiveness; it cannot be a luxury model and yet serve large numbers. Finally, it should be recognized that there can be no such thing as a "best technology" for all nonformal education. The diversity of programs, objectives, clienteles and situations is far too great to permit any standardized solutions.

We have made specific suggestions in Chapter 10 on how individual countries might usefully start off by taking a quick and rough inventory of the technologies they are already using educationally, of others that are *available* for use, and of their other valuable assets—broadcast, printing and other facilities; talents of various sorts; and specialized organizational strengths—that could be more fully harnessed in the service of rural education. We suspect that any country making such an inventory would be surprised at how many such assets it has. The real problem is how to put them to work more effectively.

The three most underutilized educational resources in developing countries are print materials, radio broadcasting, and self-instruction. The most expensive and overworked technology and the chief bottleneck to expanding and improving rural learning is traditional teacher-to-student, face-to-face oral instruction. Almost everywhere there has been, for a variety of reasons, poor deployment of scarce educational resources as between staff on the one hand and various kinds of learning aids (print materials, broadcasts, simple items of experimental equipment, paper and pencils and so forth) on the other—to the detriment of teacher productivity and student learning.

> *Recommendation:* We would urge that developing countries, with all the outside help they need and can get, pursue a strategy of rural education that puts central emphasis on *self-instruction* and on the production of well-programmed print materials and simple forms of reproduction, radio broadcasts, simple do-it-yourself learning devices and any other means that can facilitate relevant and useful learning of many sorts by many people, whether they are inside some organized education program or acting on their own.

We suggest further that a few large-scale, carefully designed and long-term experiments be undertaken in selected rural areas aimed at greatly enriching their *informal education* environment by introducing new and relevant "stuff of learning" through all sorts of low-cost means and media—newspapers, posters, bulletins, comic books, radio, and traditional forms of folk entertainment such as puppets and folk drama—and by harnessing more fully the educational potential of local institutions such as the marketplace, village council, games, fiestas and religious centers. To establish the learning objectives and guide the content conveyed by these media, the people themselves would be consulted regularly on what kinds of things they most wished to learn and how they felt about what they were being offered. Over and above whatever benefits might accrue to the community from the experiment, it would provide an extraordinary laboratory for discovering how people learn *informally* in rural areas when given a real chance. The answers might well destroy some expensive educational myths and open up previously unseen opportunities.

Our final point concerns the more efficient, effective and extensive use of educational technologies. Nonformal education programs, as noted in Chapter 10, often have a compulsion to go it alone and to have their own delivery system. This is clearly a major cause of waste and low effectiveness, especially when no one program in an area can really afford a good delivery system of its own.

> *Recommendation:* There are many opportunities, and they are not hard to find, for different nonformal programs—dealing, for example, with agriculture, health, home improvement, literacy and so forth—to combine their efforts and share facilities, broadcasts, learning materials and even staff, in ways that will help them all to do a better job. Strong encouragement, including perhaps some special incentives and rewards, should be given to the efforts of program managers, at the national level and at lower echelons, to get together, take stock of such possibilities, and take steps toward trying them out.

In this connection we also suggest that administrators and staff of nonformal education programs, who need help on developing and communicating better program content, get together with organizations (or with units of their own organization) that have special talents, know-how and facilities in the field of information and communication. Some talented writers, for example, who are bored with writing press releases and annual reports, might welcome the chance to do some lucid and appealing educational scripts. Radio station managers who have trouble filling the air time with good programs might welcome some lively and attractive new programs that were both entertaining and educational.

Finances, Costs, and Evaluation

One of the major potential advantages of nonformal education is its unusual capacity to mobilize resources and support in a great many forms (many nonmonetary) and from a variety of sources, including many unconventional ones (see Chapter 11). It is basically for this reason that we concluded, as noted earlier, that even the poorest country could mobilize support for a sizeable enlargement of rural nonformal education, provided that the political climate is favorable and the leaders and people strongly determined to build a better life. This is also one reason why decentralization is so important: where local initiatives are encouraged, the chances of mobilizing local resources and enthusiasm for getting things done are much greater.

This does not mean, however, that a massive expansion of rural nonformal education would leave unscarred the general treasury or formal education's budget. Any national program financed in whole or major part by government obviously would require additional public funds for any appreciable expansion. Agricultural extension programs are a case in point and there are many others. But it is noteworthy that, in contrast to formal education, the extra funds for expansion would not all have to come out of the pocket of one ministry but from many pockets, which could have its advantages.

Formal education would feel the budgetary competition mainly from those nonformal education programs financed by the Ministry of Education (for example, adult literacy programs), or from other publicly financed programs for children and youth that more or less paralleled or substituted for formal education. But this still leaves a wide range of nonformal programs that would scarcely be budgetary competitors of formal schooling, except insofar as all claimants to the public budget are competitors.

Few generalizations can safely be made about the costs of nonformal education because of the great diversity of programs. The costs can be very modest (as in Nigeria's Vocational Improvement Centres), but some are ridiculously high (especially in programs that copied formal educational methodologies). Most nonformal programs have low capital costs, mostly because they use labor-intensive technologies, but also because they are borrowers of under-utilized facilities. However, programs that are substantial users of modern educational technologies—such as ACPO in Colombia with its heavy reliance on print and broadcast media—are much larger capital users.

It is difficult to make direct cost comparisons between formal and nonformal education because the objectives, content, clients and duration are so different. But for getting certain jobs done, particularly in skill training, there is not much doubt that nonformal approaches have a decided advantage. Moreover, nonformal programs have many cost-saving advantages not usually available to formal education, such as the use of borrowed facilities (including schools) and of volunteers and part-time instructors.

The central issue, of course, is not costs as such but the relation of costs to results. This raises the question whether cost-effectiveness and cost-benefit analyses are feasible and appropriate in evaluating nonformal education programs.

Our answer is a decided yes, but with qualifications. Such analysis is not only feasible (as our case studies show) but absolutely essential to any rational diagnosis, planning or evaluation in the field of nonformal education. It is rarely possible, to be sure, to make refined rate-of-return calculations that have much meaning or validity. It is also virtually impossible in integrated programs to segregate the benefits attributable to education from those of other complementary components. But such statistical calculations are secondary. What is basically important when assessing any nonformal program is to view it in a cost-effective and cost-benefit framework. This requires seeing it broadly in its socioeconomic context and keeping a close eye on the relationships between its resource costs and the results it appears to be producing, both immediate and longer term, and both economic and noneconomic.

Unfortunately, few administrators of nonformal programs ask searching questions about the efficacy of their programs or try to collect evidence for answering such questions. Hardly any training programs, for instance, keep track of the employment record of their former trainees, which is one of the essential ingredients in forming any judgment of their cost-benefit record. The moral is that the planning and management of nonformal education require improvement—our next topic.

Toward Better Planning, Management, and Staffing

Planning and management (see Chapter 12) are at the vortex of all the critical issues of nonformal education touched on in this report, above all the central issues of integration, decentralization and equity which have been stressed throughout.

Steps Toward Better Integration of Effort

One of the most visible aspects of nonformal education in every country is the great diversity of organizational arrangements by which different programs are created, supported and operated. By its very nature, nonformal education is and should be an integral part of every action program aimed at development, ranging from agriculture, industry and commerce to health, family improvement and community development.

To try to separate the educational components from other components of such action programs and to consolidate them tidily under one organization— to try, in other words, to make nonformal education into a separate system and sector analagous to formal education would be a disastrous error, totally at odds with the conclusions of this study. This applies at the international as well as the country level.

The fact that nonformal education is sponsored by a great number of public and private agencies and takes a great variety of organizational forms is actually a major source of strength. Nonformal education programs can be directly tied into specialized pools of talent, knowledge, facilities and administrative strengths far greater than what any one organization could possess or manage. But diverse sponsorship, as we have seen, has also imposed on nonformal education severe problems of fragmentation. The individual pieces created by various sponsors have not added up to a coherent whole. Moreover, many of the individual programs have been founded on a specialized and narrow vision of rural development and of education.

Amelioration of the bad effects of this fragmentation requires first of all that those responsible for the separate pieces acquire a larger and common vision of the whole, that they see more clearly how their particular pieces fit into this whole and interact productively with other pieces, and that they become convinced of the disadvantages of going it alone and the mutual benefits of closer collaboration.

As more and more people and organizations—local, national and international—acquire this larger vision it will be possible to devise means and methods for achieving better integration and enhancing the effectiveness of the total effort.

The recent moves of the UNDP to establish "country programming," of Unesco, FAO and ILO to make common cause in the field of agricultural education, and of the World Bank to form strong consortia to attack selected major problems—all these are salutary examples of fresh efforts by international agencies to move in the direction of better integration. Many more such examples need to be set by international agencies, for if these agencies simply cling to their "jurisdictions" and persist in acting autonomously, they will merely reinforce the harmful bureaucratic isolationism of their counterpart agencies within the Member States.

Creative efforts to achieve better integration and fruitful decentralization are also coming out of the developing countries themselves, such as those cited in this report from India, Indonesia, Kenya and other East African countries.

All these international and national examples, however, are but the beginnings of what must be a much larger and accelerated movement toward a more coherent, integrated attack throughout the developing world on the roots of rural poverty and social injustice—a movement backed much more strongly by the richer nations than ever before.

Steps Toward Better Planning

Better planning must undergird this movement toward integration and the increased effectiveness of nonformal education: better planning of rural development as a whole, nationally; better development planning for each rural area; and better planning of each nonformal education program.

The requisites of good planning for rural nonformal education are: first, that there be a well-conceived large frame within which to plan nationally and locally; second, that those doing the planning have broad vision and the ability to view systematically all of the important factors and relationships in any situation; third, that they take both a short- and long-run view, and both an internal and external view of the particular program they are planning; fourth, that educational solutions for each situation be designed locally, not imported from a distance in some visiting expert's briefcase; and fifth, that sufficient time and resources be allowed to undertake adequate local diagnosis and planning, rather than rushing blindly into action.

Far too few nonformal education "projects" reflect this kind of planning. Many of the finely honed "project work plans" we saw during this study, drawn up for international funding and technical assistance, focused entirely on the *internal* staffing, equipment, time schedule and logistics of the proposed project, with little if any reference to clearly defined objectives, the socioeconomic context of the project, or its intended relationships to other development activities going on in the same area. They reflected *project* thinking, not *program* thinking.

Recommendations:

1. An intensive effort is needed by external agencies and developing countries, working in close concert (a) to revise existing project preparation instructions and procedures so as to invite broader perspectives; (b) to develop *through actual practice* improved techniques for planning nonformal education that can be practically applied even in the poorest countries and where reliable statistical data are sparse; and (c) to train more broad-gauged national and international personnel capable of applying these techniques.

2. We recommend that the second and third tasks above be entrusted to *existing* national and international research and training institutions already competent in economic or educational planning and sufficiently flexible and non-doctrinaire to be able to adapt to new and broader concepts and functions. To create *new* research and training institutions to specialize in planning nonformal education would be neither necessary nor desirable; it might only serve to divorce nonformal education from the other forms of education and development factors with which it needs to become more closely allied.

249

Steps Toward Improved Staffing

The effectiveness of nonformal education programs hinges critically on their ability to recruit, train, efficiently utilize, and retain able and enthusiastic personnel. A wide variety of personnel is needed, ranging from full-time, highly qualified professionals and part-time persons with special skills and talents to less qualified persons capable of learning on the job and large numbers of volunteers.

Recommendations: There are innumerable ways to improve staff, including: (1) the creation of backstopping centers to provide staff development and other central services—such as operations research, evaluation and the creation of good instructional materials—for a variety of nonformal programs, in much the same manner as good staff colleges serve a variety of governmental services; (2) better and more frequent inservice training of staff members; (3) special training for volunteers and part-time personnel; (4) practical pedagogical orientation for specialists (such as agricultural or health experts) who have much to teach but need help in how to teach it effectively; (5) development of appropriate means for grooming bright and motivated *rural* young people for important rural posts, and a reduction of the reliance of rural services on urban-oriented, academically trained personnel for such posts; and (6) amending narrow and rigid civil service rules to allow more flexible recruitment of good talent—especially rural talent—now excluded by these rules.

A Proposal for Multipurpose Centers

Conveniently located farmer training centers and other types of specialized centers, such as those found in Kenya, can be important adjuncts to extension services and other development services. However, such centers are often excessively costly, due especially to underutilization of their capacity, and the quality of their offerings often suffers because of the limited subject range of their staffs and their isolation from the mainstream of operations (see Chapters 11 and 12).

Recommendation: We suggest that serious consideration be given to specialized training centers—for rural people and field staffs—into *multipurpose development centers* that would have wider ranging staffs and that could offer good training in a variety of fields—agriculture, health and other social services, local government, and so forth. The same centers, ideally, would include nearby the field headquarters for all major rural services in the area, thereby bringing their personnel and training in closer contact with operations. These development centers could also evolve into the key planning and implementation centers for their respective districts or subdistricts. They could, moreover, serve as the hub of a network of simple, nonresidential local centers that could be all-purpose learning centers for rural people of all ages.

A few experimental multipurpose centers, based on somewhat similar concepts and principles, are currently undergoing development and testing in Kenya. We do not suggest that this sort of approach would be feasible or appropriate everywhere, but the idea would be well worth trying out in a number of places. It is the sort of forward step that a combination of national and international agencies could take in unison.

How External Agencies Can Help

This report throughout has been addressed primarily to developing countries, for they are and must be the senior partners in any development effort, with external agencies playing the role of junior partners, ready and willing to help to the best of their abilities when asked. We have noted throughout this report those problems for which external agencies might be of special help. Here, without trying to reiterate all those specific points, we offer a few general observations.

First, the various multilateral, bilateral and private organizations clearly have a great fund of experience and expertise which can be of invaluable assistance to developing countries in broadening and strengthening rural nonformal education. Moreover, they are in a unique position to undertake useful activities on a transnational basis, which individual countries cannot do alone, such as comparative research, collection and dissemination of pertinent information from different countries, certain types of advanced training that individual countries cannot afford, and the bringing together of people from different countries with common problems to learn from one another's experiences in workshops and seminars.

But there are also serious practical constraints—far more than with formal education—on what outsiders can do to assist in nonformal education. This field, for instance, involves a much greater diversity of programs, objectives and organizations; and it requires working through a variety of channels, not just one ministry. The capital requirements of nonformal education are on the whole more modest than formal education's, but they take a much wider variety of forms. Most of the manpower needs must be met by indigenous personnel; outsiders—sometimes even urban outsiders from the same country—would be total misfits.

Promising Areas for Assistance

Despite the constraints, there remains a wide range of important opportunities to assist. We suggest in particular the following promising categories of help:

1. Help in improving the techniques and the supply of personnel for planning integrated rural development and related nonformal education programs at *subnational levels.*

2. Closely connected to the above, short-term professional assistance to countries in diagnosing and sizing up their situation, with a view to formulating fresh approaches to tackling their rural development needs through nonformal education.

3. Help in creating or strengthening various facilities *above* the local level that can lend new strengths to local nonformal educational activities—such as common service facilities for staff development, research, generating good program materials and the like; or multipurpose area development centers such as suggested above.

4. Help to interested countries in evaluating their agricultural knowledge systems and in following up such an evaluation with specific help to strengthen the system at critical points.

5. Similar help in sizing up national and specific area needs for off-farm rural skills, in adapting existing training programs (including indigenous ones) to these needs, and in enlarging skill generation capacities.

6. Help in getting started on development planning for special rural areas, including the systematic development of rural hub-towns to serve as growth points for rural development and as expanding employment markets for all sorts of old and new skills.

7. Help in strengthening educational technologies for nonformal education, including the provision of special equipment, paper supplies, or the production capacity needed to support these technologies, and creative technical assistance in designing more efficient and effective ways to use educational technologies, including the cooperative use of common delivery systems by different programs.

Preparing to Help

Despite their rich background and assets for helping in this field, these outside agencies—particularly the multilateral ones—will be well advised to prepare themselves now for moving ahead in greater unison hereafter, for putting their collective weight behind a more integrated approach, for avoiding further piecemeal actions and fragmentation.

One useful step toward getting better prepared might be to form a few small task forces, made up of qualified individuals from different specialized agencies, that would respond to requests from a few selected countries for help, for instance, in evaluating their agricultural knowledge systems or in sizing up their rural training needs and resources. Such collaborative exercises, done in partnership with local experts, could combine useful technical assistance with valuable learning on the job. It could start the process of equipping both the agencies and the countries with a new cadre of "generalist" planners, capable of embracing a spectrum of educational programs in any rural development context.

Finally, most would agree that the time has come for some considerable shifts in the style and emphasis of external assistance. Many externally assisted nonformal education projects in the past have been based on conventional models developed under quite different conditions and often ill-suited to the new situation. The emphasis in the future, we suggest, should be on helping countries to design their own models, to fit their own circumstances.

Another common past practice has been to support "pilot projects" which hopefully would take root and multiply, using the country's own resources. Many of these pilots, however, have limped along and never spread, or have failed and disappeared altogether, basically because their long-term viability was never seriously assessed in the first place.

We suggest that it would be an instructive exercise for each agency to undertake an objective, critical review of a dozen or so of its own pilot projects launched several years ago to determine, if possible, the main factors that caused some to succeed—or at least to survive—and others to fail.

Our own findings prompt us to caution strongly against the further proliferation of pilot projects. There will certainly be strong justification for some, but the criteria should be tightly drawn and their rationale clearly established. On the whole, however, we believe that available resources would be more usefully spent, not on striking out in brand-new directions of dubious viability but on imaginatively modifying, strengthening and reorienting selected existing activities that already have a momentum, an indigenous coloration and assurance of strong local support.

Unfinished Business and the Future

This study has drawn a rough map of a vast and important but little explored territory that will hopefully be useful to other future investigators. It has also emerged with a variety of suggestions for more immediate action which hopefully will be of s‹ ne modest use to those who carry direct responsibilities for rural developmen

Having finished the study—at least for the moment—we are perhaps more acutely aware than anyone of its shortcomings and of the great unfinished business we have left in our wake. This whole field begs for much more research of a practical nature by many researchers and organizations. We have identified in this report what we conceive as some of the more urgent specific research needs, but these are only a small fraction of the total need.

We conclude by recalling briefly the vision of a rural learning system alluded to in earlier chapters—not as a Utopian dream but as a model of the future that could guide and inspire policymakers and planners along their way for years to come, starting immediately.

Experience has already shown beyond a doubt that the kind of education—learning—that is required to transform rural societies into a more tolerable, satisfying and hopeful place to live is *not* the kind provided by today's urban-oriented educational system whose values, prestige symbols, incentives and rewards are basically incompatible with the fundamental goals of rural development and with the not inconsiderable values of rural life. This kind of education implanted in rural areas has become mainly a transmission belt for moving talent to the cities, not a powerful instrument for changing and improving rural areas where, for as far ahead as the mind's eye can see, the great majority of peoples in the developing world will be born and live out their lives. Radically new educational conceptions and approaches are needed to meet the broad and diversified knowledge requirements and manpower needs of rural development.

The long-term goal must be to develop in each country and area a comprehensive, flexible and diversified open-access *rural learning system,* one that affords a wide range of continuous learning options—informal, nonformal and formal—to rural people of all ages, suitable to their roles, ambitions, interests and basic needs.

Such a rural learning system need not be at odds with or divorced from urban education; the two should have many common denominators and there should be many avenues of transfer from one to the other. But the rural system would not be simply a ruralized copy of the present urban-centered system—which, after all, is hardly suitable to the learning needs of most urban dwellers. It would have its own modes of learning through the environment, its own specializations appropriate to rural development, its own standards of excellence, its own prestige and rewards. Most important of all, it would unlock opportunities to rural careers for able and motivated rural young people who today are excluded from such prospects.

It remains, of course, for the countries themselves—with such sympathetic help as they need and can get from the outside—to elaborate their own vision, strategies and plans for a rural learning system. Fortunately, they do not need to start from scratch. Every one of them already possesses various institutional strengths and assets that comprise a living foundation on which to start building a better future.

The immediate task is to size up these assets—the schools, the nonformal programs and the informal learning resources—in order to determine how they should be reshaped, recombined, enlarged and supplemented by new and innovative elements in the future. Building this rural learning system must, of course, be the work of many hands and many generations, as all good education has always been. But the work *can* be started right now and then proceed by steady increments, bringing new and greater benefits each year—greater perhaps in a decade than any one now dares to hope.

EXCERPTS FROM ORIGINAL TERMS OF REFERENCE
ICED/World Bank Study
December 15, 1970

I. THE RESEARCH PROBLEM AND PURPOSE

[The research] will examine critically and systematically a substantial sample of past experience, existing projects, expert opinion, and relevant research findings with a view to developing guidelines and recommendations directly useful to planners, decision-makers and operators in this field. In particular, its aim is to help the World Bank answer two currently important questions:

- To what extent could the Bank's education financing be extended to nonformal education in rural areas, having in mind possible reinforcement of the Bank's other efforts to accelerate rural economic development and increased agricultural production?
- What would be the most promising and appropriate types of projects in this area and what sort of strategy should the Bank pursue?

II. THE RESEARCH FRAMEWORK

The research will be conducted within an analytical framework founded on the logic of systems analysis and shaped by a series of selected topics and questions important to decision-makers.

Within this framework, special attention will be given to (a) identifying the most promising types of opportunity for external assistance in this field, (b) developing criteria and methods for planning and appraising specific projects, (c) achieving effective integration of nonformal education programs with related development plans and actions in the same geographic area, and (d) identifying high payoff research questions for others to pursue.

The main topics and questions that define the framework are these (subject to possible modification as the research proceeds):

Topic 1. Differentiation of rural subareas for planning purposes.

Topic 2. Identification of priority educational clients and services.

Topic 3. Identification of learning objectives.

Topic 4. Major types of teaching-learning subsystems.

Topic 5. Causes of success or failure.

Topic 6. Costs and financing of nonformal education.

Topic 7. Appraising efficiency and productivity.

Topic 8. Opportunities for radical innovation.

III. THE RESEARCH METHODS AND SOURCES

To shed useful light on the above topics and questions will require tapping a wide range of sources and employing a variety of research methods. The following steps are envisioned:

1. Systematic examination of available documentation—published books, articles, and research reports, and particularly unpublished materials that shed light on specific projects.

2. Extensive interviews, correspondence and group discussions with knowledgeable experts in international and national aid agencies, research organizations and universities, and in a sample of developing countries.
3. Preparation of analytical papers and critiques that delve into particularly strategic topics.
4. Systematic development of case materials on selected projects or groups of projects, buttressed in some instances by direct field investigations.
5. Critical analysis and synthesis of all the foregoing evidence and the drawing of conclusions and recommendations directly useful to practitioners.
6. Submission of these findings for critical review by selected experts before final revision and submission to the World Bank.

Case Materials

Data on specific projects will provide the main empirical base for the study's conclusions. Hence such material will be systematically collected and analyzed from the outset. It seems likely that a substantial and useful picture can be put together for at least two dozen "cases" based on documentation and interviews with knowledgeable people in North America and Europe. Approximately six of these cases will be more fully developed through field investigation in a few developing countries. It will not be possible, however, within the tight time and resources limits, to write up full case studies for publication (though this could conceivably be done later). At least one such completed case study will be prepared as a model, however.

A common analytical pattern will be followed in compiling and analyzing case materials to insure systematic coverage of key points and to maximize comparability. (The ICED will encourage and assist any other research groups interested in doing case studies to adopt a similar analytical pattern.) Following are some of the main points on which data and judgments will be sought in each case:

(1) Original objectives and intended clientele of the project; any subsequent modifications.
(2) Origin and sponsorship of the project; its organizational and financial arrangements, leadership and participating groups.
(3) Its social-economic-cultural setting.
(4) How the project was planned—e.g., who did the planning; what account was taken of special local conditions; clarity of original objectives; anticipated outcomes; time horizon; integration with related economic and educational planning and major projects in the same geographic area; built-in feedback and evaluation procedures.
(5) Description of the instructional system—e.g., types of technology, personnel, materials, equipment and other inputs employed; extent of innovation and adaptation to local circumstances.
(6) Major problems encountered; efforts made to solve them, with what success.
(7) Sources of finance, level and behavior of costs.
(8) Evaluative evidence on the project's performance; e.g., identifiable learning and behavioral results relative to objectives; internal effi-

ciency; discernible economic and noneconomic benefits; contributions to related projects; attitudes of project's "constituency"—its teachers, supervisors, and participants.

(9) Plans and prospects for the future; will the project continue and if so with what modifications.

(10) Appraisal of the main causes of success (or failure); identification of the main lessons it offers for others.

Visits to Developing Countries

The project staff will make trips to at least six developing nations in Asia, Africa, and Latin America to interview selected authorities and experts, to observe projects in action and gather case materials, and to obtain other relevant information and views. To the extent possible, local consultants and assistants will be engaged to help on the local scene with gathering data and making assessments.

IV. RESEARCH COVERAGE AND ANTICIPATED END PRODUCTS

Nonformal education covers such a wide range of subjects and clientele that a careful selection must be made of what to include and what to leave out. It would be imprudent, however, to make these decisions prematurely before preliminary discussions have been held with major cooperating organizations and a determination made of what materials are most likely to be available. For initial purposes, however, it is assumed that the Bank will be especially interested in nonformal programs directly relating to employment and productivity in rural areas—particularly agriculture, fishing, forestry, small industry and construction. It should be understood that if the study's coverage is confined to these it will necessarily mean excluding such other significant areas as literacy, general primary and secondary education equivalency, health, nutrition, family planning, general community development, and the like. Even if this is the decision, however, every effort will be made to keep a watchful eye out for any striking ideas and experiences in these other fields which the Bank might find interesting.

At the conclusion of the project the Bank will receive (a) summaries of case materials on each of the projects studied, (b) a comprehensive Final Report (edited for wider distribution), (c) a confidential Special Report containing observations and recommendations specifically relating to the Bank's own program, and (d) copies of any other documents (such as annotated bibliographies and digests) generated by the project that may be useful to the Bank.

The Final Report is expected to cover such items as:

(1) Projected needs for nonformal education in rural areas: major purposes and clientele to be served to promote rural and agricultural development; relations to formal education and to economic and social development; general analytical concepts useful to diagnosis and planning.

(2) Useful classifications of (a) rural development situations, (b) priority learning clientele, and (c) priority types of learning objectives, for purposes of selecting, designing and appraising nonformal education projects.

(3) An inventory and evaluation of different types of nonformal education models, methods and technologies applicable in various types of situations.

(4) Basic factors and principles to take into account in designing and appraising specific projects and programs so as to maximize their prospects for success.
(5) Major cost and finance factors and cost behavior patterns to be considered in designing and appraising projects.
(6) Illustrative models of projects and programs—including hypothetical innovative ones—demonstrating the application of the above methods of analysis, criteria, principles and technologies in particular types of situations.
(7) Identification of most promising areas of opportunity for external assistance.

EXCERPTS FROM "GUIDELINES FOR PREPARING ICED CASE STUDIES ON NONFORMAL EDUCATION IN RURAL AREAS"
October 7, 1971

These guidelines are intended to be applied flexibly to a wide diversity of cases ranging in scope from discrete projects confined to particular localities (e.g. the Puebla Project in Mexico) to nationwide programs (e.g., Farmer Training Centers and the 4-H Club programs in South Korea). The items listed will, of course, need to be adapted to each particular case.

Despite the wide diversity among cases, every effort must be made to achieve a high degree of comparability among the studies in the following main respects: (1) consistency of analytical approach and key questions addressed; (2) types of evidence sought for answering these questions; (3) scientific objectivity and sound methodologies in handling and interpreting evidence and in presenting final results; (4) reasonable uniformity (though not rigidity) in the style and structure of presentation.

Structure and Content of Case Studies

Following is a suggested structural outline for case studies and a check list of items to be covered wherever appropriate and feasible.

A. *Introduction* (Summary)

Brief characterization of the case; why it was chosen; significant parallels or contrasts with comparable cases elsewhere; main types of lessons it offers.

B. *Origins and Context*

When, how and why the program was initiated; its general features; what needs and problems it was intended to meet; what major development goals it was related to; what organizations and individuals (domestic and foreign) played major roles in initiating it.

The economic characteristics and potential of the area (at the time the project was initiated); its stage of development; economic structure and pattern of activities; static and dynamic features; patterns of land and income distribution; economic potential of the area in light of its natural resources, population traits and other development determinants; existence or absence of local development plans and schemes relevant to the nonformal education program under study; major changes in any of the foregoing up to the present time.

Demographic, educational, social and cultural characteristics of the area when the program was launched: size, educational profile and mobility of the population; condition and extent of services of the formal educational system; other nonformal education programs already present in the area; social structure and cultural traits relevant to development; major changes in any of the foregoing up to the present.

C. Initial Planning

Description of the program as initially envisaged: structure, methods and content, duration and frequency of instruction, sharing of time between theory and practice, characteristics of staff and learners; types of facilities and equipment involved; types and role of instructional aids (printed materials, mass media, etc.); main components and functions of the educational "delivery system" above the local level.

Organizational and administrative structure (national, state, local; governmental or private) within which the program was planned and would be fitted; location of responsibilities of various types.

How and by whom the project was planned: the respective roles of national, local and foreign officials and experts in the planning process; what form the process and the resulting plan took; who finally approved it and took responsibility for implementation. Was there in fact a tangible "plan"?

Salient features of the initial plan: what specific learning objectives were set forth; what concrete results were anticipated; how clearly was the "target clientele" defined; what were the identified or assumed characteristics of this clientele (age, sex, educational background, actual or anticipated occupations, income and social status, motivations and attitudes toward different kinds of work and family and community needs); rationale for selecting this clientele. Time frame of the plan and its phasing. Were the costs and finances and tangible input requirements projected for a substantial period ahead; if so, what projection and costing methods were used? Did the plan include provisions for effective administration, for backstopping services from echelons above the local level, and for eventual local takeover of management, staffing and financial support when external assistance was phased out?

Fitness of the project to local needs and conditions: was a standard educational model adopted from another area; if so, how was it modified to fit local conditions? Or was a new model designed specifically to fit local circumstances? Was a definite effort made to integrate the new program with other local development plans and schemes, and with other nonformal and formal education in the area; if so, how was this integration to be achieved, administratively and otherwise? To what extent did the intended participants have a voice in defining their own learning needs and objectives and in shaping the new program? What, if any, research (including feedback arrangements) to test the validity of the assumed needs, the objectives and the methods to be used?

Provisions for evaluating performance and behavioral changes: What assumed or identified shortcomings in local farming techniques and practices, health and nutritional modes, entrepreneurial skills and practices, etc., was the project aimed at overcoming by altering behavior on the part of the selected learning clientele? Were criteria and evaluation procedures established at the outset for measuring the program's performance and achievements in these terms?

Appraisal of the initial planning: On the whole was the program adequately or inadequately planned; what were the major strengths and weaknesses—e.g., definition of objectives, clientele, and behavior changes sought; identification of the needs, interests, motivations of the intended learners; fitness of the educational model to local conditions; integration with other local educational processes and with local development plans, potentialities and programs; adequate projection of costs, resources and administrative requirements; provision for performance evaluation along the way; provision for eventual local take-over?

D. *Operational History and Current Functioning*

How the program evolved after its initiation: a longitudinal picture of the program's development; what initial and later problems and unanticipated conditions were encountered; how these were dealt with; what adjustments were made in the original design, objectives and action plans (see details below).

Description of the total "delivery system" at present, from local level upward; division of labor between levels; identification of components and inputs at each level; linkages with formal schools and higher institutions.

Description of clientele actually served: number, age and sex distribution, educational background, occupational background and aspirations, location, attitudes and motivations; methods of recruitment and selection; enrollment trends, drop-outs and completions; further study by "graduates".

Scope, variety and methods of educational activities: curriculum objectives and content; length of cycle, frequency of meetings, total instructional time; division of time between didactic instruction, demonstration and practice, self-study, etc.; extension and advisory services on the farm, in the home or enterprise.

Instructional aids and facilities: character and source of printed materials, radio programs, tools and equipment etc.; degree and nature of integration between them; fitness to specific local needs and conditions and to particular learners; new facilities or multiple use of existing facilities (e.g., regular schools, factories, etc.); use of demonstration farms, etc.

Characteristics and roles of administrative, instructional and advisory staff at each echelon: qualifications, how recruited, trained and upgraded; extent and role of foreign personnel; career structure and incentives; division of instructional staff time among various tasks; staff morale and turnover; extent of use of volunteers and part-time professionals (e.g. formal teachers, researchers, civil servants, etc.); geographic mobility of staff.

Follow-up to instructional program: vocational guidance; assistance in job placement; follow-up advisory services; credit facilities; further instructional sequences, etc.

Principal bottlenecks, constraints and other difficulties encountered: shortages of financial resources, staff supply, instructional materials and equipment; administrative rigidities and inefficiencies; lack of coordination with other educational and development programs; lack of learner interest and motivation; premature phasing out of external assistance; vagueness of objectives, excessive diversity of learner group; inappropriate content, etc.

Subsequent record of participants: how many left the area; how many applied the training they had received; how many participated in further nonformal or formal education; how many benefitted through better employment, improved productivity, higher income, better health, etc.?

E. *Costs, Financing and Economic Viability*

Expenditure patterns and trends: distinguish overall costs vs. unit cost per participant; capital vs. current costs (including depreciation); domestic vs. external costs; money costs vs. real resource costs; project budgetary costs vs. real costs (partly absorbed by others, such as for loaned equipment and facilities); costs borne by project budget vs. costs borne by participants (including opportunity costs for income foregone); one-time-only developmental costs vs. longer term "normal" costs; costs at local level of delivery system vs. total system costs including upper echelon components; comparison of projected costs and actual cost experience.

Sources of support, financial and in kind: financial shares coming from national, state and local public budgets; domestic vs. external contributions; contributions of voluntary organizations; value of external aid (personnel, equipment, etc.) in donor's terms vs. local terms; local contributions in kind; contributions of facilities, personnel etc. by public agencies; extent of support by participants (fees, purchase of instructional materials, etc.).

Changes in the cost and financing structure in the course of implementation.

Economic feasibility: degree to which the financial and real resource costs, as actually experienced, are compatible with long term domestic resource availabilities; comparison with possible alternative uses of the same scarce resources.

Complementarity and productivity: evidence on whether or not the educational services under study enhanced the effectiveness of complementary development actions, and vice versa (e.g., irrigation projects, farm credit schemes, producer cooperatives; improved supplies of farm inputs; land redistribution schemes, etc.,); in short, was there significant joining of forces and mutual reinforcement between education and complementary development factors that increased their collective productivity?

F. *Evaluation*

Program's sustaining power: its demonstrated capacity to survive and flourish; evidence of its acceptance and endorsement by its main constituencies (e.g., national and local leaders, past and potential participants, employers, contributing bureaucracies, contributing foreign and international agencies); record of continued attraction of financial resources, staff talent, appropriate participants.

Fitness to local circumstances: evidence on whether or not and in what specific respects the program was well suited to its objectives, well adapted to the real interests and needs of its intended beneficiaries, and to realistic local conditions and development prospects.

Internal efficiency: evidence as to whether efficient use has been made of staff, facilities, materials and other system inputs; evidence of how well the immediate specific learning objectives were achieved, judgment of overall cost-effectiveness ratio between input costs and learning outputs.

Extent and effectiveness of integration: evidence of how the particular educational program has been organically integrated with formal education; with other non-formal education programs; with agricultural and community development efforts, etc. in the same area. In what specific ways might it have been more effectively integrated? What were the apparent causes of good integration or the main obstacles?

Behavioral changes: evidence of discernible changes in the behavior of participants and the community at large along desired lines—for example, in farming techniques, crop patterns, use of new inputs and credit, investment patterns, health and nutritional practices, community cooperative self-help projects, participation in community affairs, practical use of new literacy skills, etc. Comparison of these observable behavioral changes with initial objectives of the program.

Economic and noneconomic benefits: evidence of what benefits of various sorts (both economic and noneconomic) have accrued to the participants and to the community at large as a result of the new knowledge and skills and behavioral changes induced by the educational program—for example, improved employment and higher income; reduction of illness; higher consumption standards; healthier diet; stronger self-government and local community initiatives for self-help; improved opportunities for girls and women and other disadvantaged groups; enlarged flow and use of printed materials in the community; structural changes in the economy and society resulting in more equitable distribution of income, land, opportunity and justice.

Significant side-effects and multiplier effects: spread of new and beneficial practices to non-participants in the program; impacts on neighboring communities and other areas of the country; adoption by other nations of lessons gained in the program. Other significant "halo effects."

Overall cost-benefit appraisal: taking all the apparent costs and observable benefits into account (non-economic as well as economic) do the program's results appear to have justified the investment?

What plans are there for continuing, altering, improving or expanding the program? Do these plans seem warranted in light of previous performance?

G. Significant Lessons

Causes of success and failure: What factors appear to account especially for the program's performance (good, bad or indifferent)? What changes in the initial assumptions, conception and planning or in subsequent implementation might have improved the program's performance substantially (either its internal efficiency or external productivity)? What steps have been taken or might be taken to remedy weaknesses and build greater strengths in the program?

Applicability of lessons to other situations: Which of the positive and negative factors in the present situation are likely to be applicable in a variety of other places? How transferable is this particular educational model to other situations? In the event of such transfer, what particular modifications should be especially considered and what main precautions observed?

Comparative experience with similar approaches elsewhere: If information is available regarding experience with a similar educational model applied elsewhere, what have been the comparative results? Why, for example, does it seem to have succeeded better in one place than another? Is it a type of approach that is likely to be viable (with moderate adaptation) in a wide variety of circumstances, or is it likely to work well in only a limited number of places where certain relatively unique preconditions are satisfied (e.g., a charismatic, devoted leader; a unique coluntary organization; unusually well-coordinated bureaucracies; unusual foreign aid, etc.).

Lessons for other nations: What, in summary, are the most important lessons — positive and negative — that other nations (or other areas of the same nation) can learn from this particular experience that might usefully guide their own educational and development efforts?

Table 1

Appendix C

Costs of Selected Programs

(in U.S.$)

CADU in Ethiopia

- Total cost for the whole project for the period 1967-70 was: $3,865,000.

  Includes costs for:

  Expatriate and local staff plus outside training and
  consultants $2,066,000.
  Travel, administration, materials, and other over-
  head $1,764,000.
  Feasibility studies $ 35,000.

- Revenue generated from the project during the period was $1,379,000, the net cost, therefore, was $2,487,000.
- Total annual cost for the educational activities (using 5 percent annual depreciation for building and 20 percent for equipment) was estimated at $210,000 or $3 per farm family in the project area.

IRRI in the Philippines

- Cost to the Institute per six-month course in 1971 for 35 trainees was estimated at $43,000, of which $36,000 was for instructional personnel and $7,000 for overhead.
- Cost per trainee for the Institute was $1,229. Total costs per trainee when maintenance and support and travel costs for trainees are included rose to $3,249.

ORD in the Republic of Korea

- Total ORD expenditure at the national, provincial, and
  local levels in 1971 was approximately: $10,450,000.

  Includes costs for:

  Rural Guidance $ 5,600,000.
  Research $ 3,750,000.
  General Administration $ 1,100,000.

- Operating budget for one of the 9 provincial rural guidance offices in 1971 was about $85,000, which was almost equally divided among expenditures for guidance activities, research, and general administration.
- Operating budget for one of the 140 country rural guidance offices in 1971 was about $23,000 of which about 15 percent were spent for salaries and the bulk of the rest was spent for specific extension projects.
- Average per farm-family extension cost per year (excluding research) was estimated at slightly over $2 in 1971.

PACCA in Afghanistan

- Estimated according to the Plan of Operation at about $60,000 in its third year of operation (1971) for the two development centers and the training institute for extension staff excluding salaries and other costs for the expatriate staff, which amounted to about $600,000 for the same year.

- National professional staff numbered about 78 and international staff about 16 at the end of 1971.
- Of the national costs, 90 percent was personnel costs including allowance for trainees.
- Per farm-family cost for the year (counting the total farming population in the two project areas) is $4 from the national government and $44 from both national and international sources.

Puebla in Mexico

- Costs incurred directly by Plan Puebla in 1970 were: $202,949

Includes costs for:

Salaries and perquisites	$111,785
Field operations and laboratory	$ 10,779
Statistics and data processing	$ 5,065
Rent for office and storage	$ 1,448
General expenses	$ 715
Overhead payment to CIMMYT	$ 30,958
Vehicles (maintenance and purchase)	$ 42,199

(Technical staff, including a coordinator, research, extension, and evaluation staff, totalled 11. Farmers in the project area numbered about 47,000).

MTTS in Thailand

- Cost in 1972 for 54 schools was estimated at: $1,782,000

Includes costs for:

Salaries for regular staff	$ 540,000
Overtime and fringe benefits	$ 270,000
General administrative and overhead expenses	$ 270,000
Supplies and materials	$ 540,000
Miscellaneous	$ 162,000

- Operating cost per student who successfully completed the course was about $100.

SENA PPP-R in Colombia

- Costs for PPP-R in 1971 amounted to $1,550,000 for activities under 14 regional centers. Over 300 full-time instructors were assigned for 58,000 trainees in "regular" courses and 47,000 migrant workers' courses in 1970.
- Cost per trainee (non-migrant worker) in regular courses varied in different regions ranging from a low of $9 to a high of $40. Unit costs for the migrant workers' courses were just over $1. Overall unit cost was about $12.

VICs in Nigeria

- Annual costs of the centers inspected ranged from $8,400 in 1971 (with 8-10 part-time instructors) to $20,300 in 1967-68 (with two full-time teachers and other part-time teachers), excluding the cost for an expatriate director and his assistant for the entire program.

- Annual cost per enrolled student in the lower cost Maiduguri center for the period 1968-1971 was $104; the same cost per trainee who succeeded in the trade test was $467.

Senegal Rural Training Centers

- Average cost per center in 1971 was estimated at $24,800. About $14,700 of this amount were for personnel and the rest for material and other items.
- The range of operating cost per trainee in 1970 in different centers, as estimated by the Ministry of Education, was as follows:

      Skilled Artisan   — $648   — $828
      Pilot Farmers   — $630   — $810

ACPO in Colombia

- Anticipated operating expenses for 1972 were: $4,155,000

  Includes:

Radio programs	$ 580,000
Cultural division	$ 676,000
Publishing	$ 966,000
Newspaper	$ 338,000
Administration and maintenance	$ 870,000
Regional activities	$ 725,000

Cooperative Education Program in the United Republic of Tanzania

- Annual cost in 1969-70 for the Cooperative Education College, excluding the cost for 6 expatriate staff out of 13. $157,000
- Annual operating cost in 1969-70 for the Cooperative Education Centre and 7 Wings, excluding the cost for 9 expatriate staff out of 26. $140,000

                              Total for fiscal year 1969-70 $297,000

- Estimated total operating cost for fiscal year 1972-73 for the College, the Center, and 11 Wings, and replacing all expatriate staff with local staff: $476,000

  Includes costs for:

The Cooperative College	$280,000
The Cooperative Education Centre	$ 70,000
11 Wings	$ 98,000
Added cost for replacing expatriates	$ 28,000

Rural Education Program in Upper Volta

- Total for 1970 was about $500,000 for 759 Rural Education Centers with enrollments of about 22,000 students. Major current cost is the salary of teachers. Cost per student per year was over $22.
- Cost for training in three teacher-training institutes with enrollment of 115 trainees was estimated at $64,000 in 1971-72, excluding the cost

for expatriate staff and income from agricultural products in the institutes. Taking these into account as well as dropouts, cost for training one teacher amounted to $1,250.

SOURCE: ICED Case Studies.

Table 2
Costs of Facilities and Other Capital Assets
for Selected Nonformal Education Programs
(in U.S.$)

CADU in Ethiopia
- During the first three years of the project, 1967-1970, capital costs for the entire project including educational and noneducational components were as follows:

Total	$3,285,000
Construction, including buildings and common facilities	$2,477,000
Equipment and livestock	$ 617,000
Land	$ 157,000
Roads	$ 34,000

IRRI in the Philippines
- Cost of building and furniture (in 1971) for the rice production training course (with a capacity of 35 trainees at a time) was $77,000.
- Farm plots, research facilities, libraries and other amenities of IRRI were available for the course.

ORD in the Republic of Korea
- Facilities in the national headquarters include administrative offices, research facilities, and a training center for extension staff. There are also 9 provincial offices, which include administrative offices, research facilities, and a farmer training center. Cost figures for these facilities were not available.
- The current value in 1971 of the facilities in one of the 140 country rural guidance offices was estimated at $350,000. The facilities included residential and instructional accommodation for 60 short-course farmer trainees at a time and the central facilities for extension, serving 24,000 farm families in the county with 16 staff members.

PACCA in Afghanistan
- Investment in facilities during the first three years of the project (1968-71) was estimated according to the Plan of Operation at $466,000 for two development centers (in areas that included 10,000 and 5,000 farmers) and an extension training institute with a capacity of 50 trainees at a time.

Puebla in Mexico
- Information available for 1970 shows that direct capital cost for the project was $18,000 for the purchase of vehicles.

- Facilities of CIMMYT were also available for use by the project staff. The government agriculture department provides office space in the city of Puebla and the facilities of a government center in the field.

MTTS in Thailand

- Estimated capital costs for 9 schools in 1971 was $729,000 or $81,000 per school, spent for tools, equipment and vehicles. No permanent building is included in the capital cost. Training for instructors in the Polytechnics is not included in this cost calculation. Capacity of each school in two daily shifts is 250.

SENA PPP-R in Colombia

- The 1971 "investment" budget was $128,000 spent on instructional tools and vehicles for mobile units. The transport depending on the terrain, was motorized, animal-drawn, or just mules or donkeys.
- PPP-R makes extensive use of borrowed buildings and other tools and equipment when available.

VICs in Nigeria

- Capital cost for each of the 12 VICs is estimated at $5,600 for adaptation of building and tools. The centers made use of borrowed facilities and equipment. Capacity per center is 100.

Senegal Rural Training Centers

- Capital costs as of 1971 for the 8 centers, with a capacity of 40 resident trainees in each, were as follows:

  Construction cost per center:
  a) excluding use of trainees' labor $90,000
  b) including use of trainees' labor $61,200
  Furnishings per center $10,800
  Equipment and tools per center for farming courses $22,300
  Equipment and tools per center for artisan and handicrafts courses $21,600

ACPO in Colombia

- Capital assets in 1971 included:
  - A nationwide network of radio transmission facilities
  - A record pressing plant
  - A weekly newspaper-publishing facility
  - A commercial printing and publishing plant
  - A multistoried commercial building in downtown Bogota, part of which is rented out
  - Over $3 million in endowment funds
- Total value of assets was not available.

Cooperative Education Program in the United Republic of Tanzania

- During the three years of the project (1969-1971) when the facilities for the Cooperative College and the Cooperative Education Center were established, the capital costs amounted to $650,000. The college has a capacity of 150 residential trainees. The center is the headquarters for the nationwide cooperative education system operated through 11 zonal wings. The zonal facilities including an administrative office and a meeting place are provided locally by the cooperative unions. A land-rover and audiovisual equipment for each wing are provided from the Center.

Rural Education Program in Upper Volta

- More than 500 rural education centers in existence in 1971 were built with local communities' contributions, which included voluntary labor, farm plots, construction materials, and farming and other tools worth about $1,000 for each center.
- Another 225 centers built with European Development Fund Assistance cost about $10,000 per center, excluding farm plots and equipment.
- Three separate teacher-training facilities with classrooms, dormitories, faculty-housing, animal sheds and farm plots have a total capacity of 120 trainees. Cost figures were not available.

NOTE: Cost figures in all cases are construction or purchase cost. For ORD, estimated current value of the facilities is given.

Table 3
CADU's Initial Three-Year Budget
(September 1967–July 1970)

	Ethiopian dollars (000)	Percentage of Budget
Swedish staff (January 1970, 32 persons, of whom 4 are volunteers)	3,209	23.2
Ethiopian high- and middle-level staff (January 1970, 45 persons)	668	4.8
Other locally employed staff (January 1970, 304 persons)	831	6.0
Other operating costs (Revenue is deducted)	1,261	9.1
Investment in buildings, etc.	5,945	42.9
Investment in equipment and cattle	1,480	10.7
Investment in land	458	3.3
TOTAL	13,852	100.0

SOURCE: Bengt Nekby, *CADU An Ethiopian Experiment in Developing Peasant Farming* (Stockholm: Prisma Publishers, 1971).

Table 4
Breakdown of PACCA's Initial Three-Year Budget
(1969-71)
(in U.S.$)

	1969-71	Percentage of Budget
International staff and consultants*	$1,321,420	54.9
Recurrent expenditures for local personnel*, including trainees' allowances	$ 132,600	5.5
Capital expenditures for land, building, and equipment	$ 466,000	19.4
Equipment and supplies contributed by SIDA	$ 150,915	6.3
Other expenses	$ 332,265	13.9
TOTAL	$2,403,200	100.0

*See Table 7.3, p. 7-25, for listing of PACCA's international and national professional staff.
SOURCE: Computed by ICED from data furnished by FAO.

Table 5
Direct Costs of Puebla Project 1967-70
(in U.S.$)

	1967	1968	1969	1970
Salaries and Perquisites	13,271	50,228	88,564	111,785
Field Operations and Laboratory	4,344	12,195	8,005	10,779
Statistics Collecting		1,546	5,065	5,065
Vehicles	11,976	13,787	26,238	42,199
Rent	960	1,448	1,448	1,448
General Expenses	679	666	6,279	715
Overhead for Services provided by CIMMYT	9,369	19,968	27,120	30,958
TOTAL DIRECT COSTS	40,599	99,838	162,719	202,949

SOURCE: Adapted by ICED from data furnished by Puebla.

271

Table 6
Basic Data on Puebla Project 1968-71

		1968	1969	1970	1971
Participating Farmers	No.	103	2,561	4,833	5,240
As % of potential clientele (c.47,500)	%	.22	5.39	10.18	11.05
Communities	No.	31	60	94	101
Area (Hectares)	No.	76	5,838	12,496	14,438
as % of total area under corn (c.85,000)	%	.89	6.87	14.70	17.15
Credit: Groups	No.		128	218	183
Total (U.S.%)	$	5,850	447,713	795,273	608,007
Average per ha.	$	76.97	76.70	63.64	42.11
Recuperation	%	100	.96	.96	
Yields:					
Plan Puebla Participants					
Total (metric ton)	No.	304	17,514	33,647	
Total Value (U.S.$)[1]	$	22,861	1,317,453	2,530,254	
Per Hectare (metric ton)	No.	3,894	2,765	2,670	
Value per ha.[1]	$	292.83	207.93	200.78	
Others					
Per Hectare	No.	2,091	1,791	1,917	
Value per ha.[1]	$	157.24	134.68	144.16	
Staff:					
Technical[2]	No.	7	10	11	11
Participant/Technical Staff/Ratio		20:1	233:1	439:1	476:1
Participant/Extension Agent/Ratio			640:1	967:1	1,048:1
Group/Extension Agent Ratio			32:1	44:1	37:1
Potential Clientele/Extension Agent Ratio		c.9,500:1	c.9,500:1	c.9,500:1	c.9,500:1

[1]Guaranteed Maize Price—$75.20 or 940 pesos per metric ton.
[2]Includes Coordinator, Research, Extension and Evaluation personnel.

SOURCE: Puebla Project.

Table 7
Benefit-Cost Ratios of Puebla Project
Under Different Alternatives

Different Price Assumptions for a metric ton of maize:	$49.50	$60.00	$75.20
I. Fertilizers and seeds provided by project			
Interest rate = 12%	1.18	1.45	1.84
Interest rate = 18%	1.13	1.40	1.78
II. Fertilizers and seeds provided initially by project			
Interest rate = 12%	1.40	2.01	2.88
Interest rate = 18%	1.26	1.82	2.60

SOURCE: Cano and Winkelmann, "Plan Puebla: Analisis de Beneficios y Costos" in *El Trimestre Economico* (Mexico, October 1972).

LIST OF REFERENCES

Published Material

Includes books, articles, or published reports made available for public use.

A. Agustin, S. "Vocational Training in Chile." *International Labour Review* 95(1967):452-464.

Academy for Educational Development. *Educational Technology and the Developing Countries, A Handbook.* Washington, D.C., 1972.

"Apprenticeship in Nigeria—Traditional and New Trades." *CIRF Training for Progress* 6(1967).

The Arusha Declaration and TANU's Policy on Socialism and Self-Reliance. Dar-es-Salaam: Publicity Sector, TANU, 1967.

Blinkhorn, T.A. "Lilongwe: A Quiet Revolution." *Finance and Development* 8 ([June]1971):26-31.

Boserup, Ester. *Woman's Role in Economic Development.* New York: St. Martin's Press, London: George Allen and Unwin, 1970.

Brimer, M.A., and Pauli, L. *Wastage in Education: A World Problem.* Studies and Surveys in Comparative Education. Paris: Unesco; Geneva: IBE, 1971.

Brown, Dorris D. *Agricultural Development in India's Districts.* Center for International Affairs Series. Cambridge, Mass.: Harvard University Press, 1971.

Brown, Lester. *Seeds of Change: The Green Revolution and Development in the 1970s.* New York: Praeger Publishers, 1970.

Callaway, Archibald. "Nigeria's Indigenous Education: The Apprentice System." *Odu, University of Ife Journal of African Studies* I(1964):62-79.

Los Campesinos Trabajan por el Desarrollo. Bogota: Editorial Andes, 1971.

Choldin, Harvey M. "An Organizational Analysis of Rural Development Projects at Comilla, East Pakistan." *Economic Development and Cultural Change* 20(1972):671-670.

Clark, H.F. and Sloan, H.S. *Classrooms in the Factories.* Rutherford, New Jersey: Institute of Research, Fairleigh Dickinson University, 1958.

Coombs, Philip H. *The World Educational Crisis: A Systems Analysis.* New York and London: The Oxford University Press, 1968.

de Wilde, John C. See International Bank for Reconstruction and Development.

Eicher, Carl K. *Research on Agricultural Development in Five English-Speaking Countries in West Africa.* New York: Agricultural Development Council, Inc., 1970.

Food and Agricultural Organization. *Agricultural Credit through Cooperatives and Other Institutions.* FAO Agricultural Study No. 68. Rome, 1965.

Food and Agricultural Organization. *Provisional Indicative World Plan for Agricultural Development.* 2 Vols. Rome, 1967.

Food and Agricultural Organization. *The State of Food and Agriculture, 1972.* Rome, 1972.

Foster, P.J. "The Vocational School Fallacy in Development Planning." In *Education and Economic Development,* edited by C.A. Anderson and M.J. Bowman, pp. 142-166. Chicago: Aldine Publishing Company, 1964. Also included in *Readings in the Economics of Education,* compiled by Unesco, pp. 614-633. Paris, 1968.

Gaitskell, Arthur. *Gezira: A Story of Development in the Sudan.* London: Faber and Faber, 1959.

Gillette, Arthur. "Cuba's School in the Countryside: An Innovative Hybrid." In *Training for Agriculture: Annual Review of Selected Developments,* compiled by FAO, pp. 52-55. Rome, 1972.

Goussault, Yves. "Rural 'Animation' and Popular Participation in French-Speaking Black Africa." *International Labour Review* 97(1968):525-550.

Hanning, Hugh. *The Peaceful Uses of Military Forces.* New York: Praeger, 1967.

Harbison, Frederick H. *Human Resources as the Wealth of Nations.* New York and London: Oxford University Press, 1973.

Harbison, Frederick H. and Seltzer, George. "National Training Schemes." In *New Strategies for Educational Development: The Cross-Cultural Search for Nonformal Alternatives,* edited by Cole S. Brembeck and Timothy J. Thompson, pp. 195-200. Lexington, Mass.: D.C. Heath and Co., Lexington Books, 1972.

Hoselitz, B.F. "Type and Location of Rural Industries." In *The Role of Group Action in the Industrialization of Rural Areas,* edited by J. Klatzmann; B.Y. Ilan; and Y. Levi, pp. 58-65. New York: Praeger Publishers, 1971.

Hunter, Guy. *The Administration of Agricultural Development: Lessons from India.* London: The Oxford University Press, 1970.

India, Ministry of Community Development and Cooperation. *Report of the Syllabus Committee on the Training of Rural Artisans in the Community Development Blocks.* New Delhi, January 1960.

India, Ministry of Food, Agriculture, Community Development and Cooperation, Dept. of Agriculture, Expert Committee on Assessment and Evaluation. *Modernising Indian Agriculture: Report on the Intensive Agricultural District Programme* (1960-1968). Vol. I. New Delhi, 1969.

India, Ministry of Food and Agriculture, Ministry of Community Development and Cooperation. *Report on India's Food Crisis and Steps to Meet It.* New Delhi, April 1959.

International Bank for Reconstruction and Development. See also McNamara, Robert S. and World Bank.

International Bank for Reconstruction and Development. *The Development of African Private Enterprise.* Prepared by John C. de Wilde. Report No. AW-31. 2 Vols. Washington, D.C., December 10, 1971.

International Commission for the Development of Education. *Learning to Be: The World of Education Today and Tomorrow.* Paris: Unesco; London: Harrap, 1972.

International Council for Educational Development. *New Paths to Learning for Rural Children and Youth.* Essex, Conn., September 1973. Copies may be obtained from ICED Publications, Box 601, West Haven, Connecticut 06516.

International Labour Office. *Employment Problems and Policies in the Philippines.* Employment Research Papers. Geneva, 1969.

International Labour Office. *Labour Force Projections, 1965-1985.* 5 parts. Geneva, 1971.

International Labour Office. *Towards Full Employment: A Programme for Colombia.* Geneva, 1970.

International Rice Research Institute. "Changing the Change Agent—A Step Toward Increased Rice Yields." Manila, September 30, 1967.

Jain, S.C. *Community Development and Panchayati Raj in India.* London and New York: Allied Publishers, 1967.

Johnson, A.A. *Indian Agriculture in the 1970s.* New Delhi: The Ford Foundation, August 1, 1970.

Johnson, E.A.J. *The Organization of Space in Developing Countries.* Cambridge, Mass.: Harvard University Press, 1970.

Kenya. *Adult Education in Kenya (A Historical Perspective) Decadal Report, 1960-1970.* Nairobi, Kenya: Board of Adult Education, 1971.

Khalil, H.M.M. "The Sudan Gezira Scheme: Some Institutional and Administrative Aspects." *Journal of Administration Overseas* IX(1970):273-285.

Kilby, Peter. "Hunting the Heffalump." In *Entrepreneurship and Economic Development,* edited by Peter Kilby, pp. 1-40. New York: The Free Press, 1971.

Kincaid, James M., Jr. *Strategies for Improvement of Agricultural Extension Work and Non-Degree Agricultural Training in Nigeria.* CSNRD-13. East Lansing, Michigan: Consortium for the Study of Nigerian Rural Development, Michigan State University, September 1968.

Klatzmann, Joseph; Ilan, B.Y.; and Levi, Yair, eds. *The Role of Group Action in the Industrialization of Rural Areas.* Special Studies in International Economics and Development. New York: Praeger Publishers, 1971.

Kulp, Earl M. *Rural Development Planning: Systems Analysis and Working Method.* Studies in International Economics and Development. New York: Praeger Publishers, 1970.

Lionberger, Herbert F. *Adoption of New Ideas and Practices.* Ames, Iowa: Iowa State University Press, 1960.

McClelland, David C., and Winter, David G. *Motivating Economic Achievement: Accelerating Economic Development through Psychological Training.* New York: The Free Press; London: Collier-Macmillan Ltd., 1971.

McNamara, Robert S. *Address to the United Nations Conference on Trade and Development, Santiago, Chile, April 14, 1972.* Washington, D.C.: International Bank for Reconstruction and Development, 1972.

Mayer, Albert, and Associates. *Pilot Project, India: The Story of Rural Development at Etawah, Uttar Pradesh.* Los Angeles and Berkeley: University of California Press, 1958.

Millikan, Max F., and Hapgood, David, eds. *No Easy Harvest: The Dilemma of Agriculture in Underdeveloped Countries.* Boston: Little, Brown, & Co., 1967.

Moseman, Albert H., ed. *National Agricultural Research Systems in Asia: Report of the Regional Seminar held at the India International Centre, New Delhi, In-*

dia, March 8-13, 1971. New York: Agricultural Development Council, Inc., 1971.

Mosher, Arthur T. *Creating a Progressive Rural Structure to Serve a Modern Agriculture.* New York: Agricultural Development Council, Inc., 1969.

Mosher, Arthur T. *Getting Agriculture Moving: Essentials for Development and Modernization.* New York: Praeger, 1966.

Mosher, Arthur T. *To Create a Modern Agriculture: Organization and Planning.* New York: Agricultural Development Council, Inc., 1971.

Nekby, Bengt. *CADU: An Ethiopian Experiment in Developing Peasant Farming.* Stockholm: Prisma Publishers, 1970.

Owens, Edgar, and Shaw, Robert. *Development Reconsidered: Bridging the Gap Between Government and People.* Lexington, Mass.: D.C. Heath and Co., 1972.

Polcyn, Kenneth. *An Educator's Guide to Communication Satellite Technology.* Washington: Academy for Educational Development, forthcoming.

Raper, Arthur F. *Rural Development in Action: The Comprehensive Experiment at Comilla, East Pakistan.* Ithaca, N.Y.: Cornell University Press, 1970.

Rau, S.K. "Generalities on Problems of Assistance to Small and Medium-Sized Enterprises in Member Countries of the Asian Productivity Organization." In *Promotion of Small and Medium-Sized Firms in Developing Countries through Collective Actions,* compiled by Development Centre of the Organisation for Economic Co-Operation and Development. Paris, 1969.

Rice, E.B. See U.S., Agency for International Development.

Rogers, Everett M. *Diffusion of Innovations.* New York: The Free Press, 1962.

Schramm, Wilbur; Coombs, Philip H.; Kahnert, Frederick; and Lyle, Jack. *The New Media: Memo to Educational Planners.* Paris, Unesco/IIEP, 1967.

Schramm, Wilbur. "Ten Years of the Radio Rural Forum." In *New Educational Media in Action—Case Studies for Planners,* Vol. I, compiled by the International Institute for Educational Planning, pp. 107-134. Paris: Unesco/IBE, 1967.

Sheffield, James R. *Education in the Republic of Kenya.* Washington, D.C.: U.S. Government Printing Office, 1971.

Sheffield, James R., and Diejomaoh, Victor P. *Non-Formal Education in African Development.* New York: African-American Institute, 1972.

Small Industry Training Institute. "Small Industry Extension Training Institute in India." In *Promotion of Small and Medium-Sized Firms in Developing Countries through Collective Actions,* compiled by Development Centre of the Organisation for Economic Co-Operation and Development, pp. 145-167. Paris, 1969.

Smithells, J.E. *Agricultural Extension Work Among Rural Women.* Reading, England: Agricultural Extension and Rural Development Centre, University of Reading, March 1972.

Staley, Eugene. *Planning Occupational Education and Training for Development.* New York: Praeger Publishers; New Delhi: Orient Longman, 1970.

Staley, Eugene, and Morse, Richard. *Modern Small Industry for Developing Countries.* Series in International Development. New York: McGraw-Hill, 1965.

United Nations. *A Study of the Capacity of the United Nations Development System.* Geneva, 1969.

United Nations, Department of Economic and Social Affairs, Statistical Office of the U.N. *Demographic Yearbook 1970.* New York: United Nations, 1971.

United Nations Educational, Scientific and Cultural Organisation. *Statistical Yearbook 1970.* Paris, 1971.

United Nations Educational, Scientific and Cultural Organisation, Office of Statistics. *A Statistical Study of Wastage at School.* Studies and Surveys in Comparative Education. Paris: Unesco; Geneva: IBE, 1972.

U.S., Agency for International Development. *Extension in the Andes: An Evaluation of Official U.S. Assistance to Agricultural Extension Services in Central and South America.* Prepared by E.B. Rice. Evaluation Paper No. 3. Washington, D.C., April 1971.

Valsan, E.H. *Community Development Programs and Rural Local Government: Comparative Case Studies of India and the Philippines.* Special Studies in International Economics and Development. New York: Praeger Publishers, 1970.

Watts, E.R. "Agricultural Extension in Embu District of Kenya." *Journal of Rural Development* (1969):63-81.

Weitz, Raanan. "Regional Planning as a Tool for Rural Development in Developing Countries." In *Rural Development in a Changing World,* edited by R. Weitz, pp. 86-102. Cambridge, Mass.: M.I.T. Press, 1971.

World Bank. *Education Sector Working Paper.* Washington, D.C., September 1971.

World Bank Group. *Trends in Developing Countries.* Washington, D.C., 1971.

Unpublished Documents*

Most of these references are in mimeographed form and are not readily available to the public.

Anderson, J.E. *Education for Self-Reliance: The Impact of Self-Help.* Discussion Paper No. 67. Nairobi, Kenya: Institute for Development Studies, University College, September 1968.

Anderson, J.E. *The Village Polytechnic Movement.* IDS/SRDP Evaluation Report No. 1. Nairobi, Kenya: Institute for Development Studies, University of Nairobi, August 1970.

Belshaw, D.G.R. "Planning the 'Improvement Approach': Agricultural Extension and Research." Paper read at the Third East African Agricultural Economics Conference, April 1967, at the University College, Dar es Salaam, Tanzania. Mimeographed.

Bennett, Nicholas. "A Scheme for Improving the Quality of Rural Life through Community Centered Education." Mimeographed. Paper prepared for a course given January 1973 in Cuernavaca, Mexico.

Bourgeois, Michel. "Radio at the Service of Rural Development: The Senegalese Experience of Educational Broadcasting." IIEP/S28/4. Paper read at the Seminar on Planning Out-of-School Education for Development, December 1971, at the International Institute for Educational Planning, Paris. Mimeographed.

---

*Not included are confidential and restricted documents made available to ICED.

Centre for Educational Development Overseas. "Development of Educational Mass Media in Ethiopia—A Report by the CEDO Survey Team." Mimeographed. London, 1972.

Cooperative College of Tanzania. "Notes on the Cooperative Movement in Tanzania." Mimeographed. Moshi, Tanzania, no date.

Coppen, Helen. "Educational Media for the Development of Rural Education." CRE(70)A/4. Paper prepared for the Commonwealth Secretariat Conference on Education in Rural Areas, 1970, in Ghana. London, September 1969. Mimeographed.

Food and Agricultural Organization. Report of the Agricultural Credit Mission to Afghanistan. Rome, 1967.

Green, Donald G. "Training for Indian Agricultural Development: Challenge of the 1970s." Mimeographed. New Delhi: The Ford Foundation, September 1970.

India, Planning Commission. Report of the Team for the Study of Community Projects and National Extension Services. 3 Vols. New Delhi, 1957.

International Labour Office. Assessment of Pre-Vocational Training Projects Assisted by UNICEF and ILO. 2 parts. E.ICEF/L.1272 and E/ICEF/L.1272/Add.1. New York, March 1969.

Loveridge, A.J. "A Survey of British Experience of Non-Formal Education for Rural and Agricultural Development in Developing Countries." Mimeographed. Paper prepared for ICED in cooperation with the Overseas Development Administration. London: Institute of Education, University of London, April 1972.

Myren, Delbert T. "The Puebla Project: A Development Strategy for Low Income Farmers." Paper read at the Seminar on Small Farmer Development Strategies, September 1971, in Columbus, Ohio. Mimeographed.

Platt, William J. Education by TV Satellite in Developing Countries. International Institute for Educational Planning Lecture Discussion Series. IIEP/TM/49/70. Paris: Unesco/IIEP, January 1970.

Programme on Agricultural Credit and Cooperatives. Semi-Annual Report of the Programme Manager. Technical Series No. 4. Kabul, 1970.

Prosser, Roy C. "The Development and Organisation of Adult Education in Kenya with special reference to African Rural Development, 1945-1960." Ph.D. dissertation, University of Edinburgh, 1971.

Schumacher, Edward F. "Bureaucracy, Party, and Rural Commercial Reform in Senegal: The Politics of Institutional Change, 1957-1968." Ph.D. dissertation, Columbia University, 1970.

Seago, J.A. "The Use of Media in Non-Formal Education for Rural Development: A Report on British Experience." Mimeographed. Paper prepared for ICED in cooperation with the Overseas Development Administration. Reading, England: Agricultural Extension and Rural Development Centre, University of Reading, May 1972.

United Nations Educational, Scientific and Cultural Organisation and International Bureau of Education. "Statistical Measurement of Educational Wastage: Drop-Out, Repetition and School Retardation." ED/BIE/CONFINTED/32/Ref. 1. Prepared for the International Conference on Education, 32nd Session, 1-9 July 1970 in Geneva. Mimeographed.

University of Massachusetts, School of Education, Center for International Education. "Technical Notes on the Ecuador Project." Series of papers prepared for the Ecuador Project. Mimeographed. Amherst, Mass., 1972.

"World Conference on Agricultural Education and Training: Report." 2 Vols. Papers presented at the symposium, co-sponsored by ILO, FAO, and Unesco, 17 July–8 August 1970, in Copenhagen. Mimeographed.

LIST OF ICED WORLD BANK CASE STUDIES

Title	Author
Acción Cultural Popular: Mass Media in the Service of Colombian Rural Development. April 1972.	Stephen F. Brumberg
Promoción Profesional Popular-Rural of SENA: A Mobile Skills Training Program for Rural Colombia. June 1972.	Stephen F. Brumberg
Plan Puebla/Mexico (unpublished).*	Stephen F. Brumberg
Nonformal Education and the Development of Small Enterprise in India. January 1972.	John C. de Wilde
Farmer Education Program of the Office of Rural Development in the Republic of Korea. July 1972.	Manzoor Ahmed
Mobile Trade Training Schools in Thailand. April 1972.	Manzoor Ahmed
Programs for Small Industry Entrepreneurs and Journeymen in Northern Nigeria. April 1972.	Clifford Gilpin / Sven Grabe
Senegal: Rural Vocational Training Centers (unpublished).*	Pierre Furter / Sven Grabe
The Cooperative Education System of Tanzania. April 1972.	Sven Grabe
PACCA: Education in an Integrated Agricultural Program. June 1972.	Manzoor Ahmed / Philip H. Coombs
Training Extension Leaders at the International Rice Research Institute. June 1972.	Manzoor Ahmed / Philip H. Coombs
CADU: Ethiopia (unpublished).*	Sven Grabe
The Rural Education System in Upper Volta. April 1972.	Sven Grabe

---

*Field notes not written up as formal case study.

LIST OF ICED BACKGROUND PAPERS

Title	Author
Education for Rural Development in East Bengal. April 1972.	Manzoor Ahmed
Relating Education and Training to Agricultural Development. May 1972.	Donald G. Green
Education for Rural Development in the People's Republic of China. June 1972.	Hsiang-po Lee
Training Rural Artisans and Small Entrepreneurs. April 1972.	Richard F. Tompkins
Agricultural Extension Service. April 1972.	Haile Menkerios
The Use and Production of Media in Nonformal Adult Education. July 1972.	John Bowers

Gopalaswami Parthasarathi
Vice Chancellor
Jawaharlal Nehru University
New Delhi, India

*Joseph E. Slater, President
Aspen Institute for Humanistic
Studies
New York, New York

Jan Szczepanski, Director
Instytut Filozofii
Polska Akademia Nauk
Warszawa, Potoc Staszica
Poland

Puey Ungphakorn
Visiting Professor
Wolfson College
Cambridge, England

*Member of the Executive Committee

INDEX

tional; Small entrepreneurs; Small industries
Sloan, H. S., 22fn.
Small entrepreneurs, 4, 50, 139, 147-155
Small farmers, 49, 127-138, 224-227
Small Scale Industrial Development Organization (SSIDO), See India
Small industries
  integrated programs, 154, 155
  training, 150
  See India, RIP, SSIDO
Smithells, J. E., 128fn.
South Africa, 122
South America, See Latin America
South Vietnam, 45
Sri Lanka (Ceylon): general, 3fn., 45, 121, 141fn.
  Diyagala Boys Town, 141, 145, 145fn., 183, 217
Staff use and development, 250
  agriculture, 130-132
  educational technology, 166-167, 246
  international staff, 218-219
  national staff, 214-217
  volunteer personnel, 217
  See also specific program entries under country headings
Staley, Eugene, 137fn., 138fn., 139fn.
Subsistence farmers, See Small farmers
Sudan: general, 6, 45
  Gezira Development Scheme, 6, 33, 90-92, 127, 192, 211, 224
Swanson, Burt, 45fn.
Sweden, 12
Swedish International Development Agency (SIDA), 95, 99, 105, 212

T

Tamil Nadu (Indian State), 119
Tanjore (India), 31, 119, 121, 160, 237
Tanzania, United Republic of: general, 3fn., 6, 12, 21, 36, 45
  Arusha Declaration, 80fn.
  Cooperative Education System of the Cooperative Union of Tanganyika, 6, 67, 80-84, 180, 201, 219, 223
  Moshi Cooperative College, 81
  radio correspondence courses, 159
  Tanganyika African National Union (TANU), 83
  ujamaa village, 81, 83
Technology, See Agricultural technology; Educational technology
Thailand: general, 3fn., 6, 12, 21, 45 51fn., 52fn., 76, 141

Mobile Trade Training Schools (MTTS), 6, 50, 51fn., 51-52, 53, 64, 139fnn., 143fn., 145-147, 153, 167-168, et pass. 177-227
Thompson, Timothy J., 37fn.
Training approach to rural education, See Nonformal education
Tunisia, 95

U

Uganda: general, 113, 115
  Makerere University, 131
Union of Soviet Socialist Republics (USSR), 160, 170fn.
United Kingdom, 19
United Nations, 126, 136, 212, 213
United Nations Children's Fund (UNICEF), 7, 7fn., 19fn., 23, 24, 141fn., 177fn., 185, 232
United Nations Development Program (UNDP), 23, 43, 213, 248
United Nations Educational Scientific and Cultural Organization (Unesco), 8, 18, 23, 24, 42fn., 135, 136, 212, 248
United Nations Second Development Decade, 13, 114, 114fn.
United States, 12, 22fn., 27, 45 51fn., 94, 121, 122, 126, 163, 170fn., 173
United States Agency for International Development, 24, 191
Uruguay, 10, 11
Upper Volta: general, 3fn., 10, 11, 21, 177fn., 181fn., 182
  rural school costs, 185

V

Venezuela, 115, 182
Village-level workers (VLW): India, 68-69, 94, 129, 132, 133, 161, 187
Village Polytechnics, See Kenya
Vocational Education Programs, 144
  See also Nonformal education; Occupational education
Vocational Improvement Centres (VIC), See Nigeria

W

Weitz, Raanan, 137-138fn.
Western Europe, 10, 122, 123
Winter, David G., 64fn.
Wisconsin, University of, 45fn.
Women's Programs, 128
  Ethiopia, CADU, 97
  India CD, 70

Kenya FTCs, 37
Korea, 30
World Bank, 3, 4, 4fn., 23, 108, 126, 248
World Health Organization (WHO), 23

Youths,
population, 10, 12
training programs, 145, 146, 152, 153

Y

Yen, Y. C. "Jimmy," 75

Z

Zambia, 115